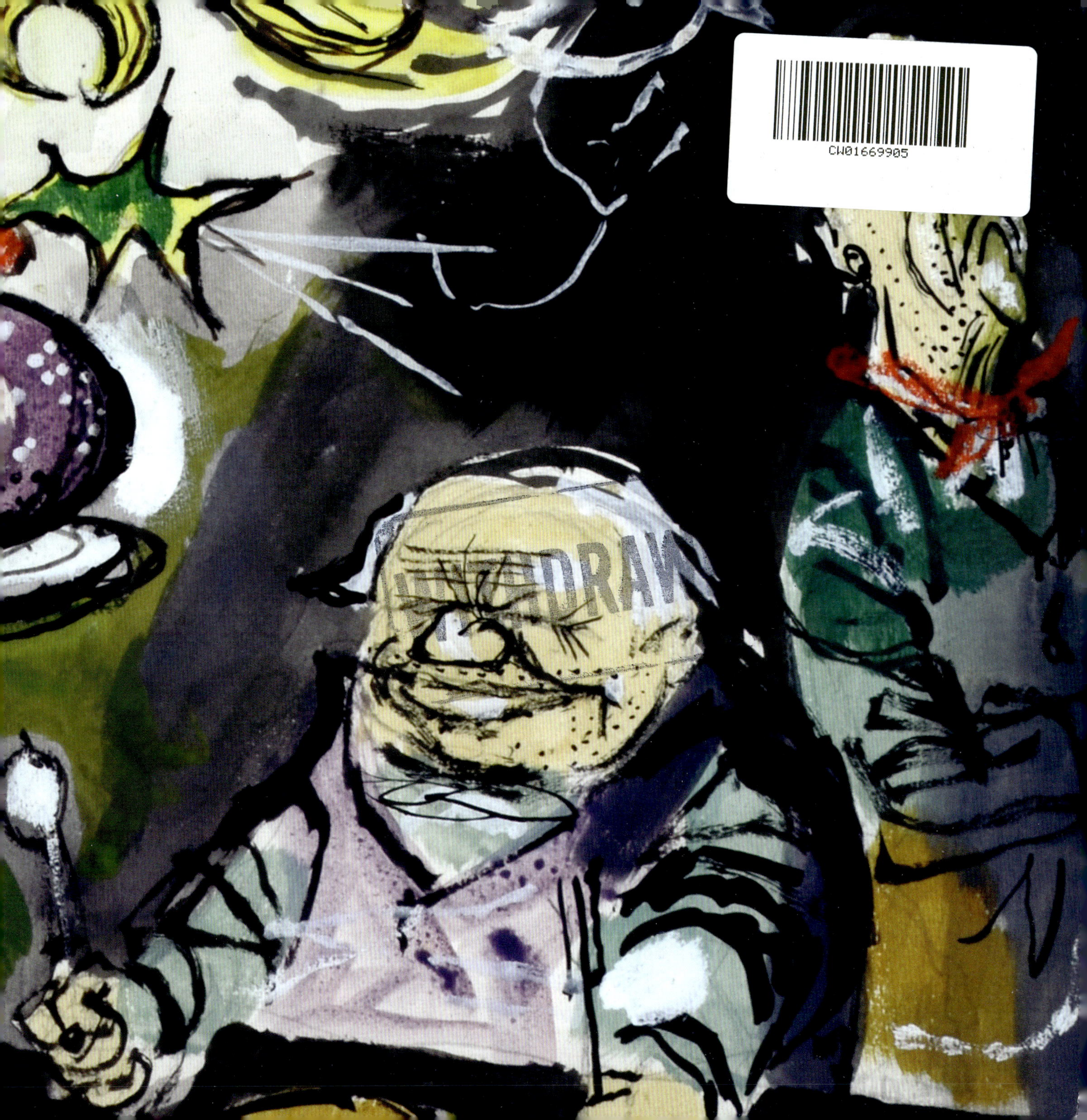

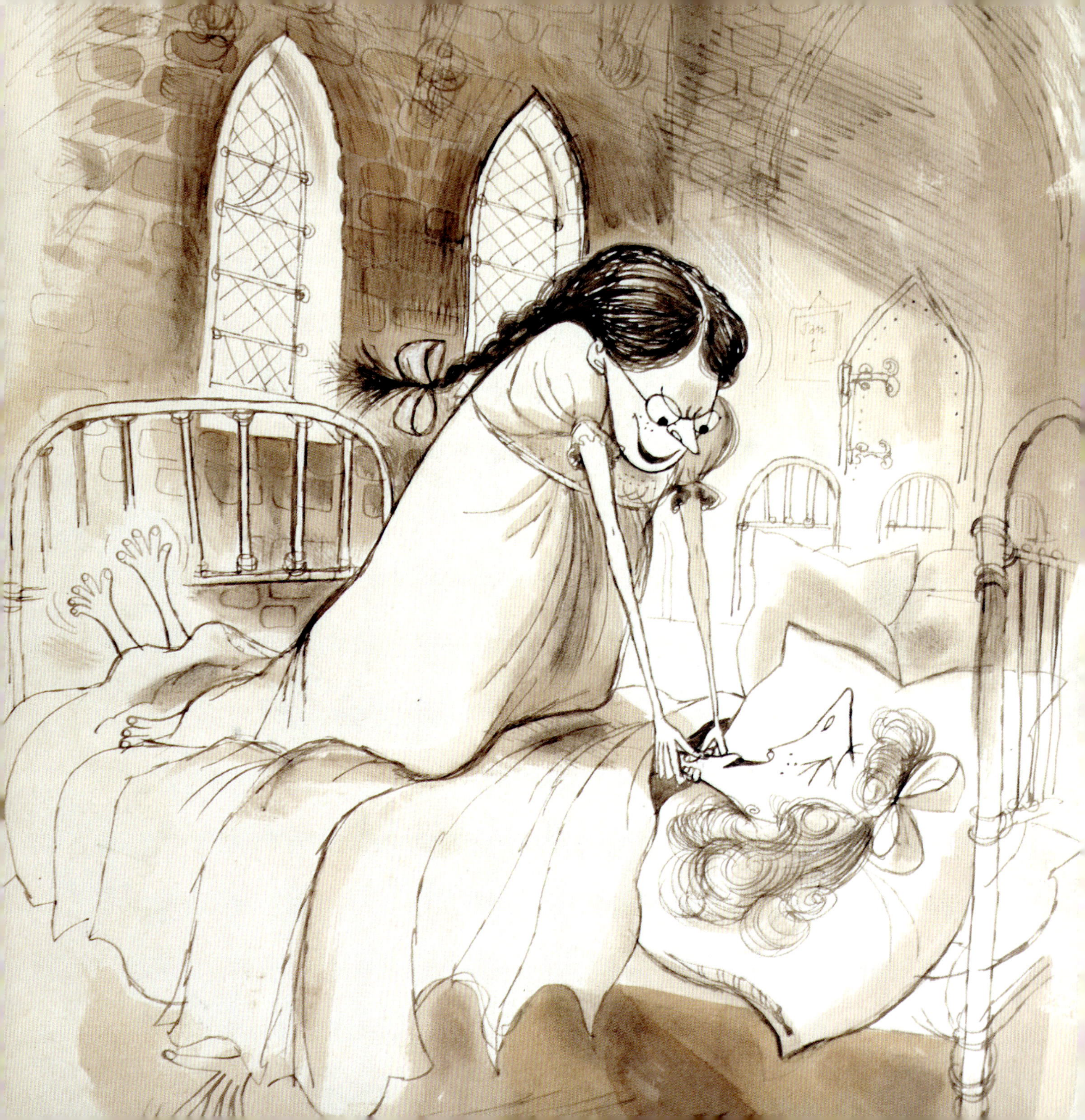
Jan
1

RONALD SEARLE REMEMBERED

(1920-2011)

England's Greatest Cartoonist

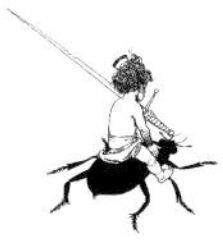

CHRIS BEETLES

8 & 10 Ryder Street, St James's, London SW1Y 6QB
Telephone 020 7839 7551 Facsimile 020 7839 1603
gallery@chrisbeetles.com www.chrisbeetles.com

8 & 10 Ryder Street
St James's
London SW1Y 6QB
020 7839 7551
gallery@chrisbeetles.com
www.chrisbeetles.com

ISBN 978-1-905738-44-1

Cataloguing in publication data is available from the British Library

Researched and written by David Wootton
Additional research by Catherine Andrews
Letters transcribed by Sandra and Gary Andrews
Edited by Catherine Andrews and David Wootton
Design by Jeremy Brook of Graphic Ideas
Photography by Julian Huxley-Parlour
Reproduction by www.cast2create.com
Colour separation and printing by Geoff Neal Litho Limited

Front cover: *The Canine Harpist* [**114**]
Front endpaper: *It was Christmas Day in the Workhouse* [**106**]
Frontispiece: *'Go on, say it – "I resolve to leave my body to science."'* [**49**]
Title verso: *Cancan Dancer* [**16**]
Contents: *Searle's-Eye View 40 – Bernard Buffet* [**340**]
Back endpaper: *The King's Breakfast. The Royal Gym* [**328**]
Back cover: *Canon Noel Duckworth Selling a Parker Pen to a Japanese Guard in Pudu Gaol* [**15**]

BOOKS FOR SALE ARE LISTED IN THIS CATALOGUE WITH A GREY BACKGROUND.

All letters, including those listed but not illustrated, are fully transcribed in the Appendix [pages 146-199].

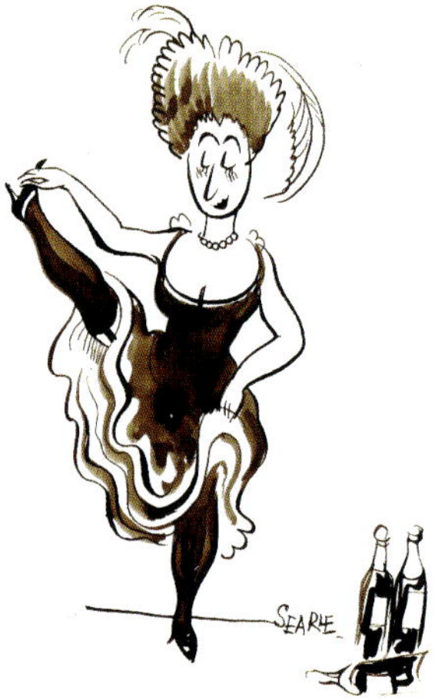

CONTENTS

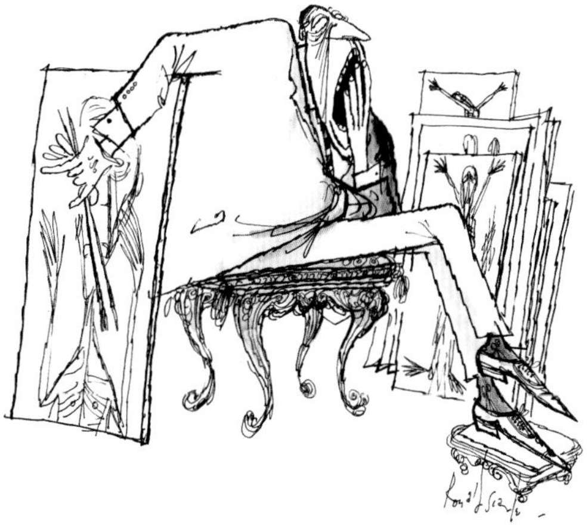

The Ronald Searle Story

For many decades, Ronald Searle was simply the most popular and most influential cartoonist-illustrator in the world. In Britain, he always remained best known for his anarchically irrepressible school children: the girls of St Trinian's and Nigel Molesworth of St Custard's. It was elsewhere – he believed – that he was more properly appreciated for his ability to apply his sharply satirical eye and incisive graphic skill to an unparalleled range of subjects: in France, where he settled in 1961; in America, which gave him so many of his later opportunities; in Germany, to which he has donated his personal collection. While his drawings are often celebratory or delightfully surreal, they are invariably shot through with a darker vision that arose out of his wartime experiences as a Japanese prisoner of war. In *Ronald Searle: To the Kwai – and Back* (1986), he wrote, 'You can't have that sort of experience without it directing the rest of your life'. He also stated that, 'to start the day with a sense of excitement, wondering where my pen will lead me this time, is the only justification for remaining on this Earth' (quoted in *The Times*, 4 January 2012, page 23).

*

Early Life

Ronald William Fordham Searle was born in Cambridge on 3 March 1920, the son of a railway station porter, who later worked as a Post Office engineer. He began drawing from an early age – with his left hand – while a pupil at St Barnabas' Church School. As he grew, he spent much of his spare time – with his younger sister Olive – at the Fitzwilliam and other Cambridge university museums, and decided to become either an archaeologist or an artist. He attended the Boys' Central School from the age of ten and, a year later, began to sing treble both in the choir of St Andrew the Great and as a soloist, spending most of his earnings on art materials. When his voice broke, he worked on Saturday mornings at Redfern's butcher's shop.

On leaving school at the age of 14, Searle was employed as a clerk with the solicitor, D R W Stevenson, Squires & Co, though was sacked after two months, because he asked for an advance on his wages to pay for evening classes at Cambridge School of Art. Nevertheless, with some help from his parents, he managed to pay the enrolment fee, which allowed him to begin his studies in September 1935. A month later, he took a position with the Co-operative Society, and at the same time began to produce weekly cartoons for the *Cambridge Daily News*. From 1936, he also contributed caricatures and sketches to *The Granta*, the leading student magazine.

A scholarship from the School of Art enabled him to begin full time studies on 15 September 1938, and in the same week he won a prize for each of his three entries to an exhibition at its Sketch Club. In 1939, his work was shown in Cambridge, at Hensher's Gallery and then the Gordon Fraser Gallery.
By the time he took, and passed, the examination for the Drawing Diploma in the June, he had enlisted in the Territorial Army, registering as an Architectural Draughtsman with the Royal Engineers.

*

The Second World War

When war broke out in September 1939, Searle was placed with the 287th Field Company of the Royal Engineers, which was stationed at various places in Norfolk and then – in January 1941 – Kirkcudbright, in Dumfries and Galloway. New friends told him stories of St Trinnean's, a progressive girls' school evacuated from Edinburgh to Galashiels, and he began to draw cartoons parodying it as 'St Trinian's' – one appearing in *Lilliput* in the October. In the same month, Searle's company embarked for the Far East – via Cape Town, Mombasa and the Chagos Islands – he making drawings all the way.

A month after Searle arrived in Singapore, in January 1942, Japanese troops attacked and occupied the island, forcing the allies to surrender. He became a Prisoner of War, and was incarcerated at Changi for over a year, contributing for a while to *The Survivor*, a camp magazine. Then, in May 1943, he was transported north to

Siam, to work as a slave labourer on the infamous Burma railway. Following a hundred mile walk, he worked 18 hours a day, breaking rocks in the stifling heat. While working in various camps, he contracted beriberi, malaria and other ailments, and his weight fell to six stone. Around him many of his friends died of disease and violent treatment.

By December 1943, Searle was so ill that he was transported to Sime Road Camp near Singapore Racecourse. Slow recovery was helped by the task of designing for the camp's Barn Theatre. In May 1944, all the prisoners were moved to Changi Gaol, built by the British eight years earlier for 600 prisoners, and now housing 10,000. For Searle, work in the prison gardens and the role of Art Editor on *The Exile*, a camp magazine, intermittently relieved continued hardship and illness. It is not too much of an exaggeration to say that his determination to keep drawing, usually secretly, and so bear witness, kept him alive. He returned to England in October 1945.

Cambridge School of Art mounted an exhibition of Searle's 'Drawings from a Japanese Prison Camp' in December 1945. Four decades later, he donated them to the Imperial War Museum and published a large selection in *To the Kwai – and Back: War Drawings 1939-45* (1986).

Post-War Britain

Living in London from late in 1945, Searle began to contribute cartoons to a wide range of magazines and newspapers, including *Punch* and *Lilliput*, the leftwing *Tribune* and the rightwing *Sunday Express*. He began a relationship with Kaye Webb, *Lilliput*'s assistant editor, who was six years his senior and married (for the second time). By the end of 1946, she discovered she was pregnant by Searle, and in the following July gave birth to twins, Kate and John. They married in March 1948, and in 1951 moved into 32 Newton Road, Paddington – a Modernist house designed by Denys Lasdun.

Searle and Webb worked together on travel books, beginning with *Paris Sketchbook* (1950), and on reportage for *News Chronicle*, initiated by a trip to Morocco in February 1951. Later the same year, *News Chronicle* started to run their series, 'Looking at London' (collected within hard covers in 1953). Then, in 1952, they founded their own imprint, Perpetua Books, originally to allow their friend, the playwright, Christopher Fry, to respond to criticism by publishing *An Experience of Critics*.

Searle's first cartoon albums – *Hurrah for St Trinian's* (1948) and *The Female Approach* (1949) – had helped make his anarchic schoolgirl characters a national institution, an overwhelming success that he soon began to regret, feeling that his skill was being pigeonholed. He tried to put an end to them in 1953, with the Perpetua publication, *Souls in Torment*, by engineering an atomic explosion in the school chemistry lab. However, they had by then achieved a life of their own, a life sustained by Launder and Gilliat's series of films (1954-80).

Rather than continue with St Trinian's, Searle offered his publisher, Max Parrish, another school-based scenario, concerning Nigel Molesworth of St Custard's. His friend, the BBC journalist, Geoffrey Willans, had used his experience as a prep-school master to create the character for *Punch*, and now they developed the delightfully misspelled record of his life and opinions in *Down with Skool!* (1953) and subsequent volumes.

Having secured a lucrative contract with *Punch* in 1956, Searle embarked on two important series for the magazine: the colour caricatures, 'Heroes of Our Time', and illustrations to Alex Atkinson's 'The New Mayhew', a study of contemporary London types (collected as *The Big City* in 1958).

In 1957, Searle was invited to the United States to make an animated film to celebrate the 75th anniversary of The Standard Oil Company of New Jersey. Working with the independent animator, Bill Melendez, he produced *Energetically Yours*. In preparation, he visited the Disney studios, in the company of Walt Disney himself. In turn, Searle's style seems to have influenced the look of *101 Dalmatians* (1961), which is set in England.

From the late 1950s, Searle underwent an increasing number of international assignments, including one, with Kaye Webb, in 1959, to refugee camps in Europe, at the invitation of the United Nations.

However, it would be the last professional trip that they would take together. Feeling overwhelmed by the social demands on his time and energy, he abandoned his family in 1961 and moved to Paris to live with Monica Koenig, a theatre designer, whom he had met three years earlier.

Receiving the Decree Absolute of his divorce in May 1967, Searle married Monica on the following day. His father had died earlier the same year and, from then on, he determined to visit Britain only to see his ageing mother.

Beyond Britain

During the 1960s, Searle gradually turned his professional attention away from Britain towards commissions for European and American publications. Assignments for *Holiday*, in particular, enabled he and Monica to live on the expenses at a time when they needed to establish new sources of income. Destinations would range from Alaska to Casablanca. In the same period, he also worked on the design element of several films, most notably the animated sequences of *Those Magnificent Men in their Flying Machines* (1965) and *Monte Carlo or Bust!* (1969), both directed by Ken Annakin. His first ever retrospective, at the Kunsthalle in Bremen, in 1965, confirmed his international reputation.

Searle's style and ideas continued to develop, often in surreal and disturbing directions, as exemplified by the drawings in his collection, *The Square Egg* (1968), and some of his cover designs for *The New Yorker* (from 1969). Eventually he would produce more covers for *The New Yorker* than for *Punch*, and by the end of the 1960s he had already priced himself out of *Punch*'s league. In 1973, the Bibliothèque Nationale mounted an exhibition of work by Searle, the first non-French living artist to be so honoured. Soon after, Pierre Dehaye, Director of the French Mint, asked him to design a self-portrait medal, and would go on to approve a whole series of medals in honour of leading caricaturists. An honorary Frenchman in so many ways, he settled in Tourtour, in Haute-Provence, in 1975, and would live there, with Monica, for the rest of his life, though refusing to take French citizenship. From 1995, he produced political cartoons for the liberal French newspaper, *Le Monde* (collected in volume form in 2002). Inevitably, Searle had pet subjects that he explored thoroughly, and with great imagination, in such later books as *Ronald Searle's Big Fat Cat Book* (1982), *The Illustrated Winespeak* (1983) and *Slightly Foxed – But Still Desirable* (1989).

Three exciting books were launched with the help of exhibitions at Chris Beetles Gallery: Jeffrey Archer's collection of short stories, *Cat o' Nine Tales* (2006), which contains 49 illustrations by the artist; and two books by Robert L Forbes: *Beastly Feasts! A Mischievous Menagerie in Rhyme* (2007) and *Let's Have a Bite! A Banquet of Beastly Rhymes* (2010), each of which contain more than 30 illustrations.

Continuing to work throughout his eighties, Searle published his last book in 2011. *Les Très Riches Heures de Mrs Mole* gathered together the drawings that he created for his wife to help her through treatment for breast cancer. A limited edition, signed by husband and wife, was sold in aid of Macmillan Cancer Support, while the original drawings were exhibited at the Cartoon Museum, London. Monica died in July 2011, and Searle himself five months later, in Draguignan, on 30 December 2011. He is survived by his children.

Searle was widely honoured for his work. He won numerous awards, including the American National Cartoonists Society's Advertising and Illustration Award in 1959 and 1965. He was appointed a Royal Designer of Industry in 1988, CBE in 2004 and a Chevalier of the Légion d'honneur in 2007. He received an Honorary Doctorate from Anglia Ruskin University in 2008, and was awarded the German Order of Merit in 2009.

His work is represented in numerous public collections, including the British Museum, the Victoria and Albert Museum, and the Bibliothèque Nationale. In 2010 he announced his intention to leave his personal collection to the Wilhelm Busch Deutsches Museum für Karkatur & Zeichenkunst in Hannover.

David Wootton, May 2012

1: EARLY WORK

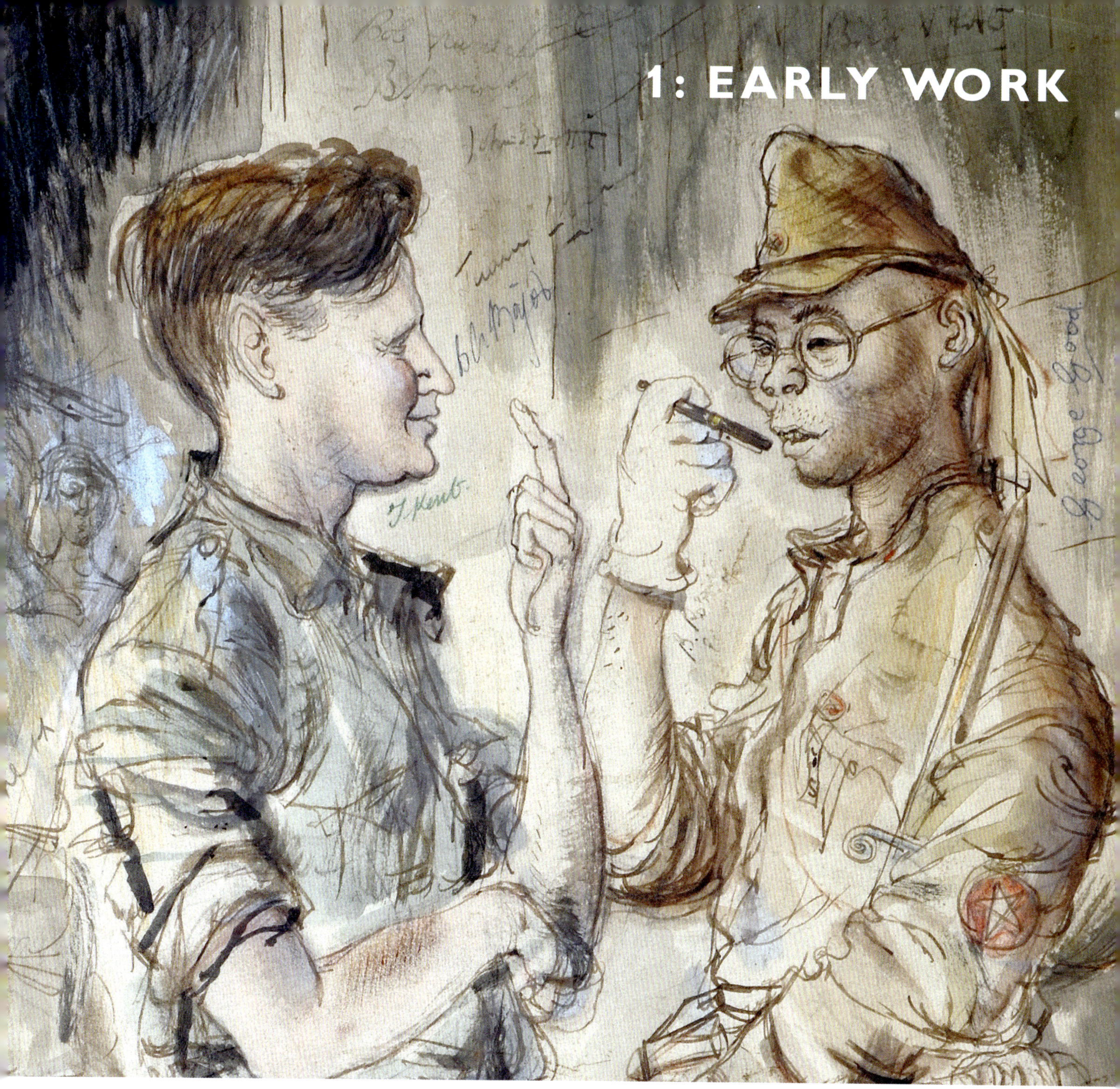

This catalogue quotes extensively from the revised edition of Russell Davies, *Ronald Searle. A Biography*, London: Chris Beetles Limited, 2003

1939: Cambridge School of Art

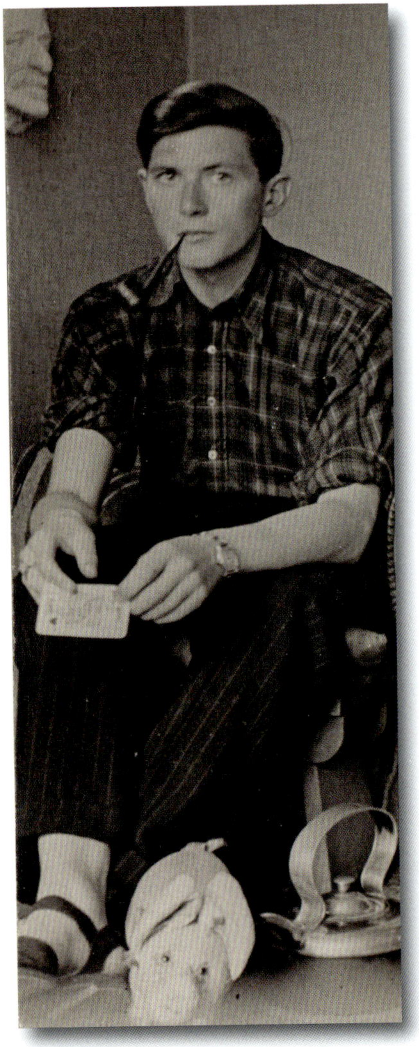

Ronald Searle at Home, 29 Collier Road, Cambridge, September 1939
Ronald Searle was a full-time student at Cambridge School of Art for the year beginning September 1938. During that time, he was living at home with his parents and younger sister, Olive.

01-07 Provenance:
Anne Dewing

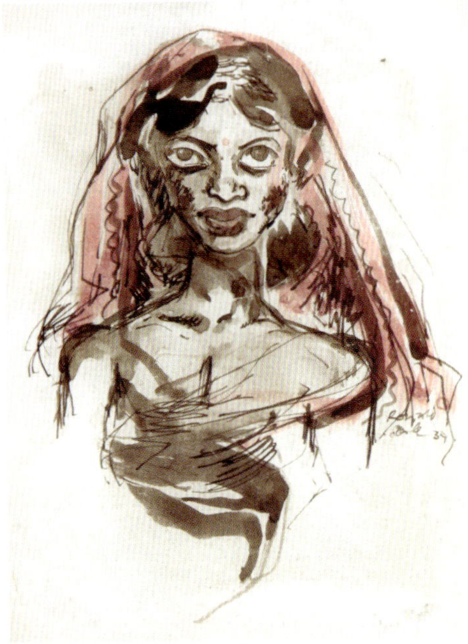

01 INDIAN WOMAN
signed and dated '39
pen ink and watercolour
8 ¾ x 6 ¼ inches

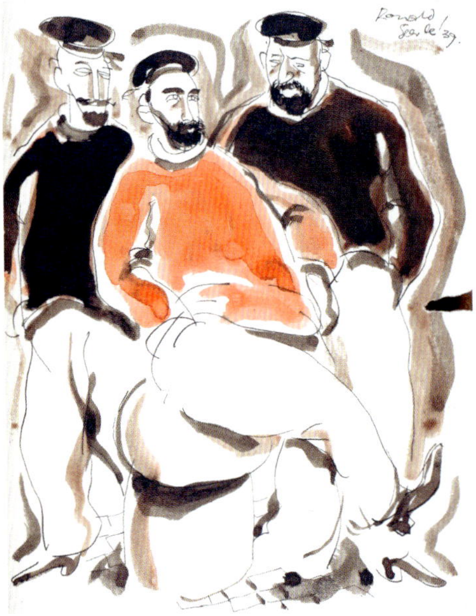

02 MERCHANT SAILORS
signed and dated /39
pen ink and watercolour
6 ¾ x 5 inches

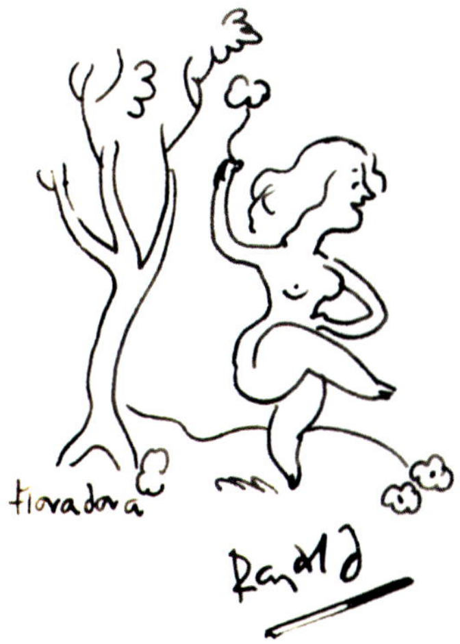

03 FLORADORA
signed 'Ronald' and inscribed with title
photograph of Ronald Searle on reverse
pen and ink
3 ¼ x 2 ¼ inches

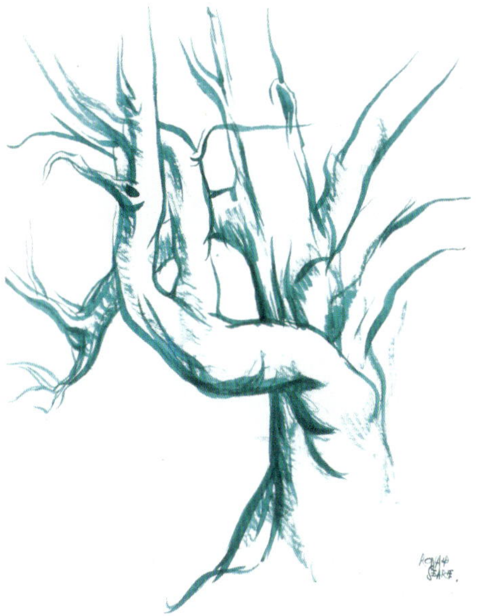

04 THE TREE
signed
ink
7 x 5 ½ inches

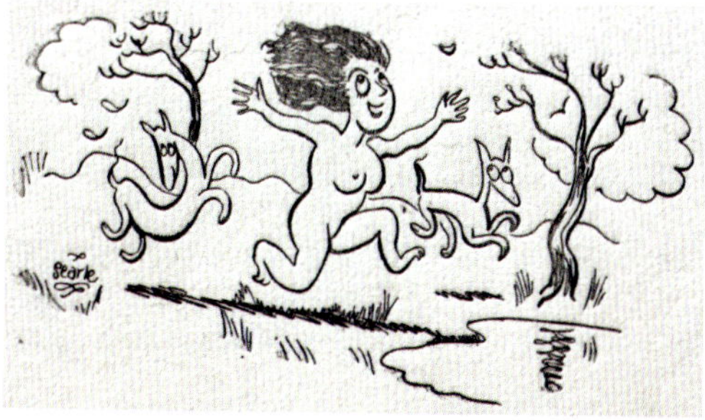

05 FROLICKING FEMALE
signed on block
linocut
2 ½ x 3 ½ inches

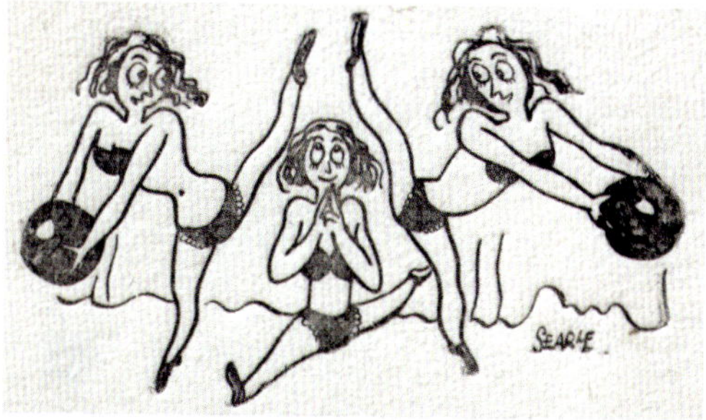

06 THREE FEMALE ENTERTAINERS
signed on block
linocut
2 ½ x 3 ¼ inches

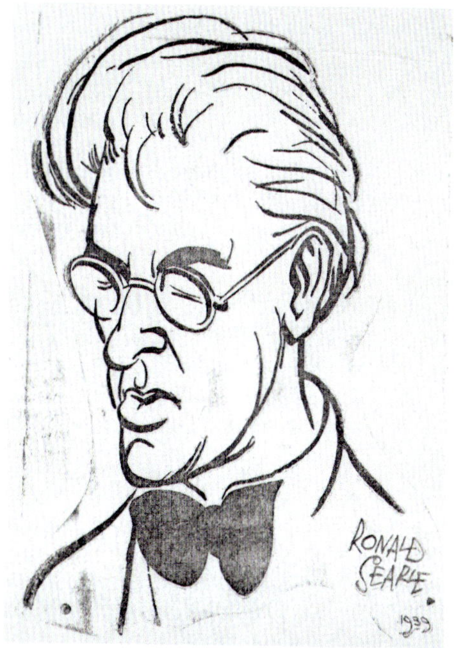

07 YEATS
inscribed with title
signed and dated 1939 on block
linocut
5 x 4 ½ inches
Illustrated: *The Granta*, 1939
Literature: *Ronald Searle. Graphic Master*, London: Cartoon Museum, 2010, page 8

1940-45: The Second World War

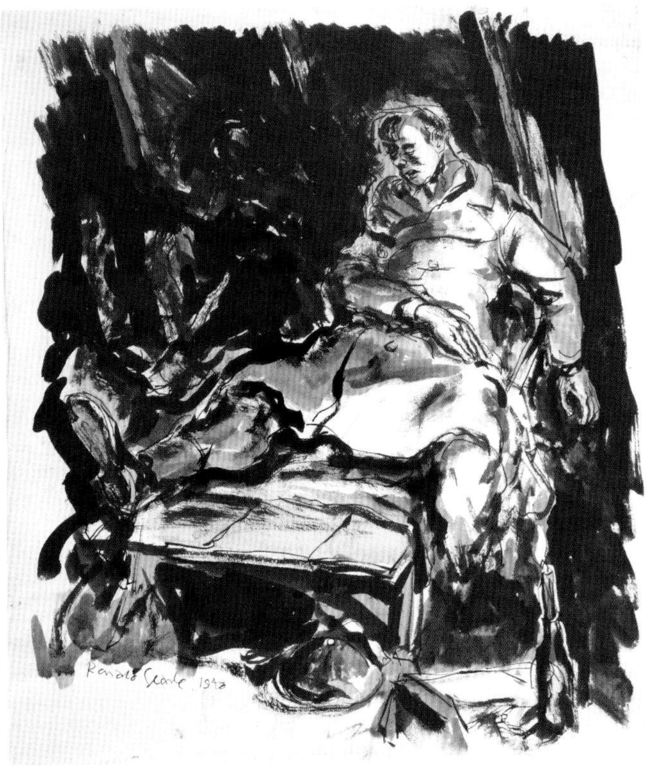

08 TIRED SOLDIER
signed and dated 1940
inscribed with title below mount
pen ink and watercolour
16 ½ x 14 inches
Provenance: Anne Dewing

'I've started already sending stuff away – lots of cartoons and prison drawings that I brought back with me. I shall bring some up – with me for you to see and I shall also try to carry your picture of the soldier back to it's rightful home!'

(Ronald Searle, in a letter to Anne Dewing, 29 October 1945)

It is now an accepted fact, even a truism, that Ronald Searle's experiences as a prisoner of the Japanese during the Second World War were the making of him as an artist. His ability and urge to draw kept him alive, and brought rare moments of pleasure to his fellow inmates. The resulting drawings comprised his first exhibition and prompted his first collection, *Forty Drawings* (1946). And much of what he observed and underwent was transformed into the black comedy of his most famous creations, notably the girls of St Trinian's.

Searle spent over three years as a prisoner of the Japanese. Incarcerated in various camps and forced to work on building the notorious Siam-Burma railway, he became exhausted, half-starved, and continually and dangerously ill. Nevertheless, he made time for and preserved energy to draw; as a result, he both produced a vital visual record of prison life, and provided many entertainments for the prisoners, including illustrations for camp magazines, set designs for shows, greetings cards and calendars. Though discipline varied within and between each camp, it remains extraordinary both that these works were made at all and that they have survived. Set against the more documentary drawings, of malnourished bodies in crowded conditions, and of their guards, these lively little drawings reveal memories of and hopes for an ordinary life, in which humour can take a more natural, almost casual part.

The Siam-Burma railway, built by prisoners of war, was completed on 23 October 1943. Searle was one of the few to survive this ordeal, though he was hardly unscathed. He was taken down to Kanchanaburi in a poor medical condition and, after some nursing from fellow prisoners, 'delivered back' to Singapore Island. Just before Christmas, he arrived at Sime Road Camp, a temporary place of rest for the incapacitated. Though he became ill again, he was at least settled and able to draw and, as his health improved, he became involved in productions at the 'Barn Theatre', both as a designer and a performer. However, on 4 May 1944, the prisoners were moved again.

On arriving at Changi Gaol, Searle was placed in Cell C1B, in the company of 200 other prisoners. Seriously ill for some months, he only gradually became well enough either to undertake manual work or to apply his artistic skills to the diversion of his fellow prisoners. He was then involved with theatrical productions, at 'Coconut Grove' and the 'Playhouse', and the camp magazine, *The Exile*.

Searle was known by his captors to be an artist, indeed all ranks of Japanese soldiers attended the shows that he designed and advertised. Nevertheless, he kept his work as private as possible, employing tiny 'easy to swallow' sketchbooks, and finding ingenious hiding places for his more 'subversive' documentary images. He particularly feared visits from members of Kempei-Tai, the Japanese Gestapo. However, the one 'request' by Captain Takahashi, the prisoner administrator, to see his drawings, in July 1944, transpired to have stemmed from the interest of one artist in another; Takahashi had been studying in Paris when he was called home to serve in the war. As a result of his inspection of Searle's drawings, he allowed him 60 sheets of good quality paper. Takahashi was himself replaced in July 1945, and the following months, the last of the war, proved especially hard, Searle spending much of that time in a hospital hut. But Searle did survive, being liberated on 28 August 1945, and returning to England two months later. Some of the cartoons that he brought back with him were worked up immediately for publication, while his experience of such an extreme conjunction of humanity and inhumanity influenced all his subsequent work.

09-13 Provenance: Stan Mesmer

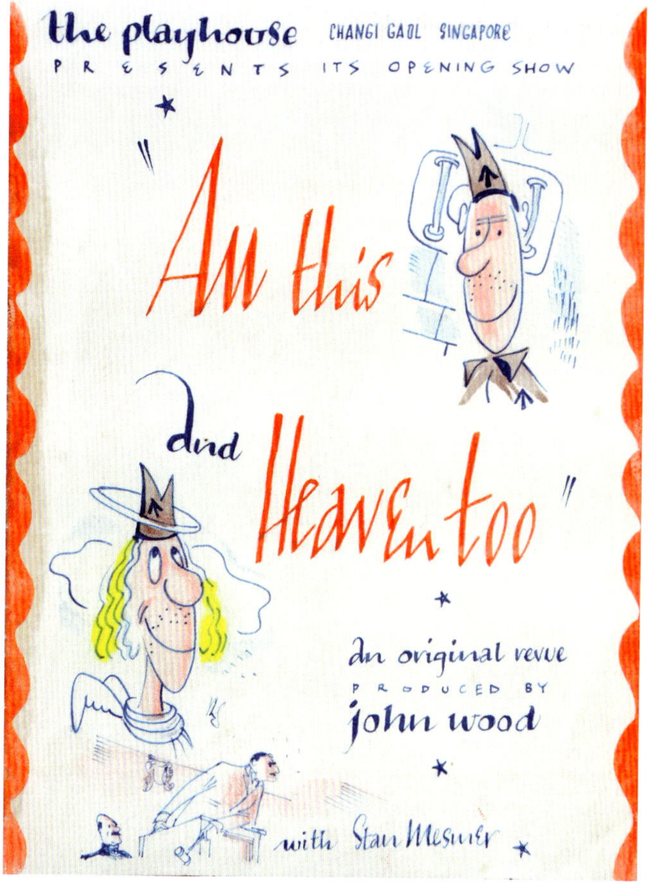

09 ALL THIS AND HEAVEN TOO
THEATRE PROGRAMME
pen ink, watercolour and coloured pencil with printed interior
7 x 5 ¼ inches folded

All This and Heaven Too

This programme was designed for a show that was produced by the Australian actor, John Wood, and starred Stan Mesmer. It was performed at the Playhouse, Changi Gaol, Singapore, in September 1944. Ronald Searle designed the production as well as the programme.

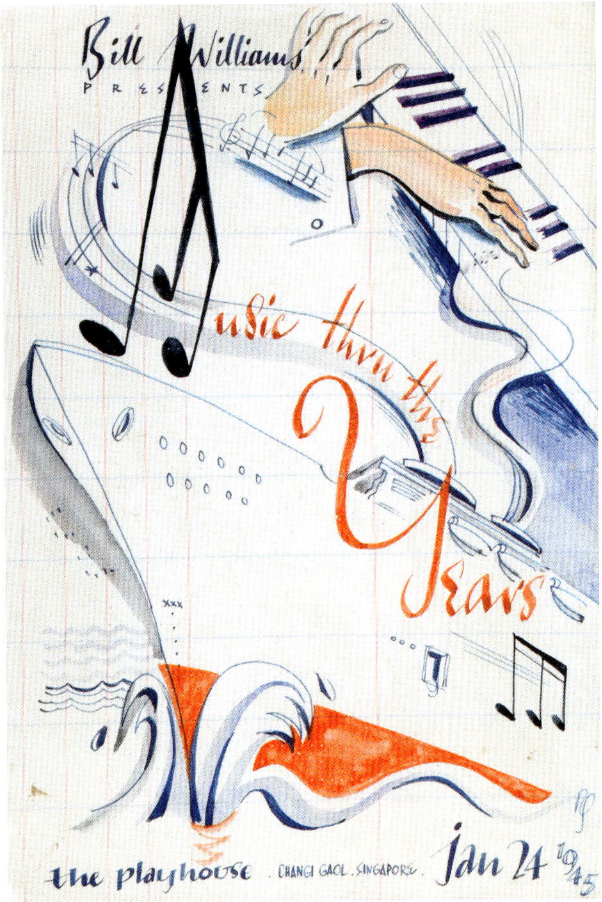

10 MUSIC THRU THE YEARS
THEATRE PROGRAMME
signed with initials
pen ink and watercolour with printed interior
8 ¾ x 6 inches folded

Music Thru the Years

This programme was designed for a show that was produced by Bill Williams. It was performed at the Playhouse, Changi Gaol, Singapore, from 24 January 1945. Ronald Searle designed the decorations and ballet costumes as well as the programme. The production was stopped by the Japanese, in March 1945, allegedly because it caused them offence.

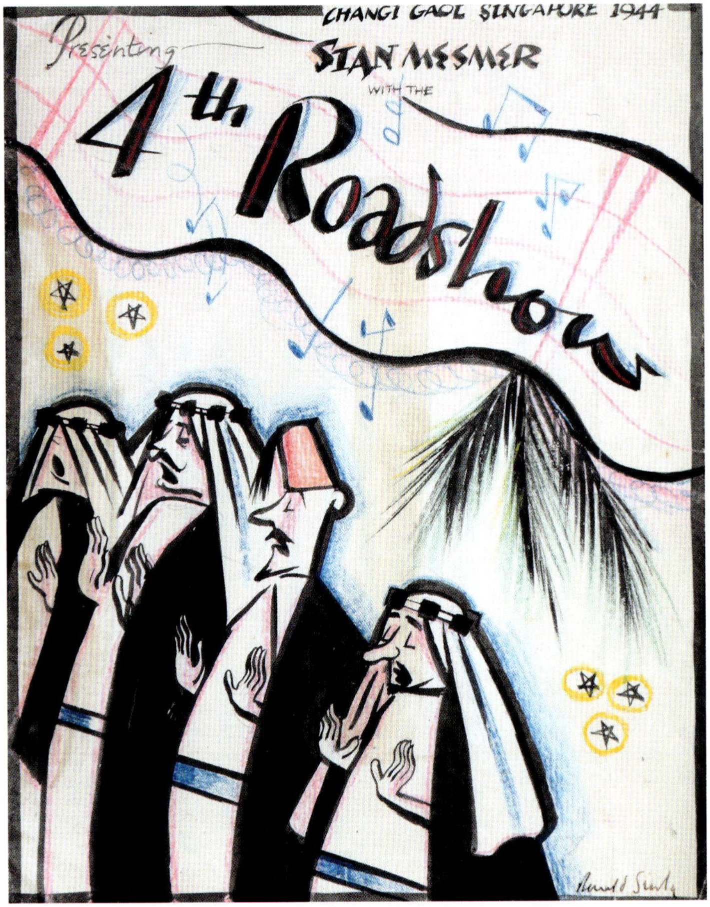

11 4TH ROADSHOW
THEATRE PROGRAMME
signed
pen ink and crayon on the reverse of an official leave roster, with printed interior
8 ½ x 6 ¾ inches folded

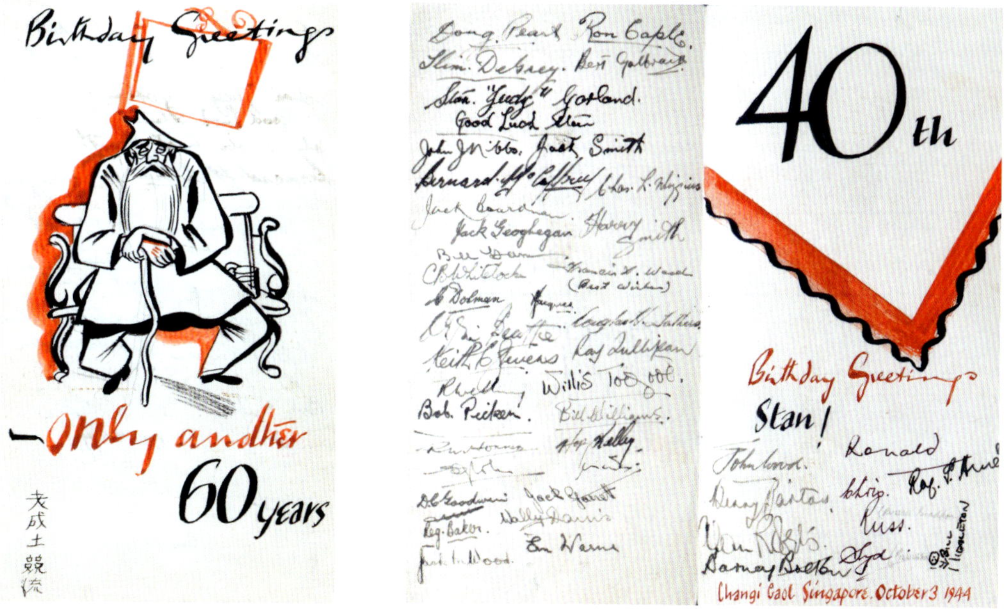

12 BIRTHDAY GREETINGS TO STAN MESMER – ONLY ANOTHER 60 YEARS
signed, inscribed 'Changi Gaol, Singapore' and dated 'October 3 1944', and further signed by 44 fellow prisoners including Russell Braddon and Syd Piddington, all on reverse
pen ink and watercolour
8 x 8 ¼ inches

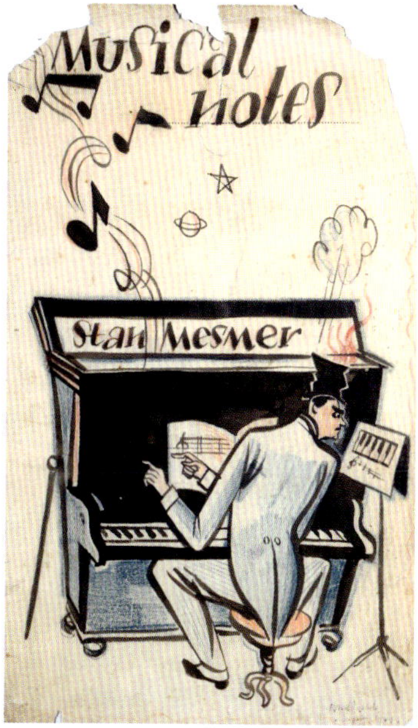

13 MUSICAL NOTES
signed and dated 'Singapore 1944'
dummy keyboard drawn on reverse in another hand
pen ink and crayon
12 ½ x 7 ¾ inches

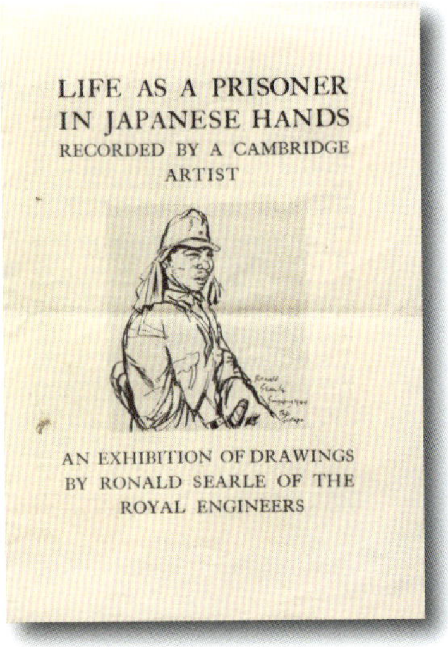

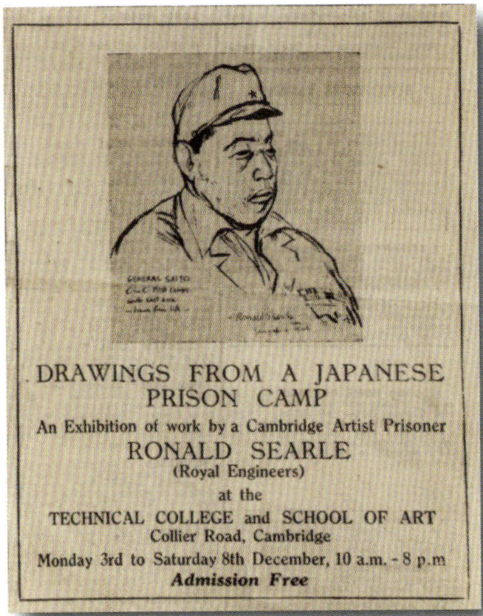

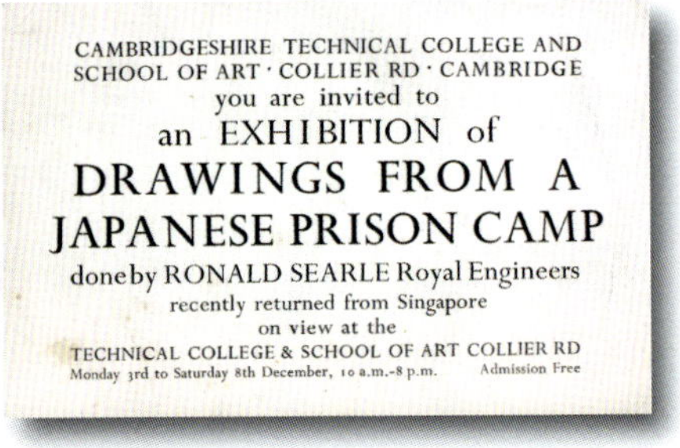

Drawings from a Japanese Prison Camp
Ronald Searle's first exhibition, 'Drawings from a Japanese Prison Camp', was held at the Technical College & School of Art, Collier Road, Cambridge, from Monday 3 to Saturday 8 December 1945.

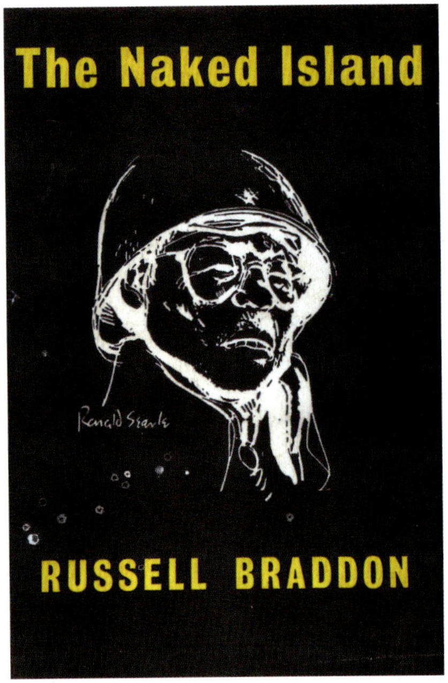

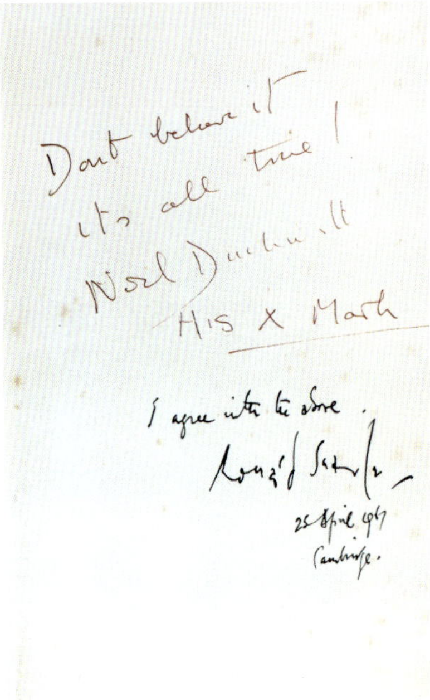

BOOKS FOR SALE ARE LISTED IN THIS CATALOGUE WITH A GREY BACKGROUND.

14 THE NAKED ISLAND
Russell Braddon
The Naked Island
London: Werner Laurie
1960
twentieth impression
[first edition 1952]
hard cover with dust jacket
266 pages
8 ¾ x 6 inches
signed and inscribed by Noel Duckworth 'Don't believe it's all true!' and signed, inscribed 'I agree with the above' and dated 'Cambridge 25 April 1967' by Ronald Searle

Canon Noel Duckworth Selling a Parker Pen to a Japanese Guard in Pudu Gaol

Educated at Cambridge, where he proved a notable coxswain, Noel Duckworth (1912-1980) became curate at the Church of the Transfiguration, Hull, following his ordination. At the outbreak of the Second World War, he was appointed Chaplain to the 2nd Battalion of the Cambridgeshire Regiment, and served in Malaya from 1941. Taken prisoner during the Battle of Muar in January 1942, he was first held at Pudu Gaol, Malaya, before being transferred to Changi Gaol, Singapore (where he met Ronald Searle). He was sent up into Thailand with the 'F' Force in April 1943, and later crossed the border into Burma to a camp called Tambaya – a hospital camp, where he stayed until April 1944. He returned to Singapore, remaining there until liberated in August 1945. He would become Canon of Accra in 1955 and first Chaplain of Churchill College, Cambridge, in 1961.

In *The Naked Island*, Russell Braddon described Duckworth as 'the most outstanding personality in Pudu Gaol' who, among many achievements, stayed with the wounded even during action, kept up the morale of prisoners and 'founded the gaol's black market' (*The Naked Island*, London: Werner Laurie, 1952, page 133). His achievements were celebrated in an edition of the BBC television programme, *This is Your Life*, on 12 January 1959. Searle appeared on the show, and presented this watercolour to him at that time.

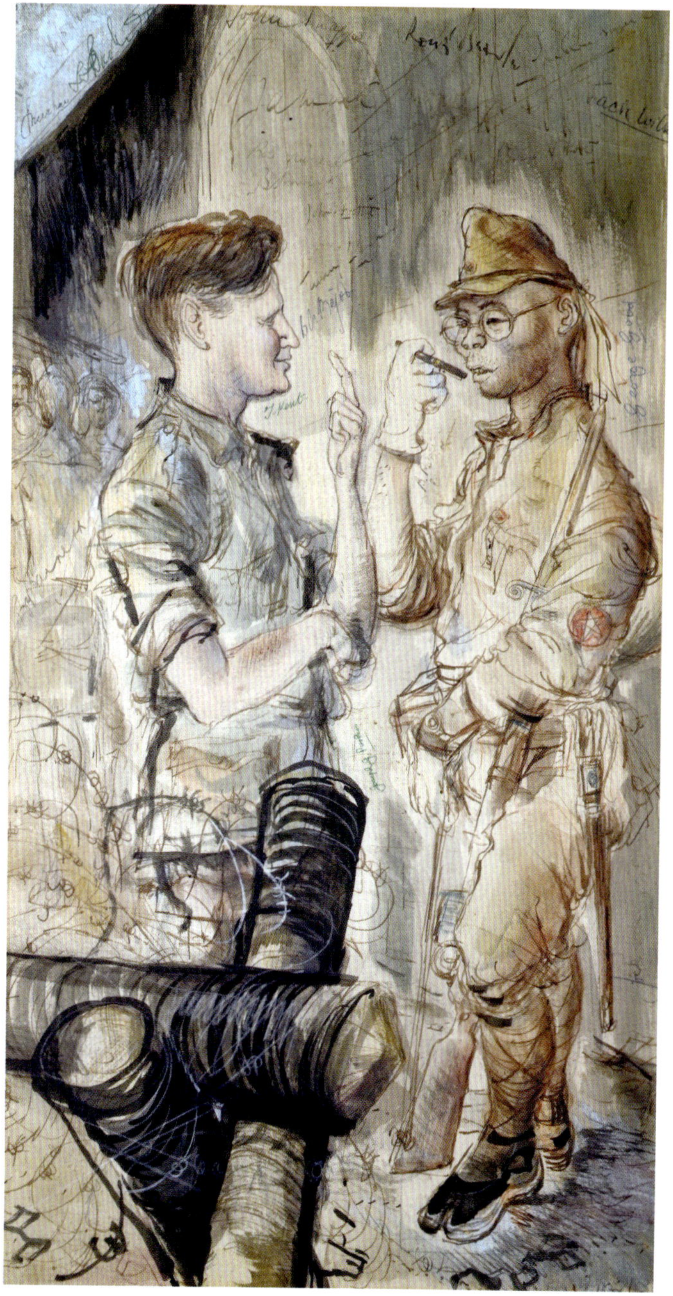

15 CANON NOEL DUCKWORTH SELLING A PARKER PEN TO A JAPANESE GUARD IN PUDU GAOL
signed, and further signed by various prisoners of war
pen ink and watercolour with crayon
17 ¼ x 9 inches

1945-50: After the War

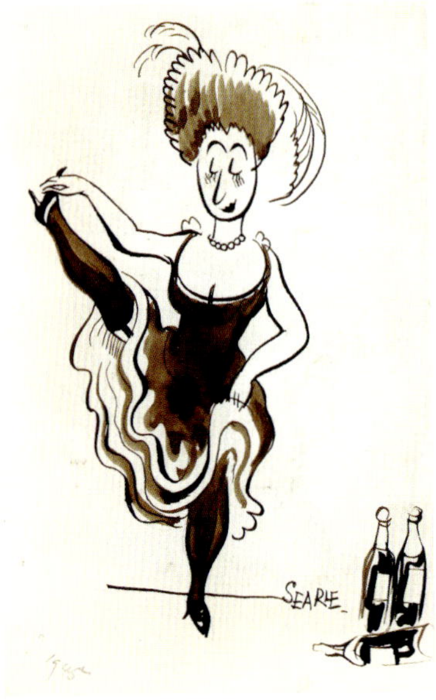

Cancan Dancer
Exemplifying his early cartoon style, and drawn by 1939, Searle used this Cancan Dancer on his first ever headed paper, while he was still living with his parents at 29 Collier Road, Cambridge. It appears above his head in a photograph of him from that year, in which he sits in mock Gothic gloom, accompanied by two skulls.

16 CANCAN DANCER
signed
pen and ink
5 x 3 ¼ inches
This drawing appeared on Ronald Searle's letterhead

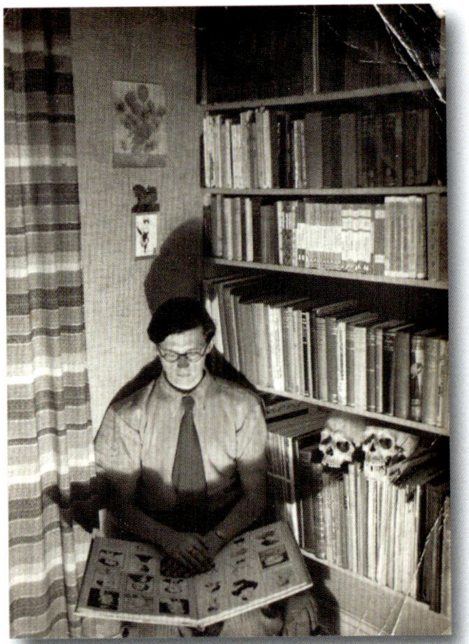

Ronald Searle at home, 29 Collier Road, Cambridge, 1939

Within a fortnight of his return to Cambridge, on 26 October 1945, Searle left for London in order to establish himself as an artist, going home to 29 Collier Road only intermittently, at weekends and for holidays. His various addresses – as seen on his letter headings – chart his progress. Initially, he stayed with his 'old art-school colleagues Pamela and Bernard Lucas' (Davies, page 74), at 3B Edith Grove, Chelsea. He discovered that periodicals were short of humorous artists, and soon became a figure of interest in his own right, being photographed for a feature in *Illustrated* magazine [see **29**]. Then, in New Year 1946, Chelsea Town Council 'allotted him a room at 34 Tite Street' (Davies, page 75), because of his status as a former prisoner of war. (Number 34 had once been 16, and thus the home of Oscar Wilde.) As a result of a bout of malaria, in the March, one of his letters to Anne Dewing was written from Princess Beatrice Hospital, Earls Court [**31**], though he continued to live in Tite Street until the July. Increasing commissions from magazines enabled him to move to 77 Bedford Gardens, off Kensington Church Street, taking over Studio Two from a Belgian painter named Cluysenaar [see **39**]. 77 Bedford Gardens was a proper artists' colony: 'the painter Jankel Adler lived upstairs and the two combative Roberts, Colquhoun and Macbryde, on the floor below. Eddie Wolfe had a room right at the top; John Minton was also in residence; and Keith Vaughan frequently called by' (Davies, page 78). The confident drawing of a woman in a headscarf – perhaps an Indian female at Colombo [see **26**] – that now emblazoned his writing paper emphasised his arrival on the artistic scene.

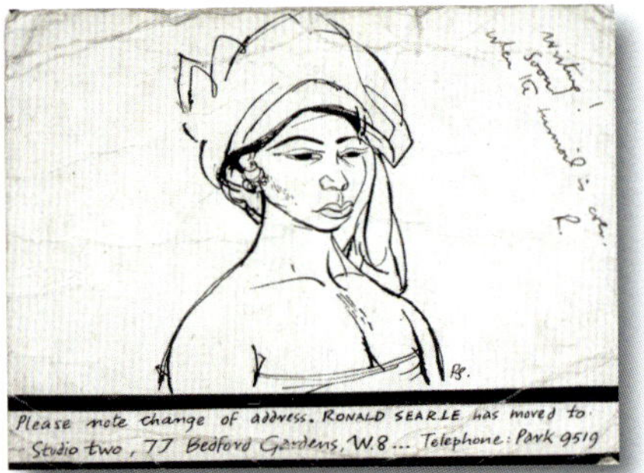

Change of address post card, July 1946

Letters to Morley Stuart
As Editor of the *Cambridge Daily News*, Morley Stuart gave Ronald Searle his first opportunities to publish cartoons on a regular basis, during the years 1935-39. They developed a good relationship, and resumed contact when Searle was released from Changi Gaol at the end of the Second World War. Over the next three years, Searle kept Stuart up to date with his burgeoning career through an occasional correspondence.
In 1948, Stuart became the dedicatee of Searle's cartoon collection, *Hurrah for St Trinian's* as '30 Years Editor of the "Cambridge Daily News", who published my first 200 drawings'.

For transcriptions of these letters, see pages 146-199

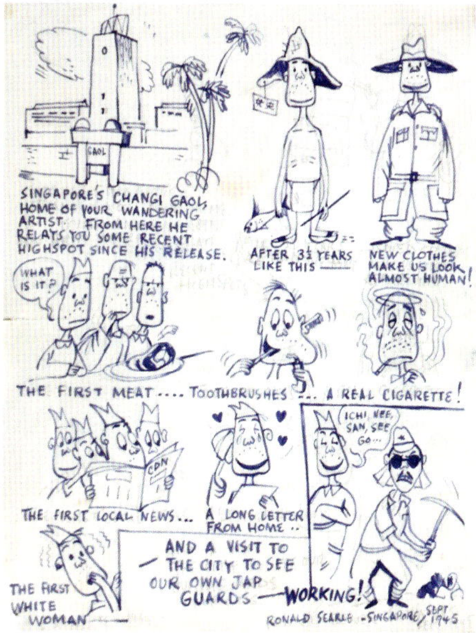

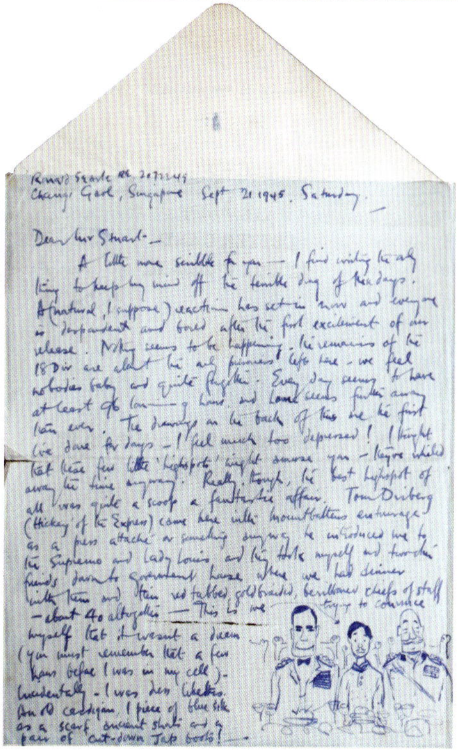
Ronald Searle [illegible]
Changi Gaol, Singapore Sept 21 1945. Saturday. –

Dear Mr Stuart –
A little more scribble for you – I find writing the only thing to keep my mind off the terrible drag of these days. A (natural, I suppose) reaction has set in now and everyone is despondent and bored after the first excitement of our release. Nothing seems to be happening – the remains of the 18 Div are about the only prisoners left here – we feel nobodies baby and quite forgotten – Every day seems to have at least 96 lo—ng hours, and home seems further away than ever. The drawings on the back of this are the first I've done for days – I feel much too depressed! I thought that these few little 'highspots' might amuse you – they've whiled away the time anyway. Really, though, the best highspot of all was quite a scoop a fantastic affair. Tom Driberg ('Hickey' of the Express) came here with Mountbatten's entourage as a press attaché or something anyway, he introduced me to the Supremo and Lady Louis and they took myself and two other friends down to government house where we had dinner with them and their red tabbed, gold braided, bemedalled chiefs of staff – about 40 altogether – This is me trying to convince myself that it wasn't a dream (you must remember that a few hours before I was in my cell) – Incidentally – I was dressed like this. An old cardigan, 1 piece of blue silk as a scarf, ancient shorts and a pair of cut-down Jap boots! –

17 LETTER TO MORLEY STUART ESQ
CHANGI GAOL, SINGAPORE, SATURDAY
21 SEPTEMBER 1945
autographed signed letter
written in pen and ink
on folded 'Air mail letter card'
6 ¾ x 10 ½ inches
includes two pen and ink drawings

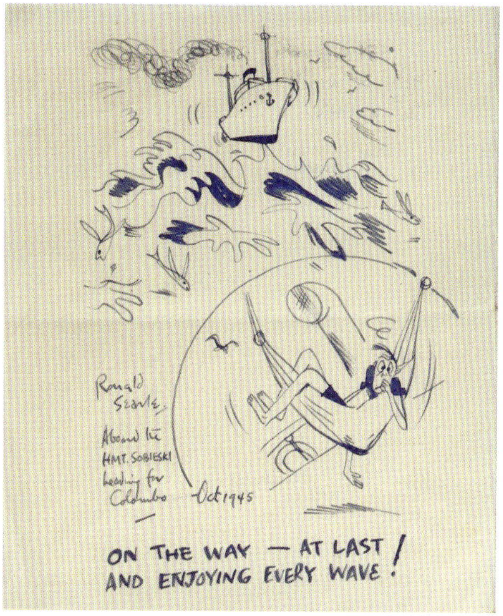

18 LETTER TO MORLEY STUART ESQ
HMT SOBIESKI, MONDAY
1 OCTOBER 1945
autographed signed letter
written in pen and ink
on folded 'Air mail letter card'
6 ¾ x 10 ½ inches
includes a signed pen and ink drawing, inscribed 'On the way – at last and enjoying every wave!' and 'Aboard the HMT Sobieski heading for Colombo', and dated 'Oct 1945'

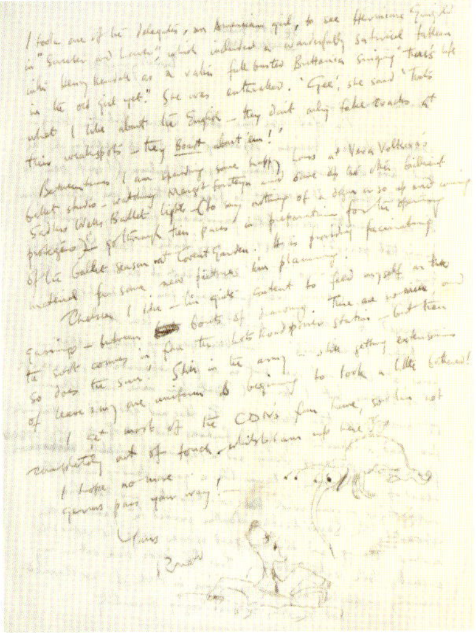

19 LETTER TO MORLEY STUART ESQ
MONDAY NIGHT [1946]
autographed signed letter
written in pen and ink
on two sides of one sheet
8 ¼ x 6 ½ inches
includes a pen and ink drawing

20 LETTER TO MORLEY STUART ESQ
WEDNESDAY (not illustrated)
autographed signed letter
written in pen and ink
on two sides of one sheet
5 ½ x 8 ¾ inches

21 LETTER TO MORLEY STUART ESQ
25 SEPTEMBER 1947 (not illustrated)
autographed signed letter
written in pen and ink
on two sides of one sheet
10 x 8 inches

22 LETTER TO MORLEY STUART ESQ
18 APRIL 1948 (not illustrated)
autographed signed letter
written in pen and ink
on two sides of one sheet
10 x 8 inches

Letters to Anne Dewing

Anne Dewing was the fiancée of Ronald Searle's close friend, Stuart Ludman, who died in Changi Gaol of cerebral malaria on 2 March 1945; Noel Duckworth [see **15**] was with him at the time of his death. Stuart and Searle had enlisted at the same time, and were together in Changi Gaol, both working on the camp magazine, *The Exile*. In his letter to Mrs Ludman, Searle wrote that during his last days 'Stuart's spirits were high always. He read a lot and kept up his studies of Music, and we talked together many times about our homes and letters' [**23**].

Anne Dewing (1915-1973) was born in Staffordshire, the daughter of a Methodist minister. Following his death, in 1930, the family moved to Norwich, and lived at Riverside Road. Training in London at Camberwell School of Art, Anne returned to Norwich to become the art teacher at Angel Road Senior School. While there, she made a puppet theatre with amazing and bizarre puppets so that the pupils could put on shows. For a number of years, she also acted at the Maddermarket Theatre, at which amateur actors worked under a professional director. It was probably through the Maddermarket, that she met Ronald and Stuart, both of whom were stationed in Norfolk during 1940.

After Stuart's death, Searle remained close to Anne. They continued to correspond following his move to London to develop his career, and she visited him and his family following his marriage to Kaye Webb. They lost touch once he moved to Paris. In her later years, Anne was Vice Head of Downham Market Girls' School, Norfolk, as well as their art teacher. Though she never married or had children, she is remembered by her niece as 'a real character and a great story teller, often having us kids on the edge of our seats, or in stitches with her yarns'.

Many thanks to Hilary Dewing for help in compiling this note.

23 TYPED LETTER TO MRS LUDMAN
CHANGI GAOL, SINGAPORE,
17 SEPTEMBER 1945 (not illustrated)
typed letter
on two sides of one sheet
7 x 5 ¼ inches

24 LETTER TO ANNE DEWING
CHANGI GAOL, SINGAPORE,
17 SEPTEMBER 1945 (not illustrated)
autographed signed letter
written in pen and ink
on folded 'Air mail letter card'
7 ¼ x 9 ¼ inches

25 LETTER TO ANNE DEWING
HMT SOBIESKI, MONDAY 1 OCTOBER 1945 (not illustrated)
autographed signed letter
written in pen and ink
on folded 'Air mail letter card'
6 ¾ x 10 ½ inches

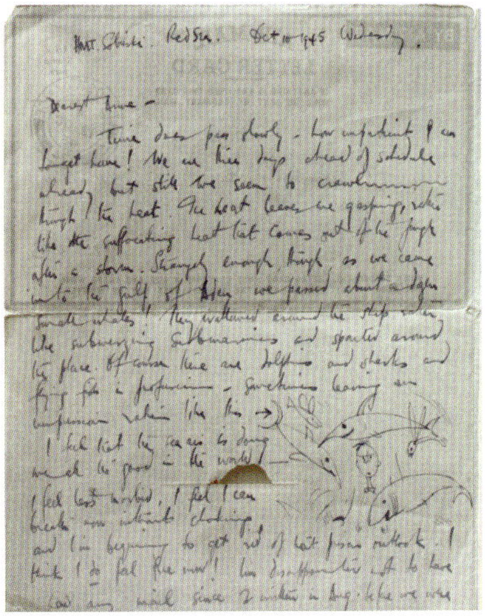

26 LETTER TO ANNE DEWING
HMT SOBIESKI, RED SEA, WEDNESDAY
10 OCTOBER 1945
autographed signed letter
written in pen and ink
on folded 'Air mail letter card'
6 ¾ x 10 ½ inches
includes a pen and ink drawing

27 LETTER TO ANNE DEWING
SUNDAY NIGHT OCTOBER 1945
autographed signed letter
written in pen and ink
on six sides of three sheets
7 x 5 ¼ inches
includes two pen and ink drawings
[with stamped addressed envelope]

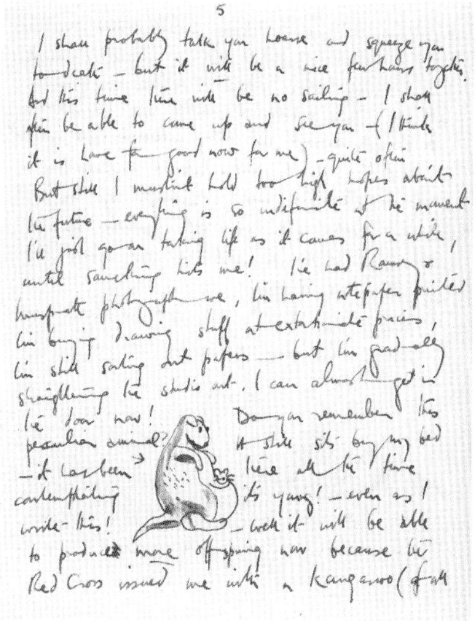

5
I shall probably take you home and squeeze you to death – but it will be a nice few hours together. But this time there will be no sailing – I shall often be able to come up and see you – (I think it is here for good now for me) – quite often. But still I mustn't hold too high hopes about the future – everything is so indefinite at the moment. I'll just go on taking life as it comes for a while, until something hits me! I've had Ramsey & Muspratt photograph me, I'm having notepaper printed, I'm buying drawing stuff at extortionate prices, I'm still sorting out papers – but I'm gradually straightening the studio out. I can almost get in the door now! Do you remember this peculiar animal? – it has been contemplating → It still sits by my bed here all the time its young! – even as I write this! – well it will be able to produce more offspring now because the Red Cross issued me with a kangaroo (of all

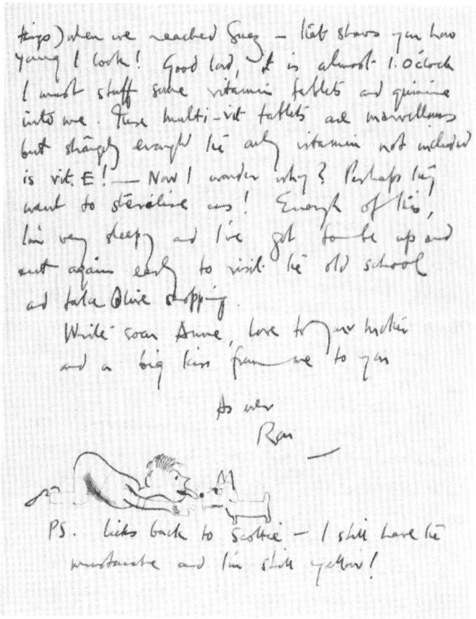

things) when we reached Suez – that shows you how young I look! Good lord, it is almost 1.0'clock I must stuff some vitamin tablets and quinine into me. These multi-vit tablets are marvellous but strangely enough the only vitamin not included is vit. E! — Now I wonder why? Perhaps they want to sterilise us! Enough of this, I'm very sleepy and I've got to be up and out again early to visit the old school and take Olive shopping.

While soon Anne, love to your mother and a big kiss from me to you

As ever
Ron

PS. licks back to Scottie – I still have the moustache and I'm still yellow!

28 LETTER TO ANNE DEWING
FRIDAY (not illustrated)
autographed signed letter
written in pen and ink
on two sides of one sheet
8 ¾ x 5 ½ inches

29 LETTER TO ANNE DEWING
WEDNESDAY 7 NOVEMBER 1945
(not illustrated)
autographed signed letter
written in pen and ink
on two sides of one sheet
6 ¾ x 5 ¼ inches

30 LETTER TO ANNE DEWING
COLLIER ROAD, 5 DECEMBER 1945
(not illustrated)
autographed signed letter
written in pen and ink
on reverse of an invitation card for an exhibition of 'Drawings from a Japanese Prison Camp' Cambridgeshire Technical College and School of Art, Collier Road, Cambridge, December 1945
3 ½ x 5 inches

31 LETTER TO ANNE DEWING
WARD A, PRINCESS BEATRICE HOSPITAL, TUESDAY 5 MARCH 1946
(not illustrated)
autographed signed letter
written in pen and ink
on one side of one sheet
11 x 8 ½ inches

32 LETTER TO ANNE DEWING
CAMBRIDGE, SUNDAY 24 MARCH 1946
(not illustrated)
autographed signed letter
written in pen and ink
on two sides of two sheets
10 x 8 inches

33 LETTER TO ANNE DEWING
GOOD THURSDAY 1946
(not illustrated)
autographed signed letter
written in pen and ink
on two sides of one sheet
10 x 8 inches

34 LETTER TO ANNE DEWING
CAMBRIDGE, SUNDAY 5PM MAY 1946
(not illustrated)
autographed signed letter
written in pencil
on four sides of two sheets
10 x 8 inches
[with stamped addressed envelope]

35 LETTER TO ANNE DEWING
SATURDAY NIGHT
(not illustrated)
autographed signed letter
written in pen and ink
on seven sides of six sheets
6 ¾ x 4 ¼ inches

36 LETTER TO ANNE DEWING
SATURDAY
(not illustrated)
autographed signed letter
written in pen and ink
on two sides of one sheet
10 x 8 inches

37 LETTER TO ANNE DEWING
THURSDAY NIGHT (not illustrated)
autographed signed letter
written in pen and ink
on two sides of one sheet
10 x 8 inches
includes a pen and ink drawing

38 LETTER TO ANNE DEWING
WEDNESDAY (not illustrated)
autographed signed letter
written in pen and ink
on two sides of one sheet
10 x 8 inches

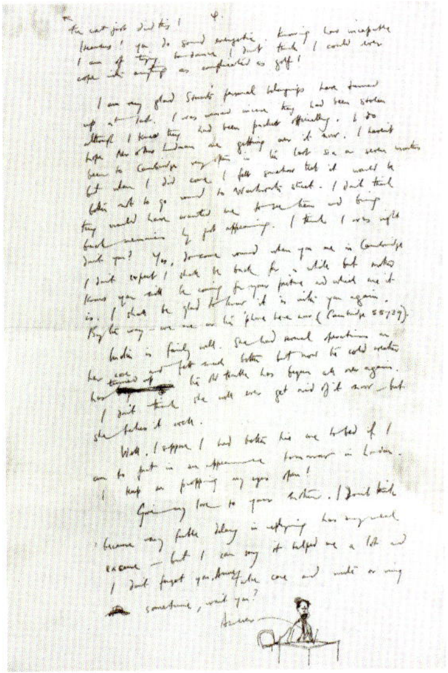

39 LETTER TO ANNE DEWING
CAMBRIDGE, SUNDAY
autographed letter
written in pen and ink
on two sides of two sheets
14 ¾ x 9 ¾ inches
includes a pen and ink drawing

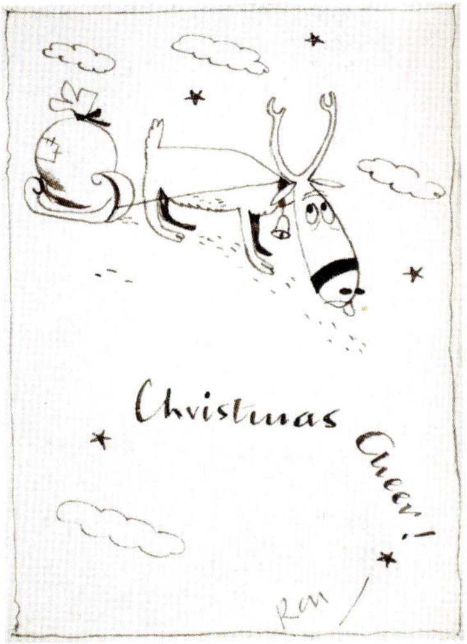

40 CHRISTMAS CHEER!
signed 'Ron' and inscribed with title
inscribed 'Writing any moment now!' on reverse
pen and ink
5 ½ x 3 ¾ inches
Provenance: Anne Dewing

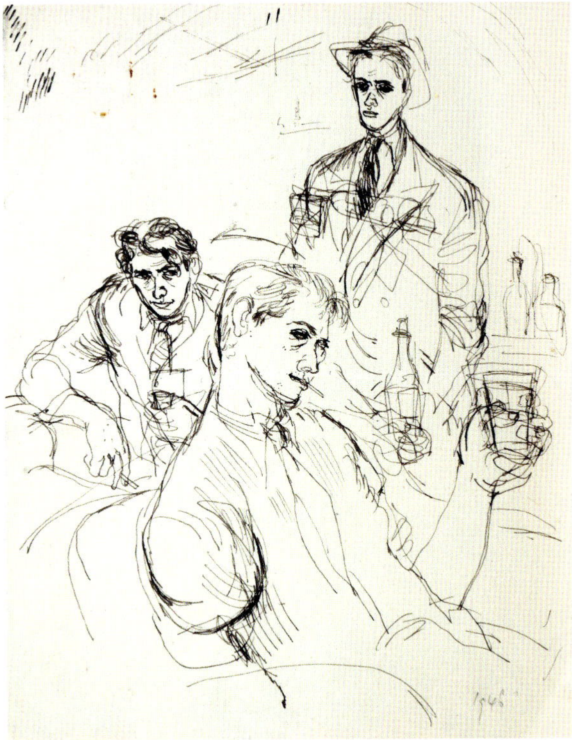

41 THREE MEN IN A BAR
pen and ink drawing of a
witch's hat on reverse
pen and ink
9 x 6 ¾ inches

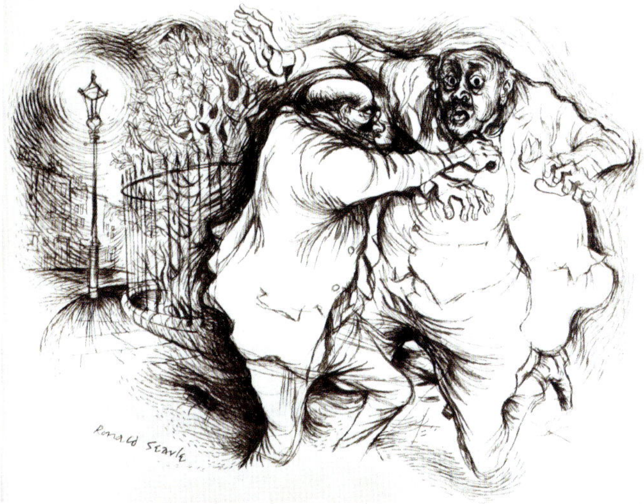

42 HE SLIT HIS THROAT
signed
pen and ink
8 x 10 ¼ inches

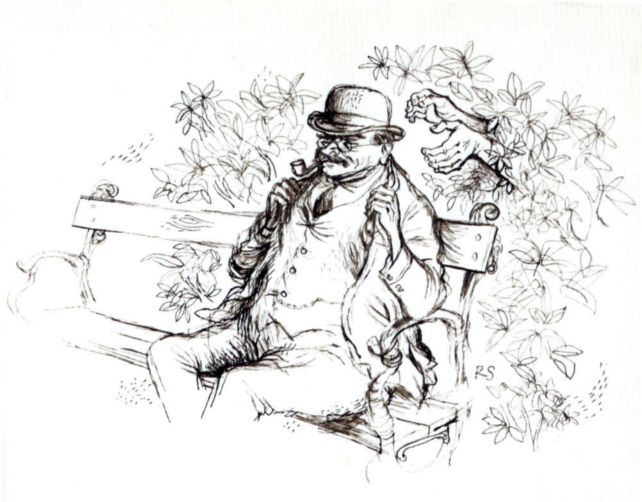

43 THE HANDS APPEARED BEHIND HIM
signed with initials
pen and ink
7 x 9 inches

44 IN SUSPENSE
inscribed 'Fuchs Trial'
inscribed with ideas for a picture for *The Saturday Book*, ideas and sketches for a cartoon called 'The Cat O' Nine Tales' for *The Tribune* and notes on the Fuchs Trial on reverse
pen ink and pencil
9 ½ x 15 ¼ inches
Preliminary drawing for *Leader Magazine*, Special Supplement, 18 March 1950, page 2

In Suspense

In 1950, *Leader Magazine* commissioned Ronald Searle to attend the Old Bailey trial of the German-British theoretical physicist Klaus Fuchs (1911-1988). Fuchs would be convicted of supplying the USSR with information about American, British and Canadian atomic bomb research. As Davies explains, Searle brought back 'drawings of Fuchs' pale figure in the dock; sketching within courts was illegal, but Searle's visual memory was already trained to reproduce scenes after the event' (page 91).

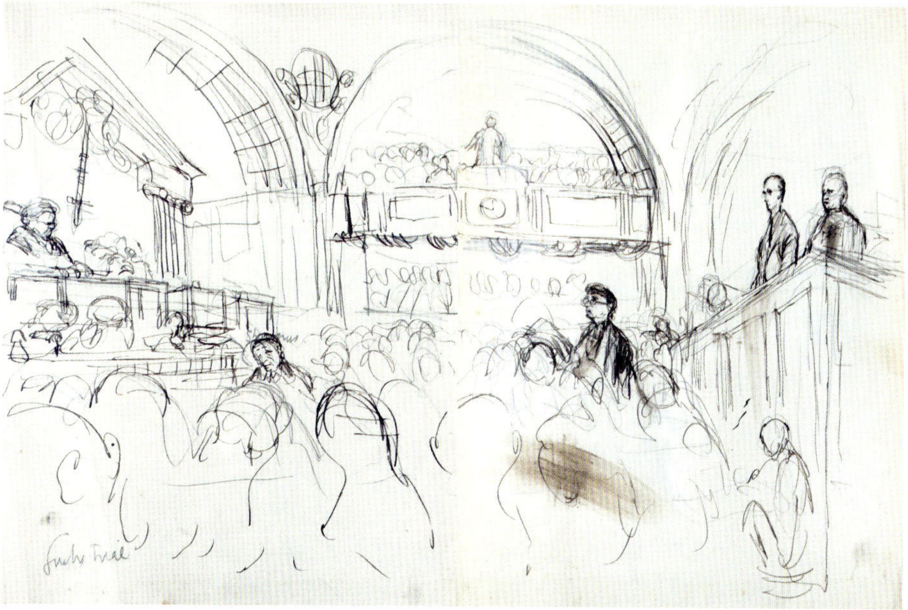

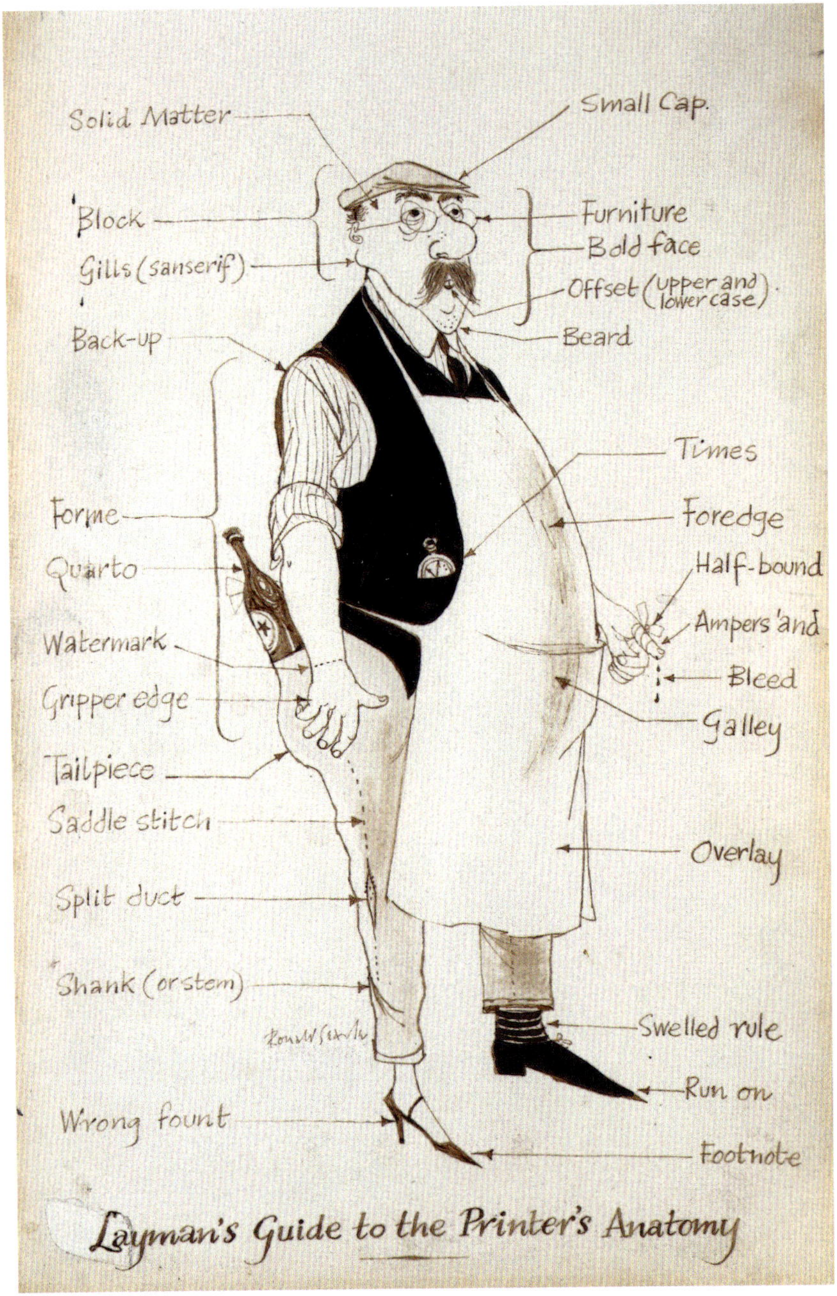

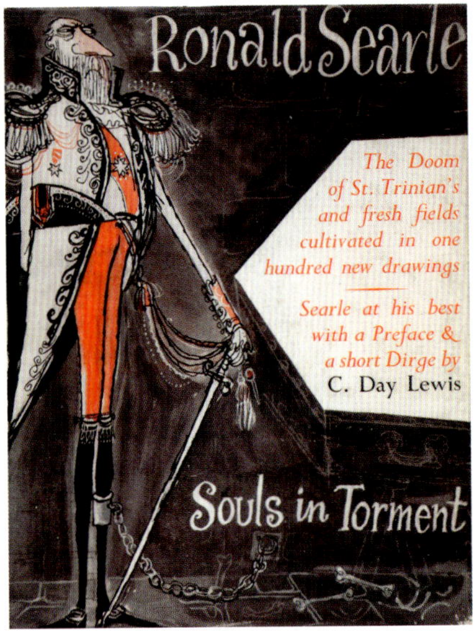

45 SOULS IN TORMENT
Ronald Searle
Souls in Torment
London: Perpetua
1953
first edition
hard cover with dust jacket
96 pages
10 x 7 ½ inches

46 LAYMAN'S GUIDE TO THE PRINTER'S ANATOMY
signed
stamped with artist's address, copyright details and '2 Jan 1950' on reverse
pen and ink
13 x 8 ½ inches
Illustrated: Ronald Searle, *Souls in Torment*, London: Perpetua Books, 1953, page 38, 'Morbid Anatomies'

2: 1950s

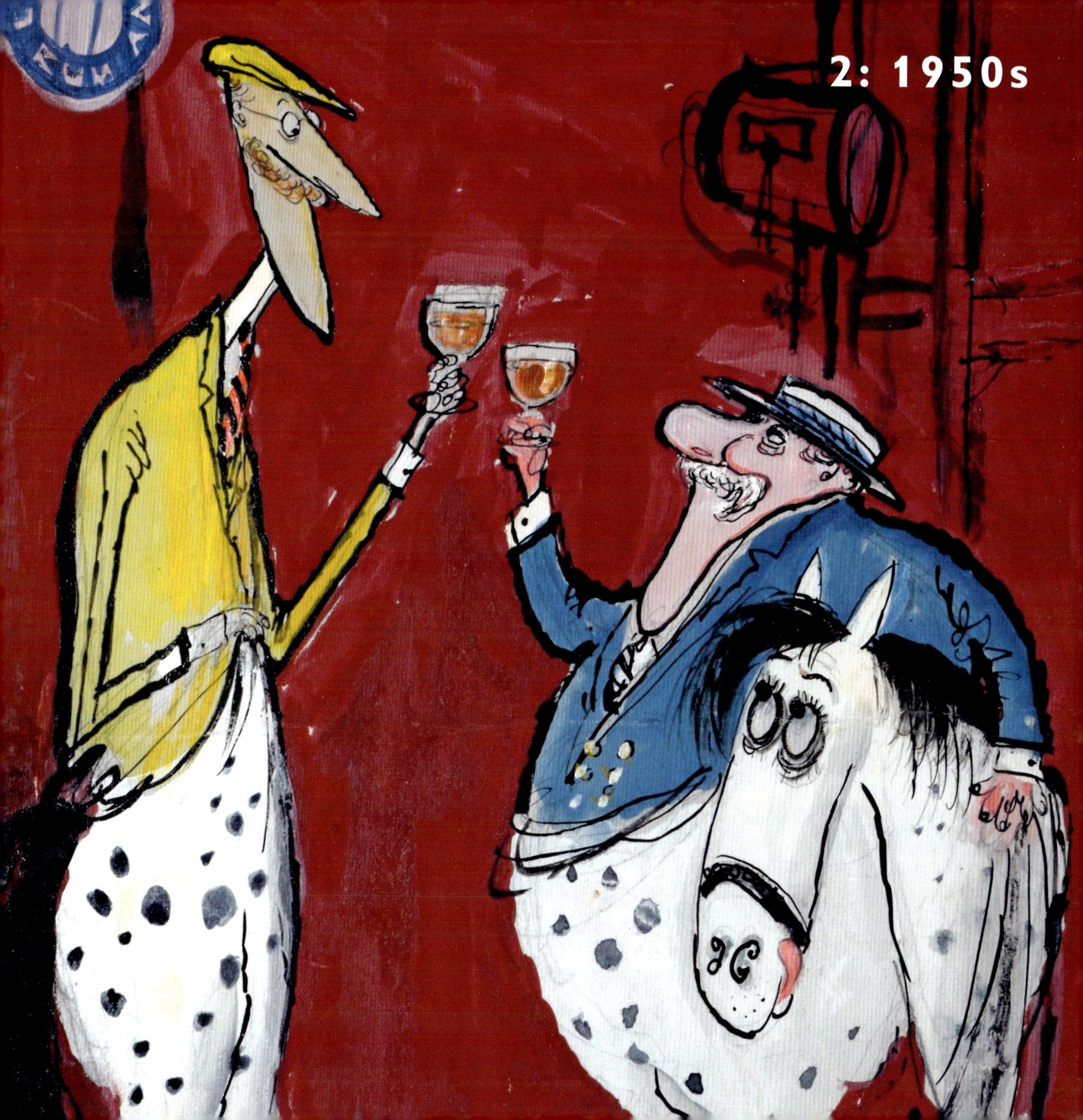

1950-60: St Trinian's

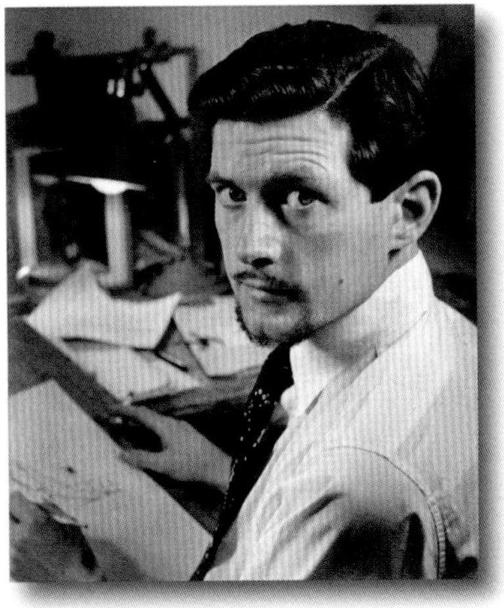

Ronald Searle by the photographer, Wolfgang Suschitzky (born 1912), who worked along side him on *Lilliput* magazine

'It is interesting to note how men of Searle's generation – Spike Milligan being another notable example – translated the unimaginable trauma of the war into stuff like St Trinian's or The Goon Show. And how distinctly unsettling it is when you look out at the drawings he produced in secret on the Burma railway, and then see direct visual quotations of torture and beheadings in his later St Trinian's cartoons.'

(Martin Rowson, *Guardian*, 4 January 2012)

It is only since Searle's death in 2011 that his inspiration for St Trinian's has been fully revealed. On 5 January 2012, the weekly newspaper, *Cambridge First*, quoted from a letter that Searle wrote to the Perse School in 1993:

> *As you know, I was born in Cambridge, and St Trinian's emerged from an amalgam of local schoolgirls.*
>
> *My sister apart, I think we could say that the main influences were certainly the Perse and the Cambridge High School for Girls.*
>
> *The Perse School for Girls was a positive source of inspiration for St Trinian's but I hope the school won't hold that against me so many years after the crime!*

However, it took another experience, during the Second World War, to provide a catalyst for these childhood memories, and so lead Searle to develop them into cartoons.

While serving with the Royal Engineers, in Kirkcudbright, early in 1941, Searle made friends with the Scottish artist, Bill Johnston, his wife, Dorothy, and their daughters, Cécile and Pat. The girls were pupils of St Trinnean's, a progressive Edinburgh school that was evacuated to Galashiels for the duration of the war. They shared stories of the school with Searle, and – in the words of Russell Davies – 'to their great delight' he 'made free with the traditions of this institution, not only Anglicizing its spelling but representing it as a forcing-house for juvenile delinquency of a positively Sohoid raffishness' (Davies, page 49).

Producing a number of St Trinian's drawings for Cécile and Pat, Searle published his first cartoon on the subject in *Lilliput* in October 1941. However, he did not get to see it in print until February 1942, when he found a tatty copy of the magazine on a Singapore street, while under fire from the Japanese. Though it is a gentle image, Searle would develop the theme of the girls' school in a much blacker direction, influenced by his treatment as a Japanese Prisoner of War. The second St Trinian's cartoon to appear in *Lilliput*, in April 1946, had a more characteristically violent caption: 'Hand up the girl who burnt down the East Wing last night'.

Originally appearing in *Lilliput*, the St Trinian's cartoons were then gathered by Macdonald & Co in mixed collections of cartoons: *Hurrah for St Trinian's! and Other Lapses* (1948), *The Female Approach, with Masculine Sidelights* (1949) and *Back to the Slaughterhouse, and Other Ugly Moments* (1951). The last of these includes a succinct example of physical and psychological bullying – 'Go on, say it – "I resolve to leave my body to science"' – in which one girl virtually strangles another into submission [**49**].

By 1951, Searle was already beginning to tire of the subject, dismissing 'these awful St Trinian's schoolgirls that I do' to a young Quentin Blake, who was one of those who questioned the artist when he appeared on the BBC radio programme, *Under-20 Parade*. Nevertheless, the following year, he did allow his *News Chronicle* colleague, 'Timothy Shy' (D B Wyndham-Lewis), to write a narrative about the school, and illustrated the resulting comic romance, *The Terror of St Trinian's*, with such vigorous drawings as *Debagging Old Flannelpants* [**50**]. The great success of this *jeu d'esprit* – published by Max Parrish – was fuelled by a publicity stunt in which a group of young women, dressed as schoolgirls, and headed by the actress, Hermione Gingold, invaded Foyle's bookshop.

From that point, Searle attempted to bring his involvement with St Trinian's to an end, refusing, for instance, to provide Max Parrish with a sequel to *The Terror of St Trinian's*. Then, in 1953, he published *Souls in Torment*, through his own imprint of Perpetua Books, which he 'explicitly intended as a funeral rite for St Trinian's' (Davies, page 101), bringing the school to an end in an atomic explosion, and employing his friend, the poet, C Day Lewis, to write 'a short dirge'.

However, once Frank Launder and Sidney Gilliat were allowed to produce a film inspired by Searle's drawings, in 1954, St Trinian's developed a life of its own, making it impossible to quash. Starring George Cole, Joyce Grenfell and Alastair Sim, *The Belles of St Trinian's* immediately entered the popular imagination and, for many people, remains the point of entry to exploring the best-known girls' school in the world. Furthermore, Searle was directly involved in the film and its three most immediate sequels, providing drawings for their title sequences and designing posters to advertise them.

In 1959, Searle's first wife, Kaye Webb, attempted another full stop by compiling *The St Trinian's Story* as 'the whole ghastly dossier', and publishing it under the Perpetua imprint in the autumn. The dust jacket described it as 'a monumental warning to any budding Frankenstein not to create a monster – however small and spotty'. Two years later, Searle took more drastic action to divorce himself from his native reputation as the creator of St Trinian's, leaving Kaye and their children, and settling in France.

St Trinian's Schoolgirls
Ronald Searle dedicated this drawing to the Manchester born artist, Oscar Pollak (1907-1980). Pollak worked in England and Argentina as a caricaturist, illustrator, printmaker and sculptor. Apparently, he was a great friend of Walt Disney, who offered him several positions within the Disney Studios.

47 ST TRINIAN'S SCHOOLGIRLS
signed with initials and inscribed 'For Oscar Pollak, from the artist' and dated 'Sept 1950'
pen and ink
4 ½ x 3 ½ inches
Provenance: Oscar Pollak
Illustrated: Ronald Searle, *The Female Approach. With Masculine Sidelights*, London: Macdonald, [1949], half title page and page 72

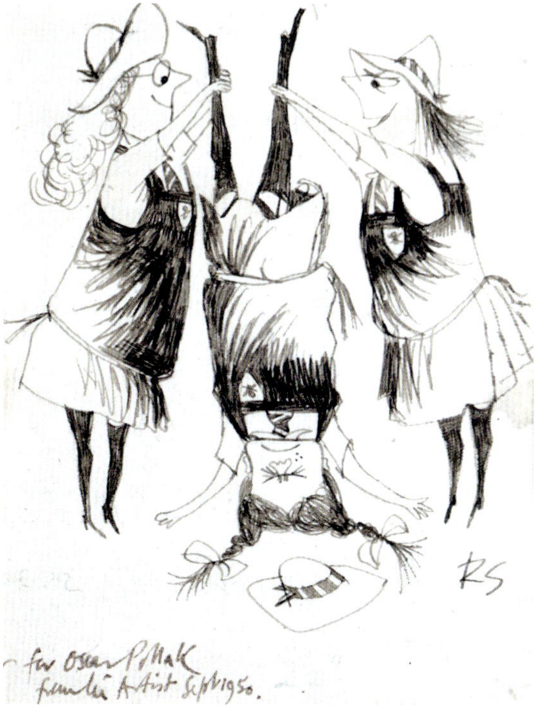

48 THE FEMALE APPROACH. WITH MASCULINE SIDELIGHTS
Ronald Searle
The Female Approach.
With Masculine Sidelights
London: Macdonald
[1949]
first edition
hard cover with dust jacket
96 pages
8 x 5 ¼ inches

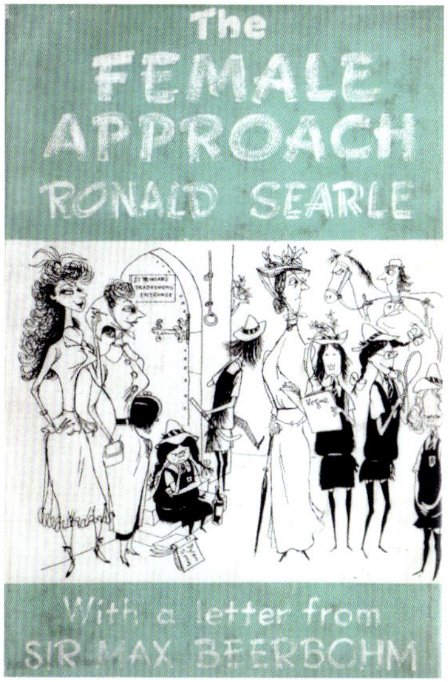

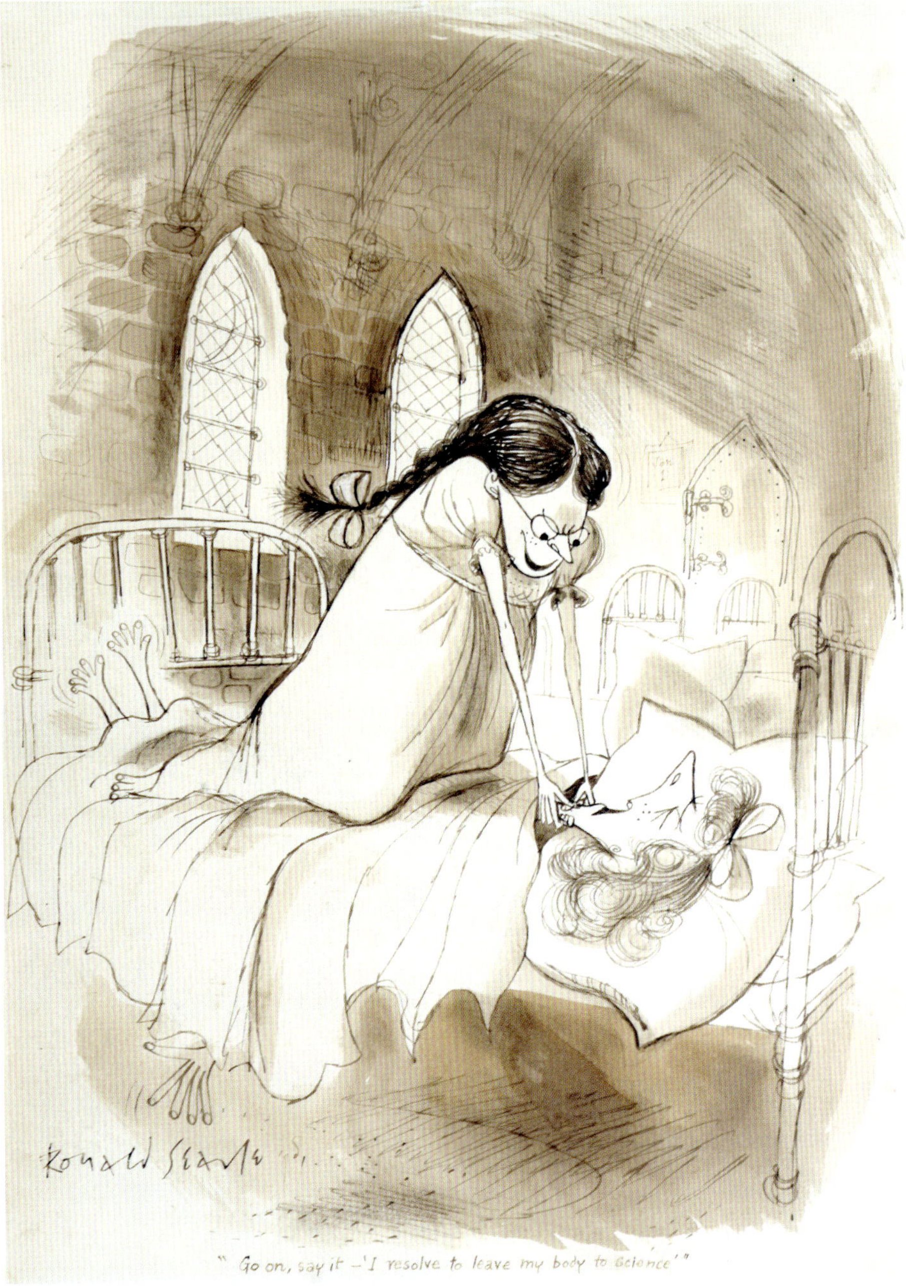

49 'GO ON, SAY IT – "I RESOLVE TO LEAVE MY BODY TO SCIENCE."'
signed, inscribed with title and dated 1951
stamped with artist's address and copyright details on reverse
pen ink and watercolour
13 ¼ x 9 ¼ inches
Illustrated: *Lilliput*, January 1951, 'Go on, say it – "I resolve to give you all my sweets this year"';Ronald Searle, *Back to the Slaughterhouse and Other Ugly Moments*, London: Macdonald, 1951, page 63; Kaye Webb (compiler), *The St Trinian's Story*, London: Perpetua, 1959, page 81; *Ronald Searle in Perspective*, London: New English Library, 1984, page 31; *Ronald Searle's Golden Oldies 1941-1961*, London: Pavilion Books, 1985, page 92
Literature: *The Curse of St Trinian's, The Best of the Drawings*, London: Pavilion Books, 1993, [unpaginated]
Exhibited: Better Books, London, (15gns)

50 DEBAGGING OLD FLANNELPANTS
signed, inscribed with title and 'The Terror of St Trinian's (p 29)' and dated 1952
pen and ink
6 ½ x 9 inches
Illustrated: Timothy Shy and Ronald Searle, *The Terror of St Trinian's*, London: Max Parrish, 1952, page 29; Kaye Webb (compiler), *The St Trinian's Story,* London: Perpetua, 1959, page 28 (excluding the right-hand girl)

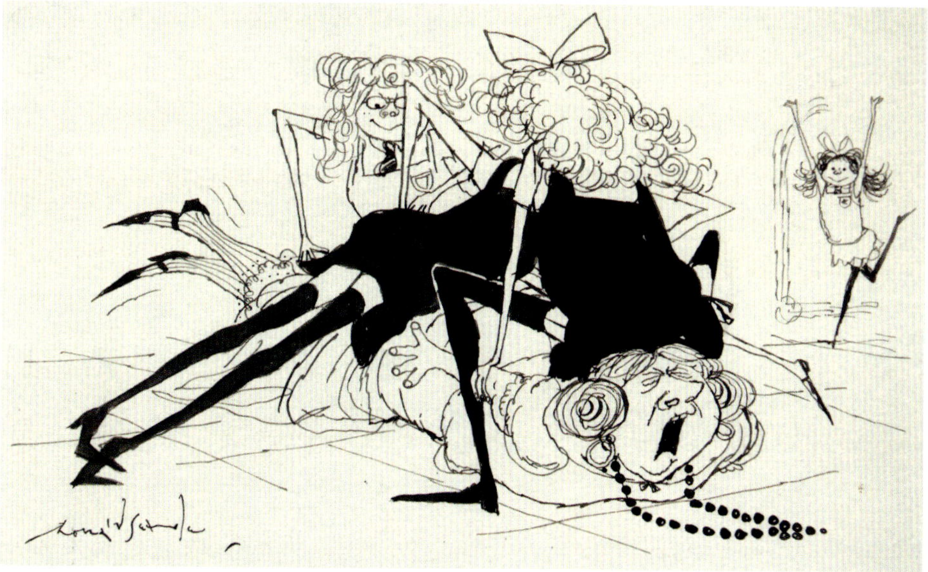

51 BACK TO THE SLAUGHTERHOUSE AND OTHER UGLY MOMENTS
Ronald Searle
Back to the Slaughterhouse and Other Ugly Moments
London: Macdonald
1951
first edition
hard cover with dust jacket
96 pages
8 x 5 ¼ inches

52 THE TERROR OF ST TRINIAN'S OR ANGELA'S PRINCE CHARMING
Timothy Shy and Ronald Searle
The Terror of St Trinian's or Angela's Prince Charming
London: Max Parrish
1952
first edition
hard cover with dust jacket
128 pages
8 x 5 ¼ inches

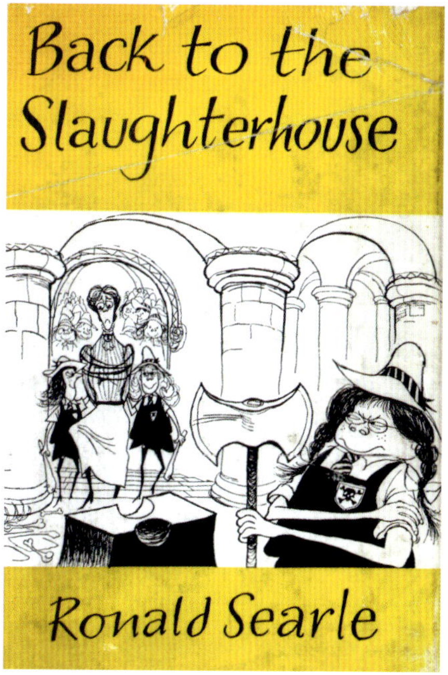

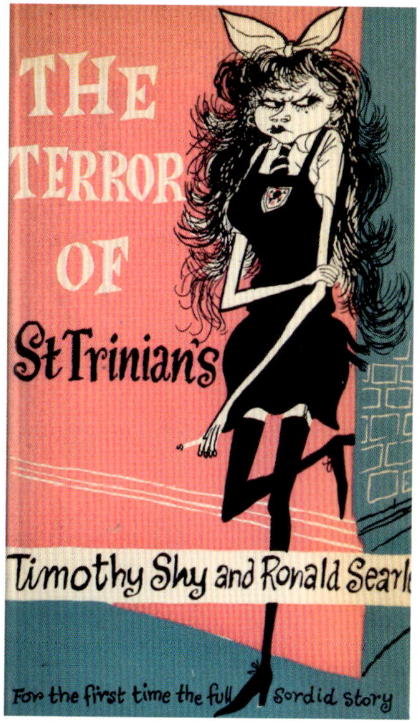

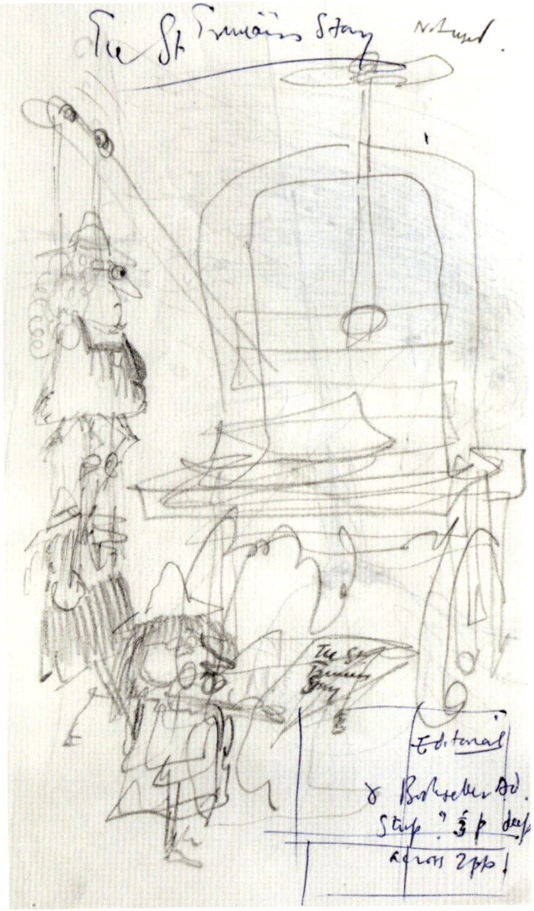

53 THE ST TRINIAN'S STORY
inscribed with title, 'Editorial & Bookseller Ad'
pencil
6 ¾ x 3 ¾ inches

reverse:
CIRCUS ACT
pen and ink
3 ¾ x 6 ¾ inches

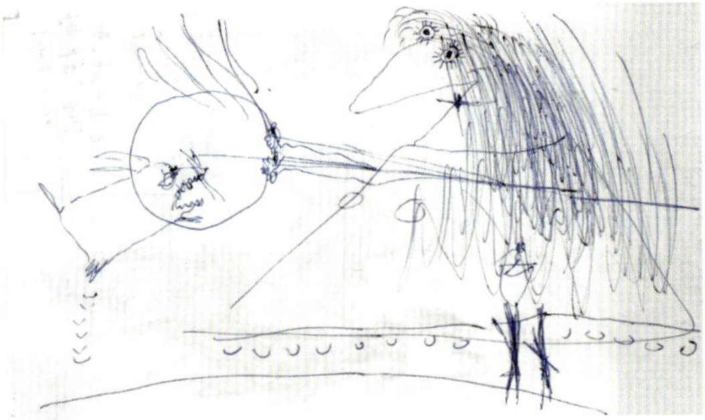

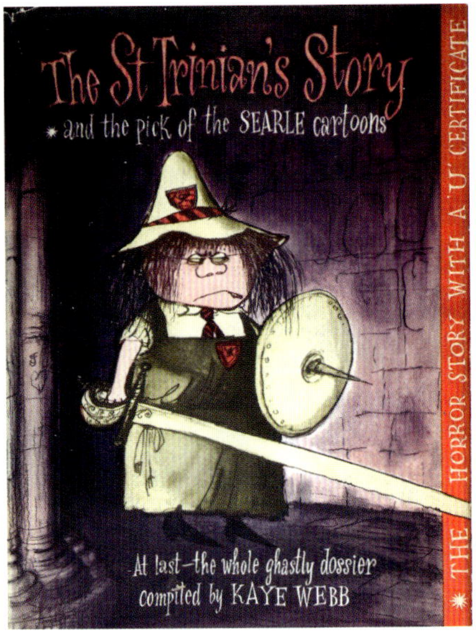

54 THE ST TRINIAN'S STORY AND THE PICK OF THE SEARLE CARTOONS
Kaye Webb (compiler)
The St Trinian's Story and the pick of the Searle Cartoons
London: Perpetua
1959
first edition
hard cover with dust jacket
118 pages
10 x 7 ½ inches

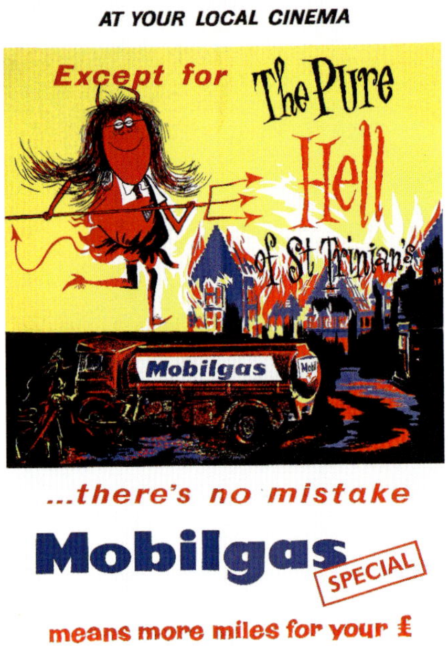

55 EXCEPT FOR THE PURE HELL OF ST TRINIAN'S
printed paper
29 ¾ x 19 ¾ inches

1951-54: News Chronicle

56 'BUT YOU CAN'T BEAT THE PORTOBELLO ROAD ON A SATURDAY'
signed
stamped with artist's address and copyright details on reverse
pen and ink
10 x 14 ¼ inches
Illustrated: *News Chronicle*, 20 December 1951; Ronald Searle & Kaye Webb, *Looking at London and People Worth Meeting*, London: *News Chronicle*, 1953, page 46

57 LOOKING AT LONDON AND PEOPLE WORTH MEETING
Ronald Searle and Kaye Webb
Looking at London and People Worth Meeting
London: News Chronicle
1953
first edition
softcover with dust jacket
96 pages
9 ¾ x 7 ¼ inches

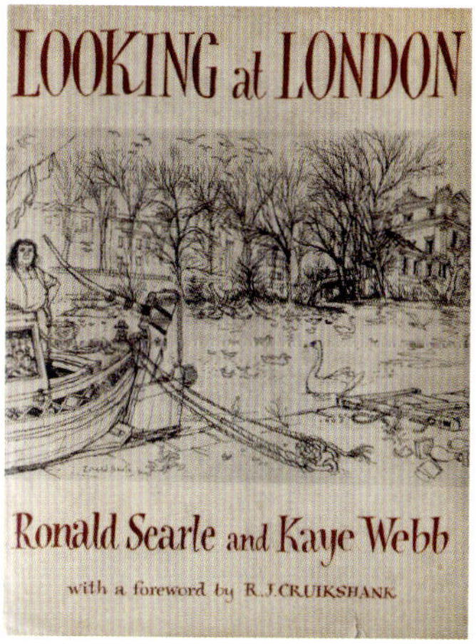

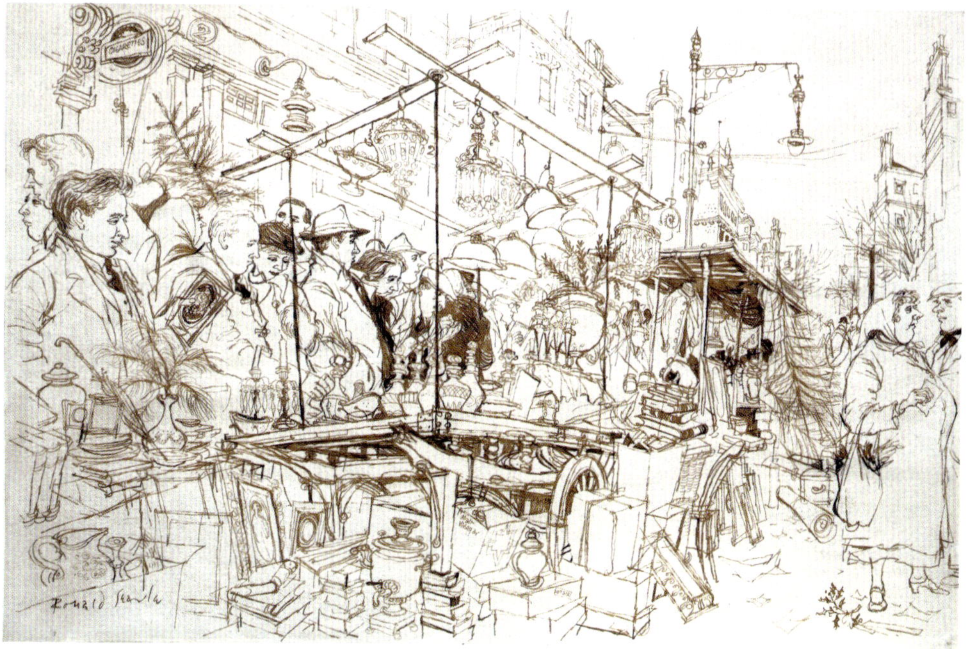

'Abandoning both political extremes at once, [Searle] left Tribune *and the* Sunday Express *in 1951 and followed his wife [Kaye Webb] to the* News Chronicle*, a six-page broadsheet costing a penny. The* Chronicle *was something of a haven for stylists of the pen. Its political cartoonist, staunchly Leftist and impatient with the paper's gentlemanly Liberalism, was Vicky (Victor Weisz). The Australian Arthur Horner contributed spot drawings and, before long, his "Colonel Pewter" strip. Richard Winnington illustrated his own film reviews with caricatures that in their dashed-off way displayed exactly what Searle meant by 'natural' instinct for a likeness. Eventually [Searle's wartime friend] George Sprod would be drafted in to do pocket cartoons. Where none of these men were at home was in reportage, which is where Searle came in; he and Kaye Webb became the newspaper equivalent of an outside broadcast unit, making a brilliant start in late October with their coverage of Dr Edith Summerskill's electioneering in Fulham …*

A week later, Searle and Webb were back with the first of a new series, Looking at London*, which grew into a book of the same name. In those years between the Festival of Britain and the Coronation there was an upsurge in Britain's affection for its surviving signs of "character". The Searles went looking for it, taking a participatory approach where possible. Instead of merely interviewing Portobello Road stall-holders, they applied for a licence themselves, learnt to say "flogging" instead of "selling", and disposed of a wide variety of bric-à-brac, including 'an ostrich-feather fan, named "Maud".'*

(Russell Davies, pages 95-96)

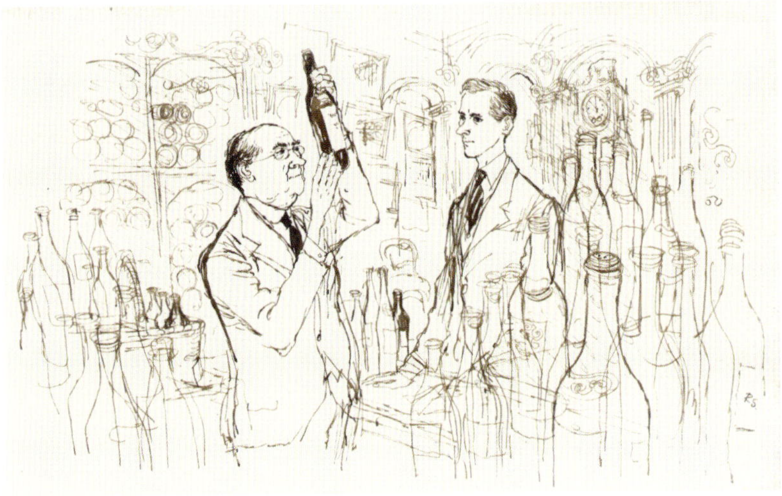

58 A GOOD VINTAGE
signed with initials
stamped with artist's address and copyright details on reverse
pen and ink
8 x 13 ½ inches

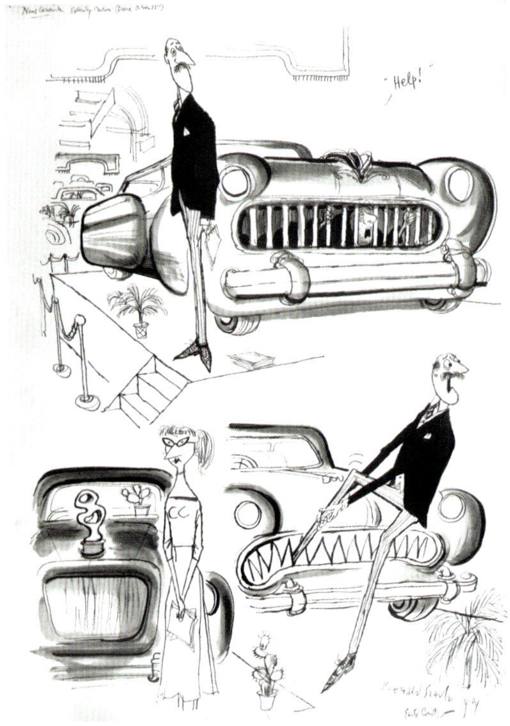

'Searle returned to the Chronicle *with an "Exclusive Saturday Sketchbook" entitled, with perhaps an ominous hint of the tyranny of the deadline, "Searle Every Saturday". This replaced Vicky's topical "Weekend Fantasia" … with a much larger and fantastical feature, very hard on the inventive faculties. Searle went for groups of visual jokes on seasonal themes: tulips, the seaside, Wimbledon, and (celebrating the end of meat-rationing) butchery.'*

(Russell Davies, page 108)

59 LONDON MOTOR SHOW, EARL'S COURT
signed, inscribed with publishing details and 'Earls Court', and dated 1954
inscribed with publishing details, stamped with artist's address and copyright details, and dated '23 October 1954' on reverse
pen ink and monochrome watercolour
21 ¾ x 15 ½ inches
Illustrated: *News Chronicle*, 23 October 1954; Ronald Searle, *Merry England, Etc*, London: Perpetua Books, 1956, page 20 (detail)

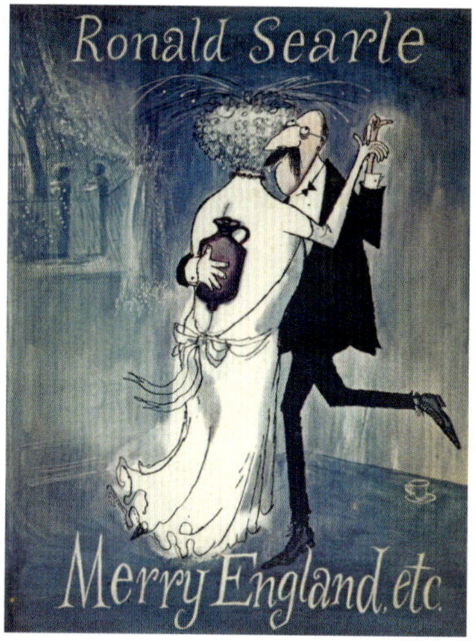

60 MERRY ENGLAND, ETC
Ronald Searle
Merry England, Etc
London: Perpetua Books
1956
first edition
hard cover with dust jacket
118 pages
10 x 7 ½ inches

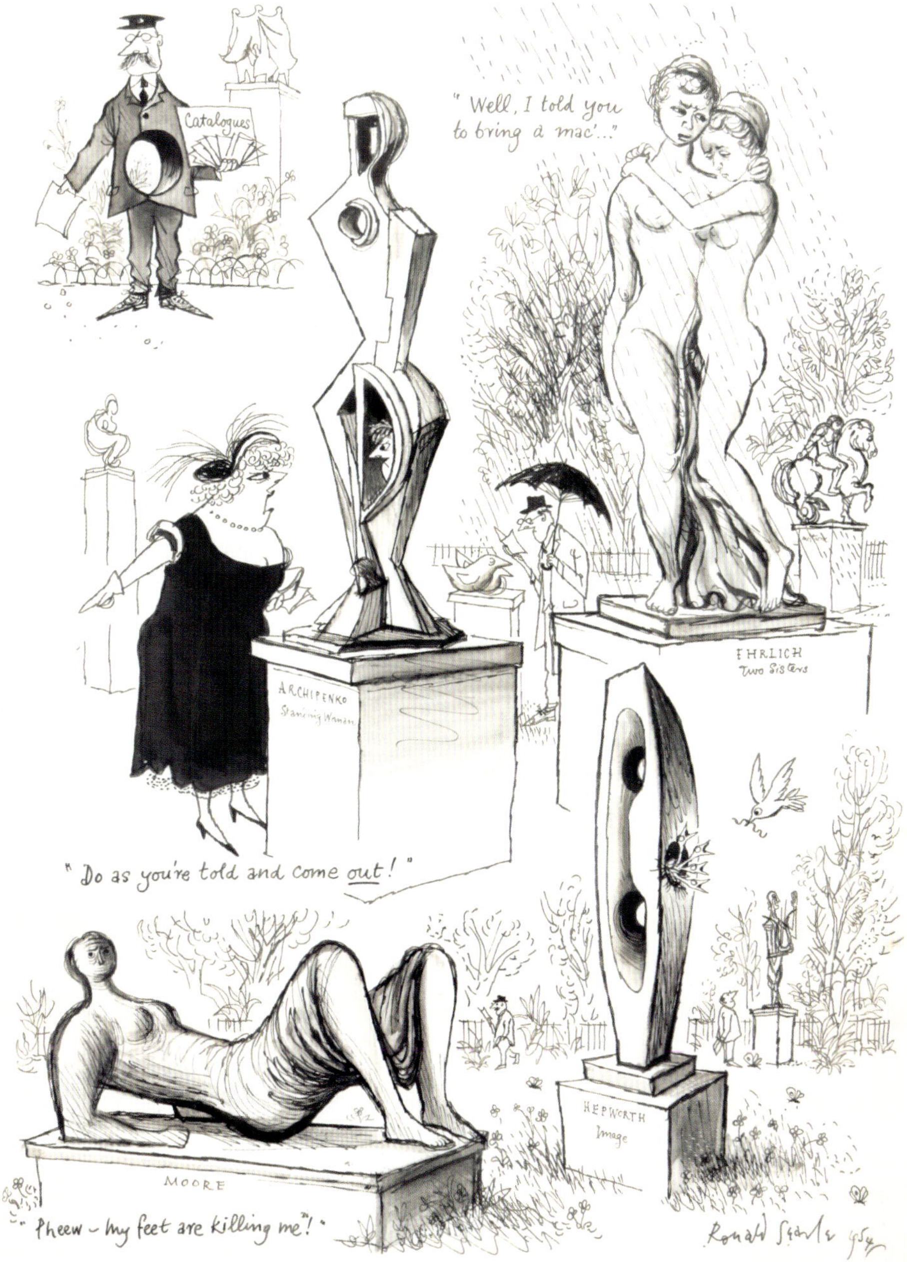

61 PRIVATE VIEW OF AN OPEN AIR SCULPTURE EXHIBITION AT HOLLAND PARK (OPENING FRIDAY 28TH UNTIL SEPTEMBER)
signed, inscribed with title and 'News Chronicle. Saturday Sketchbook (Issue May 29)', and dated 1954
pen ink and monochrome watercolour
22 x 15 inches
Illustrated: *News Chronicle*, 28 May 1954, 'Saturday Sketchbook'; Ronald Searle, *Merry England, Etc*, London: Perpetua Books, 1956, pages 80-81, 'Notes at an Open Air Exhibition'

London County Council Third International Exhibition of Sculpture, May-September 1954

The exhibitions of sculpture at Holland Park in 1954 and 1957 were two in a series of triennial exhibitions, held between 1948 and 1966, usually at Battersea Park. The series is considered to have created a much wider audience for modern sculpture. The exhibition in 1954 also celebrated the public opening of the former grounds of Holland House.

62-68 are all preliminary drawings for *News Chronicle*, 28 May 1954, 'Saturday Sketchbook' and are all taken from a sketchbook of May 1954.

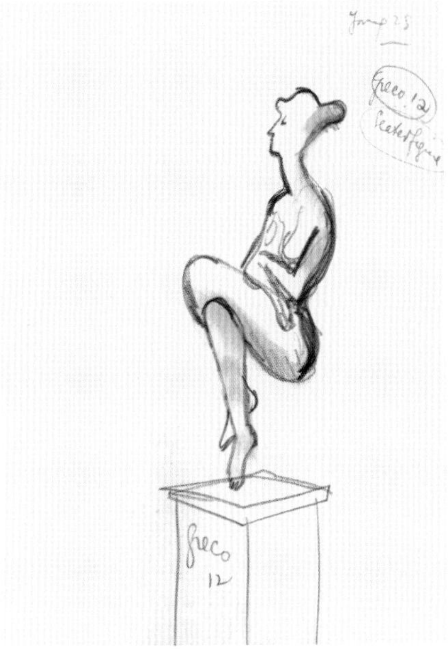

63 EMILIO GRECO, SEATED FIGURE
inscribed 'Seated figure' and 'Greco 12'
pencil
9 ¾ x 7 inches

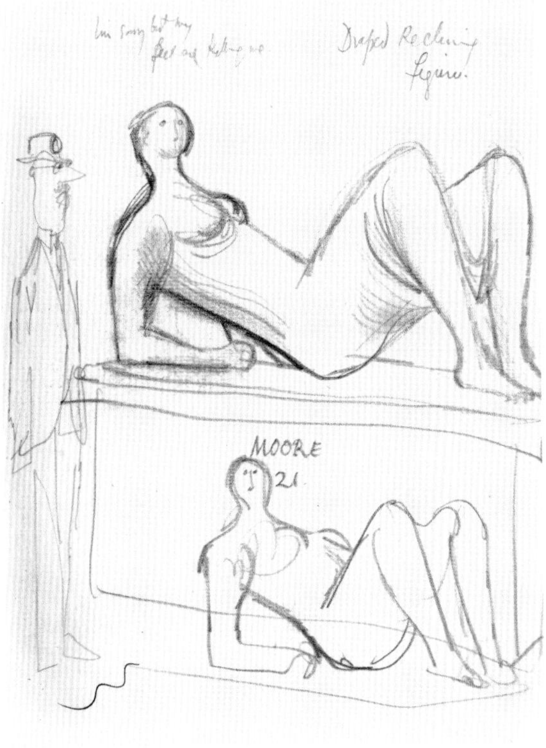

62 HENRY MOORE, DRAPED RECLINING FIGURE
inscribed 'Draped reclining figure' and 'I'm sorry but my feet are killing me'
pencil
9 ¾ x 8 inches

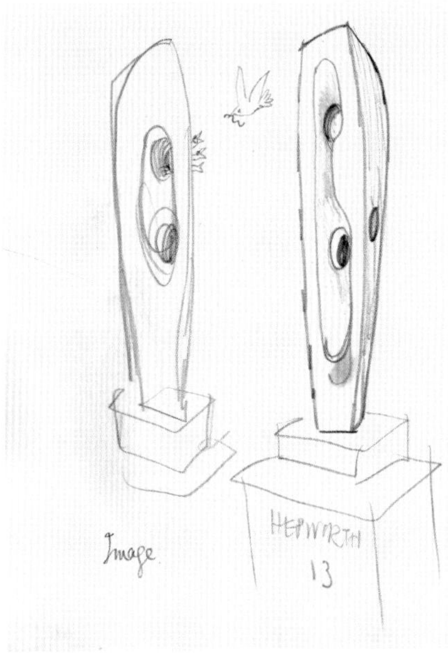

64 BARBARA HEPWORTH, IMAGE
inscribed 'Image'
pencil
9 ½ x 7 inches

65 GEORG EHRLICH,
TWO SISTERS
inscribed 'Two sisters' and 'I told you to bring a mac …'
pencil
9 ¾ x 8 inches

66 KENNETH ARMITAGE, FAMILY GOING FOR A WALK
inscribed 'Family going for a walk'
pencil
9 ¾ x 7 ½ inches

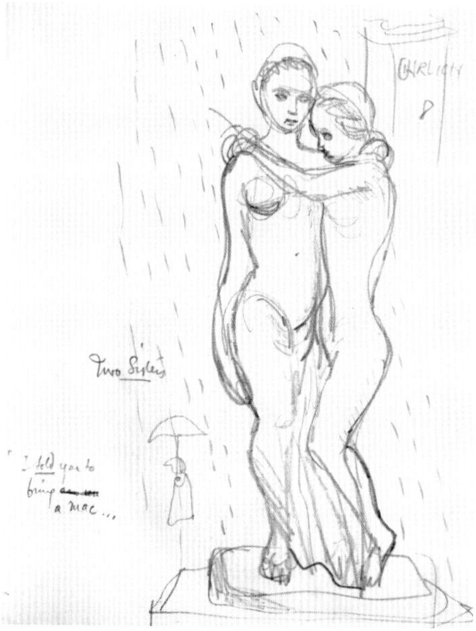

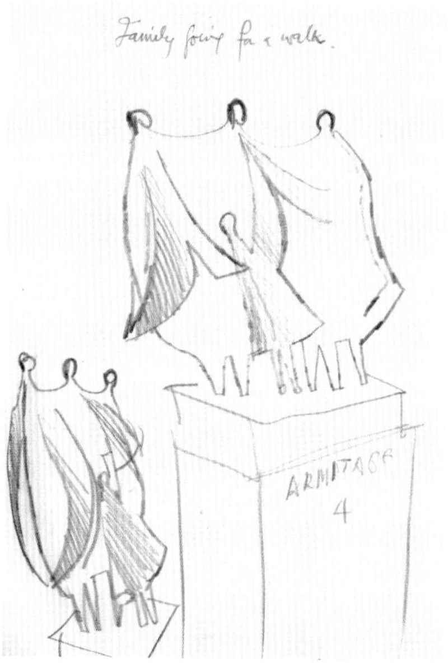

67 MARINO MARINI, HORSEMAN
inscribed 'Horseman' and 'Marini 19'
pencil
9 ¾ x 7 ½ inches

68 ALEXANDER ARCHIPENKO,
STANDING WOMAN
inscribed 'Standing woman', 'Do as you're told and come out!' and 'Do you want me to come and fetch you'
pencil
9 ¾ x 7 ¾ inches

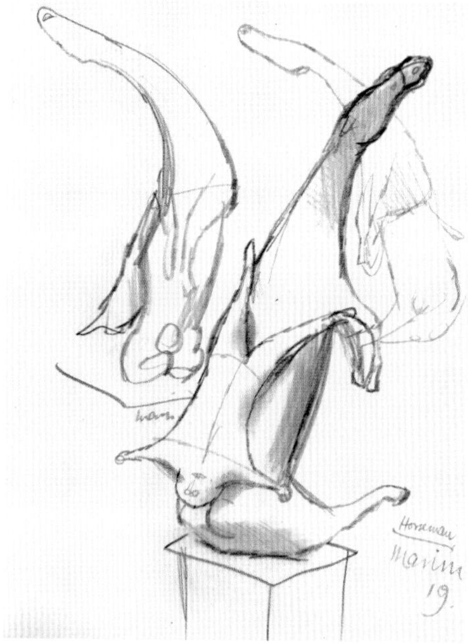

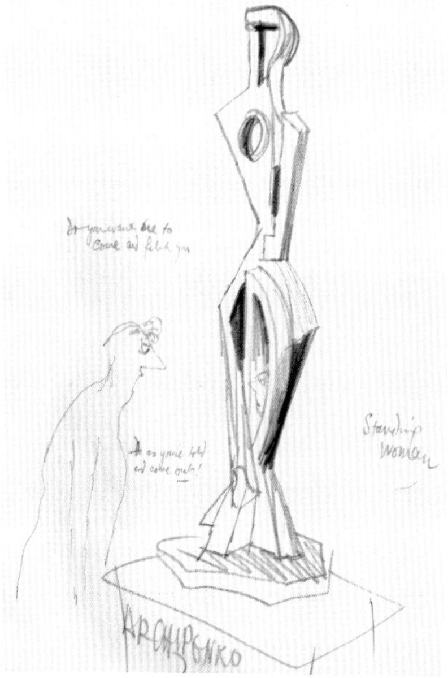

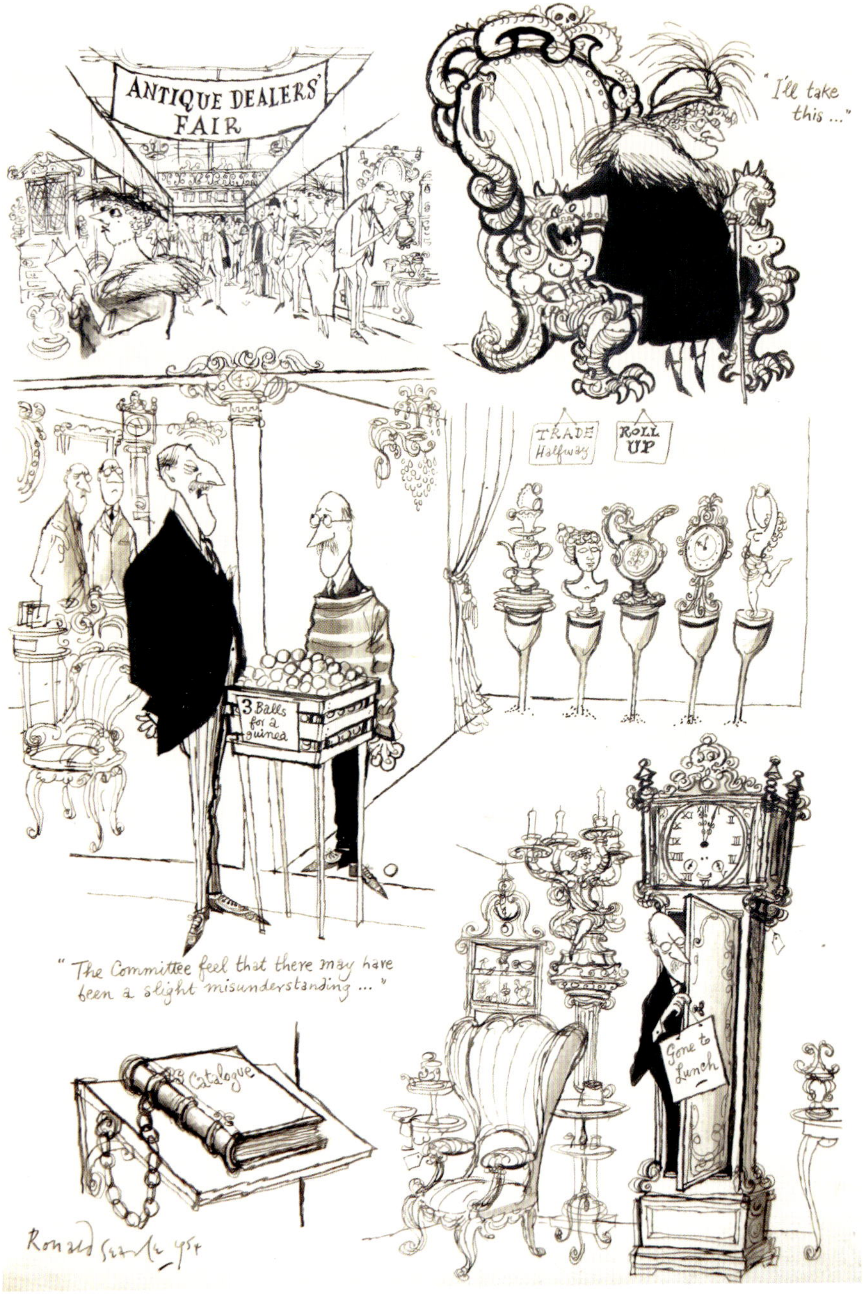

69 ANTIQUE DEALERS' FAIR
signed, inscribed with title and dated 1954
inscribed 'News Chronicle. Saturday Sketchbook (Issue June 12)' below mount
pen ink and monochrome watercolour
20 ½ x 13 ¼ inches
Illustrated: *News Chronicle*, 12 June 1954; Ronald Searle, *Merry England, Etc*, London: Perpetua Books, 1956, page 78 (detail)

1951-59: Theatrical Caricatures for *Punch*: working with Eric Keown

In *An Experience of Critics*, Christopher Fry described Eric Keown (1904-1963) as the 'most easily recognised of the critics', who 'can be seen either towering above all-comers in the gangway or collapsed scissorwise in his seat, chin resting gently between his knees. He is six feet six and a half inches tall' (London: Perpetua, 1953, page 62). He had been a theatre critic of *Punch* for 17 years, when Ronald Searle began to illustrate his column in 1949. For more than a decade, they accompanied each other several times a week to first nights in the West End, and regularly to Stratford-upon-Avon and Paris. Though Searle didn't particularly relish the task – 'the sketchbook on the knees in the stalls, the spy-glass at the ready' (Davies, page 89) – he did enjoy the anticipation, and especially the company of this 'snuff-taking Francophile' and 'unsnobbish gourmet' (Davies, page 91). Apparently, they 'actually kept each other in the job' (Davies, page 89), Searle speaking up for Keown in 1953, when the new editor, Malcolm Muggeridge considered replacing him with Kenneth Tynan. They ceased their collaboration in 1961, when Searle left England to live in France, though he and Keown shared one last spell of plays and dinners in summer 1962. Keown died of a heart attack on 15 February 1963, Searle reading of his death in *The Times*.

The drawings included here suggest the range of their theatrical experiences: English and European classics (Shakespeare and Molière), traditional entertainments (The Crazy Gang and Tommy Cooper), the modern poetic drama (Christopher Fry and Tennessee Williams), and the new wave of the kitchen sink and the angry young man (Shelagh Delaney and John Whiting). Acting talent spanned Ernest Thesiger, still performing in his mid 70s, and Laurence Harvey, new to theatre in his mid 20s. Leading directors included Tyrone Guthrie, Joan Littlewood, Peter Brook and the newly emergent Peter Hall. This range gave Searle – and *Punch* – the opportunity to engage properly with caricature, R G G Price believing that Searle was 'the first *Punch* contributor for many years to produce real caricatures' (*A History of Punch*, London: Collins, 1957, page 312).

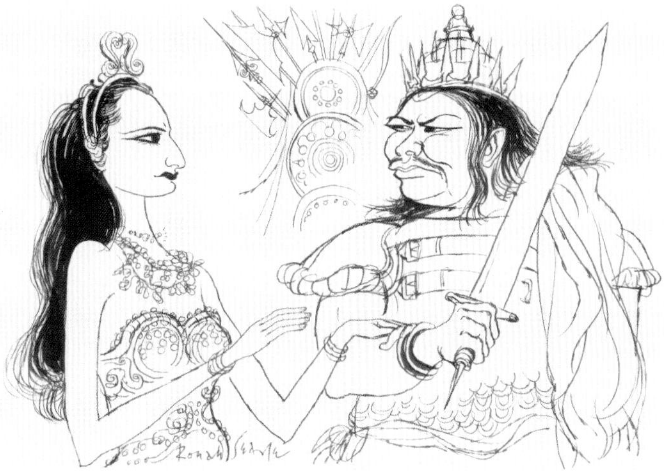

70 DEVIL'S DISCIPLE
ZENOCRATE ... MISS JILL BALCON. TAMBURLAINE ... MR DONALD WOLFIT
[TAMBURLAINE THE GREAT]
signed and inscribed with title
inscribed 'Punch Theatre' below mount
stamped with artist's address and copyright details and dated 1951 on reverse
pen and ink
9 ¾ x 12 ¾ inches
Illustrated: *Punch*, 10 October 1951, page 416, 'At the Play' by Eric Keown

Tamburlaine the Great

Searle's caricature marks a groundbreaking production of Christopher Marlowe's *Tamburlaine the Great* (1587-88): the first production in a professional theatre since the seventeenth century. Tyrone Guthrie directed the Old Vic company in an abridgement of the two parts as a single play, with Donald Wolfit as Tamburlaine, Jill Balcon as Zenocrate and Leo McKern as Bajazeth. Eric Keown wrote that 'imaginative production by Mr Guthrie and a surging performance from Mr Wolfit leaves us more conscious of the wild strength of Marlowe at his best than of the windy rhetoric that sometimes plugs the gaps' ('At the Play', *Punch*, 10 October 1951, page 416).

A review in *The Times* stated that 'It is a vibrant figure of pure theatrical flamboyance that Mr Donald Wolfit plays Tamburlaine ... It is at rough grandeur that he aims, giving the base-born conqueror a street-arab delight in cruelty and in all the dazzling appurtenances of power' (26 September 1951).

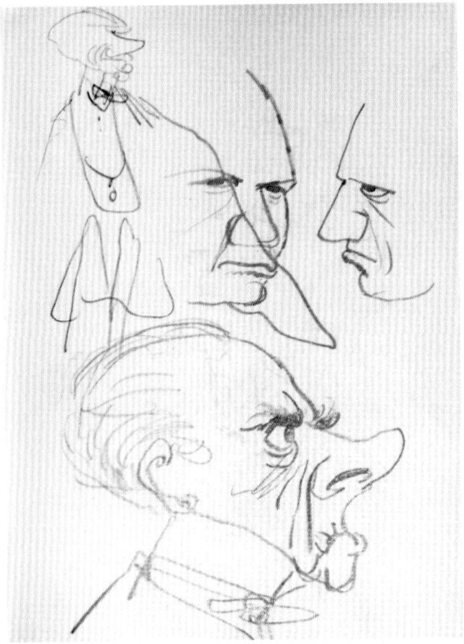

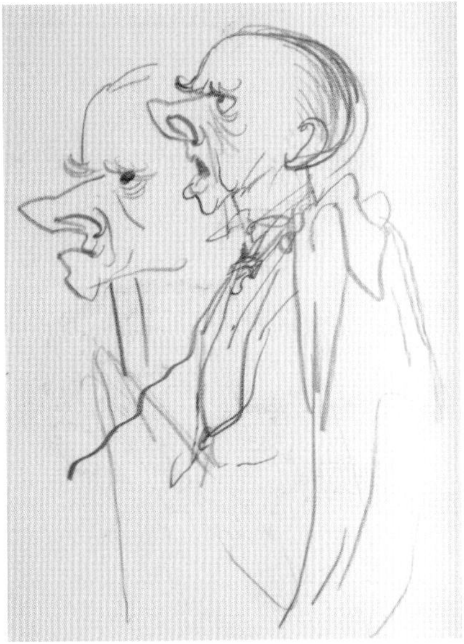

71-100 are all preliminary drawings for *Punch*, 'At the Play' by Eric Keown and are taken from four sketch books of theatre drawings, April-May 1954, January-March 1959, April-June 1959 and April 1960.

71 ROBERT FLEMYNG AS RUPERT FORSTER AND ERNEST THESIGER AS CHANCELLOR CADMUS
pencil
8 ¾ x 6 ¾ inches

reverse:
ERNEST THESIGER AS CHANCELLOR CADMUS
pencil
8 ½ x 6 ¼ inches

Preliminary drawings for *Punch*, 21 April 1954, page 507

Marching Song
Marching Song by John Whiting (1917-1963) originally premiered at the Bristol Old Vic early in 1954. It opened in London at the St Martin's Theatre on 8 April, in a production directed by Frith Banbury and designed by Reece Pemberton.

'Marching Song ... *centred round an individual under psychological pressure, in this case a General Rupert Forster [Robert Flemyng] who is guilty of war crimes involving the slaughter of innocent children. His relationships with a mistress and young girl [Diana Wynyard and Penelope Munday] add to the complex states of feeling which ultimately lead him to commit suicide. It is a symbolic play with little dramatic action but great emotional force and intellectual weightiness*'

(Philip Barnes, *A Companion to Post-War British Theatre*, London: Croom Helm, 1986, page 260)

The Prisoner

The Prisoner by Bridget Boland (1913-1988) opened at the Globe Theatre (now the Gielgud Theatre) on 14 April 1954. It was directed by Peter Glenville and designed by Felix Labisse, with music composed by Roberto Gerhard.

Bridget Boland's psychological drama was inspired by the plight of the Roman Catholic Cardinal, József Mindszenty (1892-1975), an opponent of Fascism and Communism. In 1948, he actively opposed the plan of the Communist regime in Hungary to nationalise all Catholic schools. He was found guilty of treason and imprisoned. The resulting play, much admired in its time, comprised a complex debate between spiritual qualities and materialism. A film version, also directed by Peter Glenville and starring Alec Guinness, followed in 1955.

The experience of playing the Cardinal confirmed Alec Guinness in his decision to convert to Roman Catholicism. On 24 March 1956, he 'was received into the Catholic Church, followed independently, by his wife' (Obituary in *The Times*).

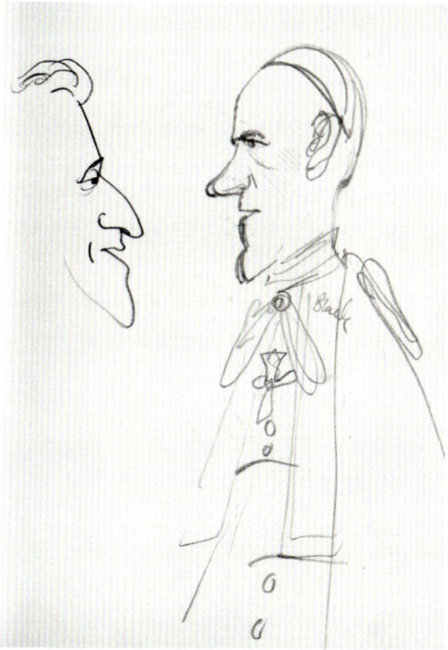

72 ALEC GUINNESS
AS THE CARDINAL (I)
inscribed 'Black'
pencil
8 ¾ x 6 ¾ inches

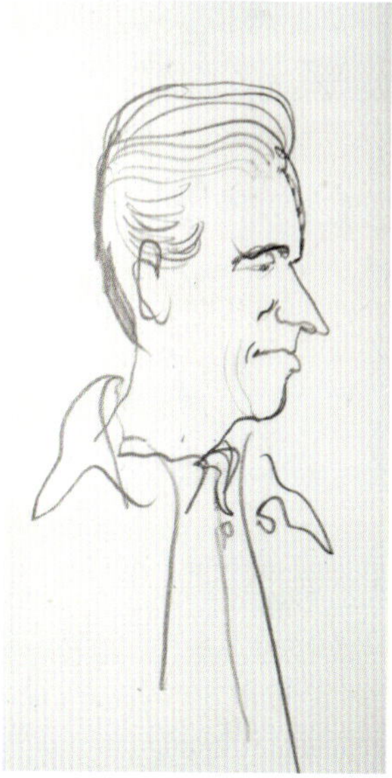

reverse:
NOEL WILLMAN AS
THE INTERROGATOR
pencil, 7 ½ x 5 inches
Preliminary drawings for *Punch*, 28 April 1954, page 535

73 ALAN DENT
signed
inscribed with title, 'The critic at the theatre as seen by' and dated 1953 in another hand
pen and ink
9 ½ x 8 inches
Illustrated: Christopher Fry, *An Experience of Critics and the Approach to Dramatic Criticism*, London: Perpetua Books, 1952, page 43

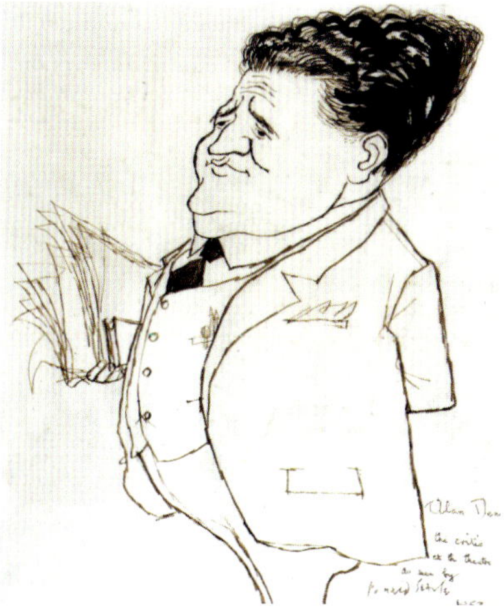

74 AN EXPERIENCE OF CRITICS AND THE APPROACH TO DRAMATIC CRITICISM
Christopher Fry
An Experience of Critics and the Approach to Dramatic Criticism
London: Perpetua
1952
second impression
hard cover with dust jacket
64 pages
7 ½ x 5 inches

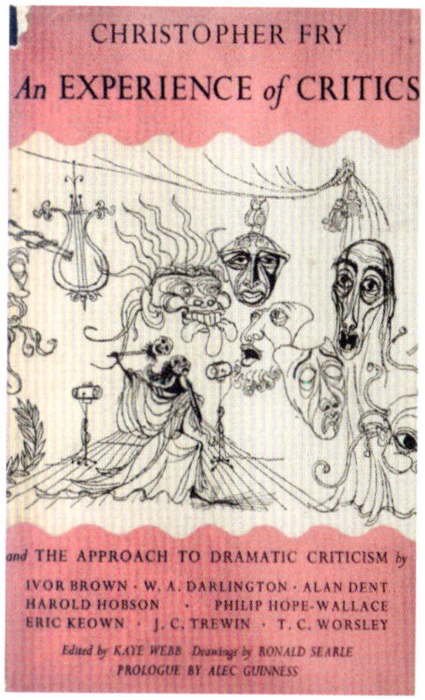

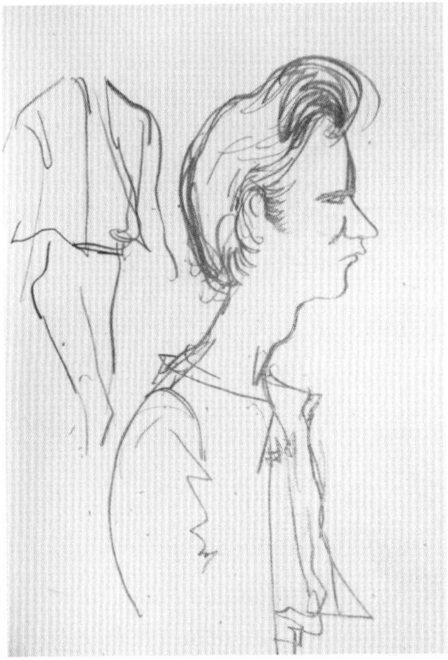

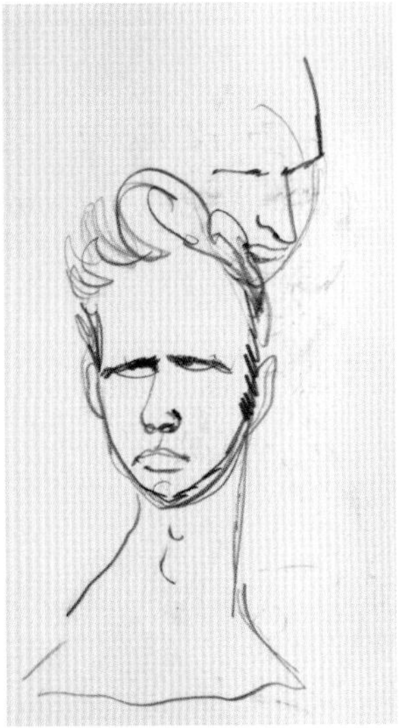

75 LAURENCE HARVEY AS ROMEO
pencil
8 ¼ x 6 ½ inches

reverse:
LAURENCE HARVEY AS ROMEO
pencil
7 ½ x 5 ½ inches

Preliminary drawings for *Punch*, 5 May 1954, page 563

Romeo and Juliet

Romeo and Juliet opened at the Royal Shakespeare Theatre, Stratford-upon-Avon, on 27 April 1954. It was directed by Glen Byam Shaw and designed by Motley.

'It is melancholy to continue saying so, but Stratford is still out of sorts. In Glen Byam Shaw's Romeo and Juliet *the need for a more mature cast is as clear as it was in the season's earlier plays … LAURENCE HARVEY's Romeo, outwardly a romantic figure, visibly burns with passion, but we remain insulated from its heat; and ZENA WALKER's Juliet, though possessing all the charm of a forthright schoolgirl, carries us no farther than that suggests'.*

(Eric Keown, 'At the Play', *Punch*, 5 May 1954, page 563)

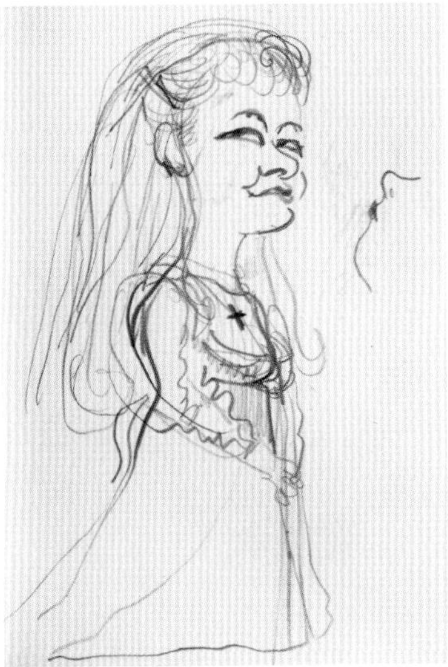

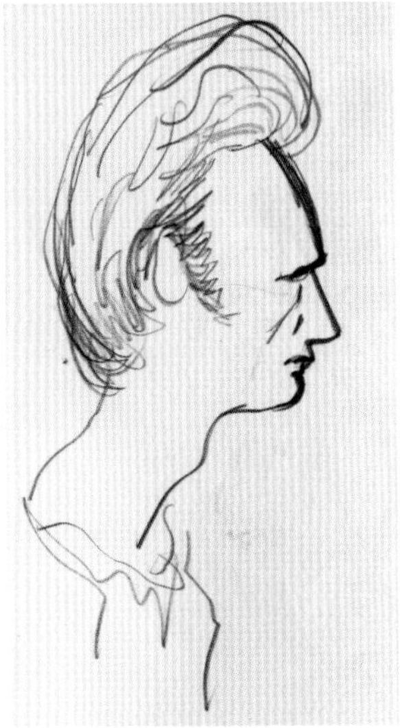

76 ZENA WALKER AS JULIET
pencil
8 ¾ x 6 ½ inches

reverse:
LAURENCE HARVEY AS ROMEO
pencil
7 x 4 ½ inches

Preliminary drawing for *Punch*, 5 May 1954, page 563

77 JAMES DONALD AS RICHARD GETTNER
pencil
8 ¾ x 6 ½ inches

reverse:
JAMES DONALD AS RICHARD GETTNER AND EDITH EVANS AS COUNTESS ROSMARIN OSTENBURG
pencil
8 ¾ x 4 inches

Preliminary drawings for *Punch*, 12 May 1954, page 591

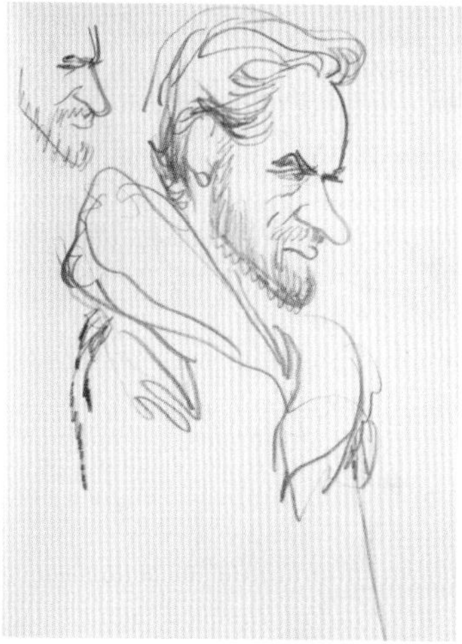

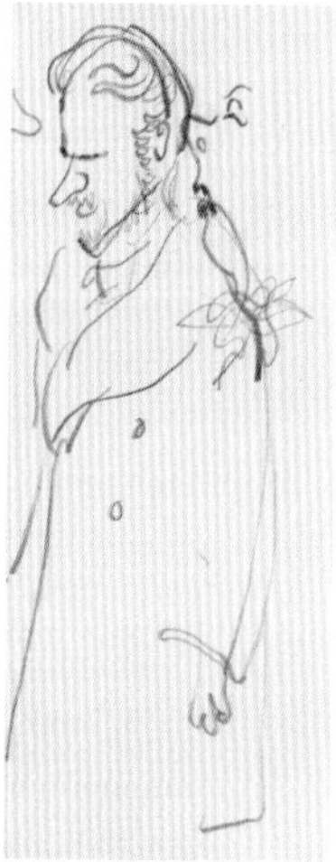

The Dark is Light Enough

The Dark is Light Enough by Christopher Fry (1907-2005) opened at the Aldwych Theatre on 30 April 1954. It was directed by Peter Brook and designed by Oliver Messel.

Described by Fry as 'A Winter Comedy', *The Dark is Light Enough* was the third in a quartet of verse plays with seasonal resonances. It was set in the country house of Countess Rosemarin Ostenburg (Edith Evans) at the time of the Hungarian rebellion against the Austrians, in the years 1848-50. The pacifist Countess selflessly shelters Richard Gettner (James Donald), her former son-in-law and deserter from the Hungarian army. On the whole, audiences and critics received it politely rather than enthusiastically, though one review was as negative as to state that 'on the stage of the Aldwych Theatre it makes a very dull longwinded play' (Richard Findlater in the *Tribune*, 28 May 1954, page 5).

One of Fry's friends, Searle designed the dust jacket for the edition of the play published by Oxford University Press.

78 EDITH EVANS AS COUNTESS ROSMARIN OSTENBURG
pencil
8 ½ x 6 ½ inches

reverse:
EDITH EVANS AS COUNTESS ROSMARIN OSTENBURG
pencil
8 ¾ x 6 ½ inches

Preliminary drawings for *Punch*, 12 May 1954, page 591

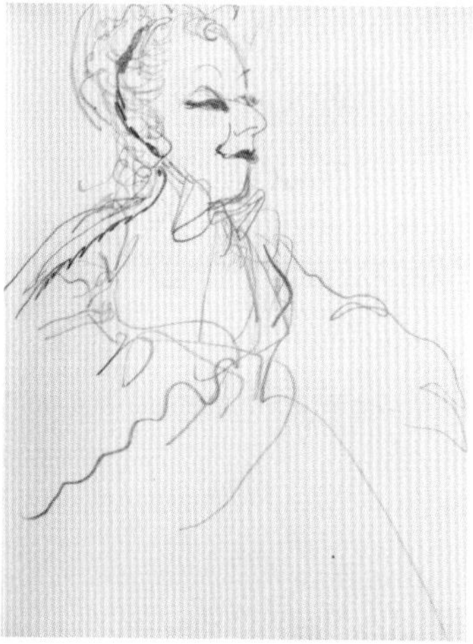

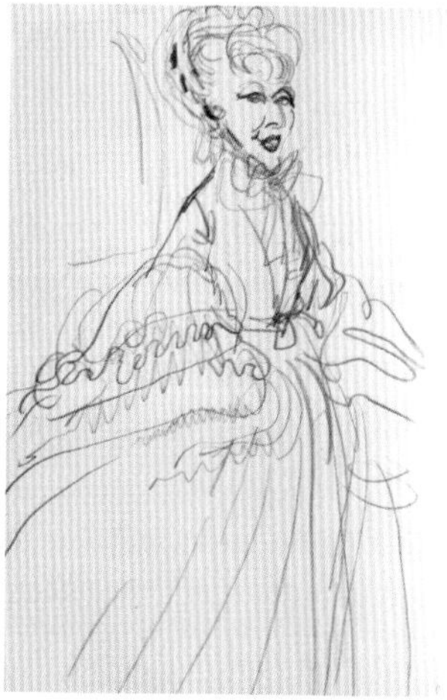

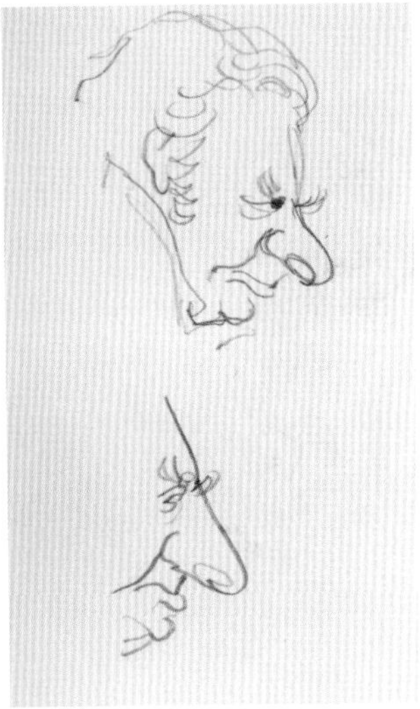

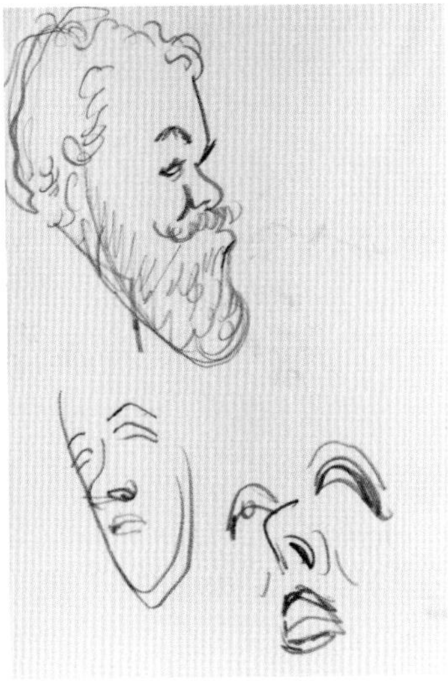

79 HUGH GRIFFITH AS BELMANN
pencil
7 ½ x 5 ½ inches

reverse:
CHARACTERS FROM 'THE DARK IS LIGHT ENOUGH'
pencil
7 x 5 inches

Preliminary drawings for *Punch*, 12 May 1954, page 591

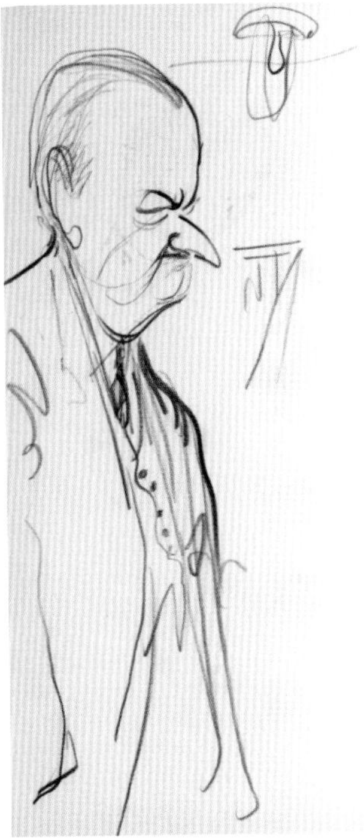

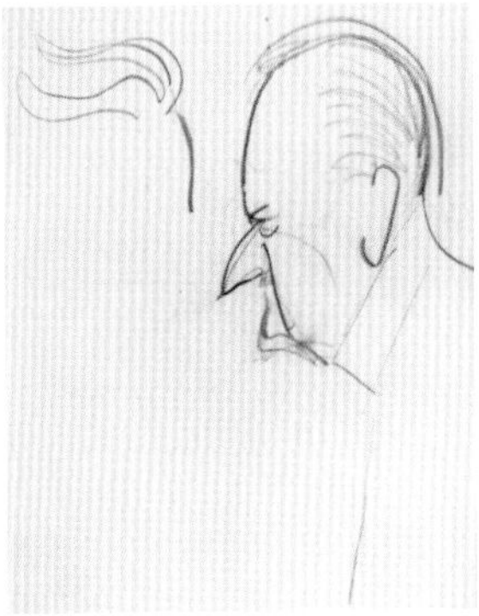

80 RAYMOND HUNTLEY AS DETECTIVE SUPERINTENDANT COATES
pencil, 8 ¾ x 4 ¾ inches

reverse:
RAYMOND HUNTLEY AS DETECTIVE SUPERINTENDANT COATES
pencil, 6 x 4 ¾ inches

Preliminary drawings for *Punch*, 28 January 1959, page 169

The Woman on the Stair

James Parish (1904-1974) based *The Woman on the Stair* on his own television play, *The Witness*, which was first broadcast in the ABC series, 'Armchair Theatre', on 24 February 1957.

The Woman on the Stair opened at the Westminster Theatre on 22 January 1959. It was directed by Jack Minster and designed by Hutchinson Scott.

'James Parish's latest thriller, The Woman on the Stair, *comes by way of TV, and shows signs of having been filled out for the stage. Its developing is very leisurely, along two lines: the capture of the flash young burglar who has murdered the old lady upstairs, and the state of mind of her friend in the flat below, a blind girl who had passed the intruder on his way down the staircase and is able to help the police …*

Miss Watford's delicate handling of this difficult part makes one eager to see her in a piece in which she can have more scope. Raymond Huntley, who always seems to me far too good an actor to be bothered by clues, is as usual an excellent advertisement for the Yard.'

(Eric Keown, 'At the Play', *Punch*, 28 January 1959, pages 169-170)

The Rose Tattoo

The Rose Tattoo by Tennessee Williams (1911-1983) originally premiered at the Martin Beck Theatre, New York, on 3 February 1951. A film version, directed by Daniel Mann, appeared four years later.

The first British production opened at the New Shakespeare Theatre, Liverpool, on 4 November 1958. Directed by Sam Wanamaker, it transferred to the New Theatre, London, on 15 January 1959.

81 LEA PADOVANI AS SERAPHINA DELLA ROSE AND SAM WANAMAKER AS ALVARO MANGIACAVALLO
pencil
8 $\frac{3}{4}$ x 4 $\frac{3}{4}$ inches

reverse:
SAM WANAMAKER AS ALVARO MANGIACAVALLO
pencil
4 $\frac{1}{2}$ x 3 $\frac{1}{2}$ inches

Preliminary drawings for *Punch*, 21 January 1959, page 138

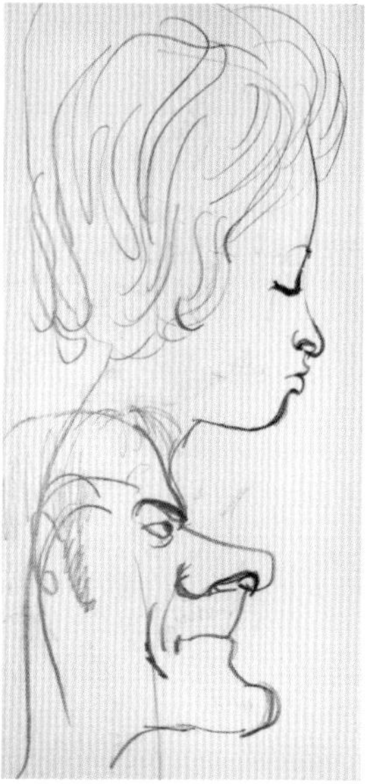

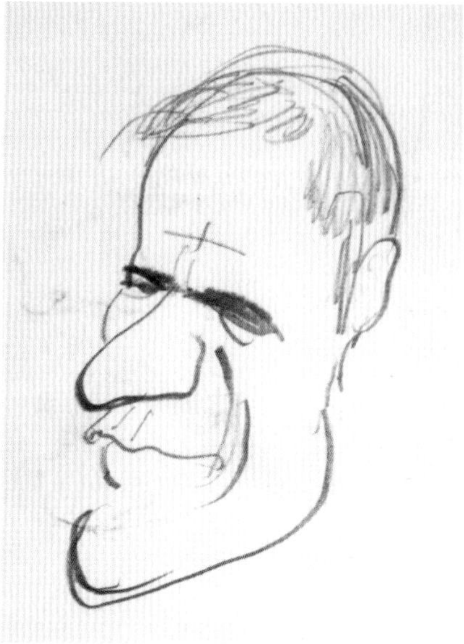

'Anyone who found the film of The Rose Tattoo, *as I did, an uncomfortably greasy exercise in earthy sex, may be relieved to hear that the play, which has been slightly chiselled by the Lord Chamberlain, is less insistently animal. It is still immensely sentimental, its sentiment to some extent congealed under the veneer of toughness engendered by Sicily and truck-driving on the highways of America. That one can observe the ironies of Tennessee Williams' central character without being repelled is largely due to the power and delicacy of an Italian actress, Lea Padovani.'*

(Eric Keown, 'At the Play', *Punch*, 21 January 1959, page 138)

82 SAM WANAMAKER AS ALVARO MANGIACAVALLO
pencil
8 $\frac{1}{2}$ x 4 $\frac{3}{4}$ inches

reverse:
SAM WANAMAKER AS ALVARO MANGIACAVALLO
pencil
8 $\frac{1}{2}$ x 4 $\frac{3}{4}$ inches

Preliminary drawings for *Punch*, 21 January 1959, page 138

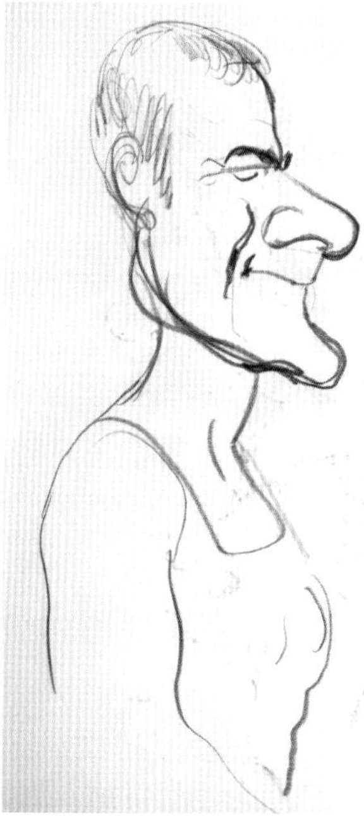

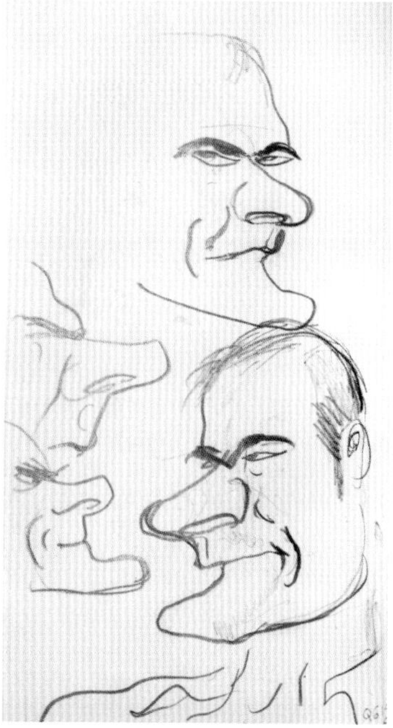

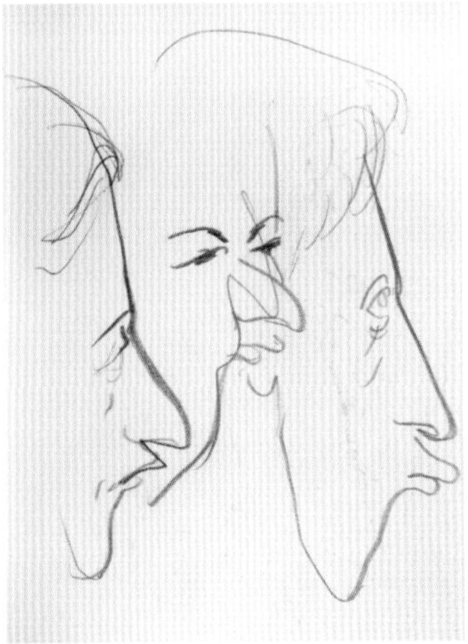

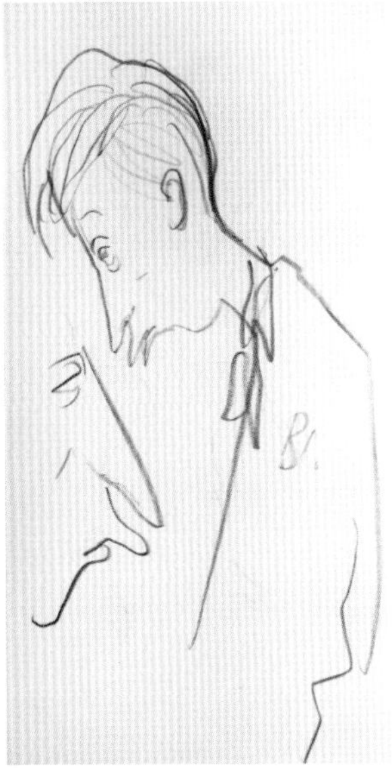

83 FRANCES CUKA AS JOSEPHINE AND MURRAY MELVIN AS GEOFFREY (I)
pencil
6 ½ x 5 inches

reverse:
MURRAY MELVIN AS GEOFFREY
pencil
8 ½ x 4 ¾ inches

Preliminary drawings for *Punch*, 11 February 1959, page 235

A Taste of Honey

A Taste of Honey by Shelagh Delaney (1938-2011) originally premiered at the Theatre Royal Stratford East on 27 May 1958, and won the Charles Henry Foyle New Play award for that year. Directed by Joan Littlewood and designed by John Bury and Una Collins, it transferred to the Wyndham's Theatre on 10 February 1959.

The 18-year-old Delaney began *A Taste of Honey* as a novel. However, on seeing Terence Rattigan's *Variations on a Theme* at Manchester's Opera House, during its pre-West End tour, she decided to transform it into a play, believing that she could write something more substantial and socially significant for the stage. Completing it in a fortnight, she sent it to Joan Littlewood, who recognised its vitality, and decided that her Theatre Workshop should produce it. Along with *Oh, What a Lovely War!* (1963), it is one of the two works for which the Theatre Workshop is best remembered.

Set in Delaney's native Salford, the play tells the story of Jo, a 17-year-old working class girl (Frances Cuka): she becomes pregnant, following a one-night stand with a black sailor, and sets up home with Geoffrey, a homosexual artist (Murray Melvin). While it originally received mixed reviews, it was praised for its accurate depiction of working class lives, and soon considered a key example of kitchen sink realism – the feminist equivalent of John Osborne's *Look Back in Anger* (1956). This association was strengthened when Tony Richardson directed a film version of it in 1961.

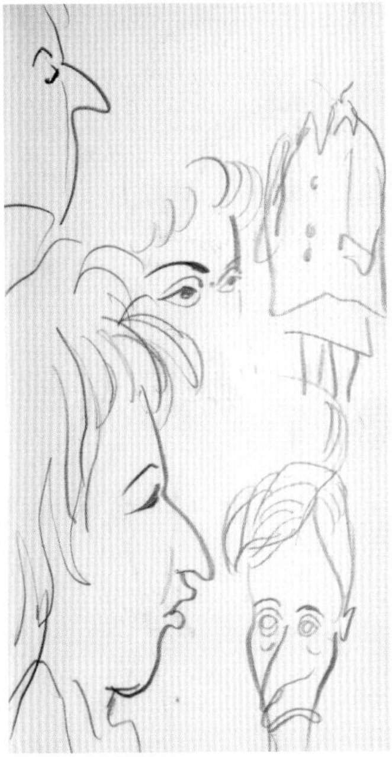

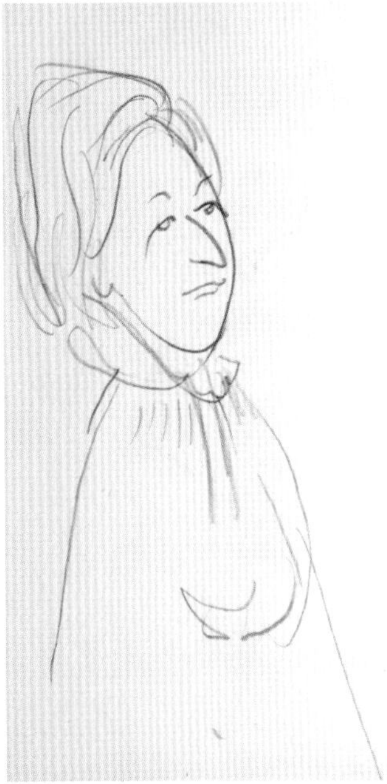

84 FRANCES CUKA AS JOSEPHINE AND MURRAY MELVIN AS GEOFFREY (II)
pencil
8 ¾ x 5 inches

reverse:
MURRAY MELVIN AS GEOFFREY
pencil
8 ½ x 4 ½ inches

Preliminary drawings for *Punch*, 11 February 1959, page 235

85 BUD FLANAGAN (I)
pencil
7 ½ x 4 ½ inches

reverse:
BUD FLANAGAN
pencil, 5 x 3 ½ inches

Preliminary drawings for *Punch*, 11 March 1959, page 364

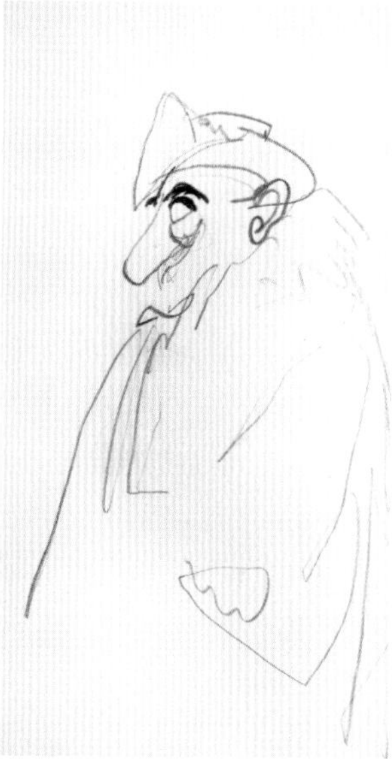

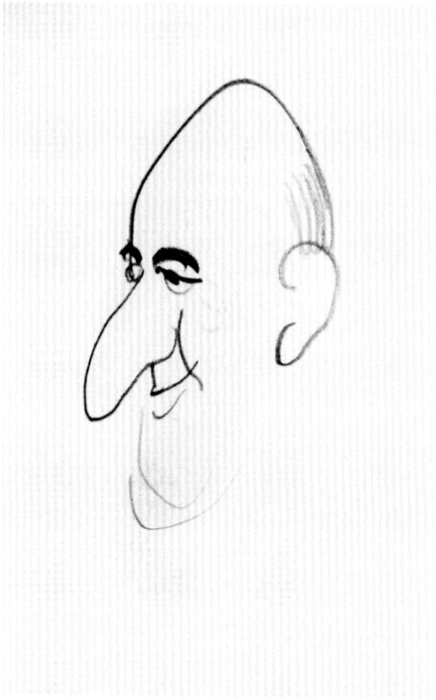

Clown Jewels

Written by Bud Flanagan, and other members of The Crazy Gang, the musical revue, *Clown Jewels*, opened at the Victoria Palace Theatre on 5 March 1959. The comedy was directed by Charles Henry; the original music and lyrics were written by Ross Parker; dances and musical numbers were choreographed by Joan Davis; the musical director was Jack Ansell; and Alan Shanks was responsible for the staging.

Adopting its name in 1937, The Crazy Gang was a group of comedians that essentially comprised three double acts: Bud Flanagan and Chesney Allen, Charlie Naughton and Jimmy Gold, and Jimmy Nervo and Teddy Knox. While making films from that year, the group was best seen on stage, and especially at the Victoria Palace between 1947 and 1962. In this, the penultimate revue in the series, the gang's sometime supporter, 'Monsewer' Eddie Gray, replaced Chesney Allen.

'The Crazy Gang are back again, casual, corny and intermittently very funny … A loose framework leaves them free to develop their lunacy as they go along; in the end the material of these six ripe old comedians matters less than what they do to it. They have a cumulative magic.

'In their funniest turn here they come on as six terrible old debutantes who have failed to make the grade, only getting as far as the Victoria Palace. This is their best lyric, and it gives ample play to their facility for representing with awful dignity the raddled elderly female.'

(Eric Keown, 'At the Play', *Punch*, 11 March 1959, page 364)

86 BUD FLANAGAN (II)
pencil
6 ½ x 4 ¾ inches

reverse:
CHARLIE NAUGHTON
pencil, 8 x 4 ½ inches

Preliminary drawings for *Punch*, 11 March 1959, page 364

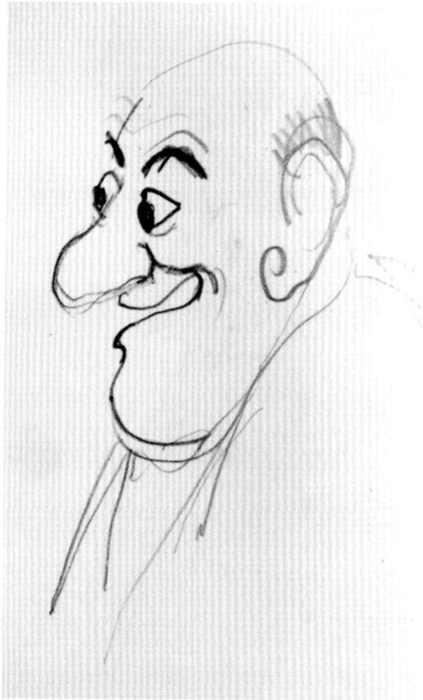

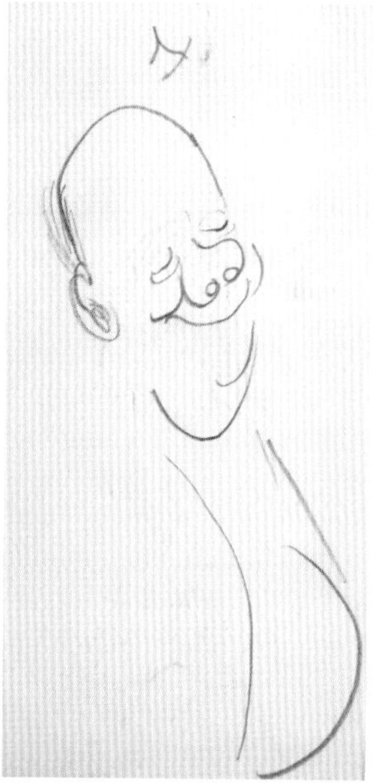

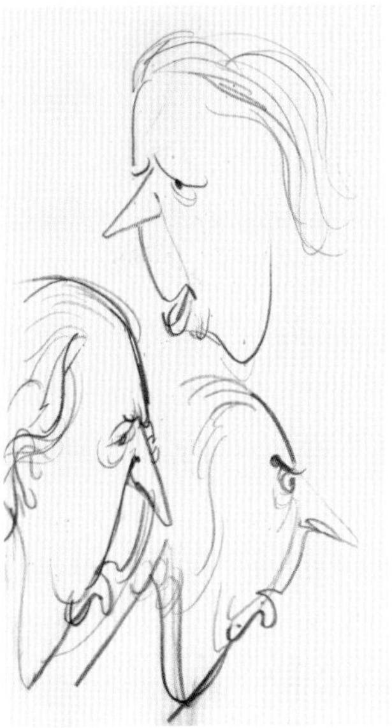

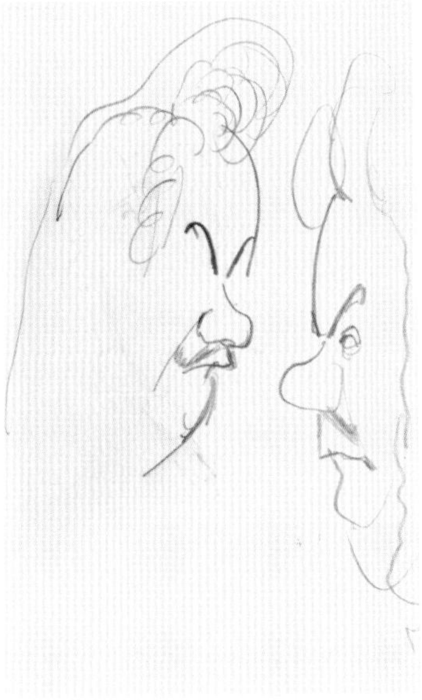

87 MILES MALLESON AS SGANARELLE
pencil, 8 x 4 ¾ inches

reverse:
DEREK FRANCIS AS GORGIBUS
pencil, 6 ½ x 5 inches

Preliminary drawings for *Punch*, 18 February 1959, page 267

Sganarelle and Tartuffe
A double bill of *Sganarelle* and *Tartuffe* by Molière, in free adaptations by Miles Malleson, opened at the Old Vic on 11 February 1959. Malleson directed the former, and Douglas Seale the latter, while both were designed by Michael Baldwin and Patrick Robertson.

'It is rather gallant of the Old Vic to try its hand at Molière, when the masters from the Comédie Française are about to show London how he should be done. Miles Malleson's free adaptations keep the spirit of Sganarelle *and* Tartuffe *in racy English dialogue; they make a festive evening, with a little wind orchestra tooting Lully's original music, and a glittering Louis ready in the royal box to receive his shower of compliments at the end of* Tartuffe.

Sganarelle *is a very slight piece about a lovers' misunderstanding, but in the name part it gives Mr Malleson an open licence for one of his fat bits of character acting, as a cowardly old husband who imagines himself cuckolded by an innocent stranger … As producer he has been less successful, allowing the complications of the plot to amble where they must race if the other characters are to keep their heads above water.*

Douglas Seale's production of Tartuffe *also suffers from lack of pace, but his cast is nearer to achieving a common style … Tartuffe himself, Molière's archetype of the psychological crook, is played very well by Derek Francis, covering the humbug's cleverness in a thick pall of solemnity'*

(Eric Keown, 'At the Play', *Punch*, 18 February 1959, pages 267-268)

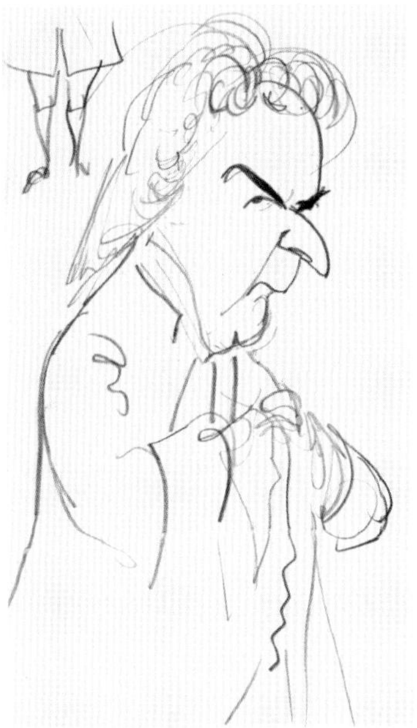

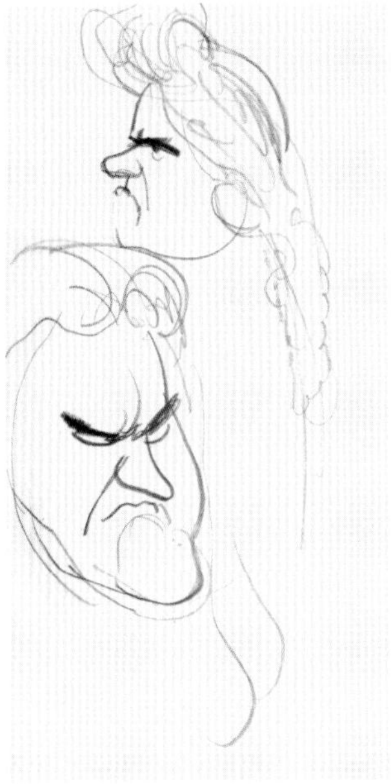

88 DEREK FRANCIS AS TARTUFFE
pencil, 8 ¾ x 4 ¾ inches

reverse:
A CHARACTER FROM TARTUFFE
pencil, 8 ¼ x 5 inches

Preliminary drawings for *Punch*, 18 February 1959, page 267

89 SHIRLEY BASSEY
pencil
8 ¾ x 5 inches

reverse:
SHIRLEY BASSEY
pencil
5 ½ x 4 inches

Preliminary drawings for *Punch*, 25 February 1959, page 300

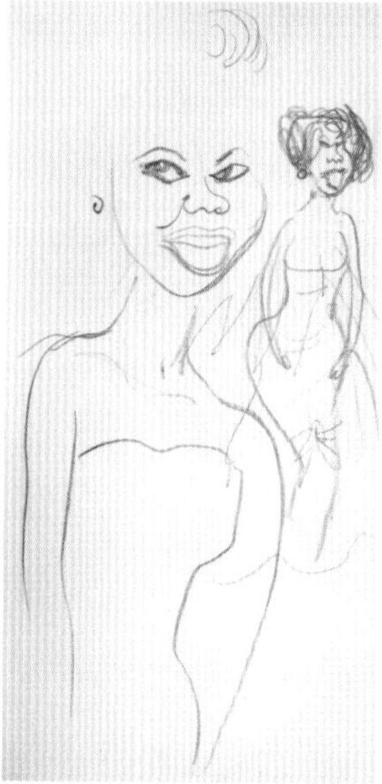

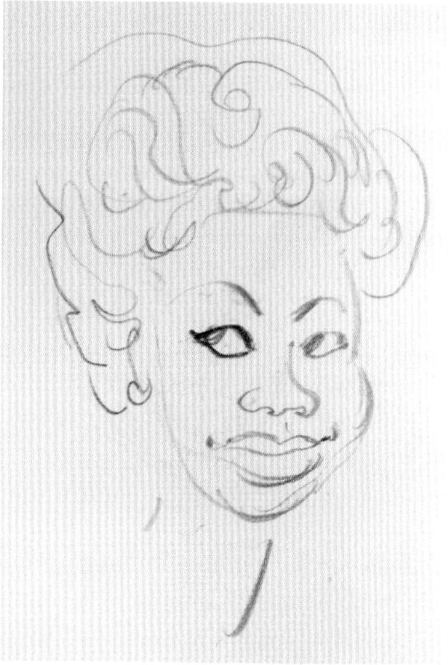

Blue Magic
Adapted from *Folies Bergère*, a Blackpool summer spectacular, *Blue Magic*, opened at the Prince of Wales Theatre on 19 February 1959. It was directed by Charles Hickman, with choreography by Malcolm Clare, and musical direction by Raymond Agoult.

'Blue Magic describes itself as a "gay new glamour revue," which means when translated that it is slanted somewhat towards sex and that no trace of satire sullies its simple innocence …

The star of the show is Shirley Bassey, who sings hot little numbers dealing with the ramifications of love …

On the side of comedy we have Tommy Cooper and Archie Robbins. Mr Cooper's line is incompetence, and he plays it rather winningly, as a great gangling ham-fisted oaf with a nerve-torn laugh and a look of desperation in his made blue eyes.'

(Eric Keown, 'At the Play', *Punch*, 25 February 1959, page 300)

90 TOMMY COOPER
pencil
8 ½ x 4 ½ inches

reverse:
SHIRLEY BASSEY
pencil
4 x 3 ½ inches

Preliminary drawings for *Punch*, 25 February 1959, page 300

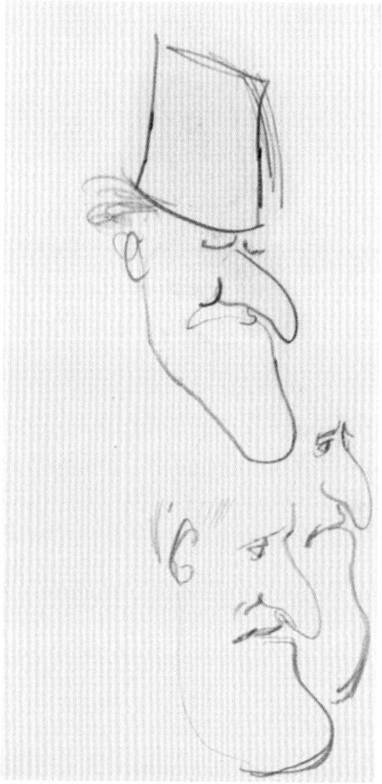

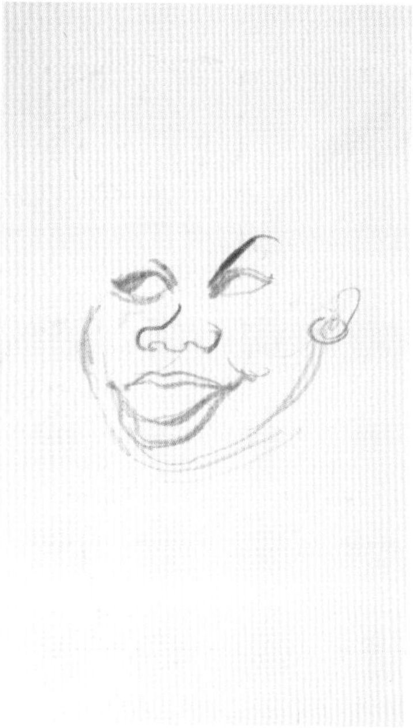

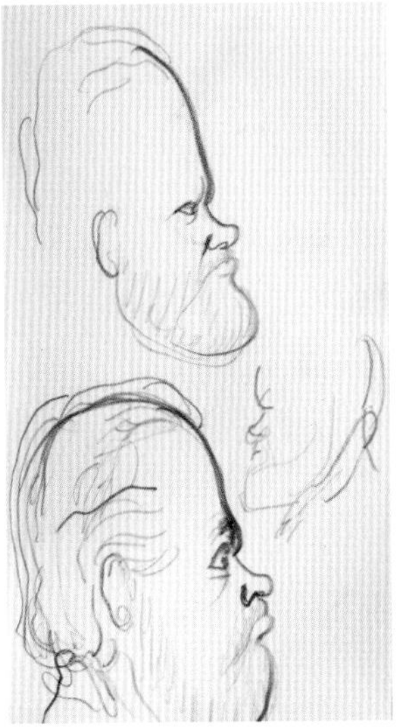

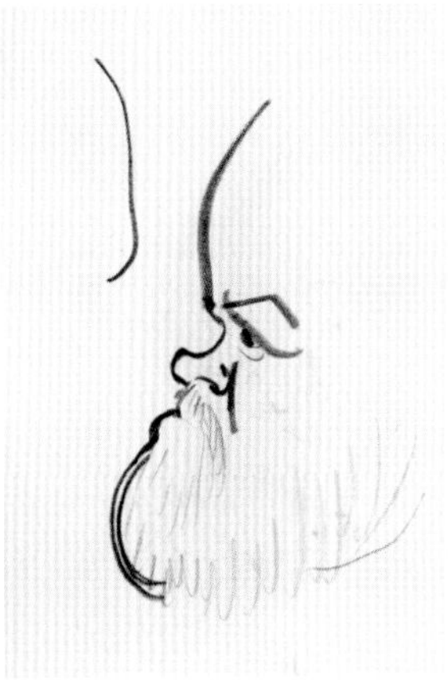

91 PATRICK MAGEE AS MAX
pencil, 8 ½ x 5 ¼ inches

reverse:
PATRICK MAGEE AS MAX
pencil, 5 ½ x 4 inches

Preliminary drawings for *Punch*, 18 March 1959, page 396

The Buskers

The Buskers by Kenneth Jupp (1928-2009) opened at the Arts Theatre Club on 12 March 1959. It was directed by Toby Robertson and designed by Reginald Woolley.

The Buskers centres on two travelling players, Guido (Gordon Gostelow), and his daughter, Julia (Wendy Hutchinson). Their surrounding circle has reacted badly to the disappearance of its former leader, Adam Cross, 'preacher and philosopher'. Guido suggests the cathartic act of re-enacting the events of the day on which he disappeared, believing that it will help each member of the troupe to understand their plight.

The writer's first play, *The Buskers*, won the International Theatre Award and a £500 award from the Arts Council. However, the reviews were generally negative, that by Eric Keown in *Punch* being characteristic.

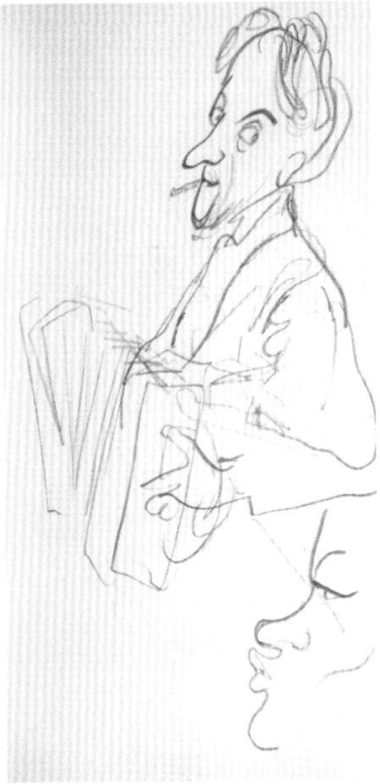

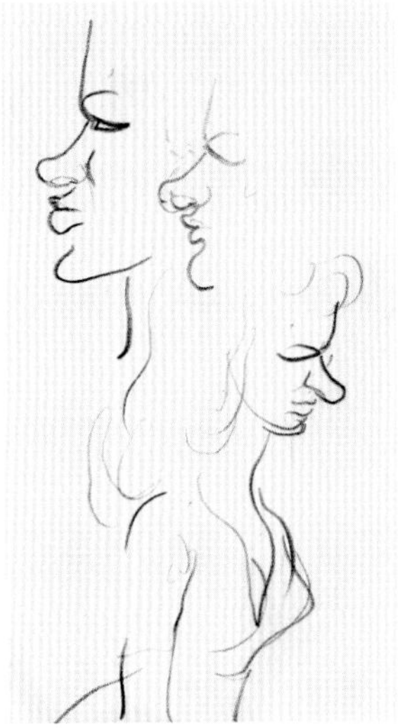

'Kenneth Jupp seems to have found his inspiration for The Buskers *in* Six Characters in Search of an Author *and in early Cold-Comfort-Farm O'Neill. It is an awkward mixture, that reaches absurdity when his least inhibited character rolls on the floor with his mother-in-law … The device of the-play-within-the-play is clumsily managed, the first part of it going on much too long. We feel tricked when at last its comedy breaks into the heavy, earthy melodrama of the second part.*

… he acting here is much better than the play. Patricia Jessel almost makes us believe in the mother-in-law, Patrick Magee has a fine dignity as the patriarch, and Gordon Gostelow is amusing as the worried little boss who does his best with such an odd menagerie.'

(Eric Keown, 'At the Play', *Punch*, 18 March 1959, page 396)

92 GORDON GOSTELOW AS GUIDO
pencil, 8 ¾ x 4 ¾ inches

reverse:
PATRICIA JESSEL AS AGATA
pencil, 8 x 4 ½ inches

Preliminary drawings for *Punch*, 18 March 1959, page 396

Othello

Othello opened at the Royal Shakespeare Theatre, Stratford-upon-Avon, on 7 April 1959. It was directed by Tony Richardson and designed by Loudon Sainthill.

This has proved to be one of the most famous Shakespeare productions of all time, though perhaps more for external reasons than for what happened in the theatre. It was both the third time that Paul Robeson had played Othello on stage and his swansong as an actor, and he arrived at Stratford in the wake of much political controversy and rumour of illness. Playing opposite him was his fellow American, Sam Wanamaker, who had also been blacklisted by the House of Un-American Activities.

Eric Keown in *Punch* was less than impressed with the result, describing Wanamaker's Iago as 'a glib salesman so obviously crooked that Othello's reiteration of his virtues begins to strike a note of farce', and Robeson's Othello as 'limited emotionally' ('At the Play', *Punch*, 15 April 1959, page 529). Searle preferred to illustrate his reviews of two theatrical offerings in Paris: Offenbach's *La Vie Parisienne* and Camus' dramatisation of Dostoyevesky's novel, *The Possessed*.

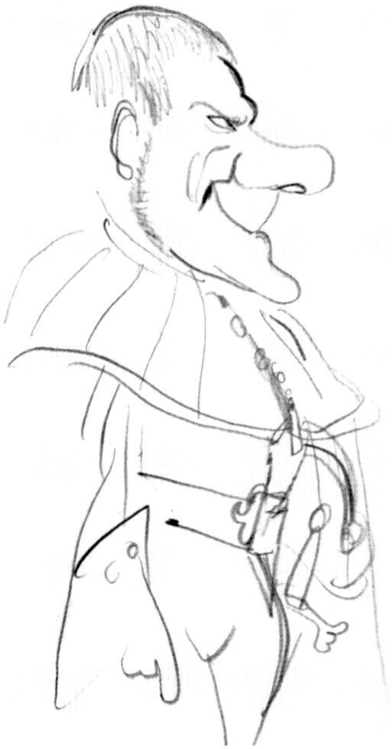

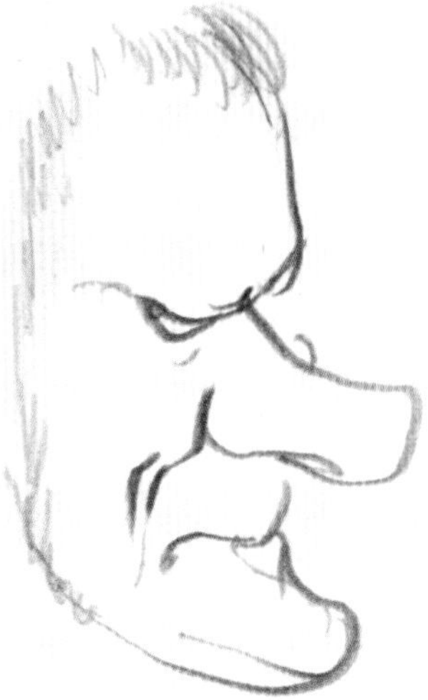

93 SAM WANAMAKER AS IAGO
pencil
8 x 4 ½ inches

reverse:
SAM WANAMAKER AS IAGO
pencil
4 x 3 inches

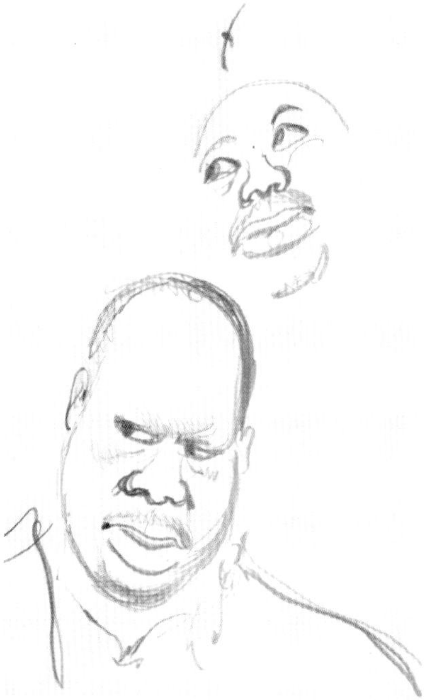

94 PAUL ROBESON
AS OTHELLO
pencil
7 ½ x 4 ½ inches

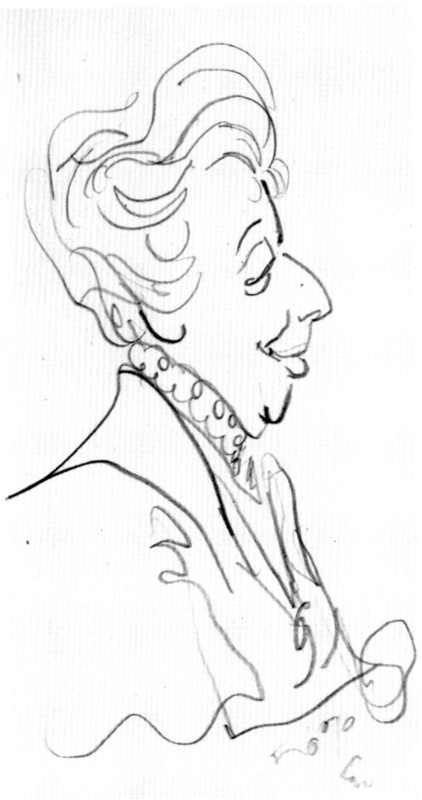

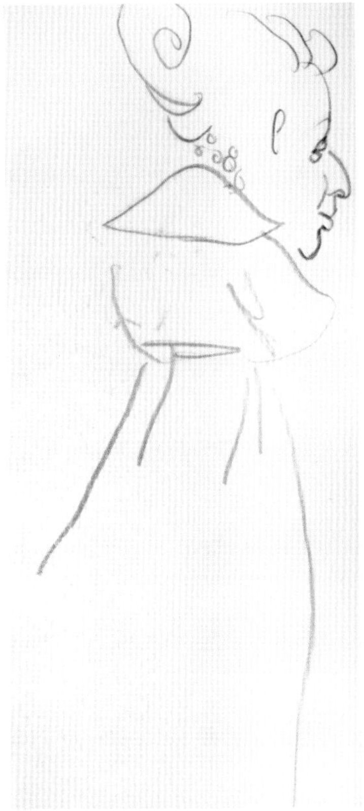

All's Well That Ends Well

All's Well That Ends Well opened at the Royal Shakespeare Theatre, Stratford-upon-Avon, on 21 April 1959. It was directed by Tyrone Guthrie and designed by Tanya Moiseiwitsch.

95 EDITH EVANS AS THE COUNTESS OF ROUSILLON
pencil
8 ¾ x 4 ¾ inches

reverse:
EDITH EVANS AS THE COUNTESS OF ROUSILLON
pencil
9 x 4 ½ inches

Preliminary drawings for *Punch*, 29 April 1959, page 593

'There are those who will be shocked at Tyrone Guthrie's flippant treatment of All's Well That Ends Well *at Stratford, but I cannot in honesty be one of them, I enjoyed it too much. The flippancy is only superficial. Mr Guthrie gets wonderful comedy from the military manoeuvres and the old women at Florence, but he takes great care to establish the drama of the court scenes and to win what sympathy he can for Helena …*

The core of the play is secure with Edith Evans, a beautifully gracious Countess Rousillon and Zoe Caldwell, who seems to me Stratford's biggest find for some time.'

(Eric Keown, 'At the Play', *Punch*, 29 April 1959, pages 592-593)

A Midsummer Night's Dream

A Midsummer Night's Dream opened at the Royal Shakespeare Theatre, Stratford-upon-Avon, on 2 June 1959. It was directed by Peter Hall and designed by Lila De Nobili.

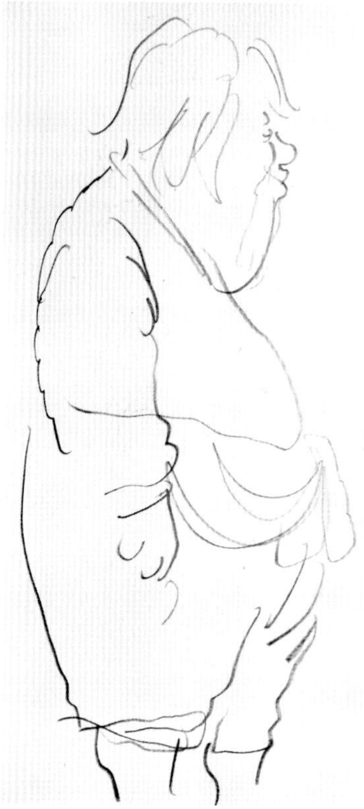

96 CHARLES LAUGHTON AS BOTTOM (I)
pencil
8 ¾ x 4 ½ inches

reverse:
CHARLES LAUGHTON AS BOTTOM
pencil
8 ½ x 4 ½ inches

Preliminary drawings for *Punch*, 17 June 1959, page 813

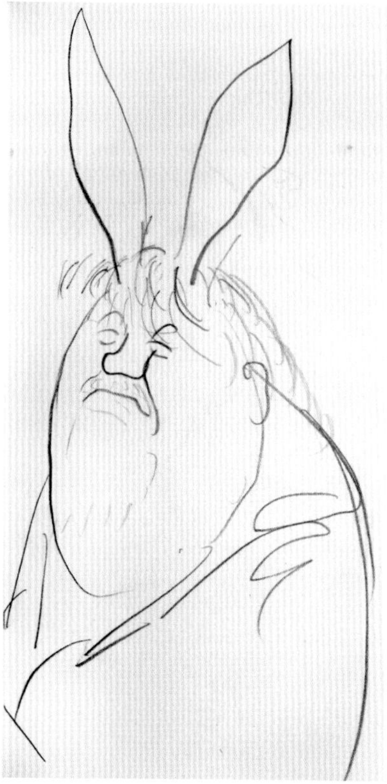

97 CHARLES LAUGHTON AS BOTTOM (II)
pencil
8 ¾ x 4 ¾ inches

reverse:
CHARLES LAUGHTON AS BOTTOM
pencil
7 x 4 ½ inches

Preliminary drawings for *Punch*, 17 June 1959, page 813

'I don't suppose there has ever been a production of A Midsummer Night's Dream *that did not arouse controversy, and Peter Hall's decision to set the play in an Elizabethan country house, with the stage strewn with rushes and a marvellously eerie forest appearing now and then behind the staircase, will obviously not please everybody. I found the conception fresh and charming.*

More eyebrows will be raised, however, at the notion of characterizing the lovers as knockabout comics … Partly as a result of this unorthodox treatment Quince's gormless Thespians emerge not as rough comics but as decent, sensible men going about their business while their betters occupy themselves in slapstick foolery … the rude mechanicals are a fairly glum lot, and Charles Laughton is allowed to make surprisingly little of Bottom.'

(Eric Keown, 'At the Play', *Punch*, 17 June 1959, page 813)

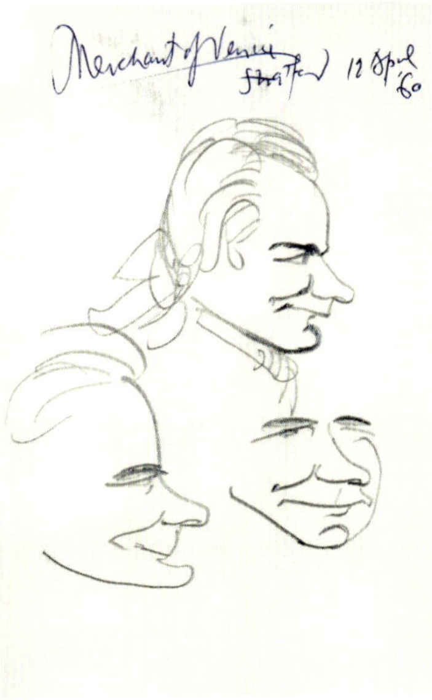

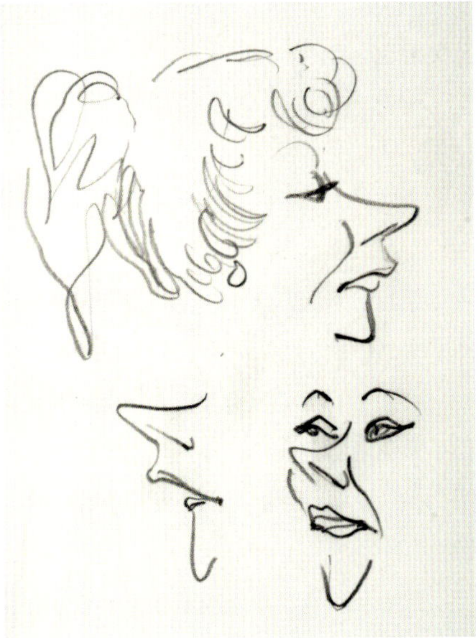

The Merchant of Venice
The Merchant of Venice opened at the Royal Shakespeare Theatre, Stratford-upon-Avon, on 12 April 1960. It was directed by Michael Langham and designed by Desmond Heeley.

98 DENHOLM ELLIOTT AS BASSANIO
inscribed 'Merchant of Venice' and 'Stratford', and dated '12 April '60'
pen ink and pencil
6 ¾ x 4 inches
Preliminary drawing for *Punch*, 27 April 1960, page 596

99 DOROTHY TUTIN AS PORTIA
pencil
6 ¾ x 4 inches
Preliminary drawing for *Punch*, 27 April 1960, page 596

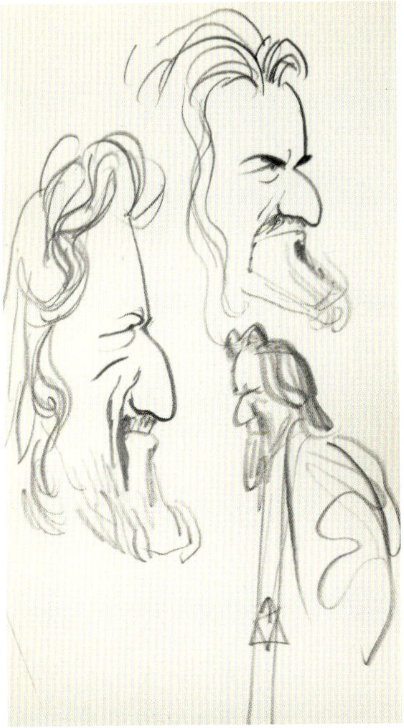

'With Michael Langham's The Merchant of Venice *Stratford makes amends for its poor opening. This production is simple and intelligent; in the main it is well acted, and Desmond Heeley's unostentatious sets and eighteenth century dresses show it off admirably. Peter O'Toole, who distinguished himself in* The Long and the Short and the Tall, *shows every sign of being a very interesting recruit to Shakespeare; his Shylock is refreshingly not a caricature of the cringing Jew of tradition but a fiercely independent fellow prepared to take on the Doge or anybody else …*

Dorothy Tutin seemed to me a delightful Portia up to and after the trial scene; there, though she went for it with the utmost gallantry, I thought her handicapped by her size and youth.'

(Eric Keown, 'At the Play', *Punch*, 27 April 1960, page 596)

100 PETER O'TOOLE AS SHYLOCK
pencil
6 ¾ x 4 inches
Preliminary drawing for *Punch*, 27 April 1960, page 596

1953-60: Punch

1953

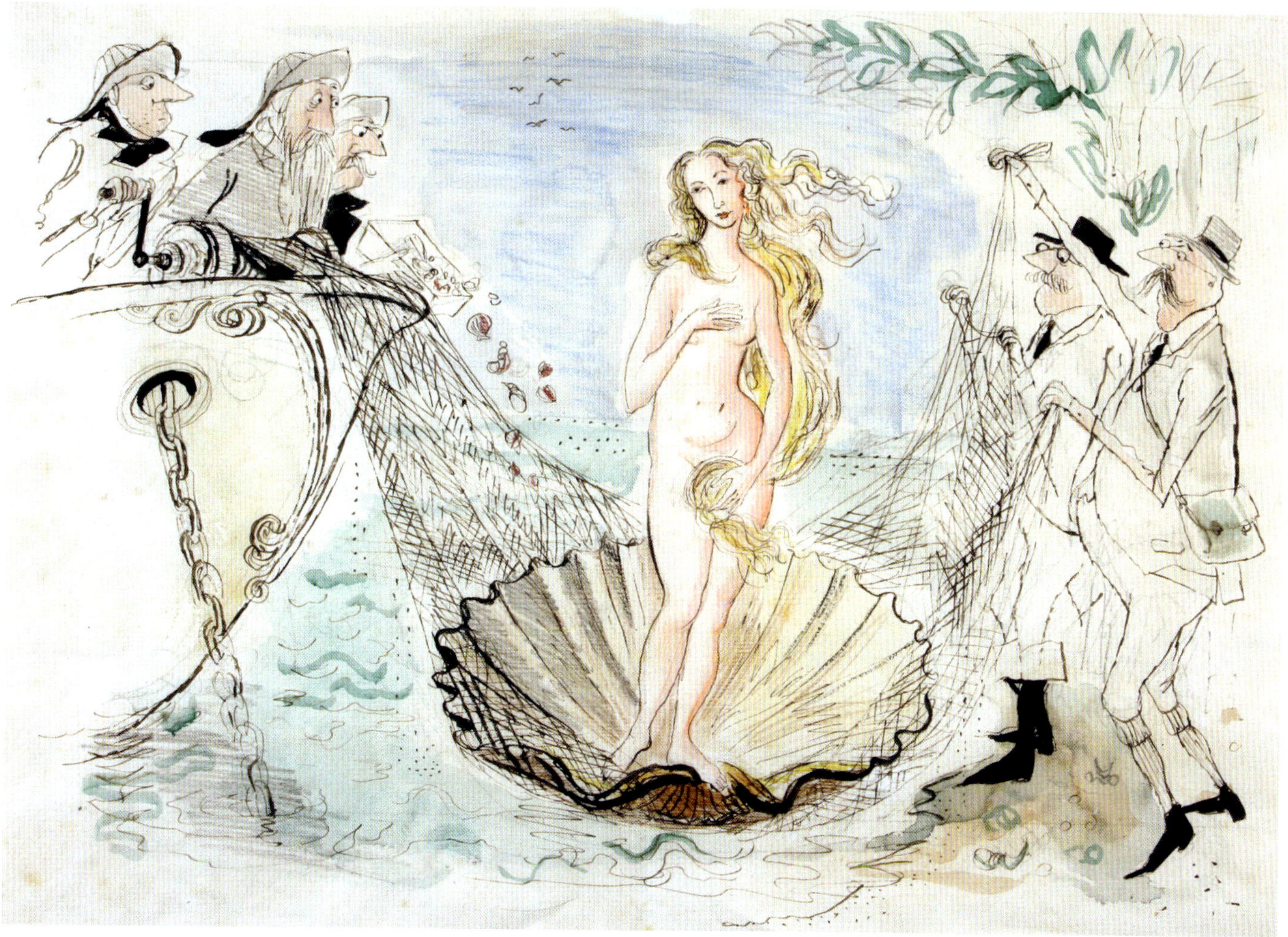

101 RISING TO THE OCCASION

THE CONCHOLOGICAL SOCIETY OF GREAT BRITAIN AND IRELAND MAKES A RECORD HAUL

inscribed 'The Society of Marine Conchologists make their greatest discovery', 'Rough' and 'Punch Coronation Issue' below mount

pen ink and watercolour with pencil

11 ¾ x 15 ½ inches

Preliminary drawing for *Punch Coronation Number*, 13 May 1953, page 31; Ronald Searle, *Merry England, Etc*, London: Perpetua Books, 1956, page 91

1953

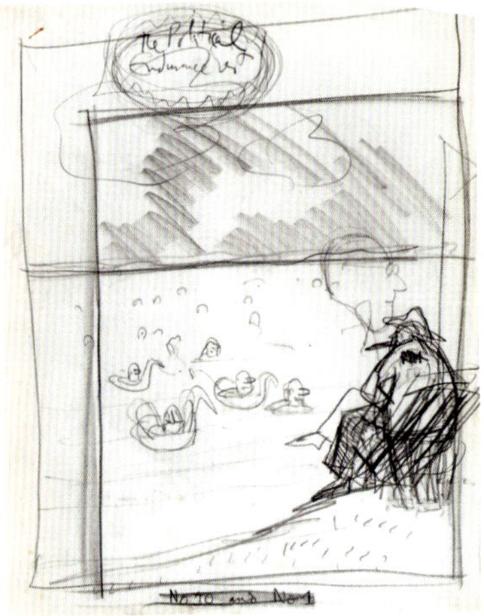

102 CROSS-CHANNEL MARATHON
inscribed 'The Political Endurance Test'
pencil
10 ¾ x 8 inches
Preliminary drawing for *Punch*, 12 August 1953, page 193

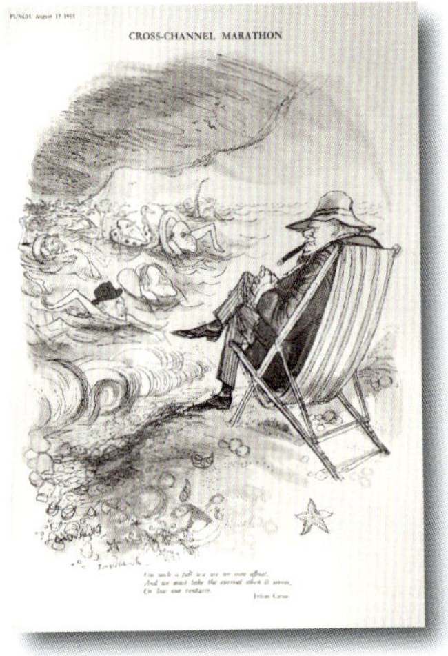

Cross-Channel Marathon

In this cartoon, Ronald Searle alluded to a forthcoming event, in which the Californian swimming coach, Florence Chadwick, would cross the English Channel for the third time. (She did so on 4 September 1953, setting a new world record of 14 hours and 42 minutes.) The Prime Minister, Sir Winston Churchill, is shown sitting in a deckchair on the beach, while watching members of the cabinet swimming towards him. He had suffered a serious stroke in June 1953 – though it was publicised as exhaustion – and was therefore thought likely to retire. He finally did so two years later, giving way to his Foreign Secretary, Anthony Eden, who appears in the foreground of the finished cartoon.

1954

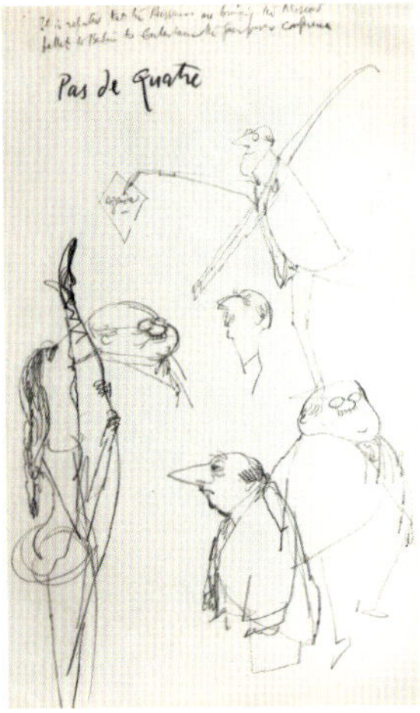

103 PAS DE QUATRE
inscribed with title and 'It is reported that the Russians are bringing the Moscow Ballet to Berlin to entertain the Four Power Conference'
pencil
13 ¾ x 8 ¼ inches
Preliminary drawing for *Punch*, 27 January 1954, page 137

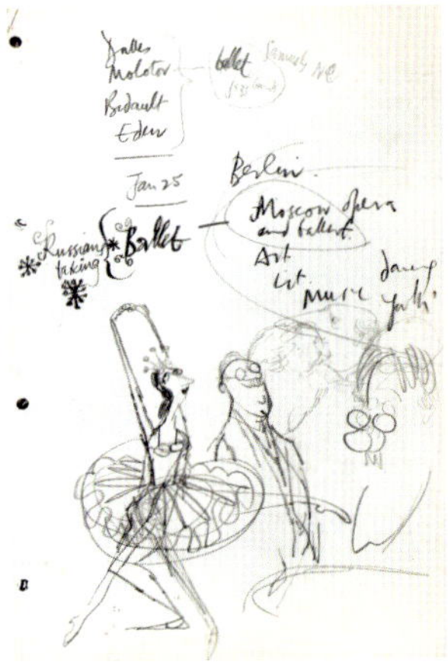

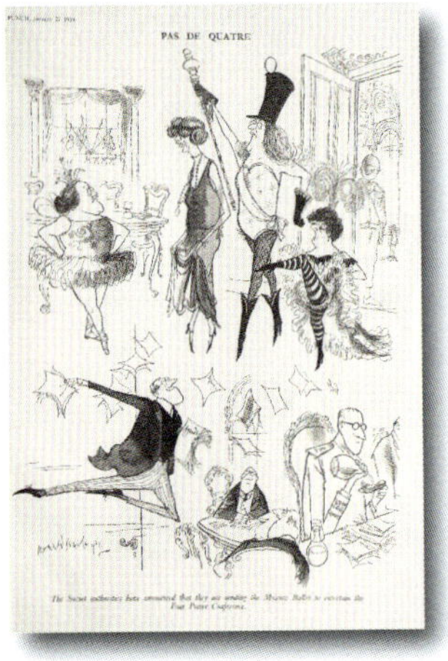

104 STUDIES FOR PAS DE QUATRE
pencil
13 x 8 ¼ inches
Annotated preliminary drawing for *Punch*, 27 January 1954, page 137

An Old Favourite ...
Private View at the Royal Academy

In this cartoon, Ronald Searle gently parodied four of the works included in the 1954 Royal Academy Summer Exhibition, which are (clockwise from the top left):
No 27: *Man in a Brown Suit*
by Ruskin Spear (1911-1990);
No 231: *The Rt Hon The Lord Simonds, Lord Chancellor, on the Woolsack*
by Lord Methuen (1845-1932);
No 162: *Alderman H B W Cresswell* by Bernard Fleetwood-Walker (1893-1965) (now in The Herbert Art Gallery, Coventry);
No 535: *The Four Queens Find Lancelot Sleeping* by Frank Cadogan Cowper (1877-1958)

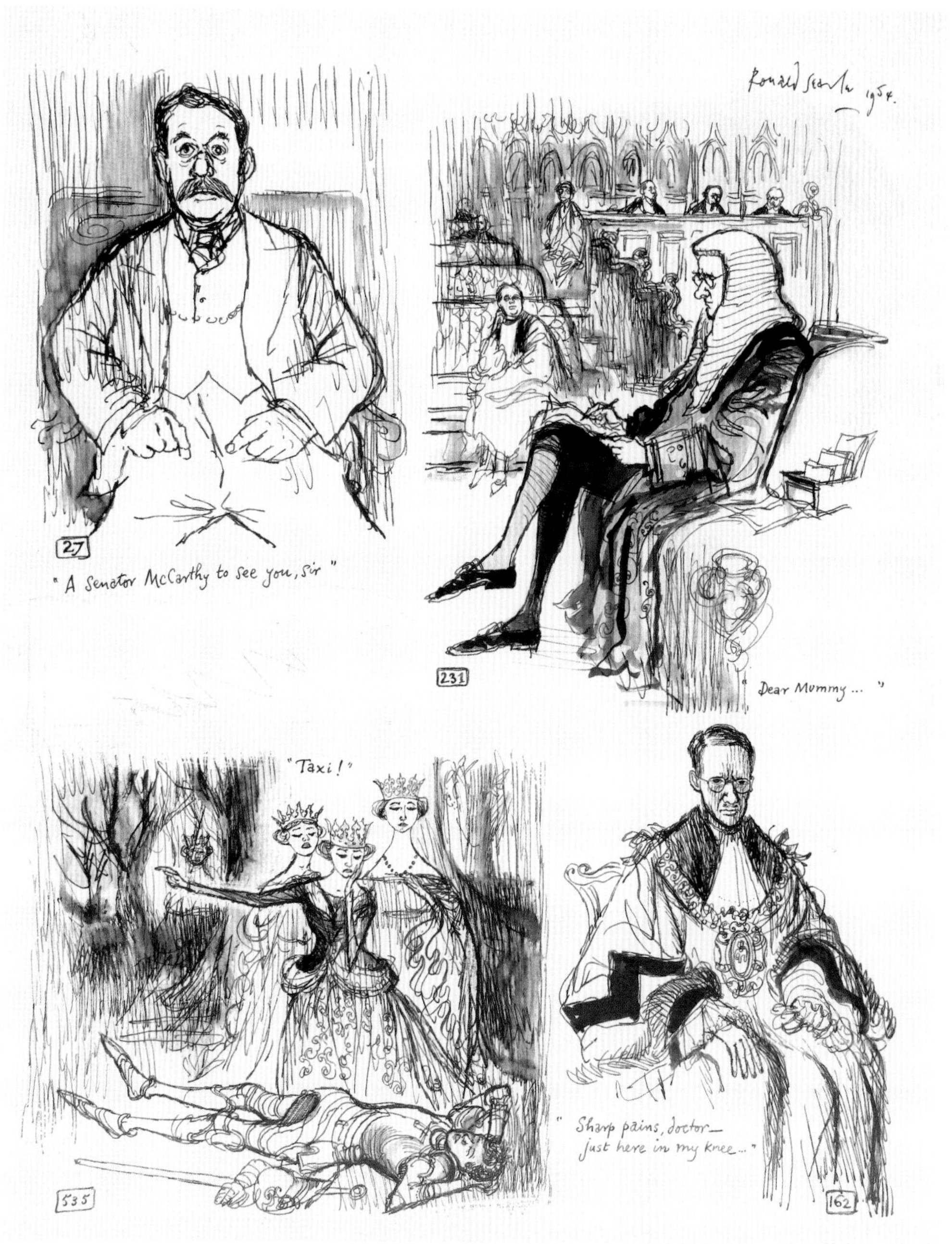

105 AN OLD FAVOURITE ... PRIVATE VIEW AT THE ROYAL ACADEMY
signed and dated 1954
inscribed 'Punch. Merry England Etc. Perpetua Books: London 1956, pp 84/85' and dated 1954 on reverse
pen ink and watercolour
19 ½ x 14 ½ inches
Illustrated: *Punch*, 5 May 1954, page 545; Ronald Searle, *Merry England, Etc*, London: Perpetua Books, 1956, pages 84-85 (excluding lower left image)

1955

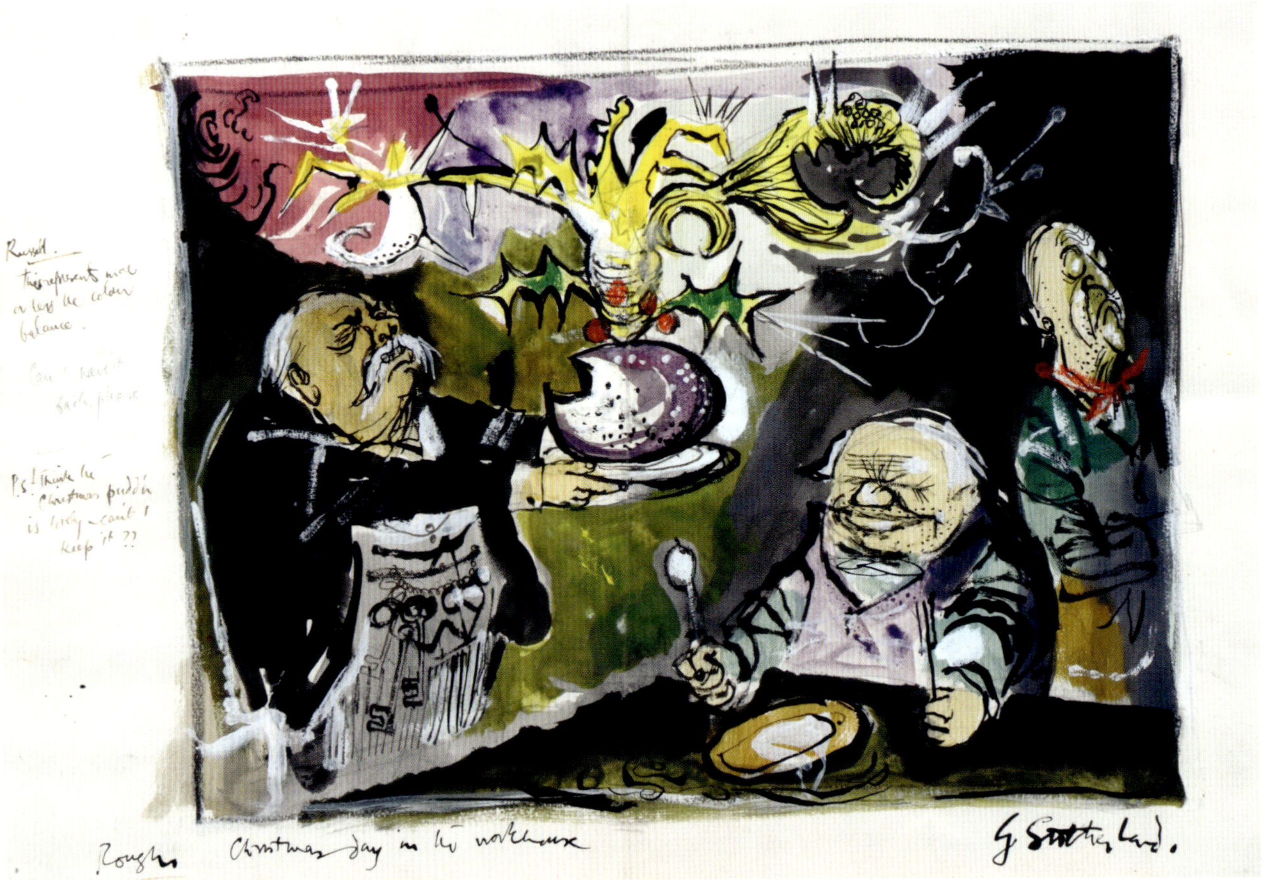

106 IT WAS CHRISTMAS DAY IN THE WORKHOUSE
signed 'G Sutherland' and inscribed 'Christmas Day in the Workhouse', 'Roughs' and 'Russell, this represents more or less the colour balance, can I have it back, please, P.S. I think the Christmas Puddin is lovely – can't I keep it??'
pen ink, watercolour and bodycolour with pencil
10 ½ x 14 ½ inches
Preliminary drawing for *Punch*, 7 November 1955, 'Almanack for 1956', page 34

It was Christmas Day in the Workhouse

This brilliant parody of the painting style of Graham Sutherland (1903-1980) was Ronald Searle's contribution to a cod competition in the 1954 *Punch* Almanack 'for the most moving painting, in water-colour or oils, on the subject "It was Christmas Day in the Workhouse"'. 'Peter Scott' (actually painted by W A Sillince), 'Edward Bawden' (Smilby) and 'Stanley Spencer' (Norman Mansbridge) submitted the other 'prizewinning entries'.

Searle's image references three of Sutherland's most famous portraits, those of Winston Churchill (1954, destroyed), Lord Beaverbrook (1951, now in the Beaverbrook Art Gallery, New Brunswick, Canada) and Somerset Maugham (1949, now in the Tate). The finished version of this composition is also in the Beaverbrook Art Gallery.

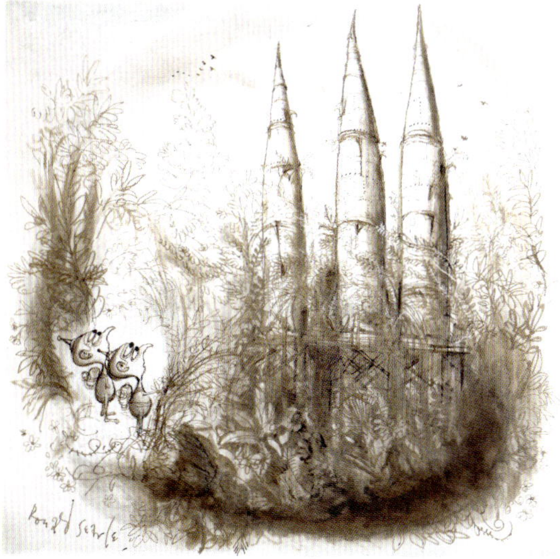

107 OBJECTS OF WORSHIP, I SHOULD IMAGINE ...
signed
inscribed with title below mount
pen and ink
13 ¼ x 13 inches
Drawn for but not illustrated in *Punch*, February 1955
(illustrating a supplied joke)

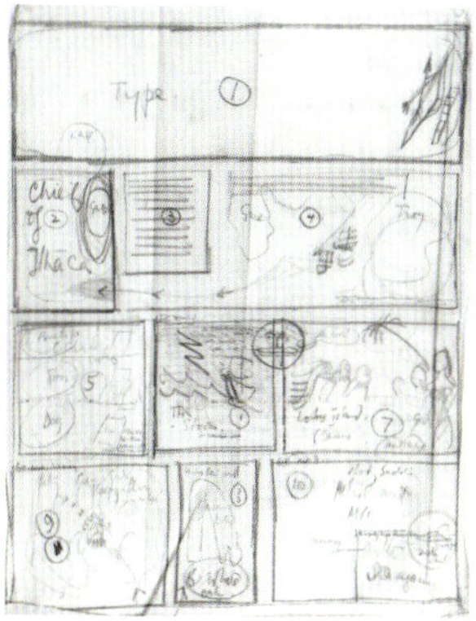

108 NOW! CAPSULYSSES
A STRIP-DIGEST OF THE CONDENSED BOOK OF THE FILM (I-V)
(only (I) illustrated)
pen ink and pencil on tracing paper
19 x 14 inches
Annotated preliminary drawings for *Punch*, 25 May 1955, pages 643-46

Now! Capsulysses
Ronald Searle produced the strip, *Now! Capsulysses*, for the 1955 *Punch* Summer Number, in response to news of the forthcoming 3-D Italian film version of Homer's epic, directed by Mario Camerini and starring Kirk Douglas.

1956

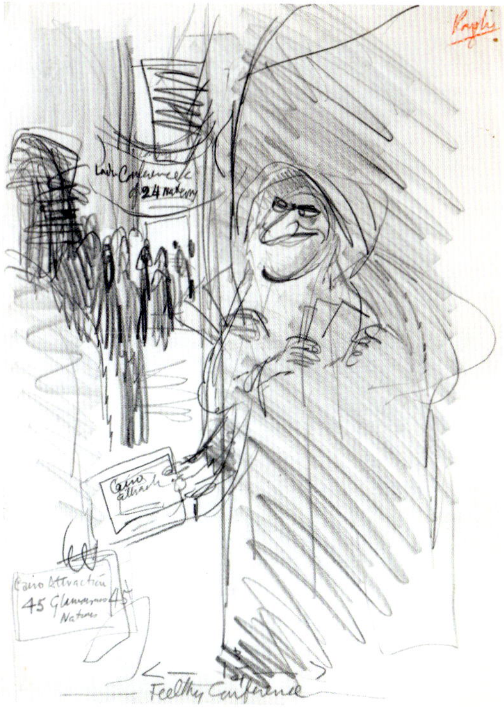

109 FEELTHY CONFERENCE ...
inscribed with title and 'Roughs'
pencil
11 x 8 inches
Preliminary drawing for *Punch*, 22 August 1956, page 201

Feelthy Conference ...
On 22 July 1956, President Nasser of Egypt announced his decision to nationalise the Suez Canal. On 16 August, 22 nations responded by coming together at Lancaster House, in London, for a week-long conference on the issue. However, Nasser refused to attend (as did any representative of Greece, which was quarrelling with Britain about Cyprus). Ronald Searle represents him in this cartoon as an Egyptian trader or tout trying to sell tickets to an alternative event. He would reject the idea – agreed by 18 of the nations present at the conference – that the canal be managed internationally. Two months later, Britain, France and Israel planned to invade Egypt. Late in the year, Searle was called on by the Department of Psychological Warfare to produce anti-Nasser propaganda.

1957

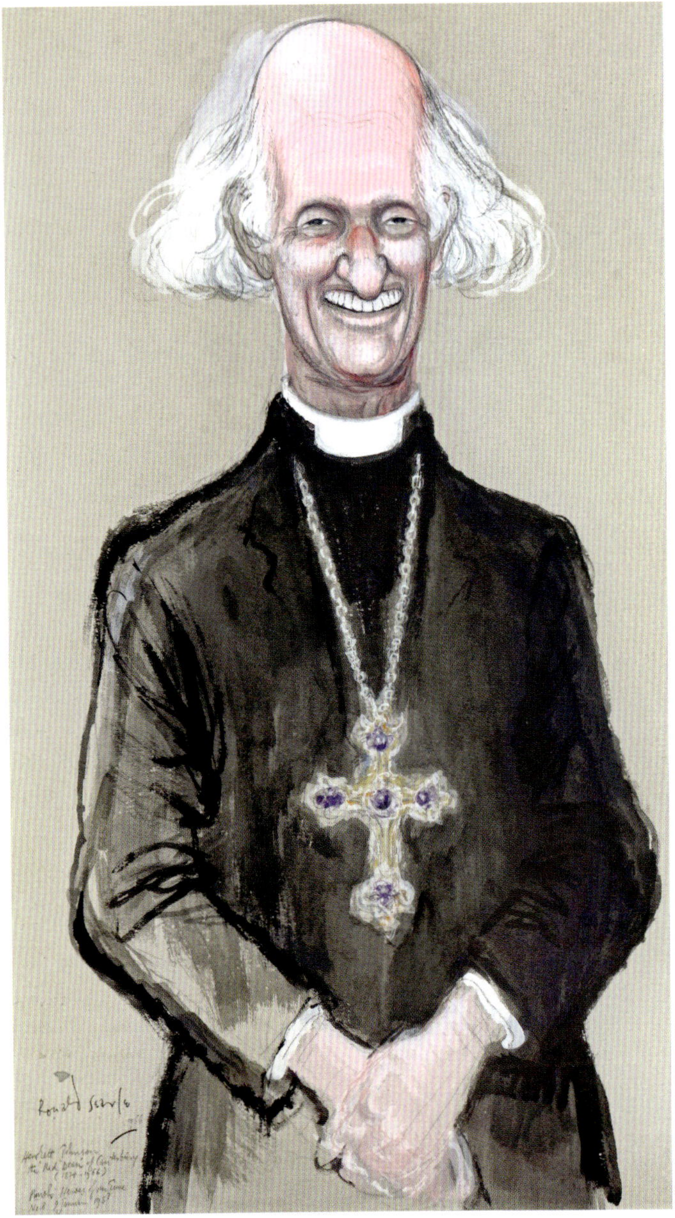

The Dean of Canterbury

The Very Reverend Hewlett Johnson (1874-1966) was appointed Dean of Manchester in 1924, and Dean of Canterbury in 1931. He came to public prominence during the 1930s, when he began to express support for the Soviet Union and its allies. Though his influence had begun to wane by the time that Ronald Searle produced this portrait, his activities remained troublesome for the British government as, internationally, he was confused with the Archbishop of Canterbury (the Most Reverend Geoffrey Fisher).

'the "Heroes of Our Time" were colour caricatures printed as a centrefold across two whole pages [of Punch*]. Among the "Heroes", there were several (notably T S Eliot, in his office at Faber's) who consented to give Ronald a brief sitting, though they must have known that heading under which they were destined to appear was heavy with irony. The selection actually divided itself between "Sacred Monsters" and "Sacred Cows". Adopting the faded palette of the age of "Spy" and "Ape", and toning down something of his natural spikiness in their honour too, Searle produced portraits which were the talk of London for weeks'*

(Davies, pages 115-116)

110 THE DEAN OF CANTERBURY
WHAT CURIOUS CREED DOES HEWLETT PREACH,
WHAT SINGULAR GOSPEL SPREAD?
PERHAPS THAT THE DOCTRINES THE CHRISTIANS TEACH
SHOULD ALL BE TAKEN AS RED
signed, inscribed 'Hewlett Johnson, the "Red Dean" of Canterbury (1874-1966)' and with publishing details, and dated 1957
watercolour with bodycolour and pencil on tinted paper
20 ½ x 12 inches
Illustrated: *Punch*, 9 January 1957, pages 98-99, 'Heroes of Our Time – 8'
Exhibited: 'Ronald Searle: A Celebration', Ruskin Gallery, Anglia Ruskin University, Cambridge, January-February 2008

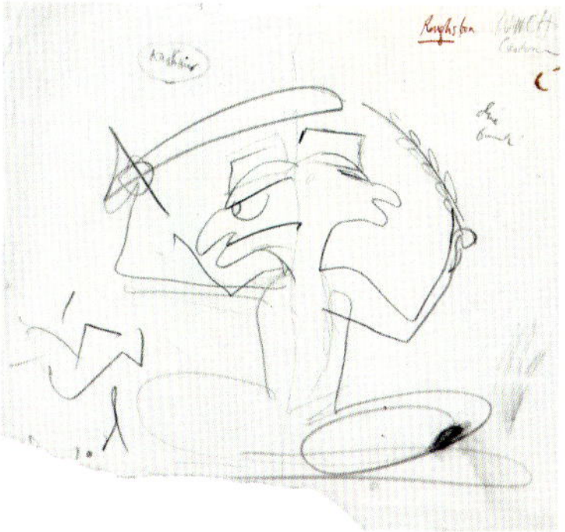

111 NEHRU
ON KASHMIR/ON SUEZ
inscribed 'Roughs box, Punch Cartoon', 'due 6 March'
and 'Kashmir'
pencil
7 ½ x 7 ¾ inches
Preliminary drawing for *Punch*, 23 January 1957, page 168

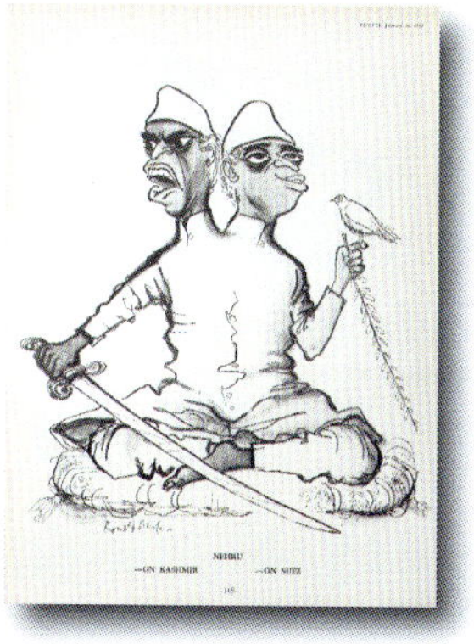

Nehru
The first Prime Minister of an independent India, Jawaharlal Nehru (1889-1964) inevitably took very different positions on the issues of Kashmir and Suez. While he criticised the invasion of the Suez Canal by Britain, France and Israel, he defended Indian Sovereignty in Kashmir (his own family originating in that region). On 23 January 1957 – the day that this cartoon was published – V K Krishna Menon, the Indian Ambassador to the United Nations, gave an eight-hour speech to the UN Security Council defending India's stand on Kashmir.

1958

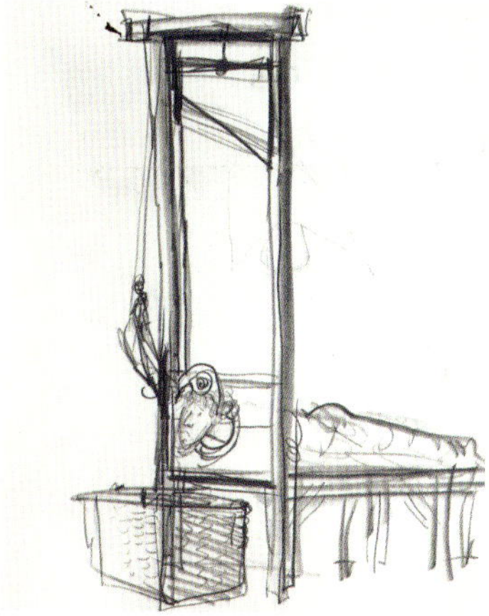

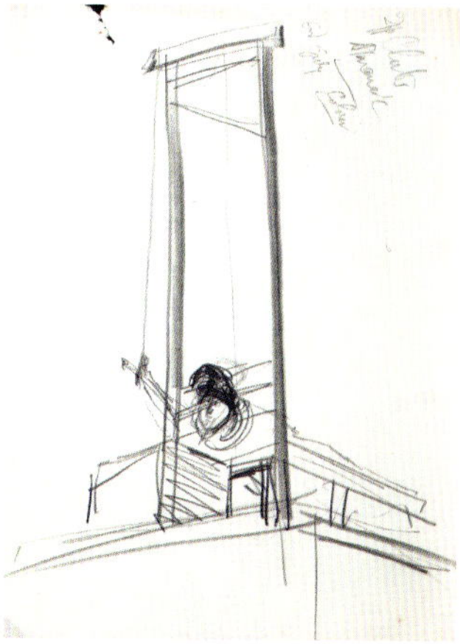

112 ALGERIAN CRISIS (I)
pencil
10 x 7 ½ inches
Preliminary drawing for *Punch*, 21 May 1958, page 665

113 ALGERIAN CRISIS (II)
inscribed '2pp, Clubs, Almanack, end July, colour'
pencil
10 ½ x 7 ½ inches
Preliminary drawing for *Punch*, 21 May 1958, page 665

Algerian Crisis
The Algerian war of independence from France began in 1954. By 1958, French army commanders had become highly frustrated at the lack of effective government support of their efforts to end the rebellion. As a result, they attempted a coup, first seizing power in Algiers on the night of 13 May. Ronald Searle represents the events of mid May through the suicide by guillotine of Marianne, the emblematic figure of France.

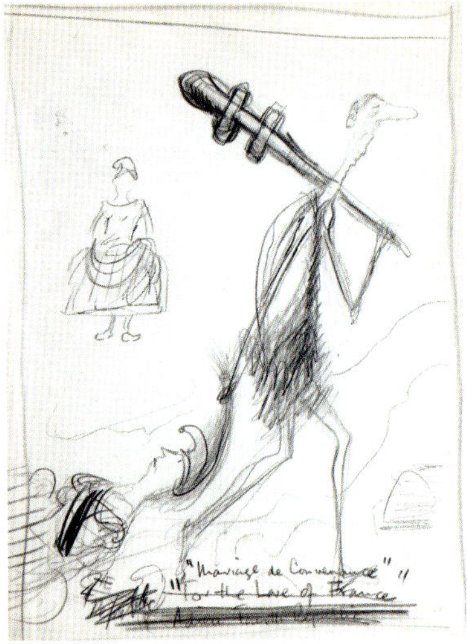

115 MARIAGE DE CONVENANCE
inscribed with title
pencil
10 ½ x 7 ½ inches
Preliminary drawing for *Punch*, 4 June 1958, page 733

Mariage de Convenance

By 1 June 1958, the French army commanders in Algeria had succeeded in their aim to force the collapse of the Fourth Republic and so return Charles de Gaulle to power. Ronald Searle represents De Gaulle as a caveman in his treatment of France (Marianne).

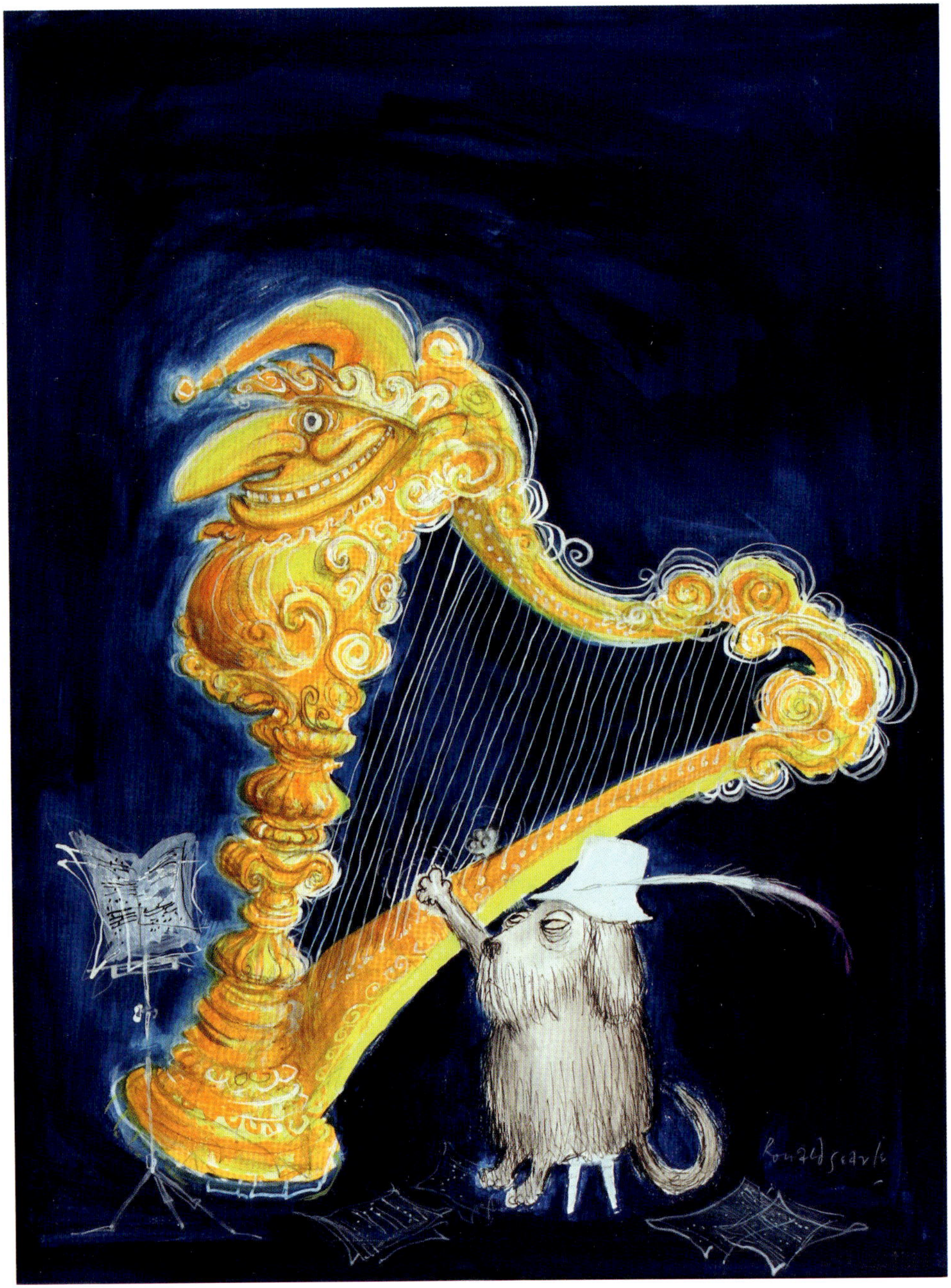

114 THE CANINE HARPIST
signed
pen ink and bodycolour with pencil
17 ½ x 13 ½ inches
Illustrated: *Punch*, 19 March 1958, front cover

Leave them alone, and they'll come home ...
Many thought Iain Macleod (1913-1970) ineffectual as Minister of Labour and National Service to the Conservative government, as unemployment and short-time working increased and overtime was reduced across the British workforce.

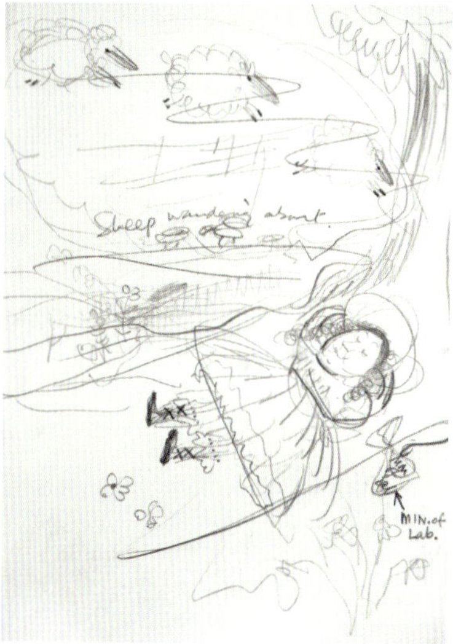

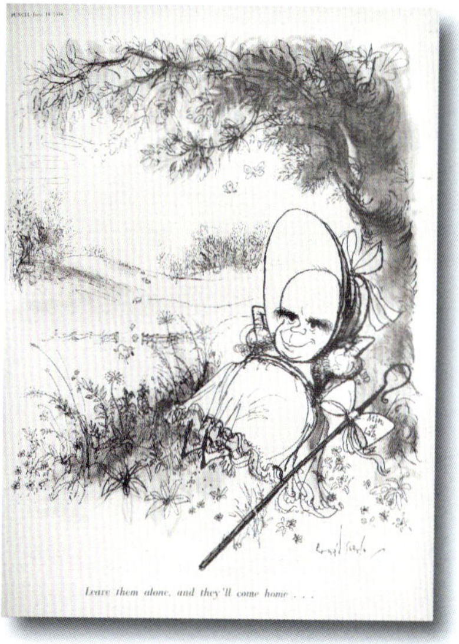

116 LEAVE THEM ALONE, AND THEY'LL COME HOME ... (I)
inscribed 'Sheep wandering about' and 'Min of Lab'
pencil
10 ½ x 7 ½ inches
Preliminary drawing for *Punch*, 18 June 1958, page 797

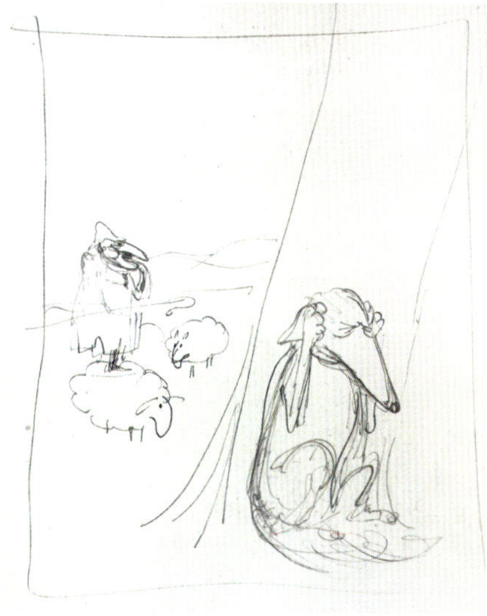

117 CALLING THE SHEEPDOG
pencil
8 ½ x 6 ½ inches
Preliminary drawing for *Punch*, 23 July 1958, front cover

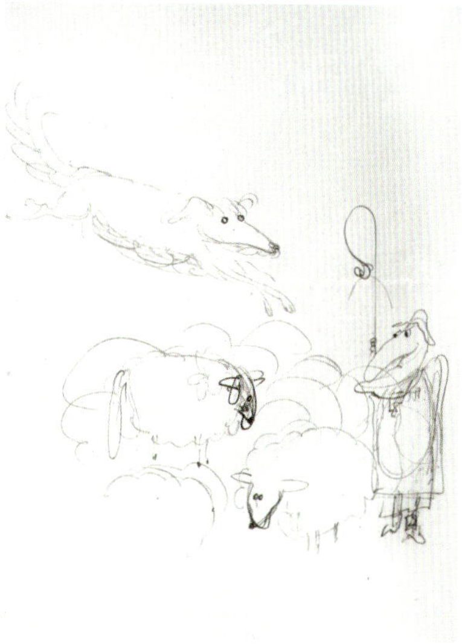

118 ROUNDING UP SHEEP
pencil
8 x 7 ½ inches
Preliminary drawing for *Punch*, 23 July 1958, front cover

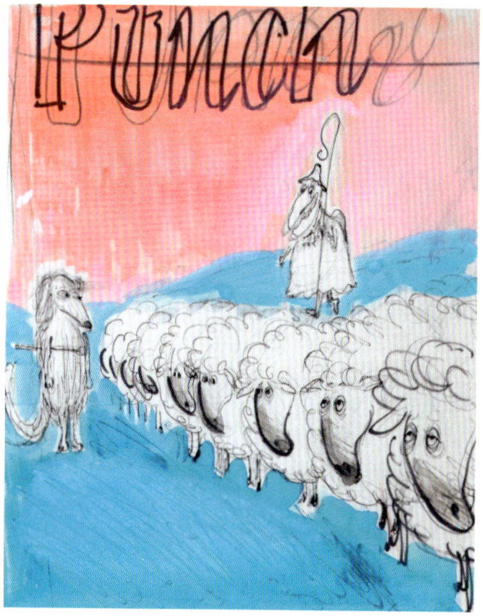

119 ALL PRESENT AND CORRECT
pen ink, watercolour and bodycolour with pencil
8 ¼ x 7 inches
Preliminary drawing for *Punch*, 23 July 1958, front cover

1958

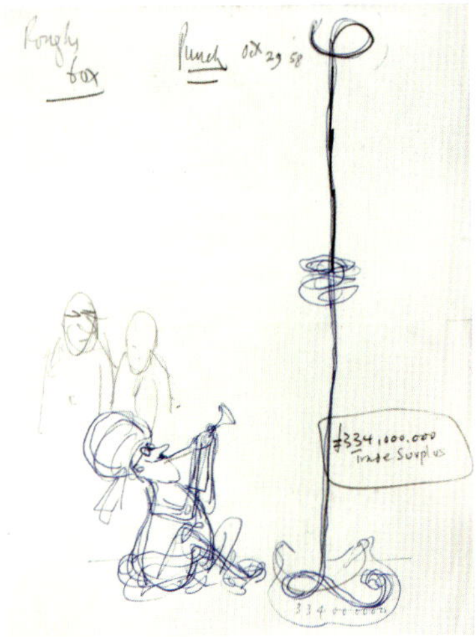

120 TRADE SURPLUS
inscribed 'Roughs box', 'Punch' and '£334,000,000 Trade Surplus' and dated 'Oct 29 58'
pen ink and pencil
11 x 8 inches
Preliminary drawing for *Punch*, 22 October 1958, page 523

Trade Surplus
Conservative Chancellor of the Exchequer, Derick Heathcoat-Amory (1899-1981), charms a rope in the shape of a pound sign out of a basket marked with the amount of trade surplus. During 1958, a substantial increase of exports to the United States more than made up for the decline in exports to countries in Western Europe and the Commonwealth.

1960

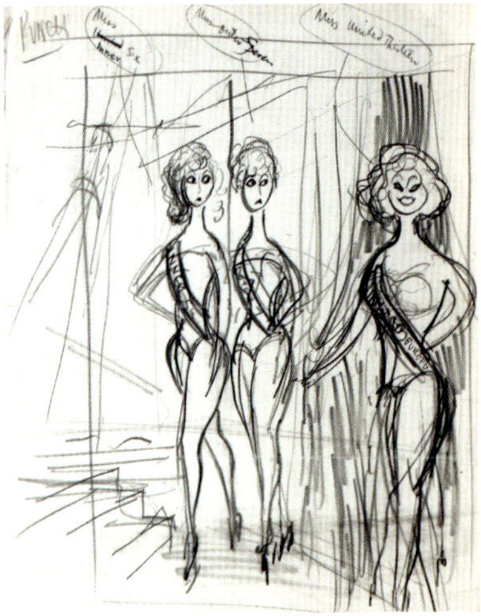

Miss Europe 196-?
This cartoon parallels the Miss Europe beauty contest (that would take place in Beirut on 11 June 1960) and the European Economic Community, at the time that Britain first applied for membership. The 'Inner Six' comprised the founding members of the EEC, while the 'Outer Seven' formed the European Free Trade Association. A leading member of the Inner Six, France, under the Presidency of Charles de Gaulle, vetoed Britain's application for fear of the indirect influence of the United States.

121 MISS EUROPE, 196-?
inscribed 'Punch' and 'Miss Inner Six, Miss Outer Seven, Miss United Thirteen'
inscribed 'Daily Sketch' on reverse
pencil
9 ¾ x 7 ½ inches
Preliminary drawing for *Punch*, 27 April 1960, page 571

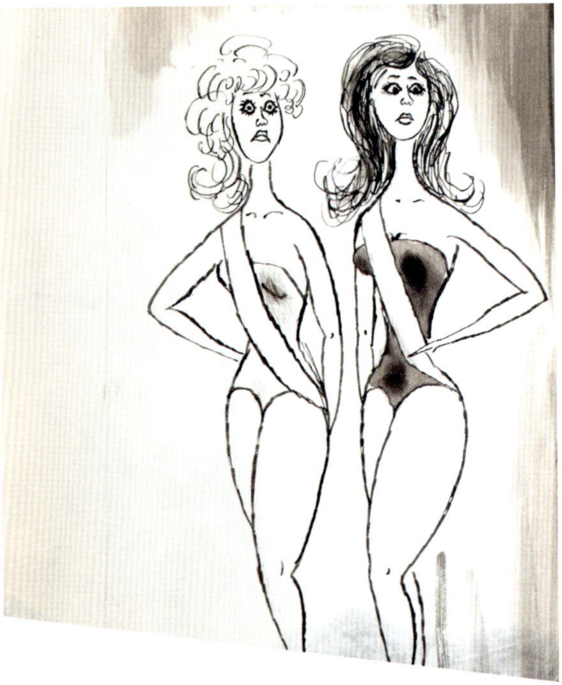

122 MISS INNER SIX AND MISS OUTER SEVEN
pen and ink with watercolour
9 ½ x 6 ½ inches
Preliminary drawing for *Punch*, 27 April 1960, page 571

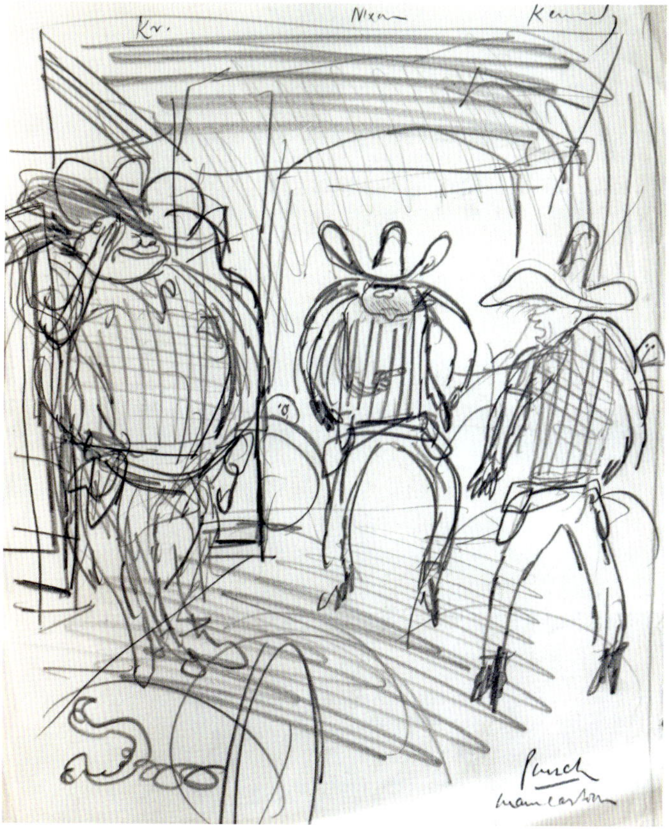

123 'HOWDY, STRANGERS!'
inscribed 'KV, Nixon, Kennedy' and 'Punch, main cartoon'
pencil
9 ¾ x 7 ½ inches
Preliminary drawing for *Punch*, 14 September 1960, page 363

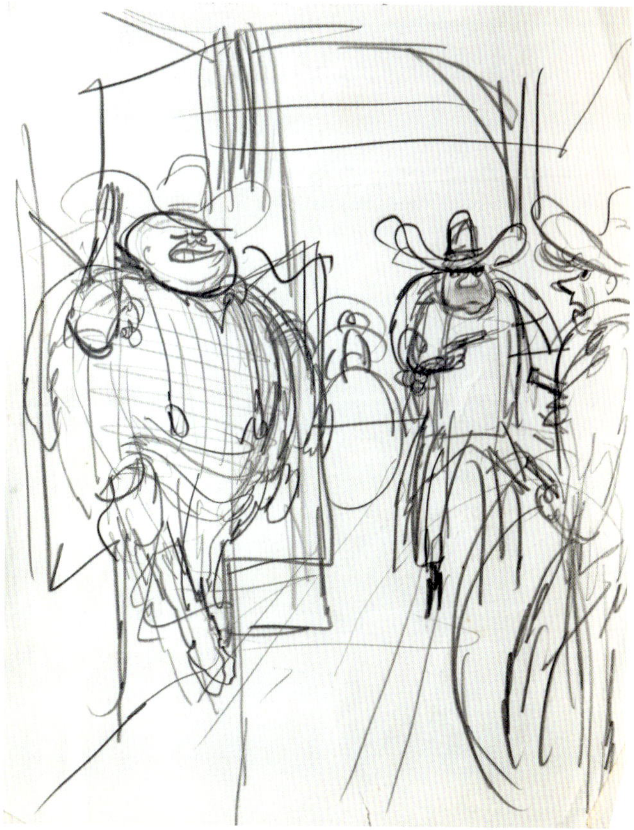

124 'HOWDY, STRANGERS!'
pencil
9 ½ x 7 ½ inches
Preliminary drawing for *Punch*,
14 September 1960, page 363

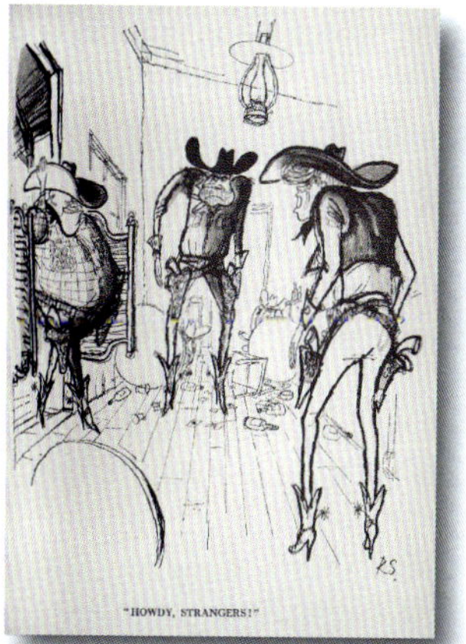

Howdy, Strangers!

In September 1960, the Soviet premier, Nikita Khrushchev (1894-1971), made his second and final visit to the United States, having appointed himself as head of the USSR's delegation to the United Nations. Ahead of his actual arrival on Monday 19 September, Ronald Searle imagined a traditional Western setting for a meeting between Khrushchev, the Republican President, Richard Nixon (1913-1994), and the Democratic candidate, John F Kennedy (1917-1963), during the lead up to the Presidential elections.

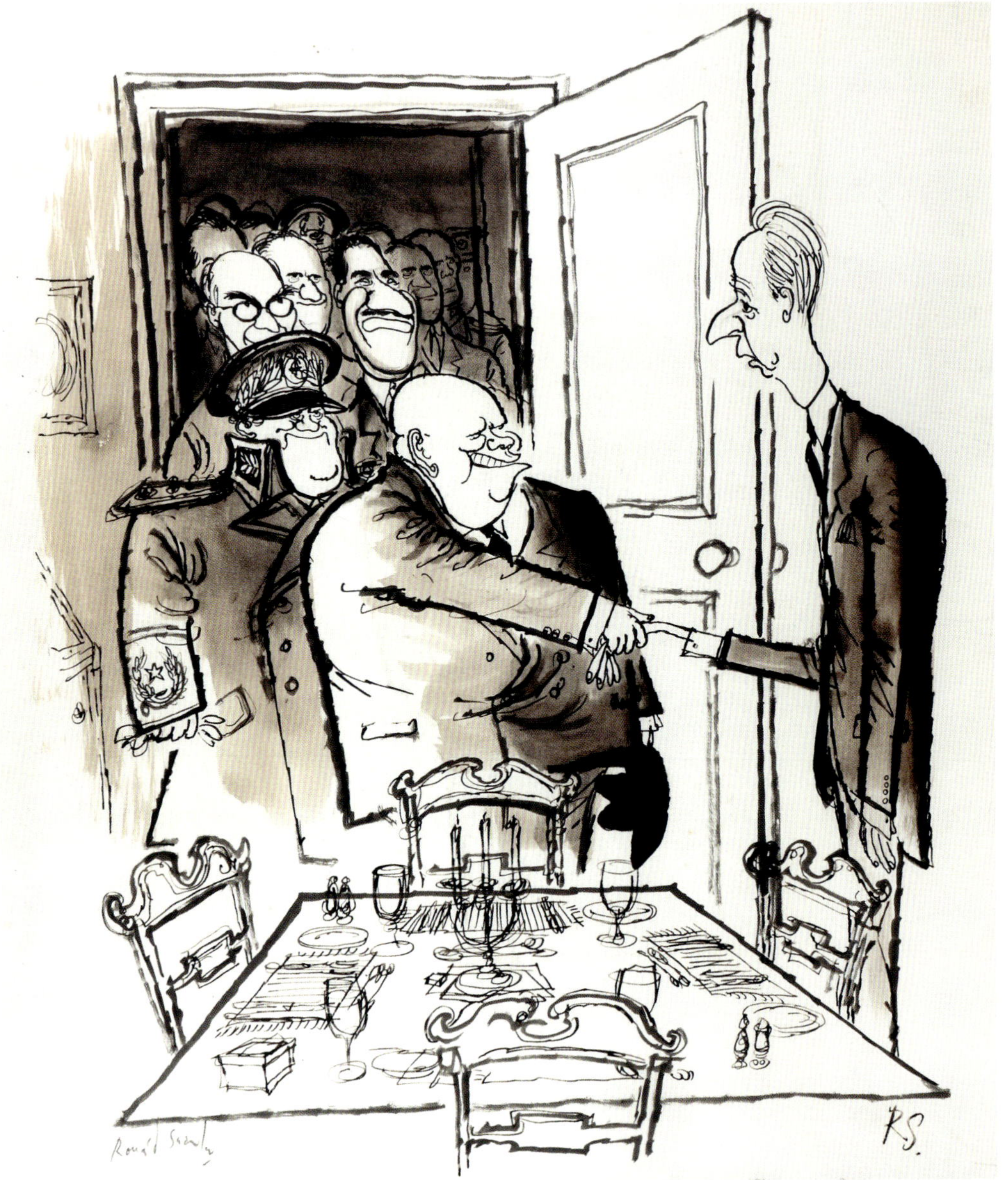

Why, of course, Mr Krushchev ...

Khrushchev spent much of his time at the United Nations wooing the leaders of such newly independent states as Egypt (Nasser), Hungary (Kádár), Poland (Gomułka), Yugoslavia (Tito), much to the bemusement of the Secretary-General, Dag Hammarskjöld (1905-1961). Khrushchev was soon disrupting meetings of the General Assembly, behaviour that culminated, on 12 October, in his banging his shoe in angry response to the accusation – by Filipino delegate, Lorenzo Sumulong – that the Soviet Union had 'swallowed' up Eastern Europe.

125 'WHY, OF COURSE, MR KRUSHCHEV, IT'S PERFECTLY ALL RIGHT BRINGING ALONG YOUR COUSIN TITO, COUSIN GOMULKA, COUSIN KADAR, COUSIN NASSER ... AND THEIR FRIENDS AND THEIR FRIENDS' FRIENDS WHO HAPPEN TO HAVE ARRIVED UNEXPECTEDLY ...'
signed and signed with initials
inscribed 'Punch FP Political Cartoon' and 'Hammarskjöld UN' and signed with initials by Russell Brockbank [Art Editor of *Punch*] below mount
pen ink and watercolour on board
17 ½ x 14 inches
Illustrated: *Punch*, 21 September 1960, page 399

Early 1950s: Preliminary Drawings

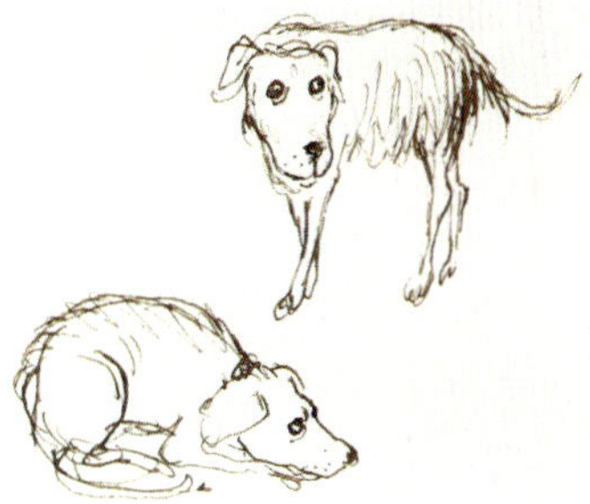

126 DOGS
pen and ink
3 ½ x 3 ½ inches

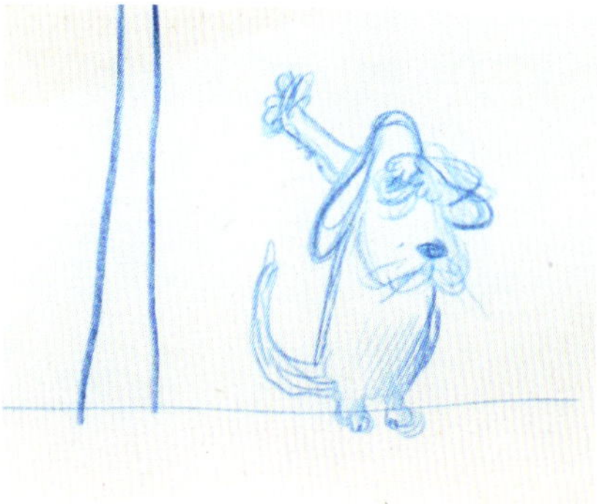

127 FOR TV CAMPAIGN AGAINST THE LAMPPOSTS (detail)
signed with initials and inscribed with title
coloured pencil on a Perpetua Ltd post card
3 ¼ x 5 ¼ inches

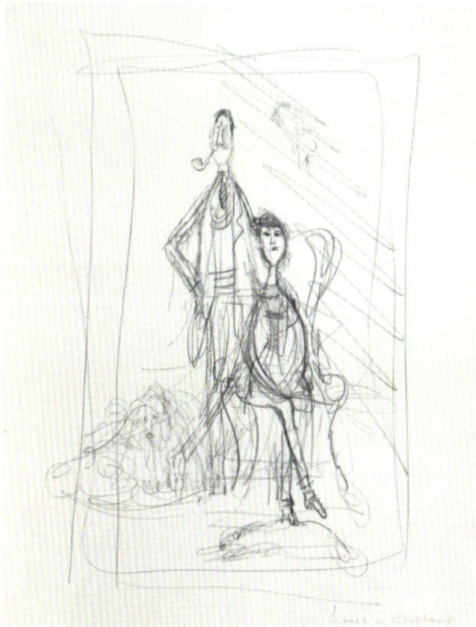

128 FAMILY PORTRAIT
inscribed 'Love in England'
pencil
10 x 8 inches

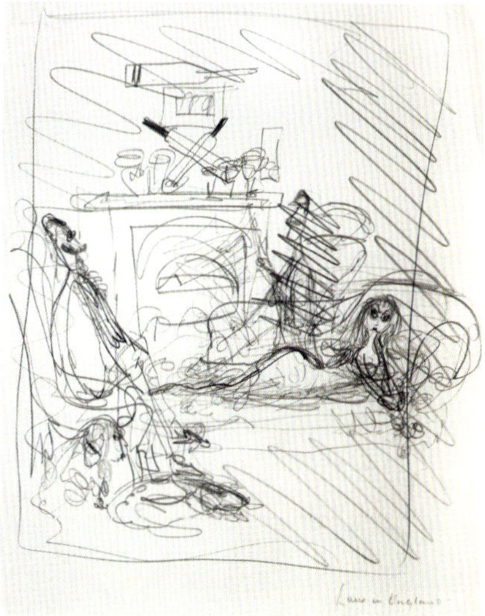

129 AT HOME
inscribed 'Love in England'
pencil
10 ¾ x 8 ½ inches

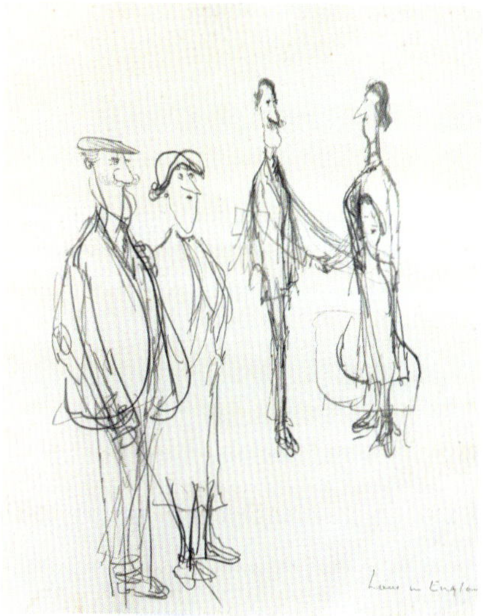

130 RELATIONS
inscribed 'Love in England'
pencil
9 ½ x 8 inches

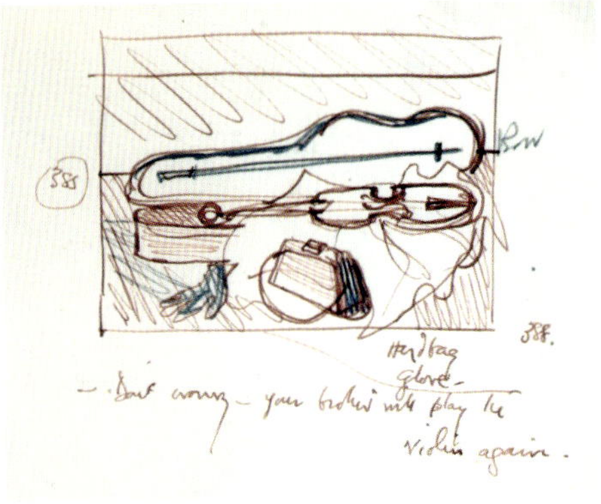

131 '– DON'T WORRY – YOUR BROTHER WILL PLAY THE VIOLIN AGAIN'
inscribed with title and 'Handbag, Glove', 'Bow', '385' and '388'
inscribed 'Roughs, Punch feature' below mount
coloured ink with pencil
3 ½ x 4 inches

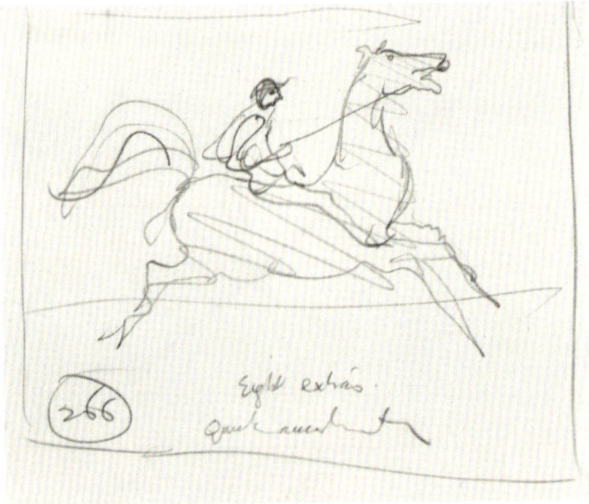

132 QUICK ACCELERATION
inscribed with title, 'Eight Extras' and '266'
pencil
4 x 4 ½ inches
Possibly a preliminary drawing for an animated cartoon

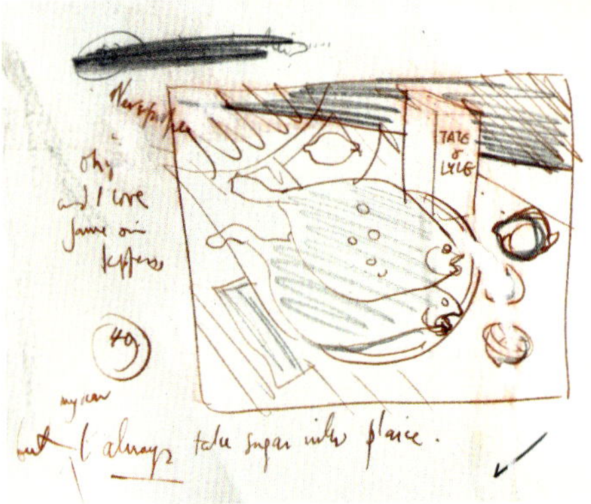

133 'BUT MY DEAR I ALWAYS TAKE SUGAR WITH PLAICE'
inscribed with title and 'Newspaper', 'Oh yes and I love jam on kippers' and '49'
coloured ink with pencil
4 x 5 inches

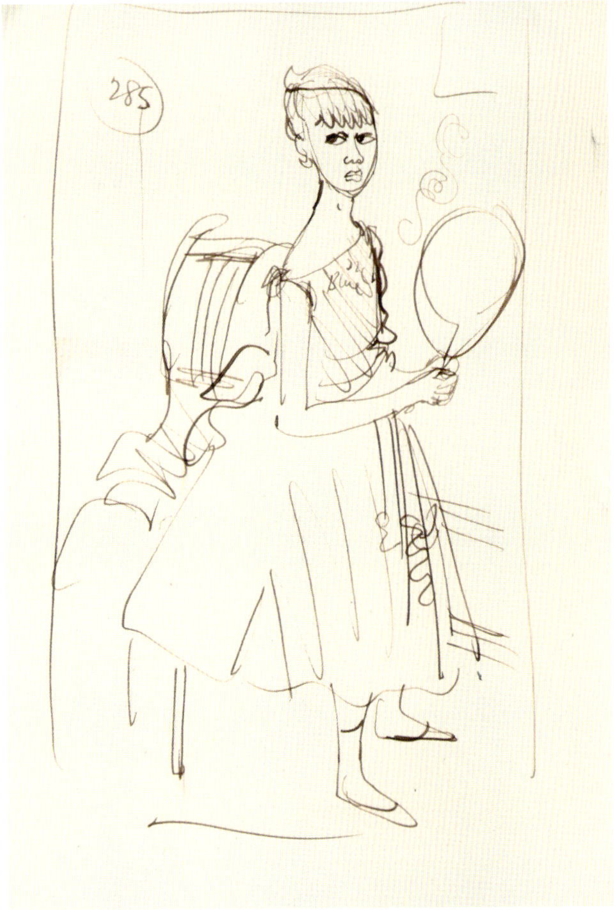

134 PICTURE AT AN EXHIBITION
inscribed '285'
coloured ink
7 x 4 ½ inches

136 CORONATION TABLEAUX (REHEARSAL)
inscribed with title, 'The Sword's Mightier than the Pen' and 'The Pen's Mightier than the Sword'
pen and ink
6 ¾ x 5 inches

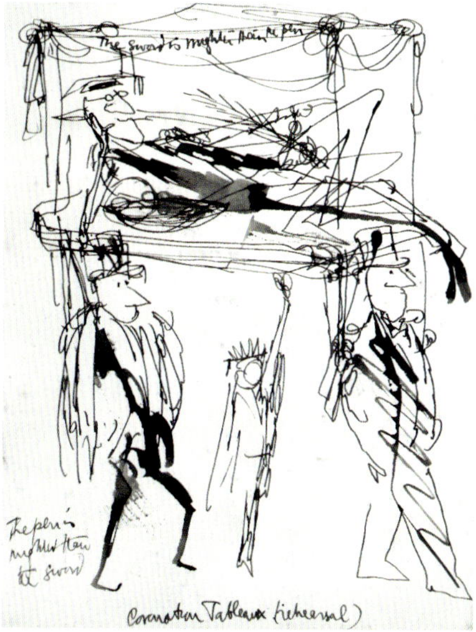

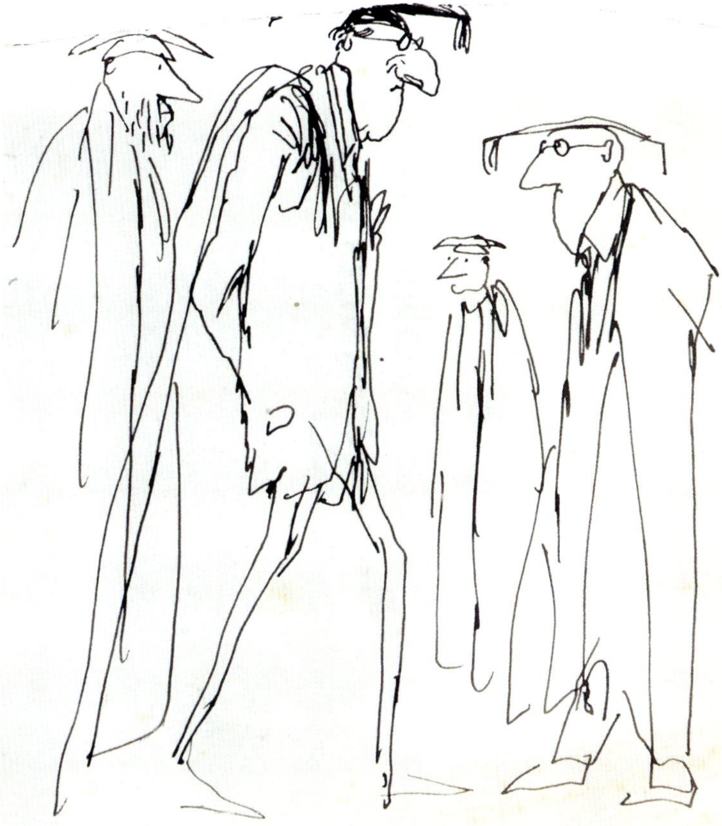

135 DONS
pen and ink
5 ½ x 4 ¾ inches

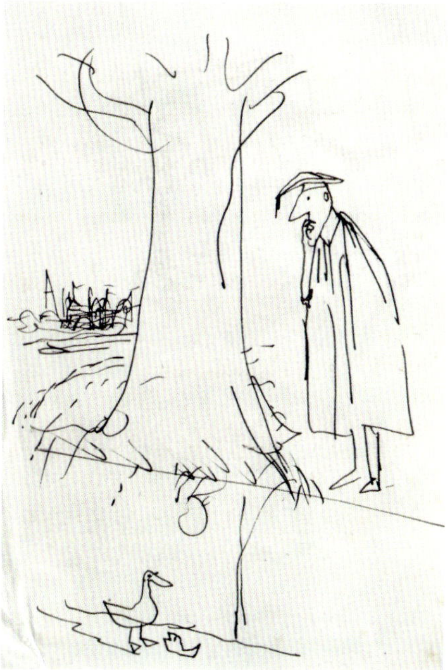

137 CONTEMPLATION
pen and ink
6 ½ x 5 inches

1951-62: Lemon Hart Rum

The distiller and importer, Mr Lemon Hart (1768-1845), of the Jewish community in Penzance, Cornwall, established his brand of rum in 1804. His family probably came from Germany, and his Christian name is likely to have been an Anglicisation of 'Lehman', though the association of lemon with rum is a happy one.

Hart may have supplied the fleet with rum, and it remained the navy's drink long after his death, and into the twentieth century. The spirit had a resurgence of popularity in Britain during the 1950s, by which time United Rum Merchants Ltd had taken ownership of Lemon Hart Rum, as well as Lamb's Navy Rum. The popularity of those two brands was greatly helped by Ronald Searle, in his 11 year contribution to advertising campaign, 'Have a Good Rum for Your Money', from 1951 to 1962.

Searle approached the campaign by presenting the brands as two men, who have been described in the following terms by Russell Davies:

> *The Holmes-and-Watson relationship of Mr Lemon Hart and his friend from Lamb's Navy Rum is distinguished by British stolidity on the latter's side, and a farouche and accident-prone tendency on the part of Mr Lemon Hart.* (page 97)

Though Mr Lemon Hart sometimes appeared alone, Mr Lamb often joined him under the slogan, 'Two in Harmony'. Searle could interpret this phrase in a positive, even affectionate way, in such images as *Picking Holly*, in which one supports the other, and *The Pantomime Horse*, in which they toast each other following a collaborative performance. However, he could also treat it ironically, as when they compete at billiards or back rival runners.

Searle was paid between £250 and £350 guineas for each image, which then appeared in a variety of formats from magazine pages to huge billboards, and on products that included booklets, calendars and glasses. He also produced drawings for some animated advertisements, including *Parents Take Hart* (1953), which was realised by Larkin Studios, London, and shown in cinemas.

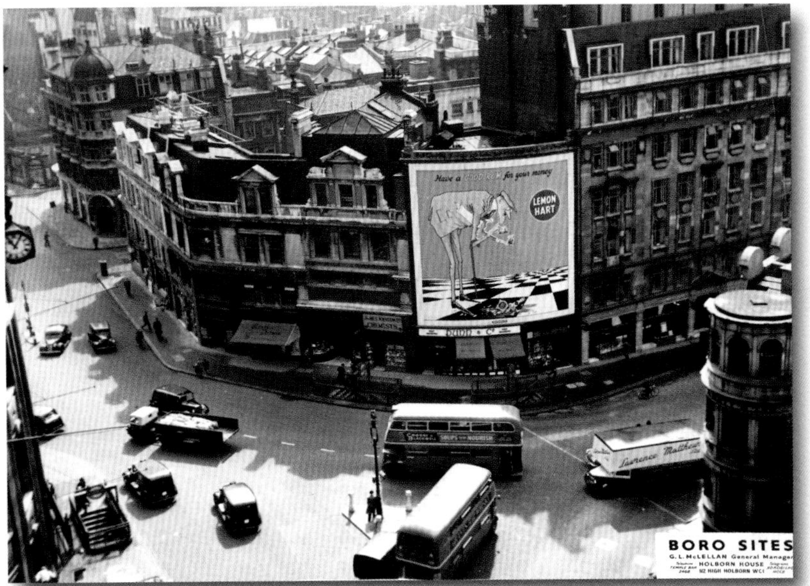

Lemon Hart Rum billboard advertisement Monument, City of London, spring 1952

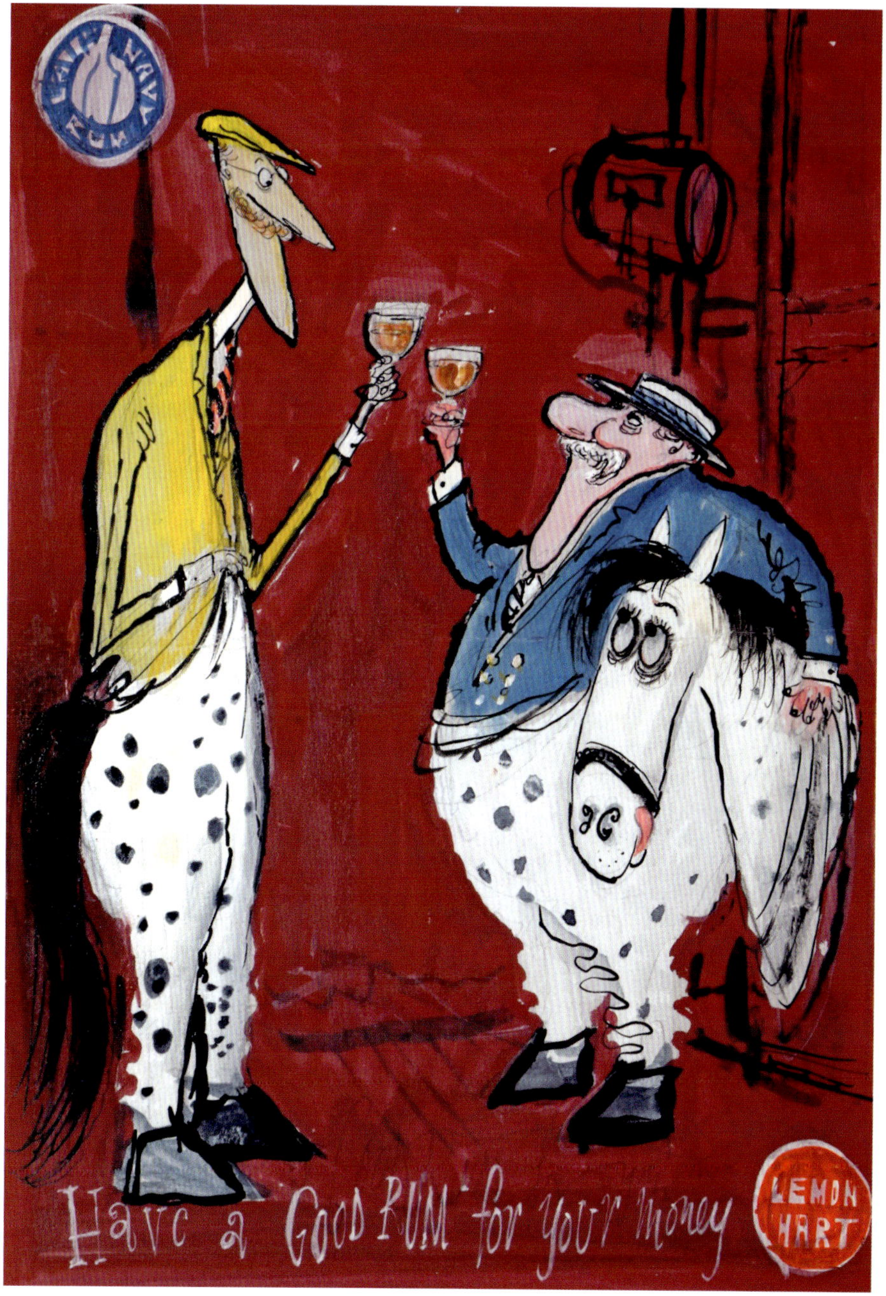

138 THE PANTOMIME HORSE
pen ink, watercolour and bodycolour
13 ½ x 9 ½ inches
Exhibited: 'Ronald Searle: A Celebration',
Ruskin Gallery, Anglia Ruskin University,
Cambridge, January-February 2008

139-142 are all preliminary drawings for Lemon Hart Rum Advertising

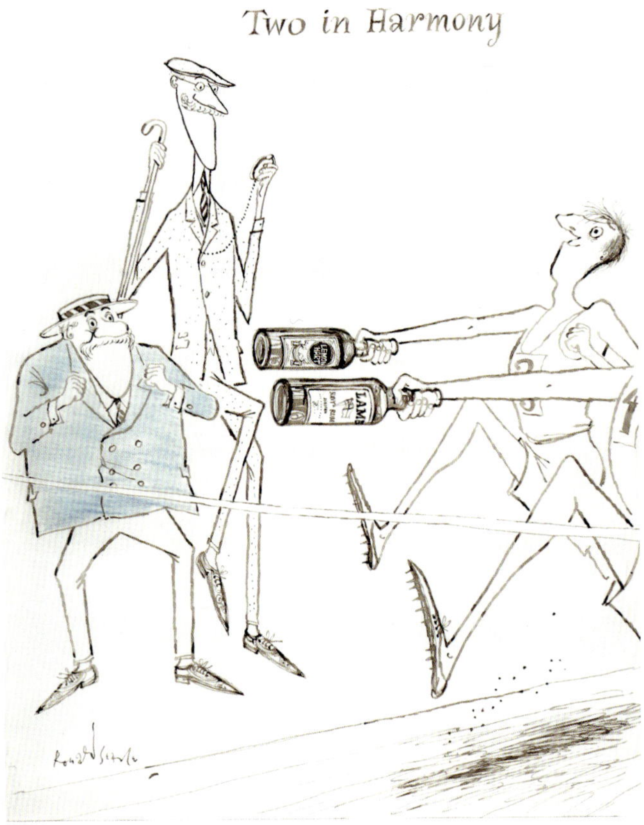

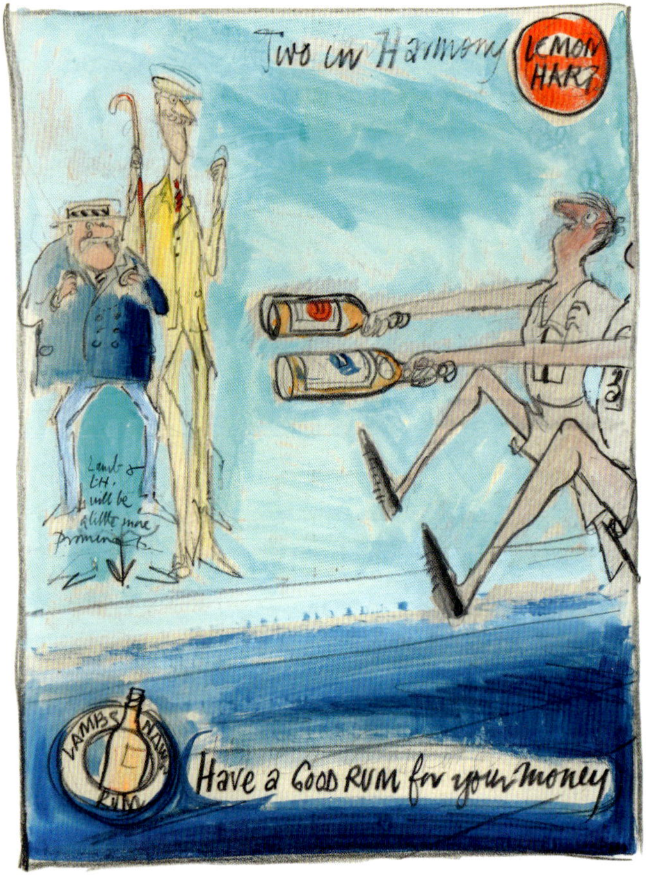

139 TWO IN HARMONY (I)
signed
pen and ink with coloured pencil
19 x 13 inches

140 TWO IN HARMONY (II)
inscribed 'Lamb & LH will be a little more prominent'
watercolour, bodycolour and charcoal with pencil
19 x 14 ¼ inches

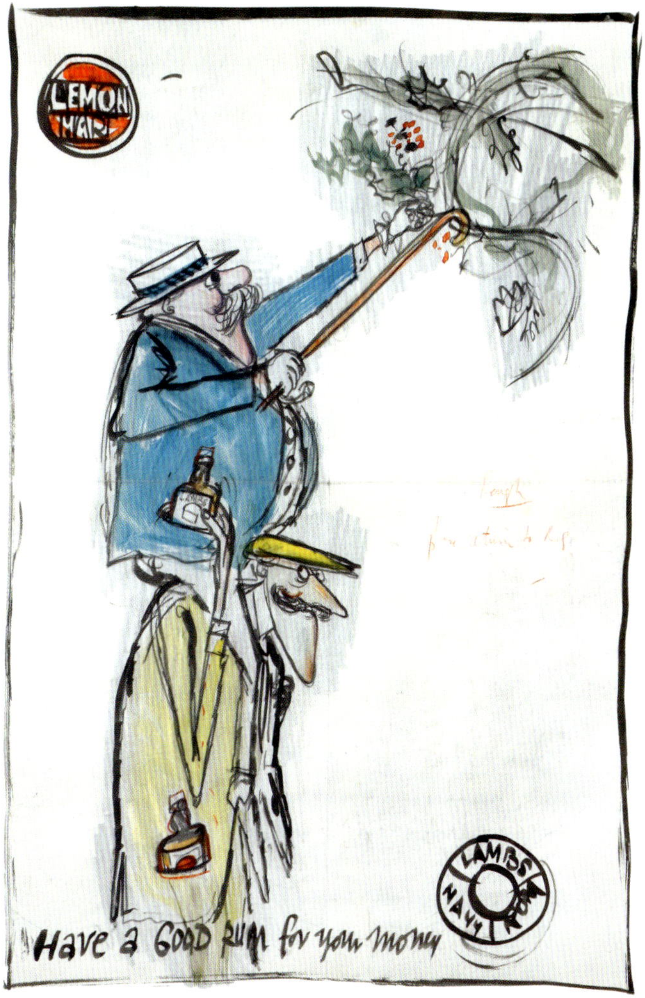

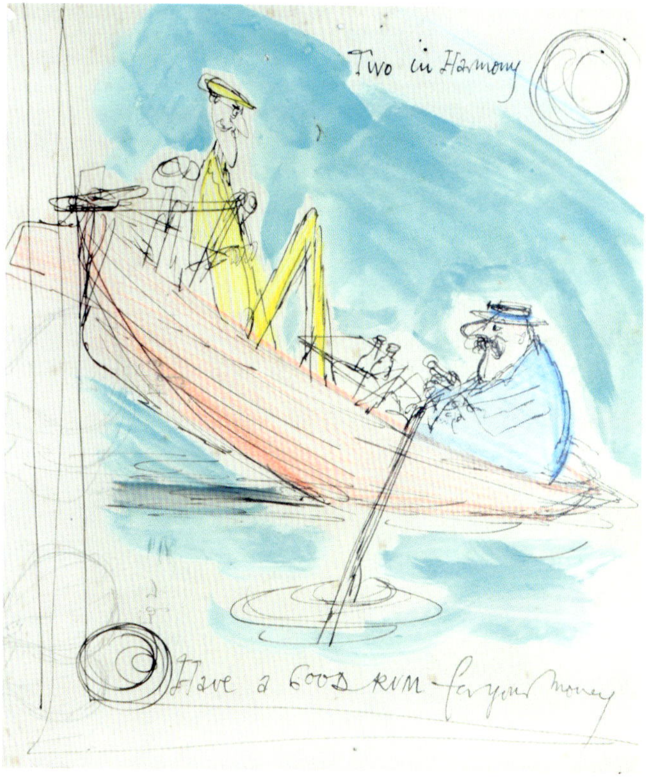

141 PICKING HOLLY
inscribed 'Rough, please return to RS'
pen ink and watercolour with pencil
12 ½ x 14 ½ inches

142 THE LEMON HART RUM BOAT
inscribed 'Two in Harmony' and 'Have a Good Rum for your money'
pen ink, watercolour and coloured pencil
7 x 6 inches

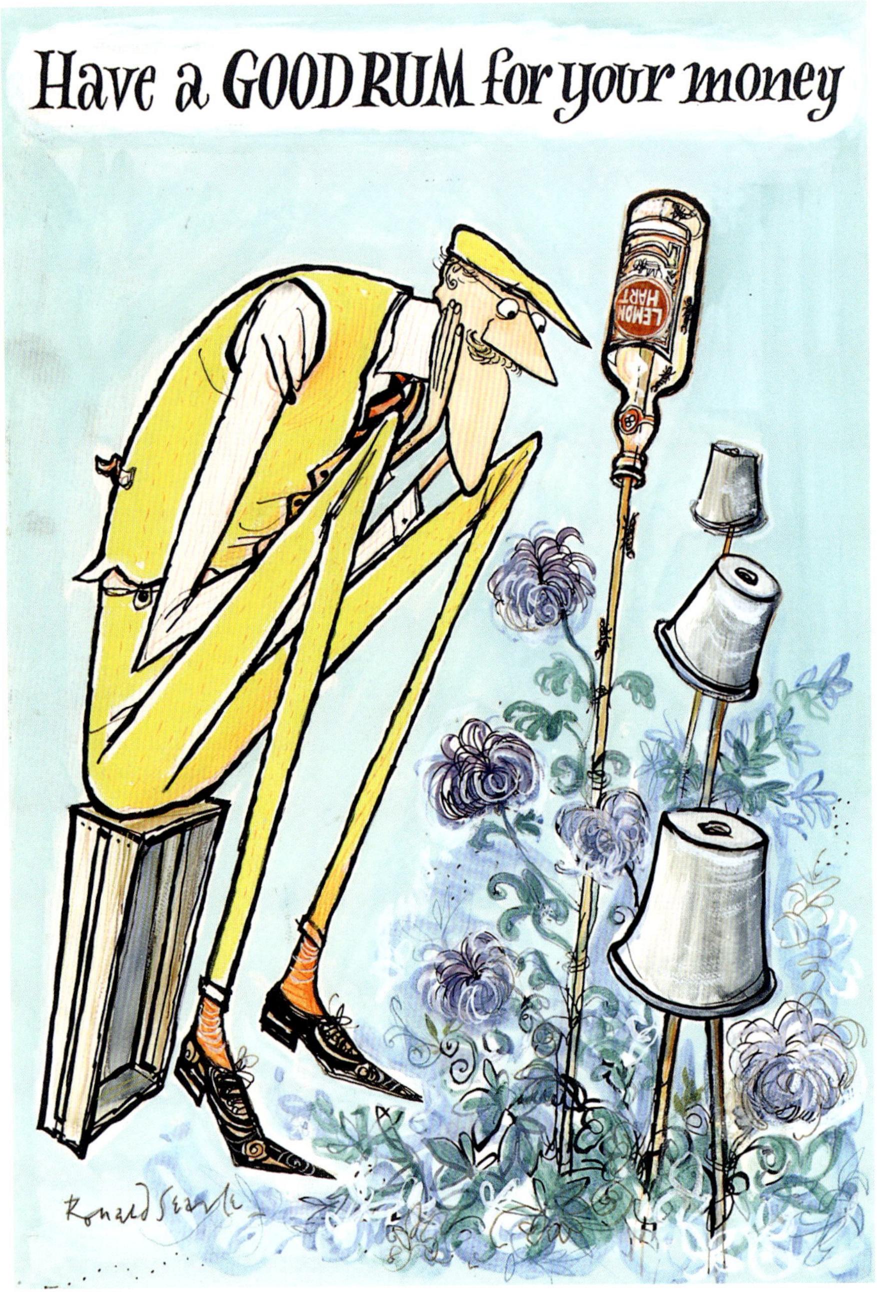

143 MR LEMON HART EARWIG CATCHING IN THE GARDEN
signed
pen ink and watercolour with bodycolour and coloured pencil
18 ½ x 12 ½ inches

144-147 are all preliminary drawings for Lemon Hart Rum Advertising

144 LEMON HART RUM – BANG ON A DRUM!
pen ink and watercolour
10 x 7 ¼ inches

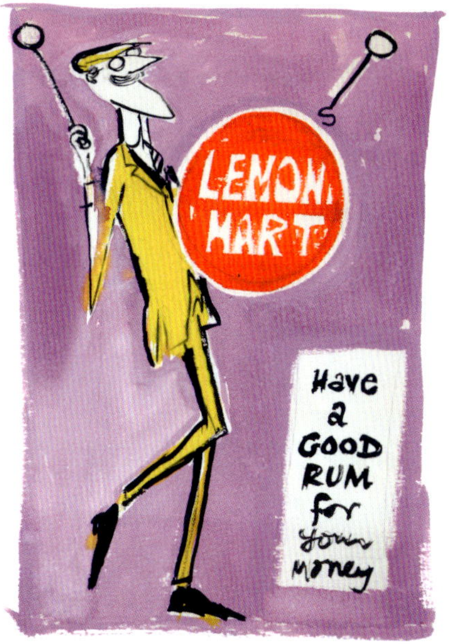

145 BALL IN THE AIR – LEMON HART'S HERE!
pen ink and watercolour with chalk and pencil
10 ¼ x 7 ¼ inches

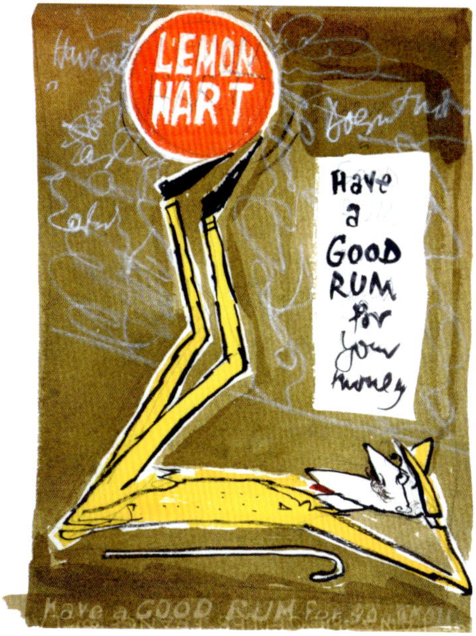

146 LEMON HART BALLOON
inscribed 'Does not linger on' and 'Easily digested'
pen ink and watercolour with chalk and pencil
10 ¼ x 7 ¼ inches

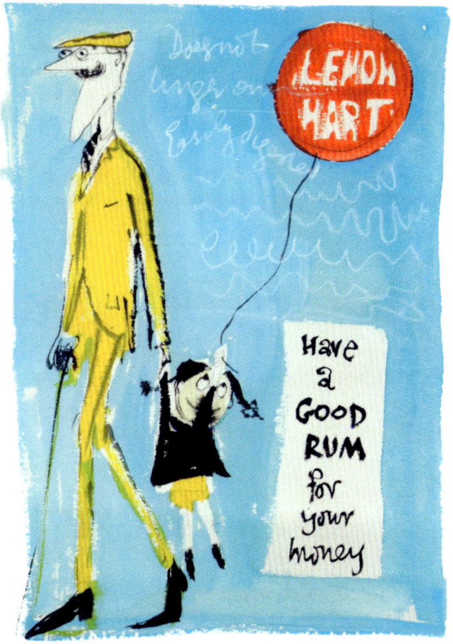

147 LEMON HART PRICE TAG
pen ink and watercolour with pencil
4 ¾ x 2 ¼ inches

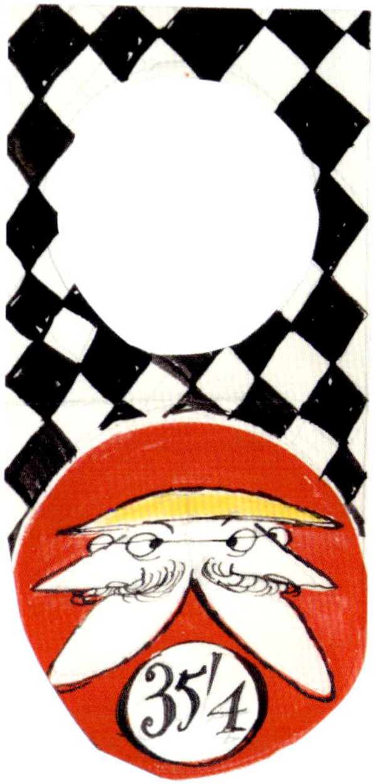

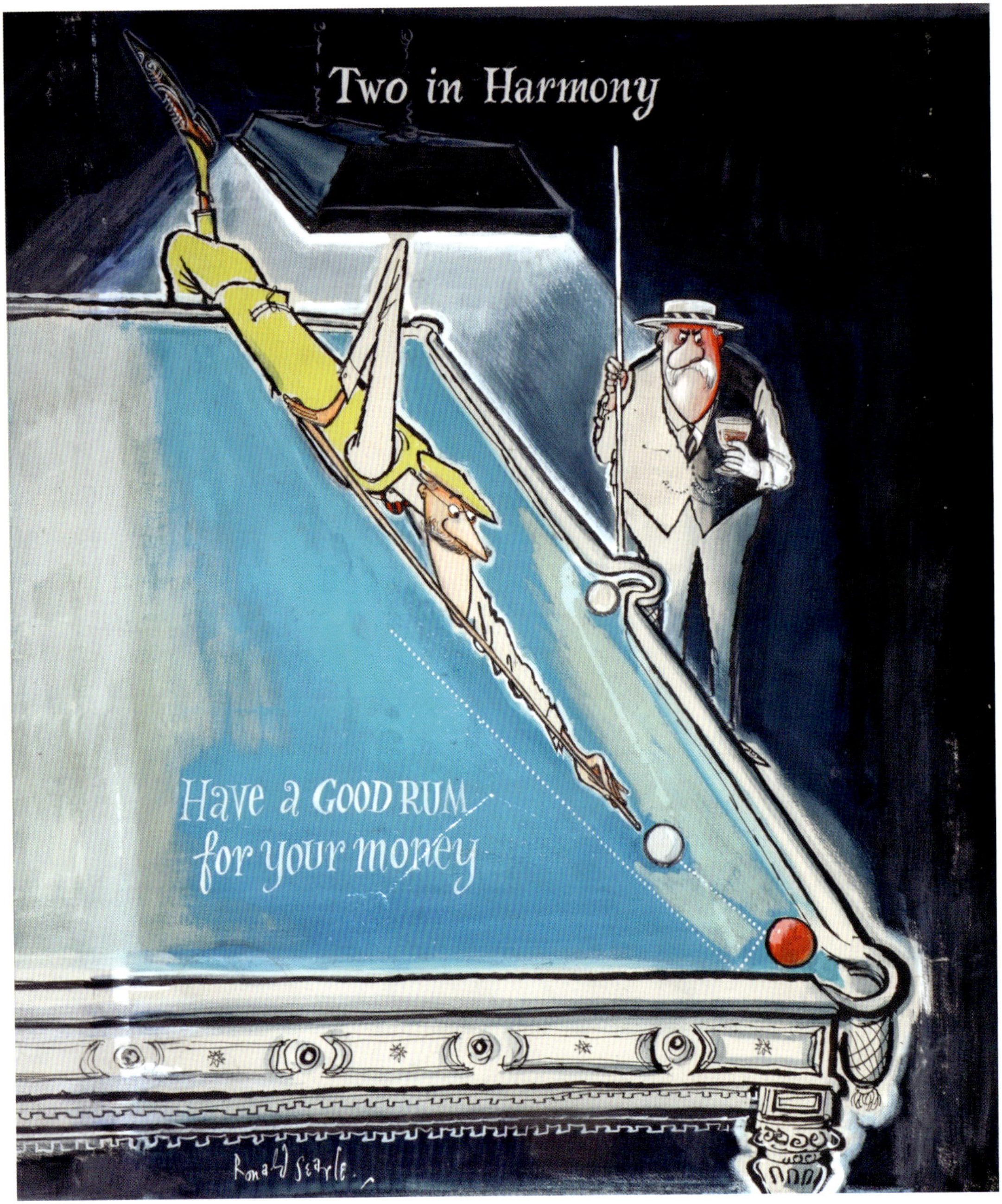

148 BILLIARDS
MR LEMON HART AND MR LAMB'S NAVY RUM
signed
pen ink, watercolour and bodycolour
21 x 18 inches
Exhibited: 'Ronald Searle: A Celebration' Ruskin Gallery, Anglia Ruskin University, Cambridge, January-February 2008

149 & **150** are preliminary drawings for Lemon Hart Rum Advertising

149 TROPICAL PARADISE
signed with initials and inscribed 'Rough Lemon Hart Ideas'
pencil
11 x 8 ½ inches

150 MR LEMON HART
pencil
8 ½ x 8 inches

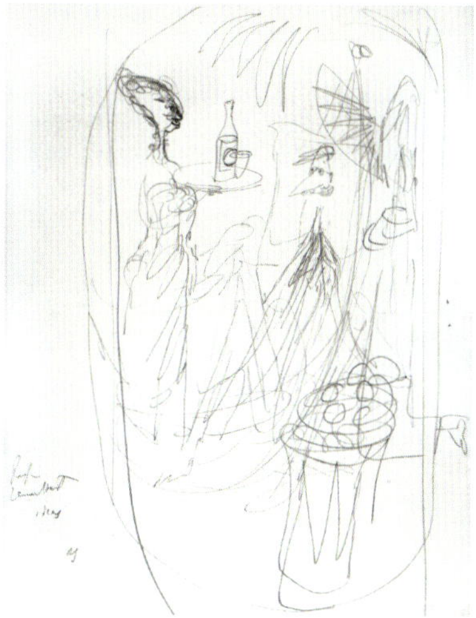

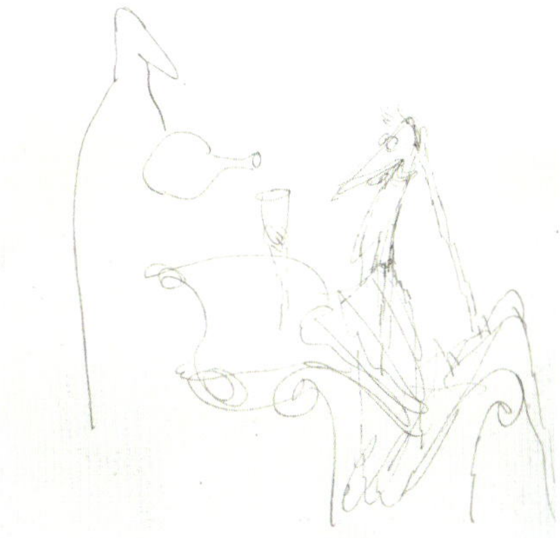

1956: Advertisements for US Royal Golf Balls

151 & **152** are preliminary drawings for a series of advertisements for the US Royal Golf Balls by United States Rubber Company, 1956

151 US ROYALS AD USA
inscribed with title
pencil on tracing paper
10 ½ x 8 inches

152 TAKE HAZARDS IN YOUR STRIDE WITH US ROYALS
pen and ink
7 ½ x 4 inches

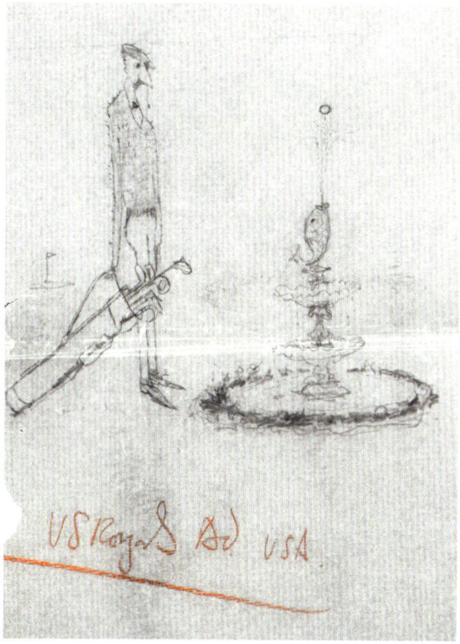

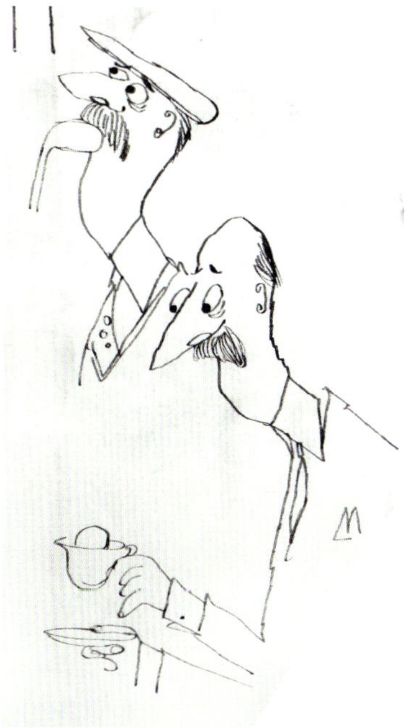

1952-59: Designs for Christmas Cards

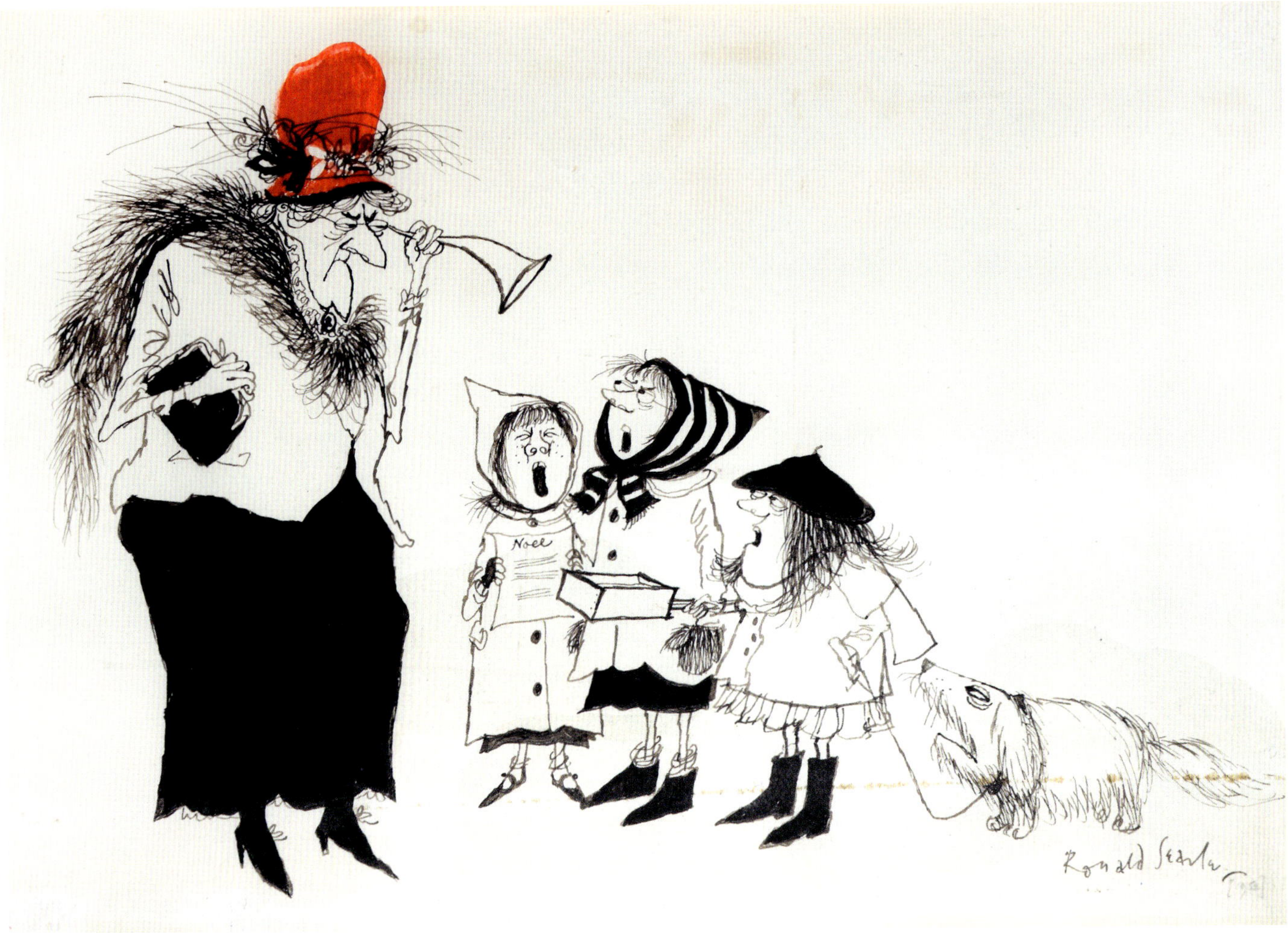

153 CAROL SINGING
signed and dated 1952
inscribed 'Design for a Christmas Card' and with medium and size, stamped with artist's address and copyright details, and dated 1952 on reverse
pen and ink with watercolour on board
10 ½ x 13 ¼ inches

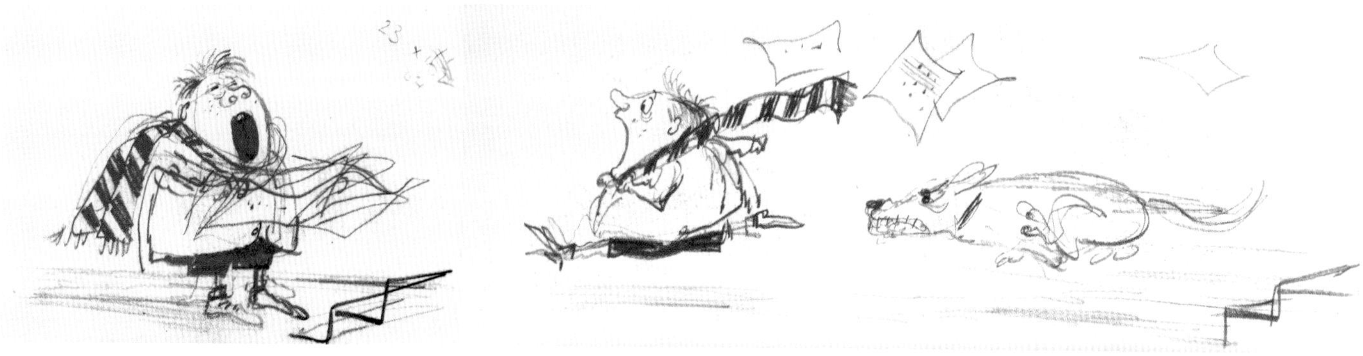

154 BEWARE OF THE DOG
pencil
4 ½ x 18 ¾ inches
Preliminary design for a Christmas Card

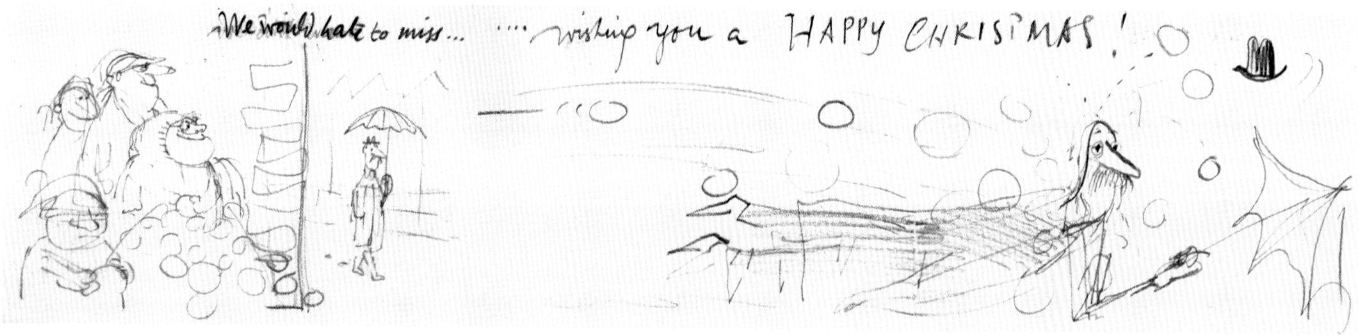

155 WE WOULD HATE TO MISS ...
... WISHING YOU A HAPPY CHRISTMAS!
pencil
4 ½ x 18 ½ inches
Unused preliminary design for a Christmas Card

156-158 are preliminary designs for Christmas Cards

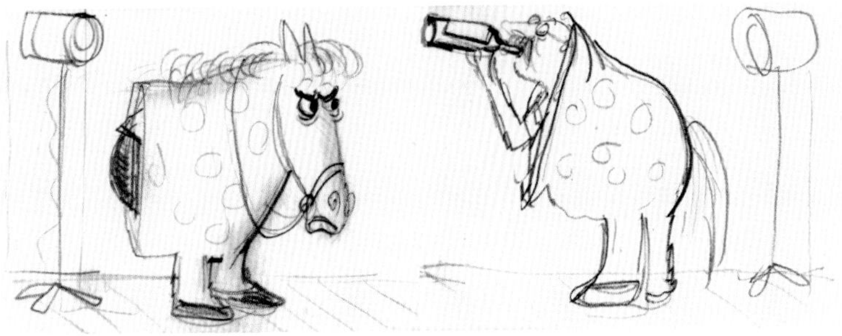

156 PANTOMIME HORSE
pencil
4 ½ x 18 ¾ inches

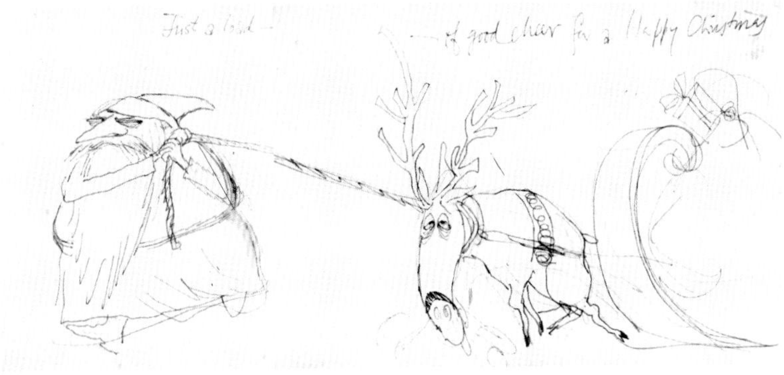

157 JUST A LOAD – OF GOOD CHEER FOR A HAPPY CHRISTMAS (I)
pen ink and pencil
6 ¼ x 14 ¼ inches

reverse:
EXPRESS DELIVERY (not illustrated)
pencil
6 x 19 inches

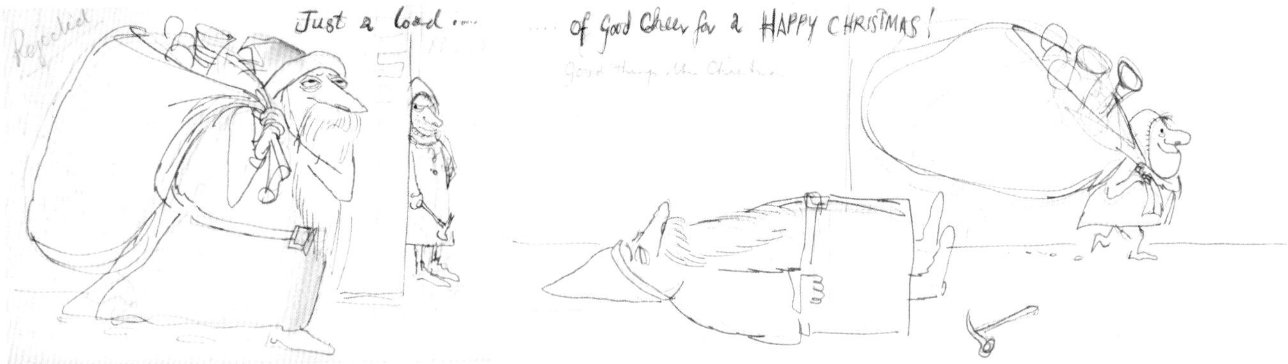

158 JUST A LOAD ... OF GOOD CHEER FOR A HAPPY CHRISTMAS! (II)
inscribed 'Bags of good things this Christmas'
inscribed 'Valentine' on reverse
pen ink and pencil
4 ½ x 18 ½ inches

1953-56: Molesworth

In 1953, Ronald Searle refused the request of the publisher, Max Parrish, to extend the St Trinian's series. Instead, he offered another equally certain bestseller for the Christmas season. For his friend, Geoffrey Willans, a BBC journalist, had decided to develop the character of Nigel Molesworth of St Custard's, the schoolboy subject he had created for *Punch* during the 1940s. Searle had been asked to collaborate and illustrate, and an unconvinced Parrish agreed to the proposal only on condition that his involvement was complete. The resulting book, *Down with Skool!* (1953), was so instant a success, selling over 50,000 copies in six months, that it proved Searle right in having confidence in his friend's project. Following Willan's early death in 1958, Searle described him as 'the sort of writer who made collaboration sheer enjoyment' (quoted in Davies, page 126). Such a sentiment sustained the quality of the Molesworth series, through *How to be Topp* (1954) and *Whizz for Atomms* (1956) to *Back in the Jug Agane* (1959).

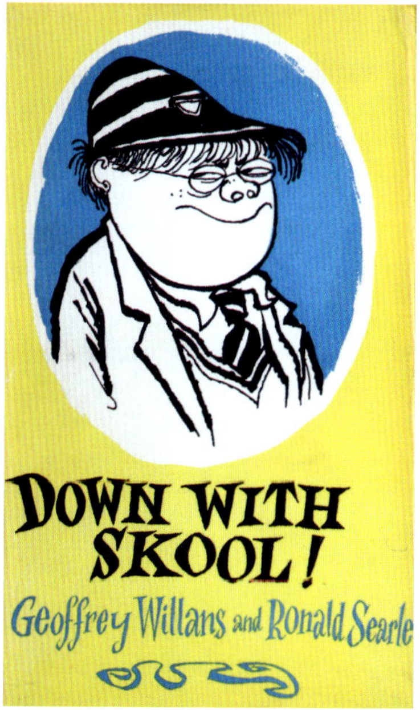

159 DOWN WITH SKOOL! A GUIDE TO SCHOOL LIFE FOR TINY PUPILS AND THEIR PARENTS
Geoffrey Willans and Ronald Searle
Down With Skool! A Guide to School Life for Tiny Pupils and their Parents
London: Max Parrish
1953
second impression
hard cover with dust jacket
106 pages
8 x 5 ¼ inches
inscribed by Ronald Searle 'From Ronald Searle for Jean E although …' and dated 'July 1954'

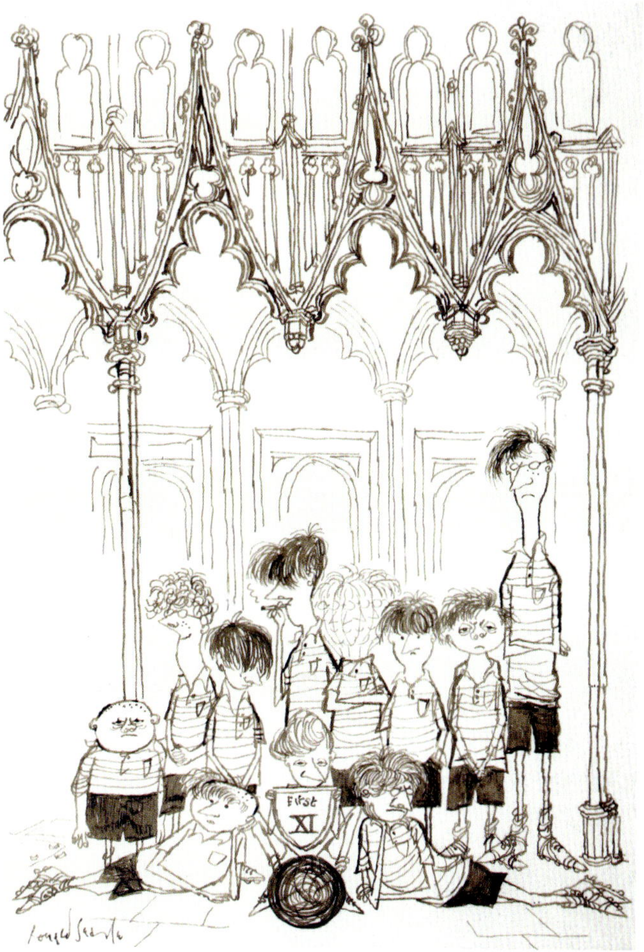

160 THE FOOTBALL TEAM
PLAYED 8. WON 0. DRAWN 0. LOST 8
signed
pen and ink
11 x 7 ½ inches
Illustrated: Geoffrey Willans and Ronald Searle, *Down With Skool!* London: Max Parrish, 1953, page 82; Geoffrey Willans and Ronald Searle, *The Compleet Molesworth*, London: Max Parrish, 1958, page 82

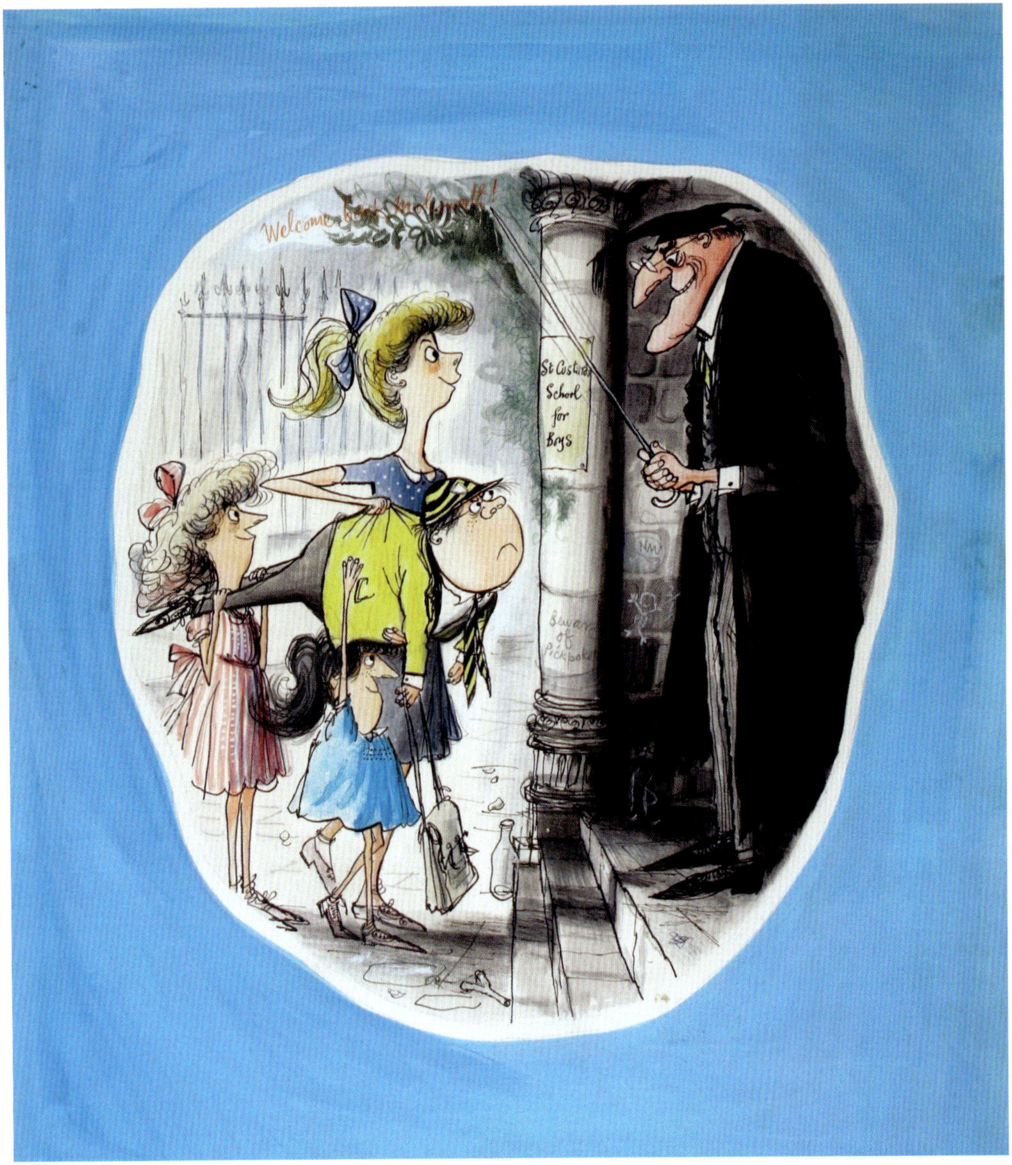

161 WELCOME BACK MOLESWORTH!
inscribed with title
inscribed 'Young Elizabethan October cover' below mount
stamped with artist's address on reverse
pen ink, watercolour and bodycolour with pencil on board
16 x 14 inches
Illustrated: *Young Elizabethan*, October 1956, front cover

1953-59: Book Illustrations

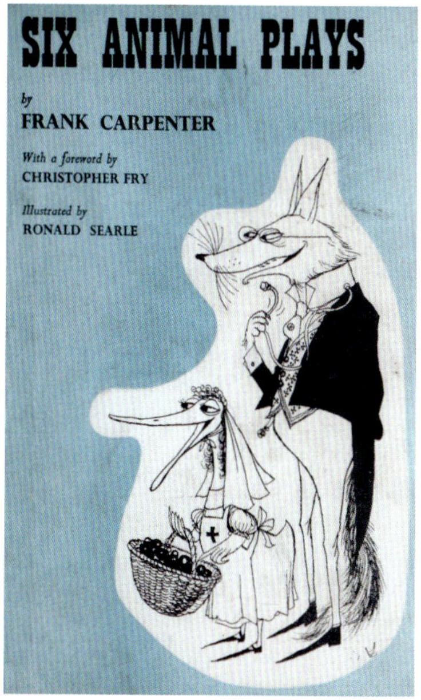

162 SIX ANIMAL PLAYS
Frank Carpenter
Six Animal Plays
London: Methuen & Co
1953
first edition
soft cover
134 pages
7 ¼ x 5 inches

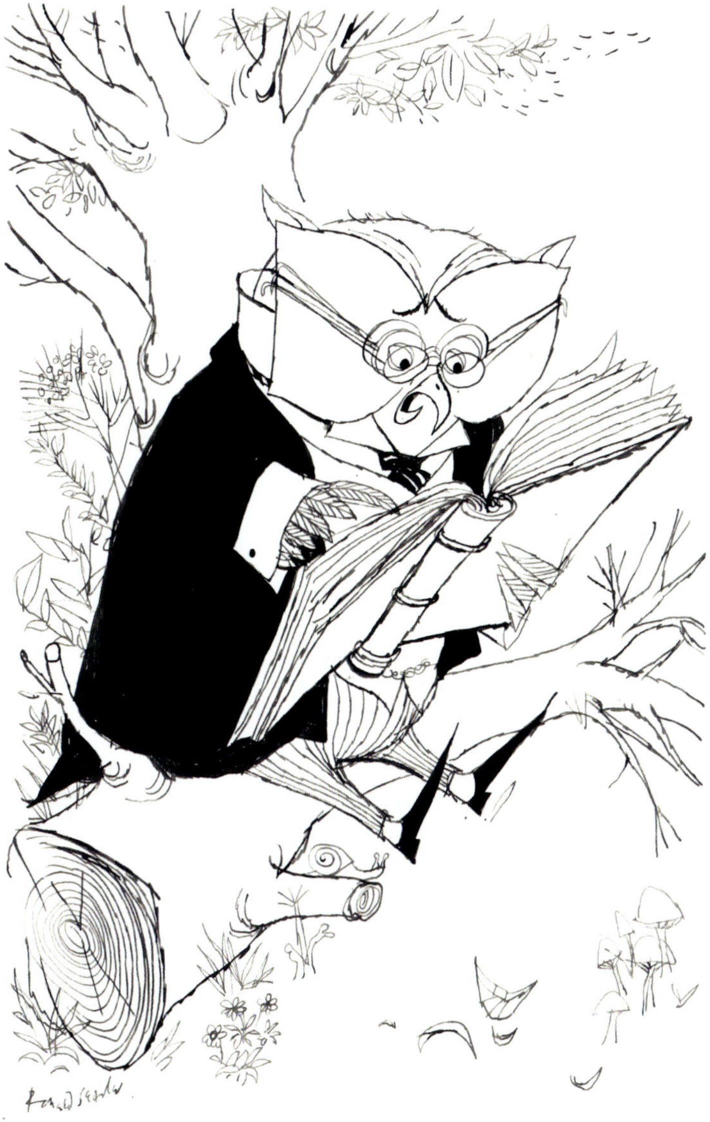

163 'I WISH I WAS CLEVER!'
signed
inscribed with title and 'The Magic Owl' below mount
stamped with artist's address and copyright details on reverse
pen and ink
14 x 10 ½ inches
Illustrated: Frank Carpenter, *Six Animal Plays*, London: Methuen & Co, 1953, page 36, 'The Magic Owl'

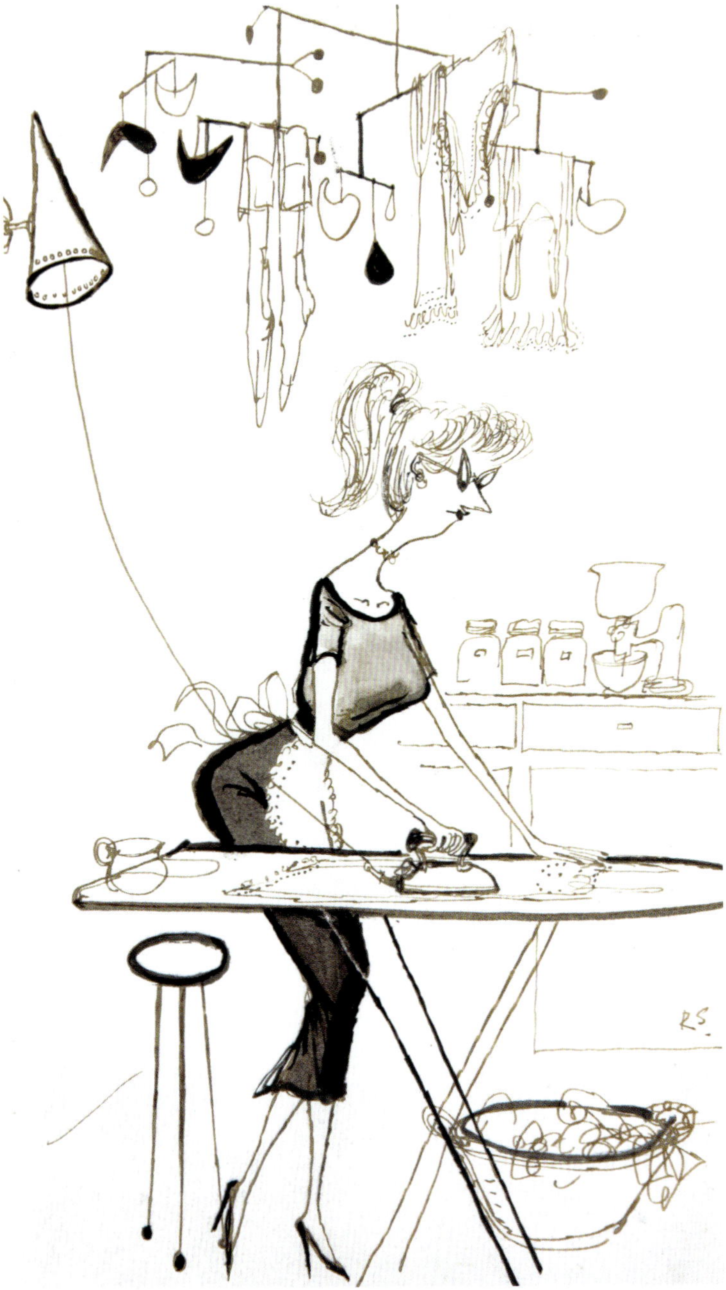

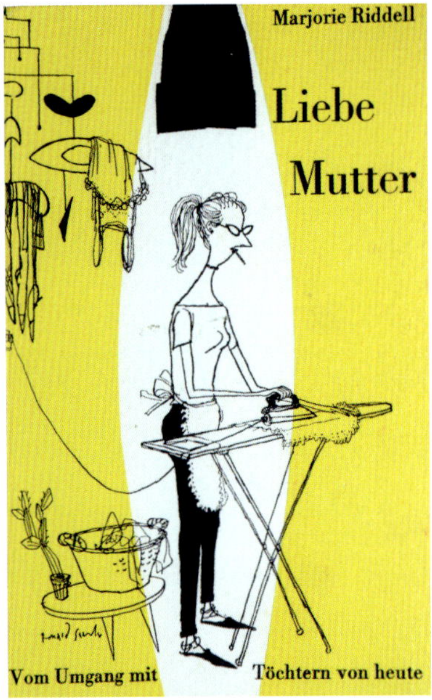

165 LIEBE MUTTER
VOM UMGANG MIT TOCHTERN
VON HEUTE
Marjorie Riddell
Liebe Mutter. Vom Umgang mit Tochtern von heute
Zurich: Sanssouci
1956
first edition
hard cover (issued without dust jacket)
79 pages
6 ¾ x 4 ¾ inches

164 A SINGLE WOMAN
signed with initials
pen and ink
14 x 7 ¾ inches
Similar to Ronald Searle, *Souls In Torment*, London: Perpetua, 1953, page 29; Marjorie Riddell, *Liebe Mutter. Vom Umgang mit Tochtern von heute*, Zurich: Sanssouci, [1956], front cover

166 THE INVESTIGATOR
Reuben Ship
The Investigator
London: Sidgwick and Jackson
1956
first edition
hard cover with dust jacket
119 pages
7 ½ x 5 inches

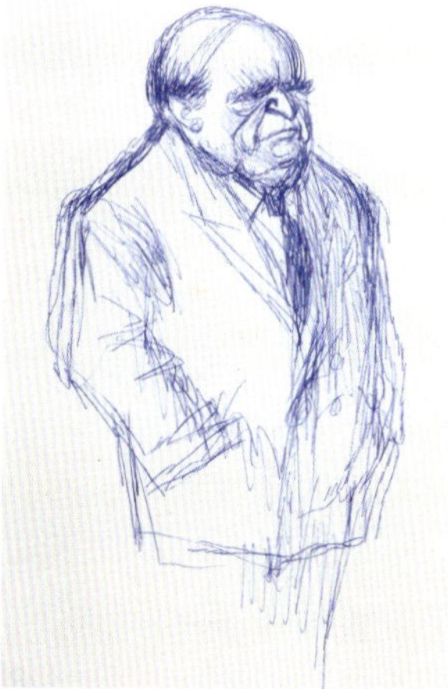

167 THE INVESTIGATOR (II)
inscribed 'Titus Oates, Tourquemada, Judge Jeffries, The Gate Keeper – Chairman'
pen and ink
12 ½ x 7 ½ inches

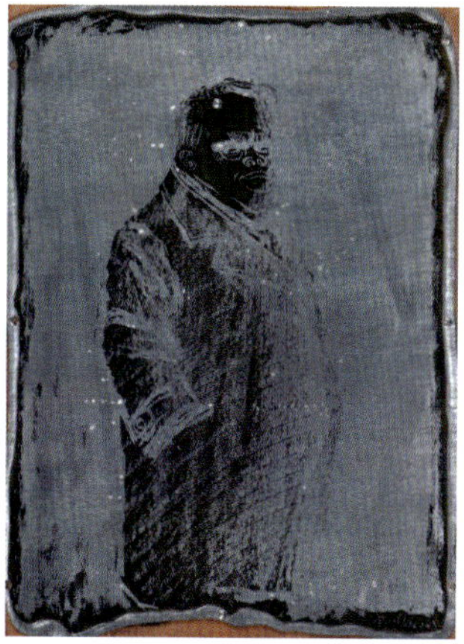

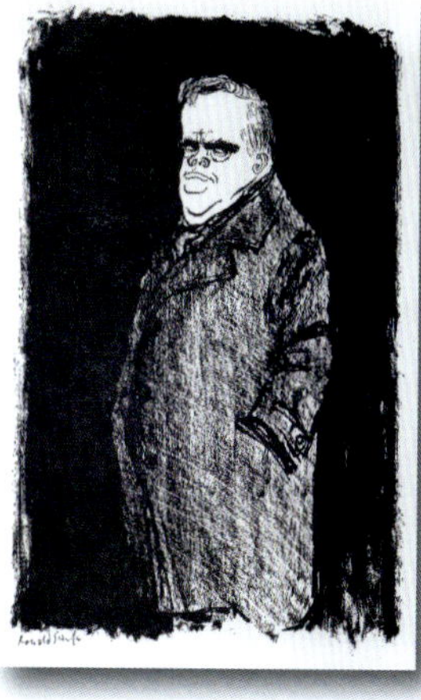

168 THE INVESTIGATOR
printer's block
6 ¼ x 4 ½ inches

167, 169 & **170** are preliminary drawings for Reuben Ship, *The Investigator*, London: Sidgwick and Jackson, 1956, rear dust jacket and frontispiece

169 THE INVESTIGATOR (I)
inscribed '4'
pen and ink
6 ¾ x 7 ½ inches

170 THE INVESTIGATOR (III)
pen and ink
12 x 7 ½ inches

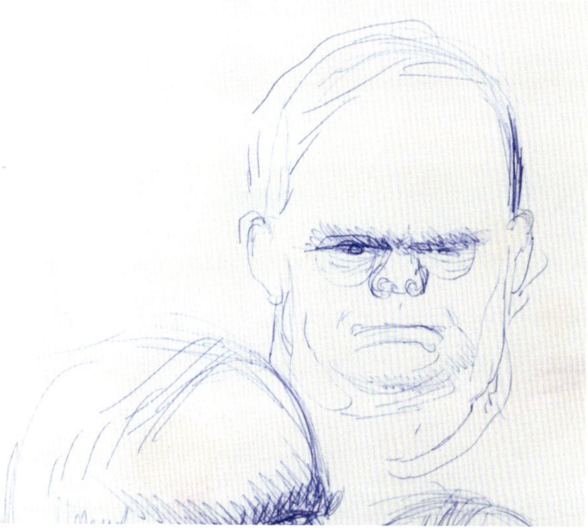

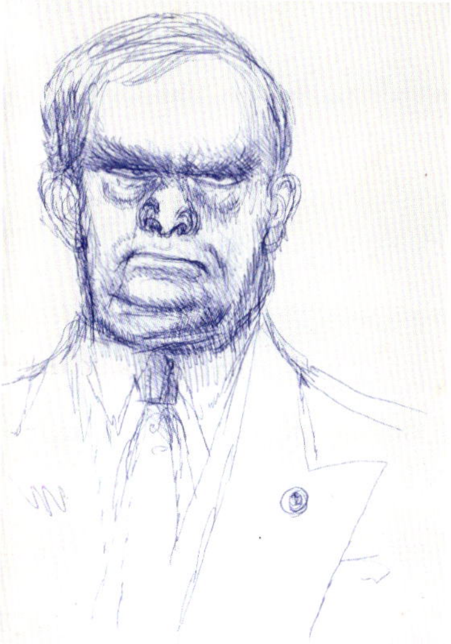

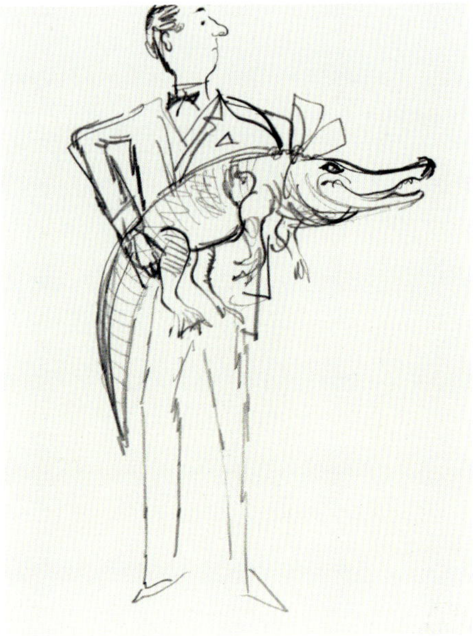

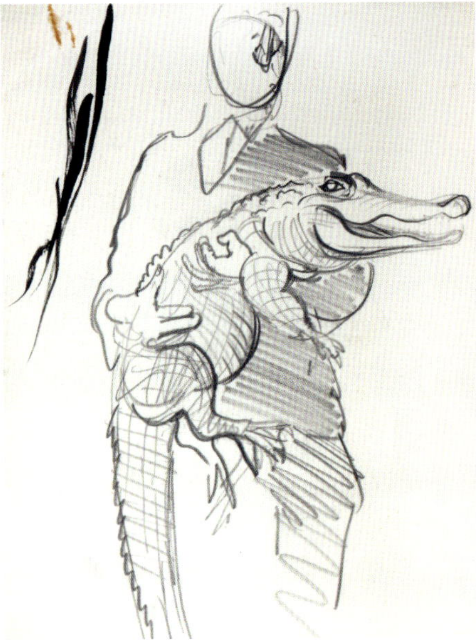

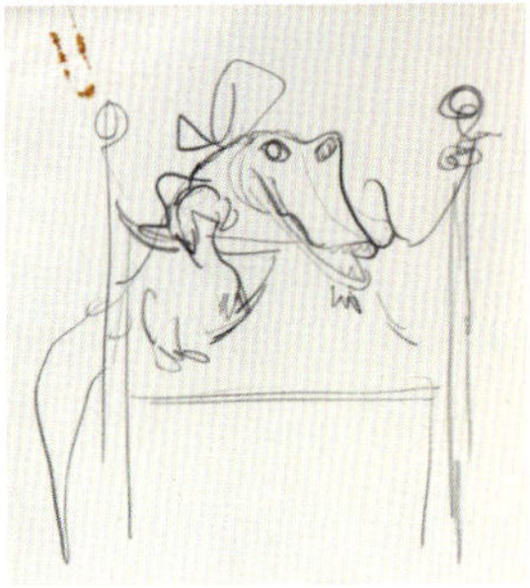

174 MARGHERITA IN BED
pencil
7 x 6 ½ inches

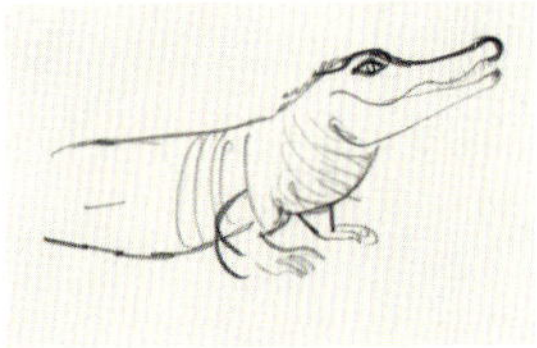

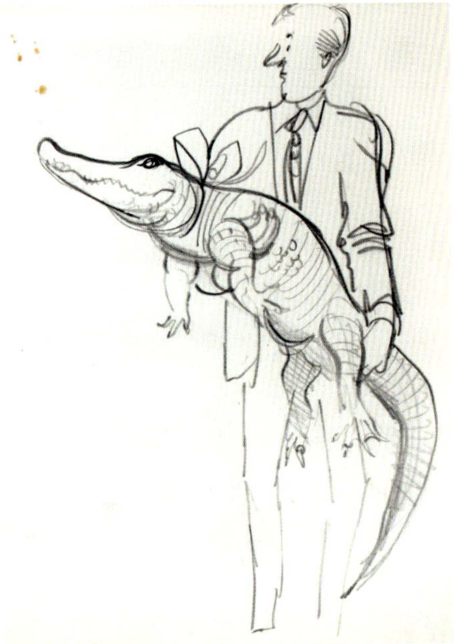

171-175 are preliminary drawings for Charles Terrot, *Un Alligatore Che Si Chiama Margherita*, Milan: Longanesi & Co, 1957, front dust jacket

171 CARRYING MARGHERITA (I)
pencil
8 ¾ x 6 ½ inches

172 AN ALLIGATOR CALLED MARGHERITA
inscribed 'Rough'
pencil with pen and ink
8 ¾ x 6 ¾ inches

173 CARRYING MARGHERITA (II)
pencil
8 ¾ x 6 ½ inches

175 MARGHERITA
pencil
4 x 6 inches

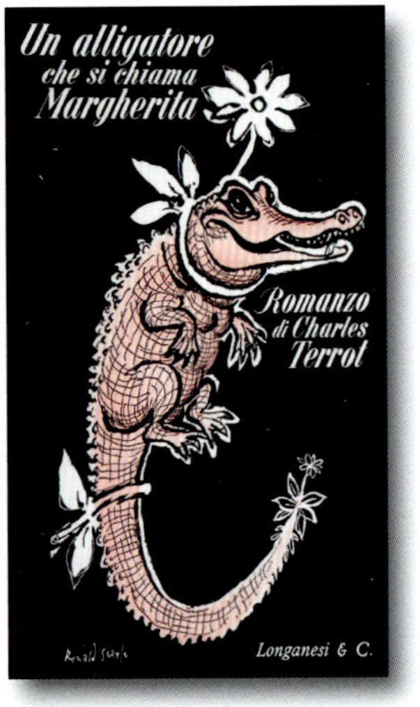

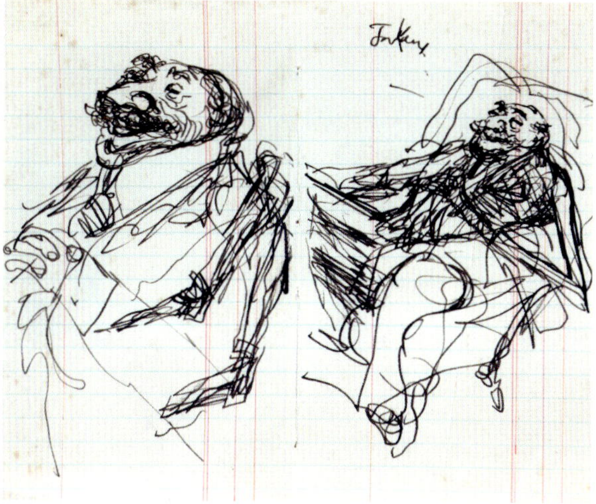

176 JORKENS
inscribed with title
inscribed with accounting calculations on reverse
pen and ink on lined paper
5 x 6 inches
Preliminary drawing for Lord Dunsany, *Jorkens borrows another whiskey*, London: Michael Joseph, 1954, front dust jacket and spine, frontispiece and chapter headings

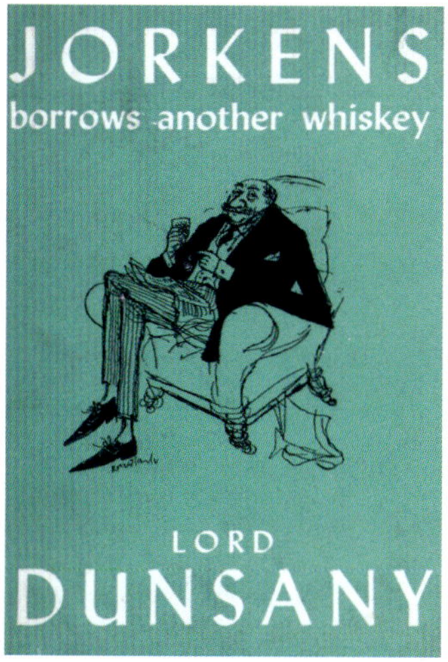

177 JORKENS BORROWS ANOTHER WHISKEY
Lord Dunsany
Jorkens borrows another whiskey
London: Michael Joseph
1954
first edition
hard cover with dust jacket
256 pages
7 ½ x 5 inches

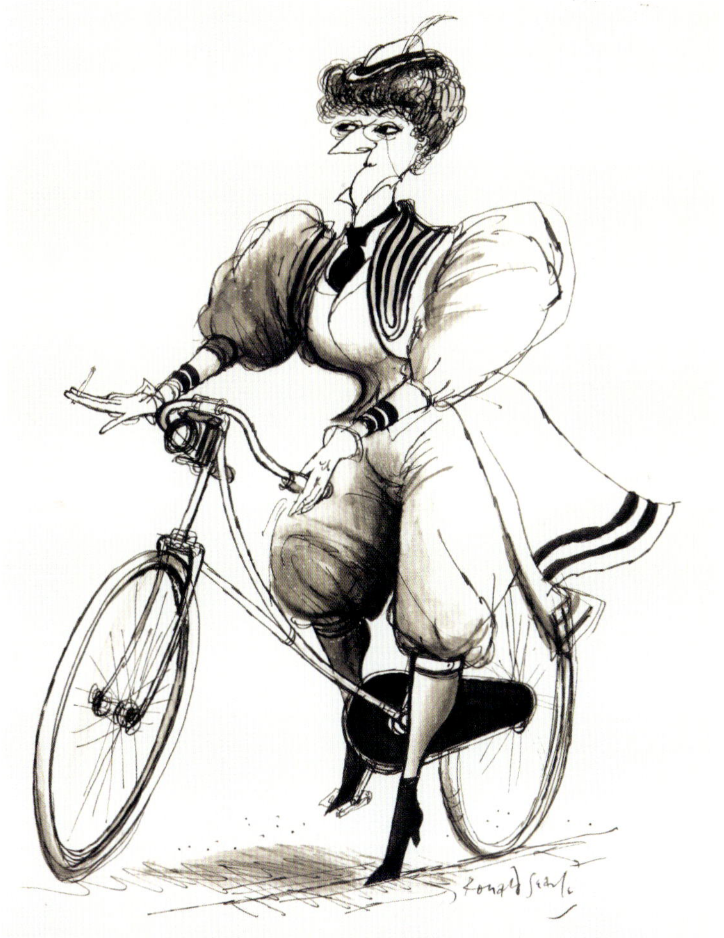

178 THE ADVANCED YOUNG WOMAN
signed and inscribed with title and 'Mr Rothman's Guide to Londoners of the Nineties'
pen ink and watercolour
15 x 12 ½ inches
Illustrated: *Mr Rothman's New Guide to London*, London: Rothman's of Pall Mall, 1958, page 26

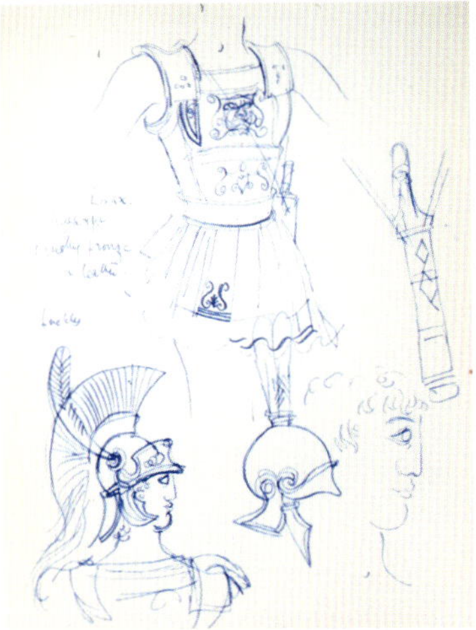

179 STUDIES FOR TEGEUS-CHROMIS
inscribed 'Thorax, Greek type, usually bronze or leather' and 'Buckles'
pen and ink, 6 ¾ x 4 ¾ inches

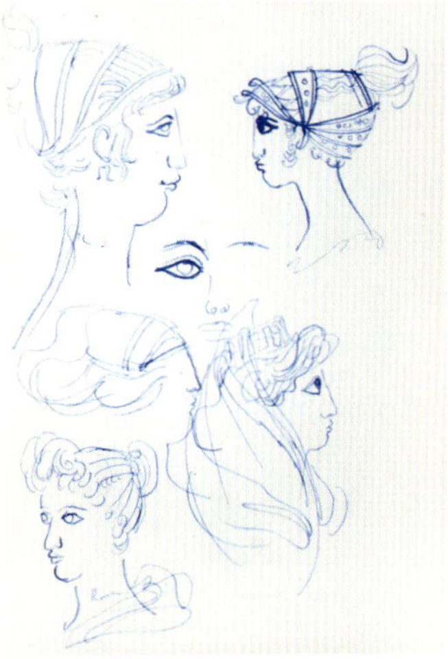

180 STUDIES FOR DYNAMENE (I)
pen and ink
7 x 4 ¾ inches

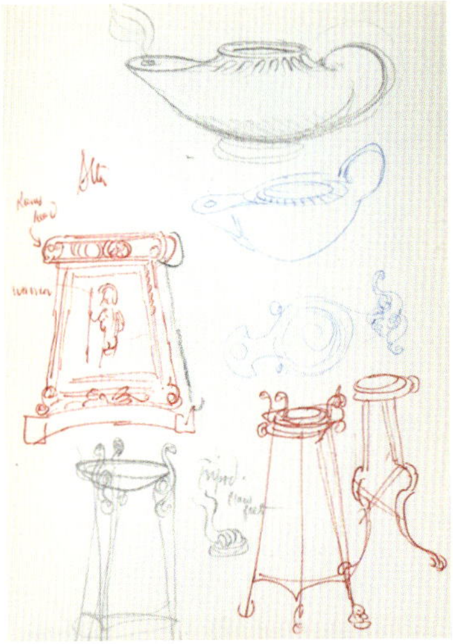

181 ROMAN LAMPS
inscribed 'Alter, Ram's Head, Warrior' and 'Tripod, Claw Feet'
pen ink, coloured ink and pencil
7 x 5 inches

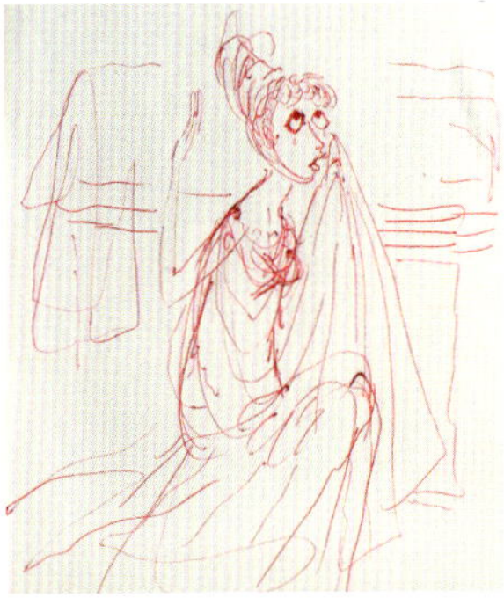

182 A PHOENIX TOO FREQUENT
Christopher Fry
A Phoenix Too Frequent
London: Oxford University Press
1955
seventh impression
(first edition 1949)
hard cover with dust jacket
43 pages, 7 ½ x 5 ¼ inches
annotated and sketched in by Ronald Searle
(showing detail of illustration on endpaper)

179-181 are taken from a sketchbook of preliminary drawings for *A Phoenix Too Frequent* by Christopher Fry, 1959

A Phoenix Too Frequent

In 1959, Ronald Searle illustrated a new edition of *A Phoenix Too Frequent*, a comedy by his friend, Christopher Fry, for Oxford University Press. In preparation for this project, he annotated and sketched in a copy of an earlier edition.

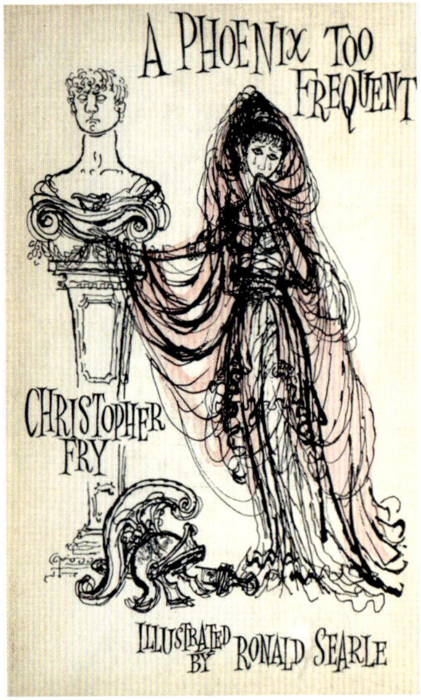

183 A PHOENIX TOO FREQUENT
Christopher Fry
A Phoenix Too Frequent
London: Oxford University Press
1959
first edition
hard cover with dust jacket
78 pages
9 ½ x 6 ¼ inches

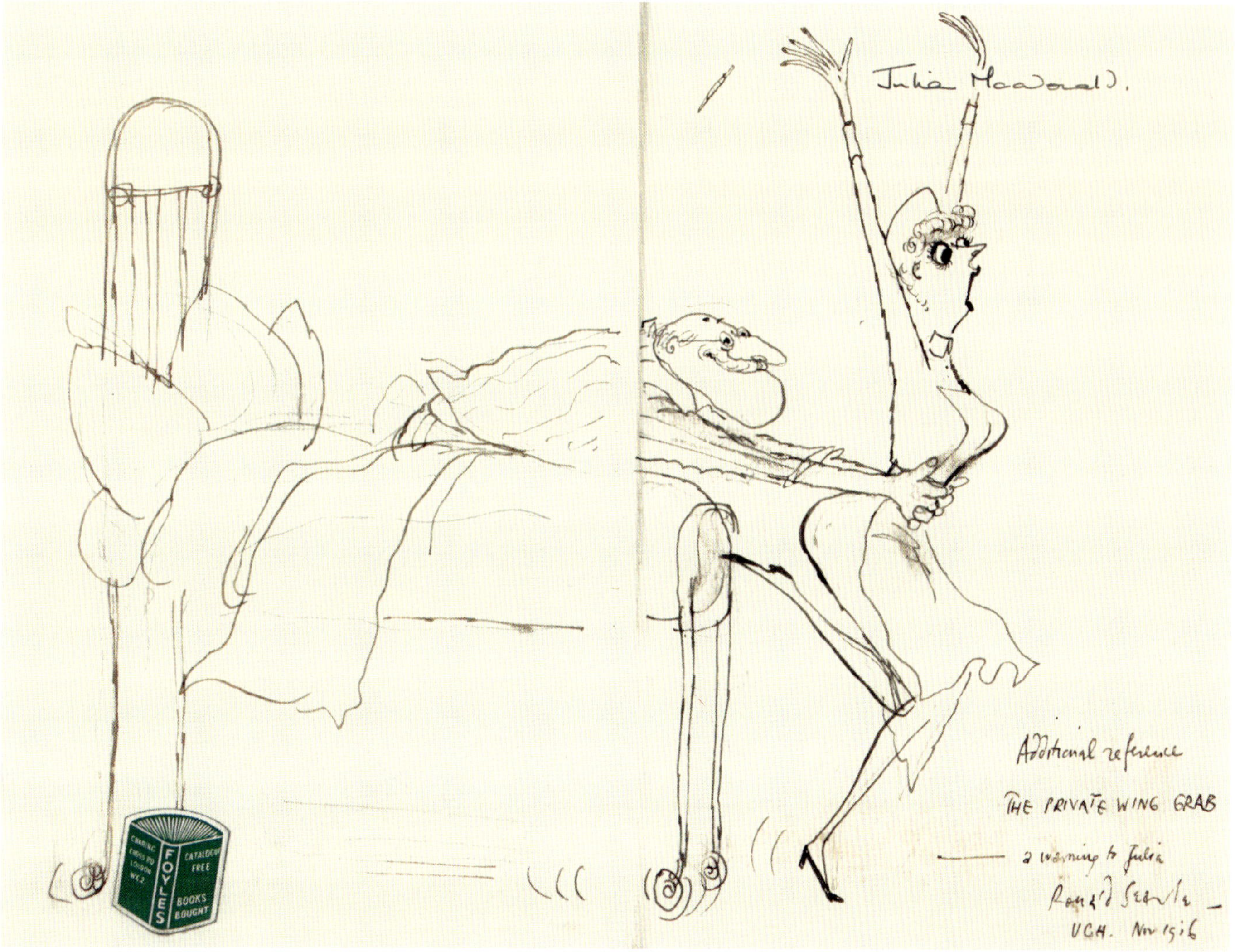

The Private Wing Grab

Not only did Ronald Searle annotate books for his research purposes – as with *A Phoenix Too Frequent* – but he also made presentation drawings in books that had been illustrated by other artists, as is exemplified here. In November 1956, he was rushed into University College Hospital in order to receive an emergency operation for peritonitis, as a result of a burst appendix. Julia, the nurse who cared for him, was rewarded with a drawing made on the front endpaper of her copy of Nina Farewell's *The Unfair Sex*, illustrated by Roy Doty.

184 THE PRIVATE WING GRAB
signed, inscribed with title, 'Additional Reference – a warning to Julia. Uch' and dated 'Nov 1956'
pen and ink
drawn on the endpapers of Nina Farewell, *The Unfair Sex. An Exposé of The Human Male for Young Women of Most Ages*, London: Frederick Muller, 1953
7 x 9 ¼ inches

1956-58: The Big City or The New Mayhew

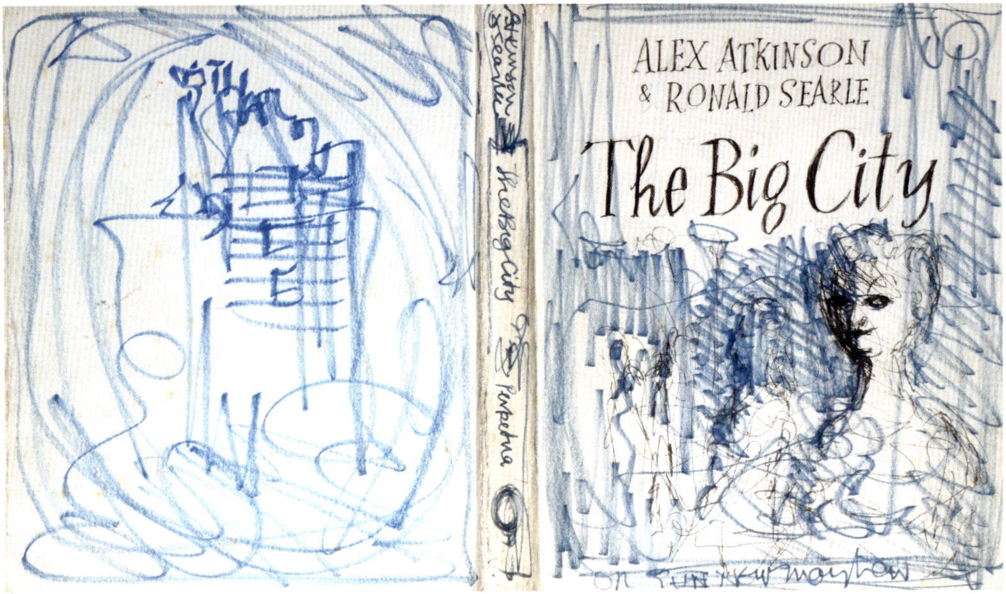

185 THE BIG CITY OR THE NEW MAYHEW DUST JACKET DESIGN
pen ink and coloured ink
inscribed 'Alex Atkinson & Ronald Searle, The Big City or The New Mayhew' on reverse
9 ¾ x 8 ¼ inches folded
Design for Alex Atkinson & Ronald Searle, *The Big City or the New Mayhew*, London: Perpetua Books, 1958, dust jacket

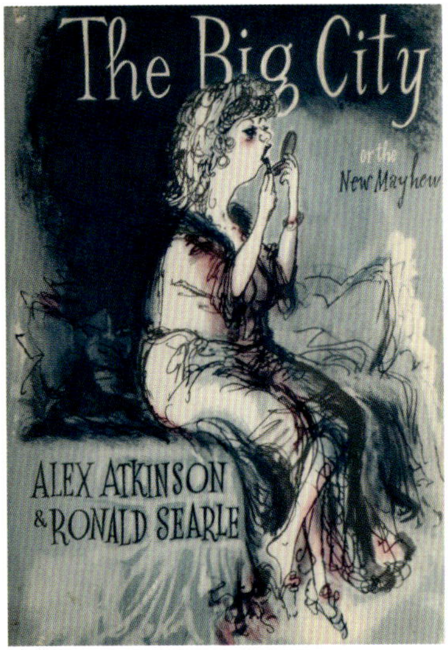

'Alex Atkinson came up with the notion of inhabiting the style of Henry Mayhew, one of the Victorian founders of Punch, *and producing a modern equivalent of his* London Labour *and the* London Poor. *There being less outright shocking squalor in mid-Fifties London … Atkinson concentrated on a class more characteristic of the age: those pathetically defiant strugglers of inner-suburban bedsitter-land, where ambition finally learns to die.'*

(Davies, pages 114-115)

186 THE BIG CITY OR THE NEW MAYHEW
Alex Atkinson & Ronald Searle
The Big City or the New Mayhew
London: Perpetua Books
1958
first edition
hard cover with dust jacket
111 pages
10 x 7 ½ inches

'It is inevitable that many more of the more unfortunate inhabitants of this great capital city should eke out their lives without attracting any but the most superficial attention from the millions that surround them; and this is especially true of those men and women of foreign birth who have sought refuge here from political or racial discrimination and oppression. For these exiles, as they are called, are not normally inclined to advertise their presence among us; being for the most part content (if, indeed, they can in such circumstances ever be accounted content) to exist quietly from day to day in some unfashionable backwater, consoled in the knowledge that footsteps upon the landing are unlikely to herald either torture or incarceration.'

(Alex Atkinson & Ronald Searle, *The Big City or the New Mayhew*, London: Perpetua Books, 1958, page 55)

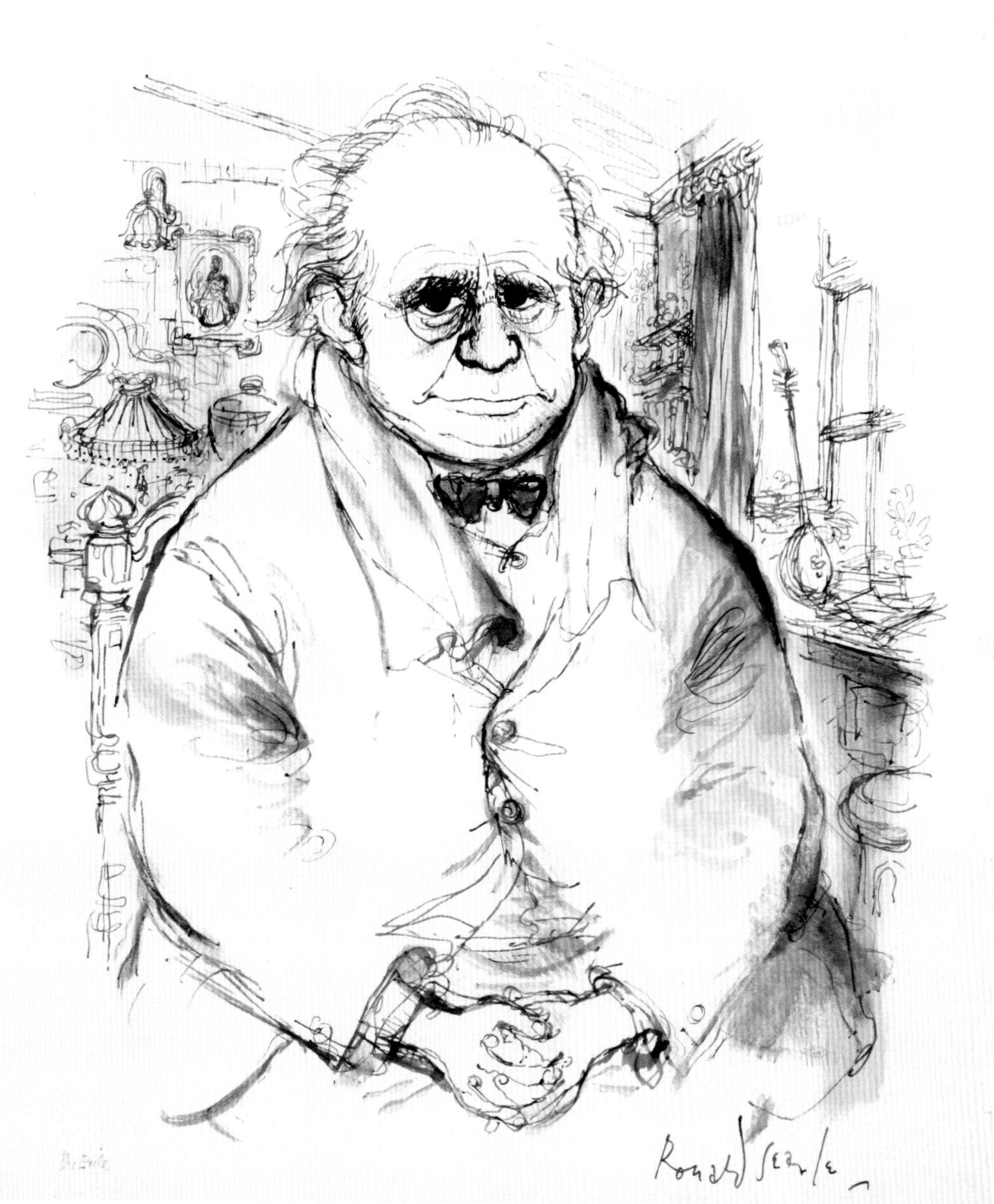

187 THE EXILE
signed and inscribed with title
inscribed with publishing details, stamped with copyright details and dated 1958 on reverse
pen and ink with monochrome watercolour on board
16 x 12 ¾ inches
Illustrated: *Punch*, 8 January 1958, page 100, 'The New Mayhew – The Exile'; Alex Atkinson & Ronald Searle, *The Big City or the New Mayhew*, London: Perpetua Books, 1958, page 57

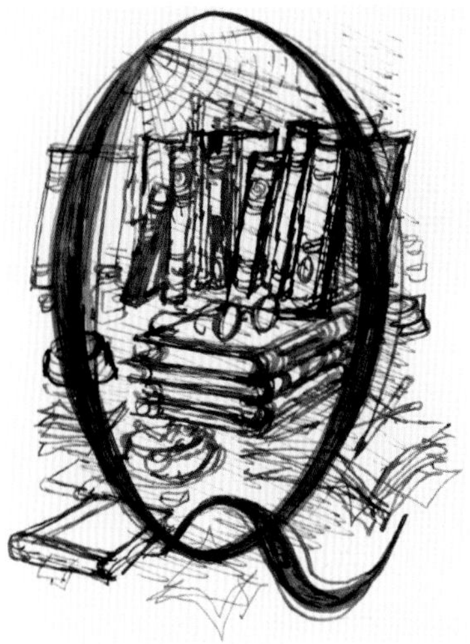

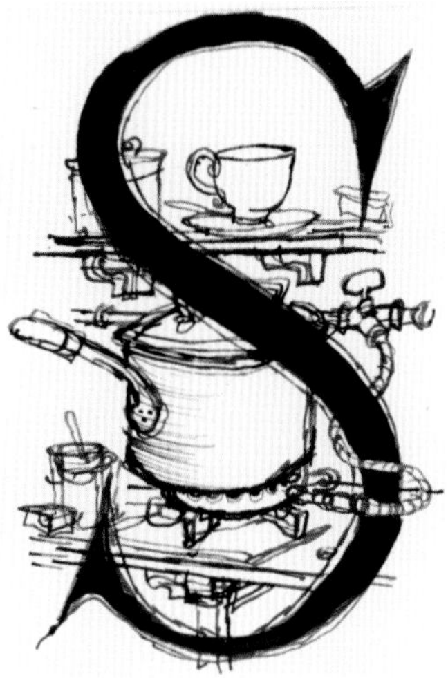

188 A LITERARY MAN
inscribed with title, 'Punch, The New Mayhew 8', 'Redrawn for book' below mount
pen and ink
5 ½ x 5 inches
Illustrated: *Punch*, 1 August 1956, page 129, 'The New Mayhew – A Literary Man'

189 AN ORPHAN STENOGRAPHER
signed with initials, inscribed with title, 'Punch, The New Mayhew 9', 'Redrawn for book' below mount
pen and ink
5 x 4 inches
Illustrated: *Punch*, 15 August 1956, page 185, 'The New Mayhew – The Orphan Stenographer'

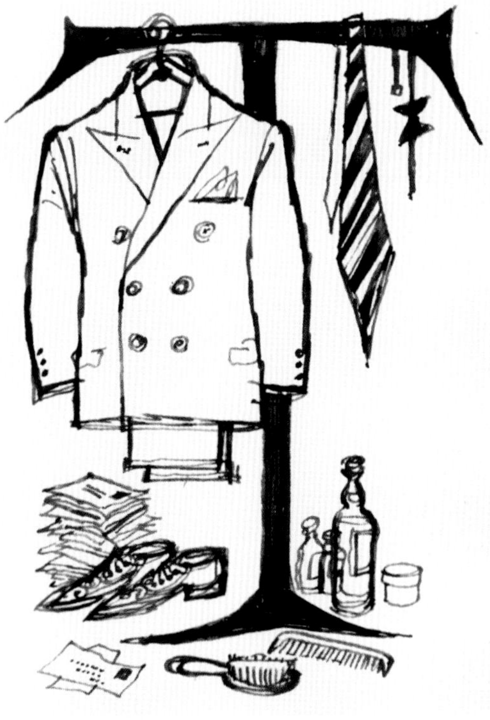

190 TELEVISION MAN
signed with initials and inscribed 'Redrawn for book' below mount
inscribed with title on reverse
pen and ink
4 ½ x 3 ½ inches
Illustrated: *Punch*, 11 April 1956, page 397, 'The New Mayhew – Television Man'

191 AN ENCYCLOPAEDIA SELLER
signed with initials
inscribed with title, 'New Mayhew 2', 'Redrawn for book'
below mount
pen and ink
4 ½ x 3 ½ inches
Illustrated: *Punch*, 23 May 1956, page 623, 'The New Mayhew – An Encyclopaedia Seller'

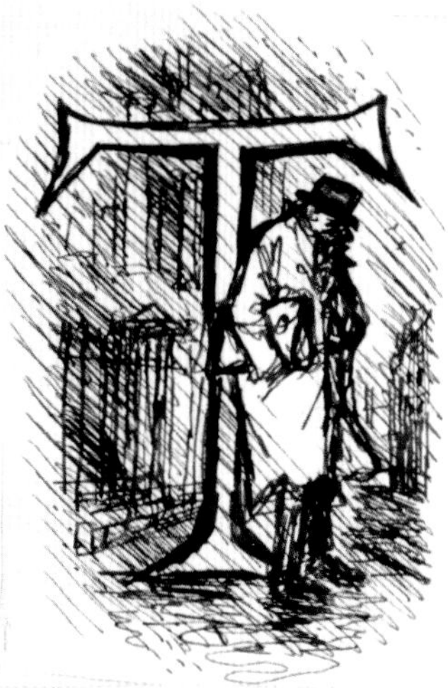

192 A NIGHT AT WRESTLING
pen and ink
7 ½ x 5 ½ inches
Preliminary drawing for *Punch*, 5 March 1958, page 321, 'The New Mayhew – A Night at Wrestling'

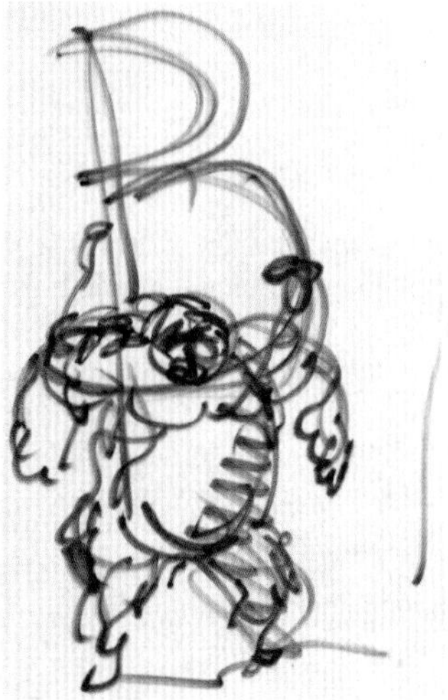

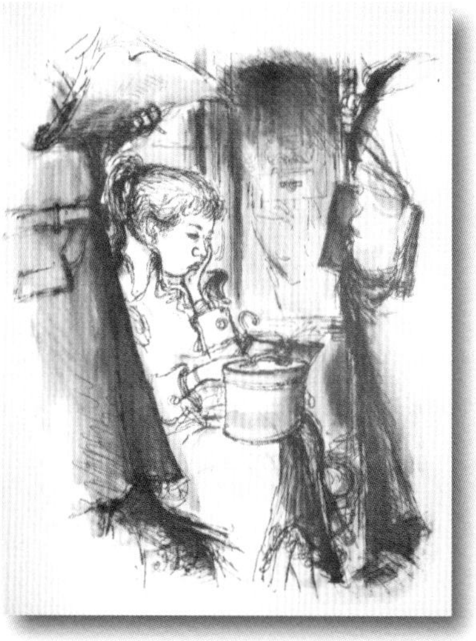

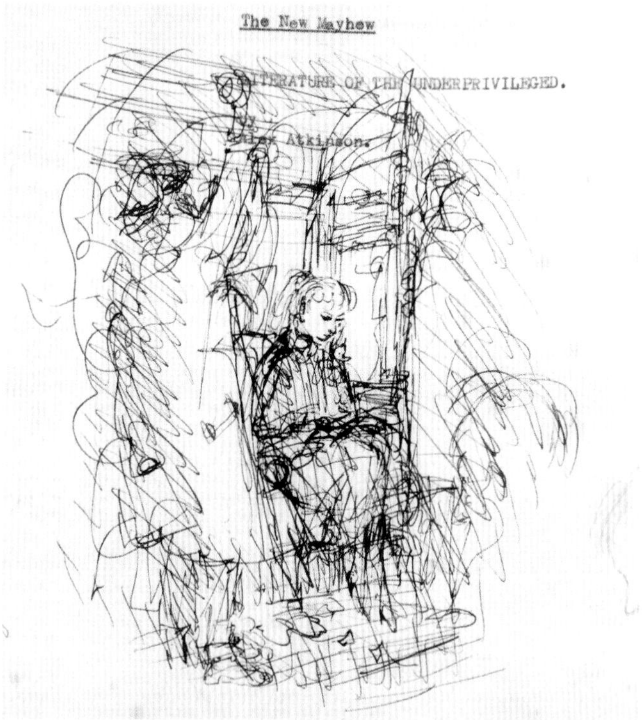

193 LITERATURE OF THE UNDERPRIVILEGED (detail)
pen ink and pencil over typed manuscript
9 ½ x 7 ¾ inches
Preliminary drawing for *Punch*, 22 January 1958, page 154, 'The New Mayhew – Literature of The Underprivileged' by Alex Atkinson; Alex Atkinson & Ronald Searle, *The Big City or the New Mayhew*, London: Perpetua Books, 1958, page 73

1957: Dr Adams Trial, Old Bailey

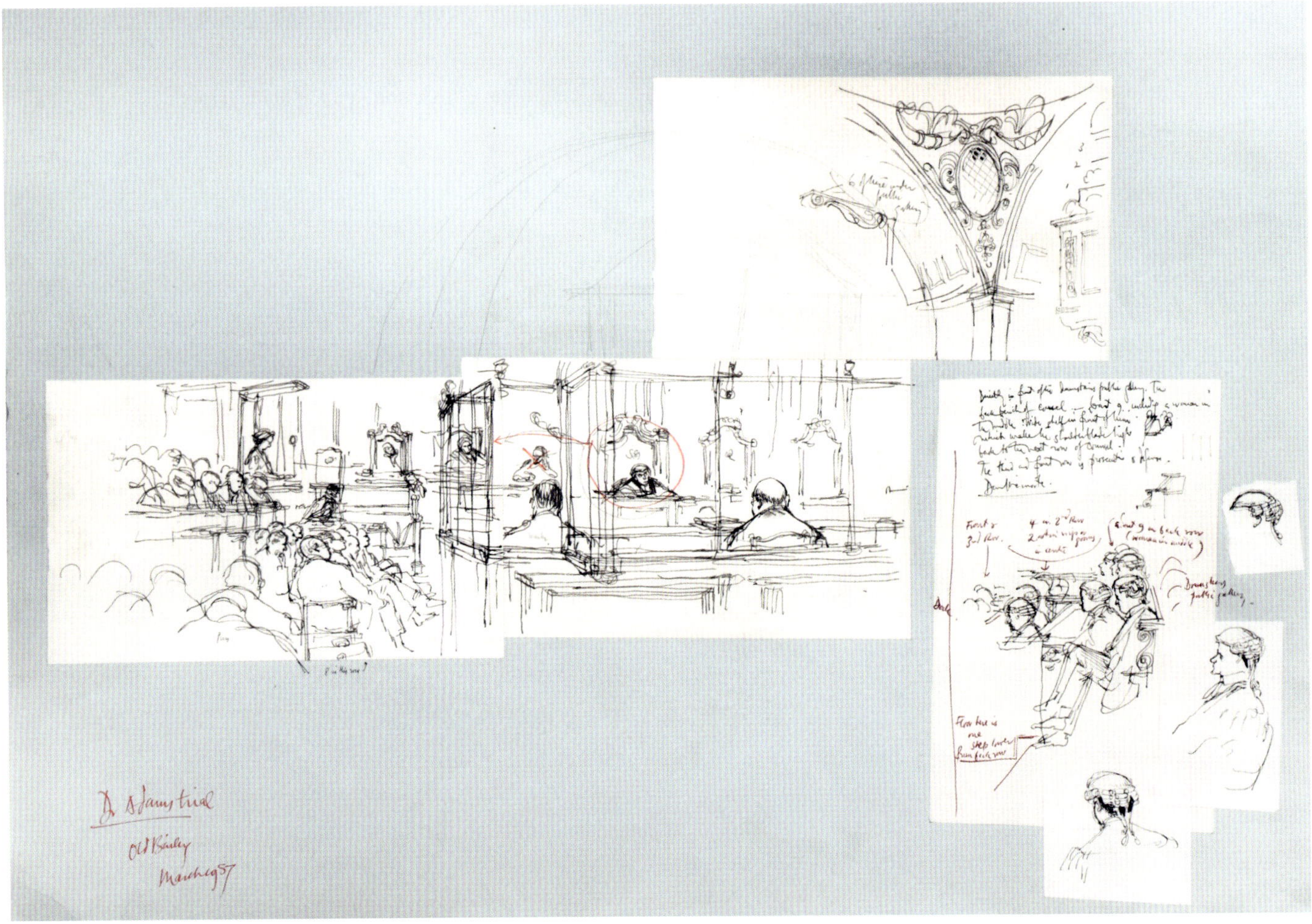

194 DR ADAMS TRIAL, OLD BAILEY
inscribed with title and descriptive notes,
and dated 'March 1957'
pen and ink with pencil on sketchbook
pages and fragments laid down on
tinted paper
15 x 20 ¾ inches

1957: Dr Adams Trial, Old Bailey

From 18 March 1957, the general practitioner, John Bodkin Adams (1899-1983), was tried at the Old Bailey for the murder of Edith Morrell, a patient from whom he inherited a Rolls-Royce Silver Ghost, a Jacobean cupboard and a chest of Georgian silver. He was acquitted on 9 April, at the end of what was then the longest murder trial in Britain, and lived on for another three decades. However, he remains suspected of the murder of 160 of his Eastbourne patients, who died during the decade 1946-56, and some of whom made him a beneficiary of their wills.

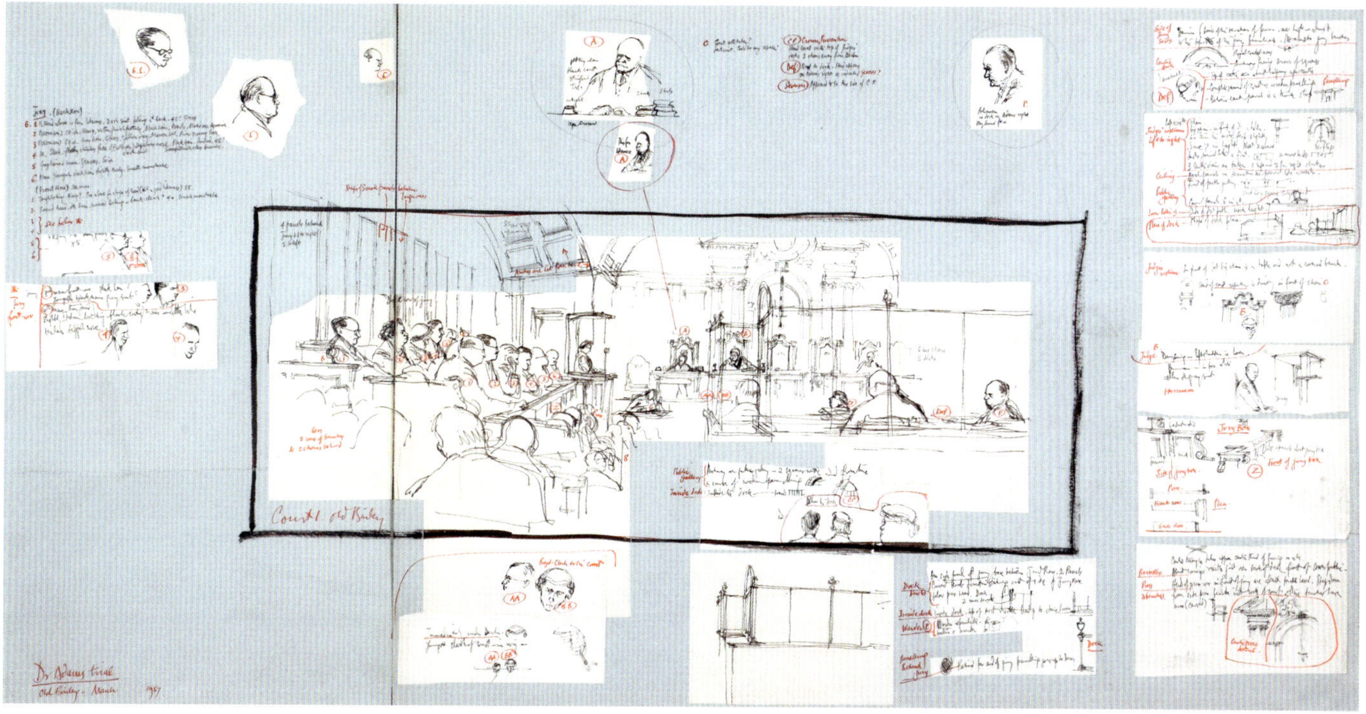

195 DR ADAMS TRIAL, OLD BAILEY

COURT I

inscribed with title and descriptive notes, and dated 'March 1957'
pen and ink with pencil on sketchbook pages and fragments laid down on tinted paper
15 x 29 ¼ inches

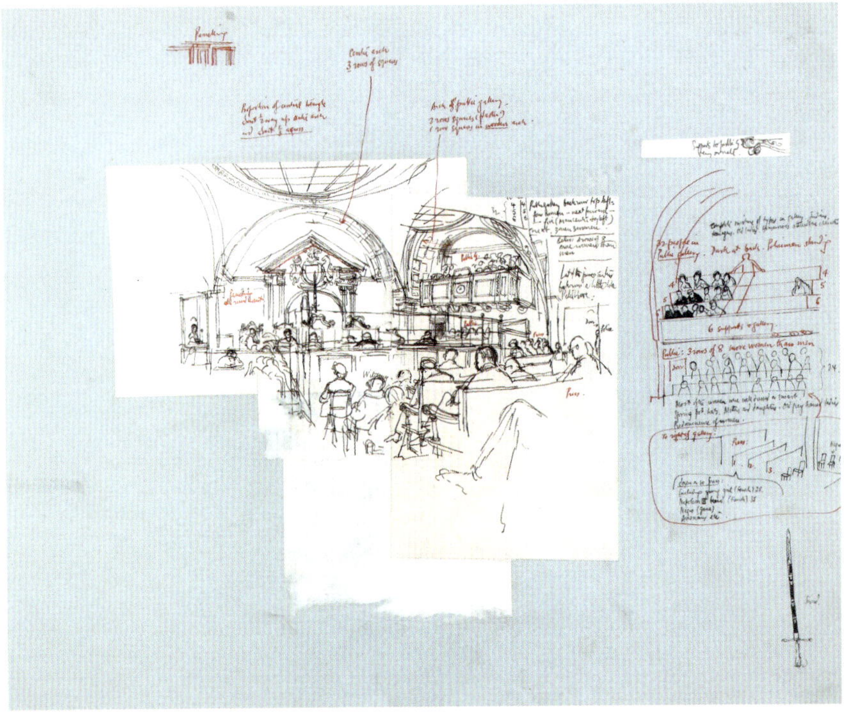

196 DR ADAMS TRIAL, OLD BAILEY
PRESS AND PUBLIC GALLERIES
inscribed with title and descriptive notes, and dated 'March 1957'
pen and ink on sketchbook pages and fragments laid down on tinted paper
15 x 20 ¾ inches

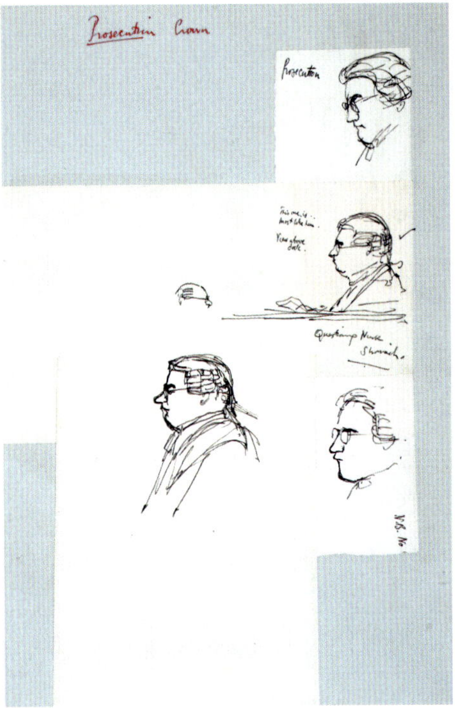

198 DR ADAMS TRIAL – OLD BAILEY
PROSECUTION CROWN
inscribed with subtitle and descriptive notes
pen and ink on sketchbook pages and fragments laid down on tinted paper
15 x 8 inches

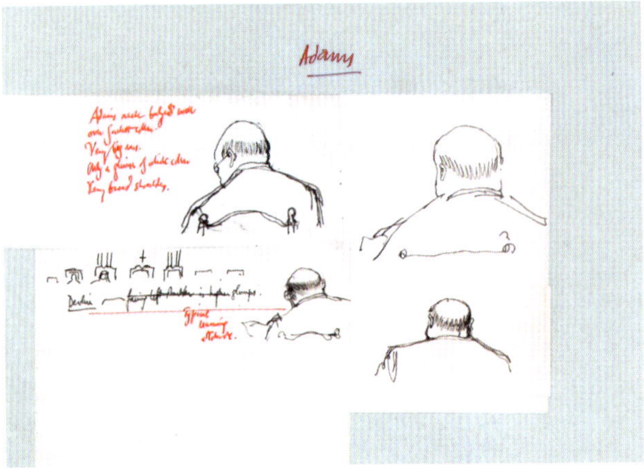

197 DR ADAMS TRIAL – OLD BAILEY
ADAMS
inscribed with subtitle and with descriptive notes
pen ink and pencil on sketchbook pages and fragments laid down on tinted paper
15 x 9 inches

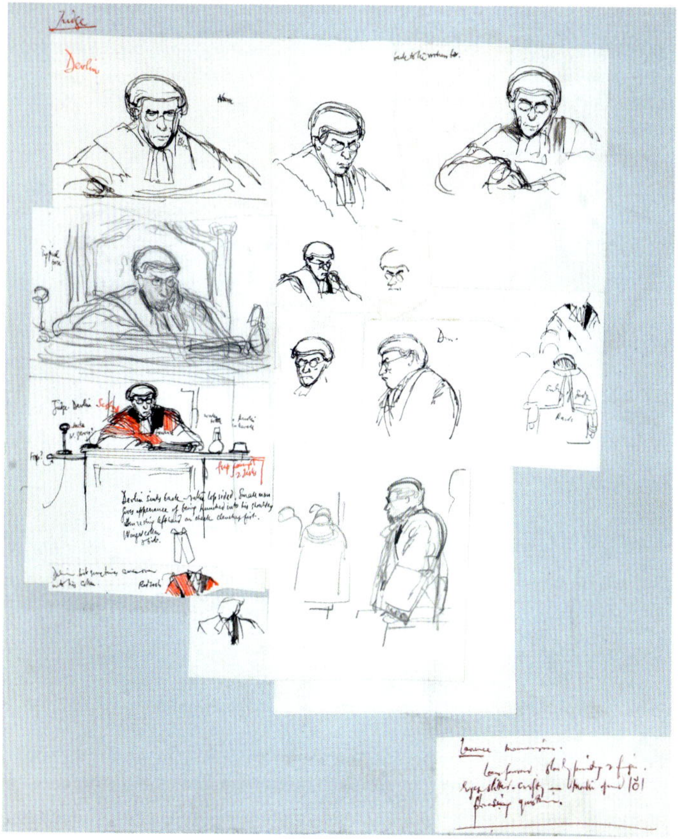

199 DR ADAMS TRIAL, OLD BAILEY
JUDGE
inscribed with subtitle and descriptive notes
pen ink and pencil on sketchbook pages and fragments
laid down on tinted paper
15 x 12 ½ inches

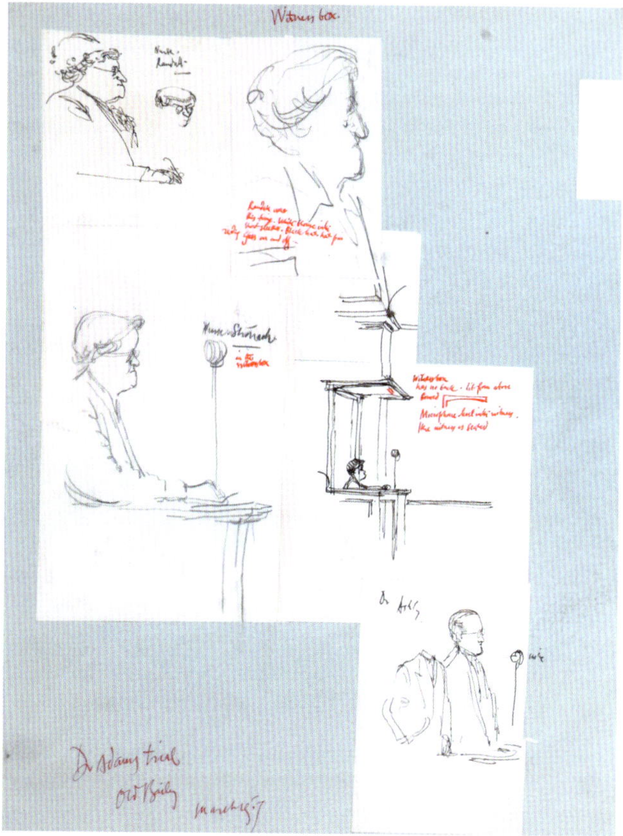

200 DR ADAMS TRIAL, OLD BAILEY
WITNESS BOX
inscribed with title and descriptive notes, and dated 'March 1957'
pen and ink with pencil on sketchbook pages and fragments
laid down on tinted paper
15 x 11 inches

1957-60: American Sketchbook Drawings

New York, June 1957

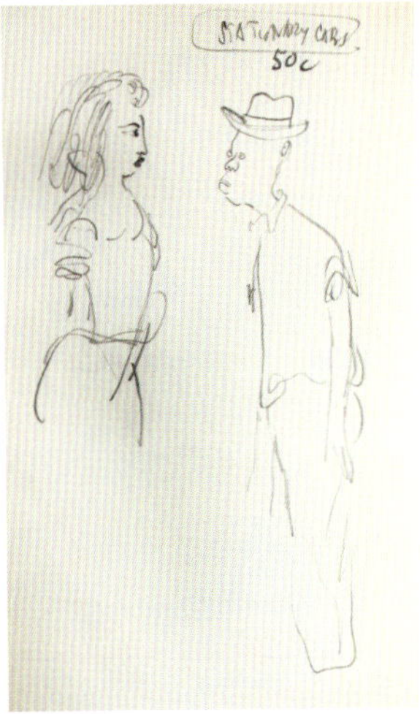

201-209 are taken from a sketchbook of New York, June 1957

'Searle had reached the age of thirty-seven without ever visiting America, where a considerable amount of his work had appeared both in magazines and books … Now at last he had a chance to go. The Standard Oil Company of New Jersey had an idea for an animated film to celebrate their seventy-fifth anniversary in business, and invited Ronald over to work on it. It would be a three-month trip – alarming for Punch*, though they would be mollified with a promise of a Searle 'Sketchbook' from the New World. Searle and his wife sailed over in mid-May …'*

(Davies, page 122)

201 NEW YORK FIGURES
pencil
7 ¾ x 5 inches

reverse:
NEW YORK SIGNS (not illustrated)
pencil
8 x 5 inches

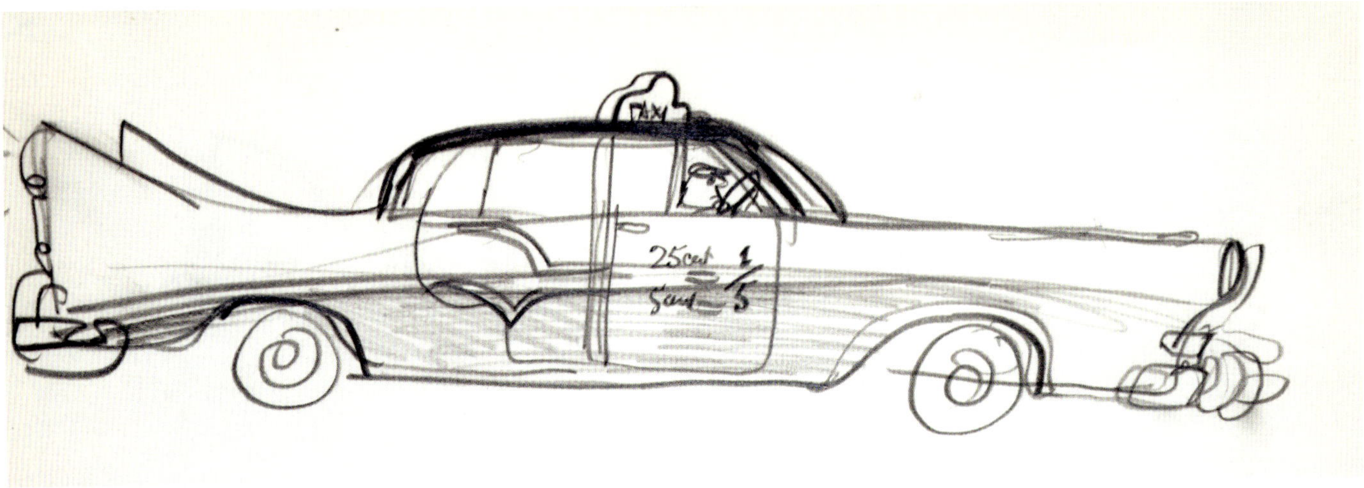

202 TAXI
pencil
3 ½ x 8 ¼ inches

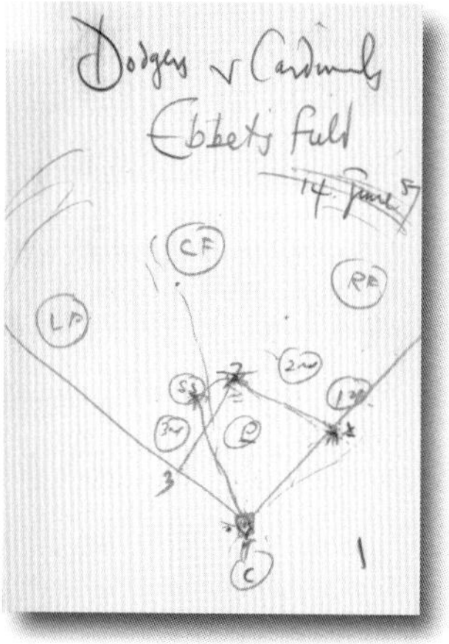

Dodgers v Cardinals
On the afternoon of Friday 14 June 1957, the Brooklyn Dodgers played and won against the St Louis Cardinals in a National League baseball game at their home stadium of Ebbets Field, Flatbush, Brooklyn.

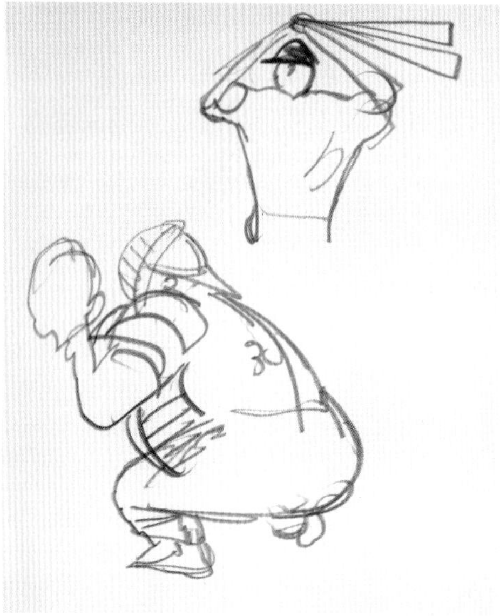

203 CATCHER
pencil
6 ¼ x 5 inches

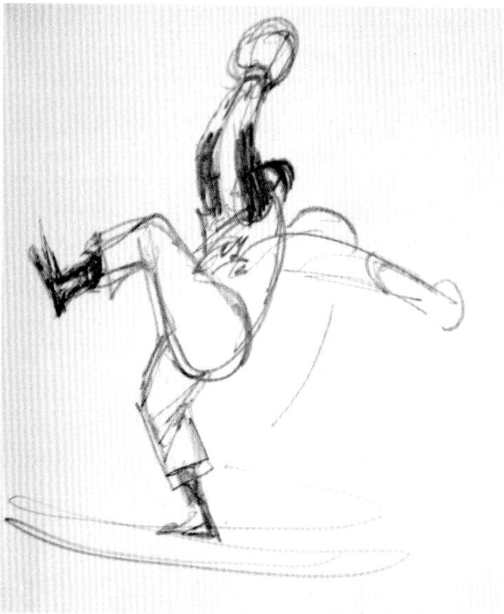

204 PITCHER
pencil
5 ½ x 5 inches

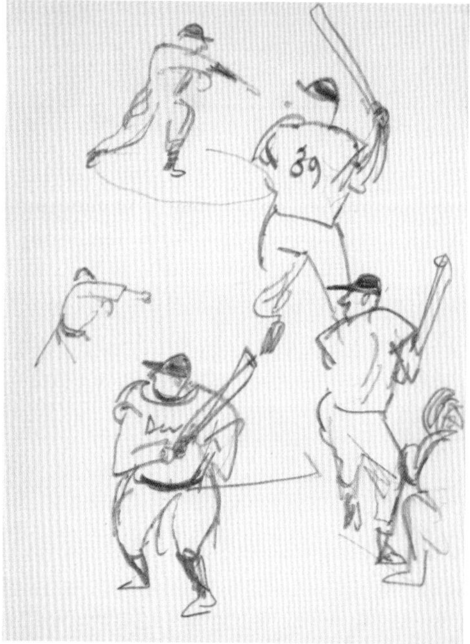

205 BATTER:
ROY CAMPANELLA
OF THE DODGERS
pencil
7 x 5 inches

Roy Campanella of the Dodgers
Roy Campanella (1921-1993) was a leading player for the Brooklyn Dodgers' between 1948 and 1957. Considered one of the greatest catchers in the history of baseball, he was selected as the National League's Most Valuable Player in 1951, 1953 and 1955. However, having had an African American mother, he had initially been barred from Major League Baseball, and was instrumental in breaking the colour barrier.

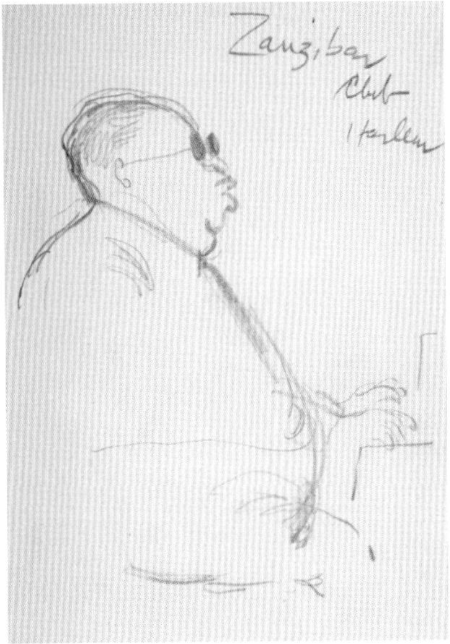

206 PIANO (I)
inscribed 'Zanzibar Club Harlem'
pencil
7 x 5 inches

207 PIANO (II)
pencil
8 x 5 inches

208 DRUMS
pencil
8 x 5 inches

209 DANCING AT THE SAVOY
pencil
6 ½ x 5 inches
Preliminary drawing for 'Savoy Dance Hall', *Punch*, 17 July 1957, page 71, 'Searle in America'

Savoy Dance Hall

While in New York, Ronald Searle managed to visit the famous Savoy Ballroom, or Dance Hall, just a year before it closed on 10 July 1958. Opening three decades earlier, on 12 March 1926 at Lenox Avenue, Harlem, it became one of the most popular dance venues of the Swing era, and was particularly associated with the Lindy Hop. The second floor dance hall, with its double bandstand, provided a space in which black and white Americans could dance together. Many leading jazz artistes performed at the hall, including Chick Webb, Benny Goodman, Dizzy Gillespie, Charlie Parker, Art Blakey and Thelonious Monk.

Searle has annotated one drawing of a pianist at the Savoy [**206**] with the words 'Zanzibar Club Harlem', a reminiscence of one of the great jazz clubs of the past, which had closed in 1947.

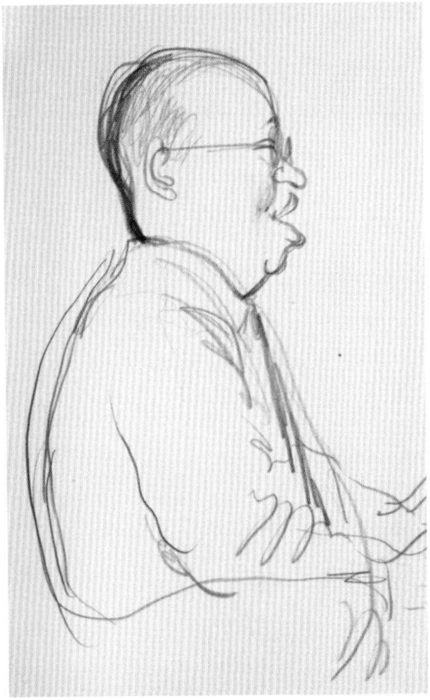

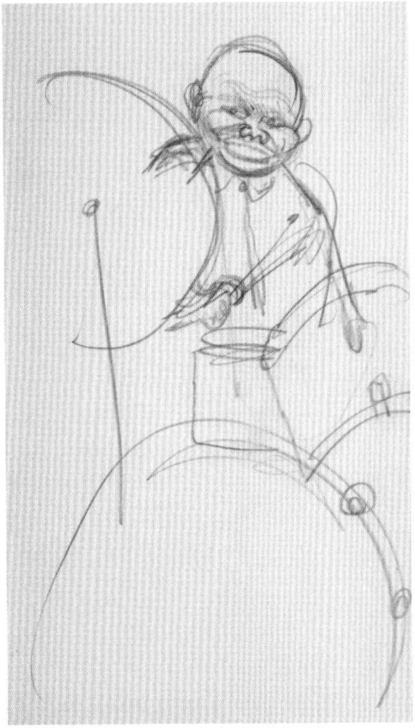

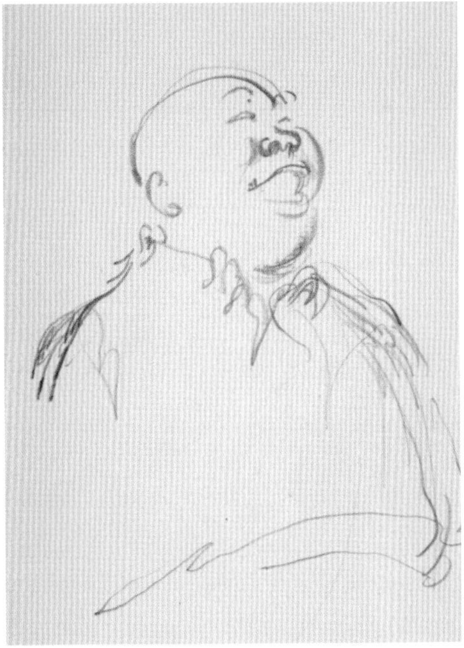

San Francisco, July 1957

Tarantino's, Fisherman's Wharf, San Francisco
Tarantino's was opened in April 1946 by J Eugene McAteer and Daniel J Sweeney Jr, who described themselves as the 'two Irishmen of Fisherman's Wharf'. Occupying the former Crab Fisherman's Protection Association, it has since become an institution among the many restaurants in the area.

210-212 are taken from a sketchbook of LA and Hollywood, July 1957

210 TARANTINO'S, FISHERMAN'S WHARF, SAN FRANCISCO
pen and ink
5 x 8 inches

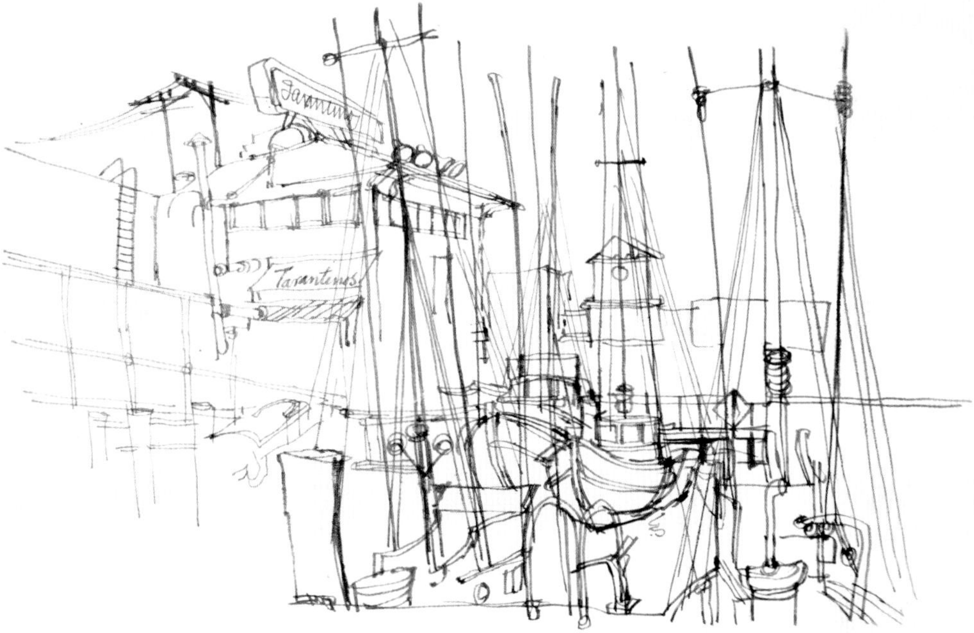

'It was the nature of the work offered that took Searle back to the United States … The real breakthrough came in July 1959, just at the time of the British printers' strike, when Holiday *ran 'By Rocking Chair Across America' as a huge summer feature … overall reaction was so positive … that Alex Atkinson was taken on the staff of* Holiday, *while Searle was invited over to enter upon a golden age of American reportage.'*

(Davies, pages 129-130)

'[He] spent most of February [1960] in America again, expanding a 'Christmas Carol' colour-feature for Life, *and driving down to New Orleans for a* Holiday *feature. [his American agent] John Locke took the wheel, covering up to 600 miles a day. It was Locke who arranged the whole American programme on Searle's behalf.'*

(Davies, page 133)

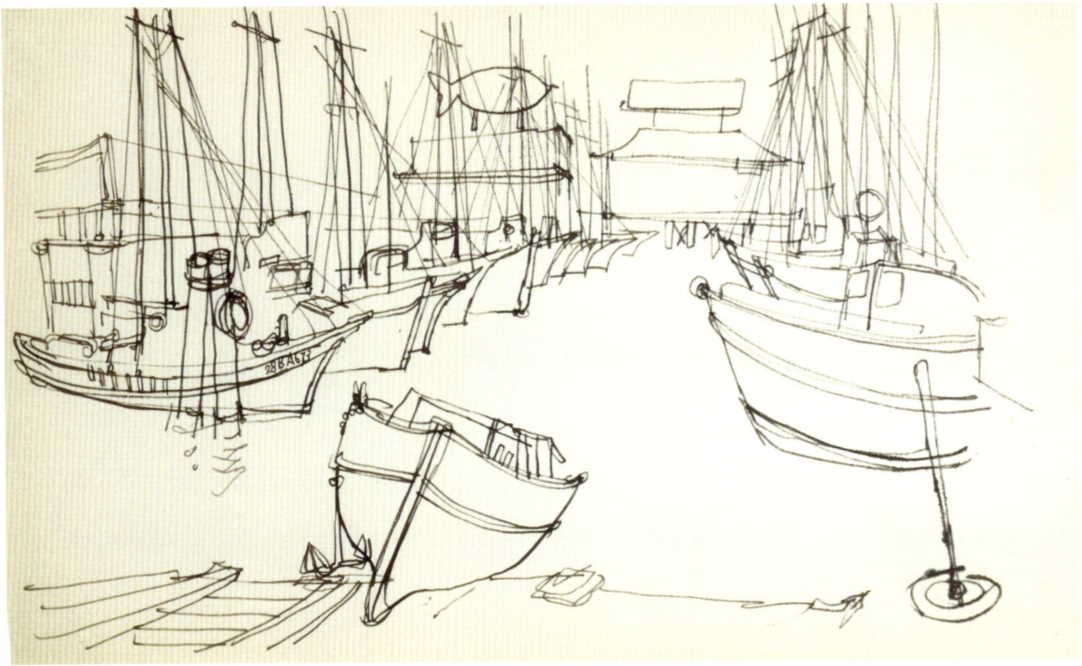

211 FISHERMAN'S WHARF, SAN FRANCISCO
pen and ink
5 x 8 ¼ inches

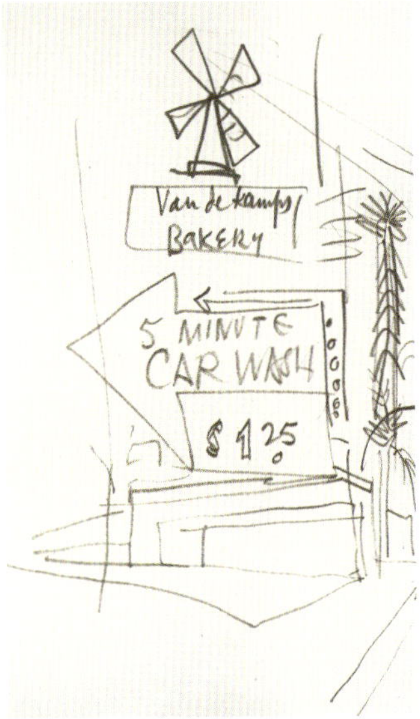

'Later [in 1960], America called again … this time predominantly with the voice of Life *magazine, who clearly felt that* Holiday *was getting too much of the pie. The proffered topic, they knew was irresistible: the Presidential Election campaign, Kennedy versus Nixon, starting with a week on the road with Kennedy.'*

(Davies, page 133)

212 AMERICAN HIGHWAY: 5 MINUTE CAR WASH
pen and ink
8 ¼ x 5 inches

reverse:
EDDIES MODERN HOTEL (not illustrated)
pencil
7 ½ x 5 inches

New Orleans, February 1960

Dan's Pier 600
Ronald Searle visited the club, Dan's Pier 600, while working on an assignment for *Holiday* magazine. Owned by Dan Levy Snr, it stood in the French Quarter at the corner of St Louis and Bourbon Street.

Searle's notes on the club recorded the following:

'Had little club in New Orleans. Wasn't a girlie place. Went up to Chicago – source for import of showgirls. Came back to New Orleans with 9 girls. One of whom was Kalantan. Practically went broke. Sold his air-conditioning unit to pay the girls ...

Features perhaps the best available Jazz in N O ...

They (the Jazz musicians) like working for me. I leave them alone and I never know what they are going to do. As it is they look forward to coming to work ...

To cut the shows in half and run audience through one door and out of the other. Announce 45 minute interval and give an actual interval of five minutes. That way can get 8-10 shows a night.'

213-228 are taken from a sketchbook of New Orleans, 1960

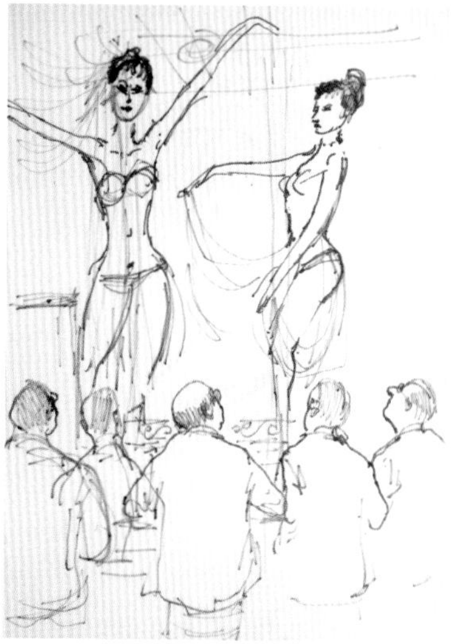

213 DAN'S PIER 600
pen and ink
12 x 8 ¾ inches

Al Hirt
The New Orleans trumpeter and bandleader, Al Hirt (1922-1999), led the band at Dan's Pier 600 for ten years. Then, in 1962, he opened his own club on Bourbon Street, which he ran until 1983. In 1963, he recorded the album, *Honey in the Horn*, which included his best-known track, the instrumental composition, *Java*.

Ronald Searle's notes recorded that 'Some say that he has an unusually big tone but he uses only two thirds volume at the club. Terrific technique and tone. Could play blues if he wanted to'.

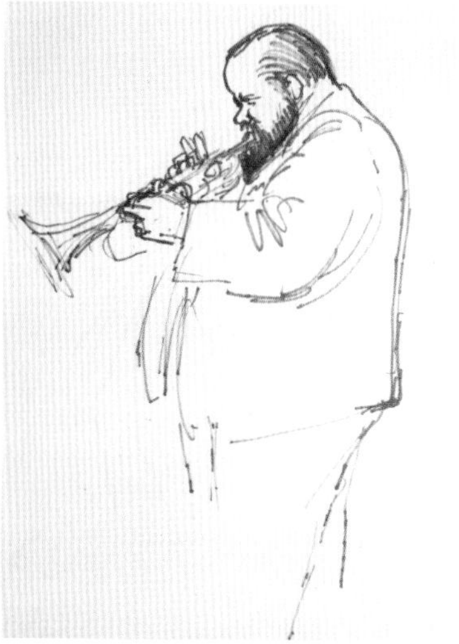

214 AL HIRT (I)
pen and ink
11 ½ x 8 ½ inches

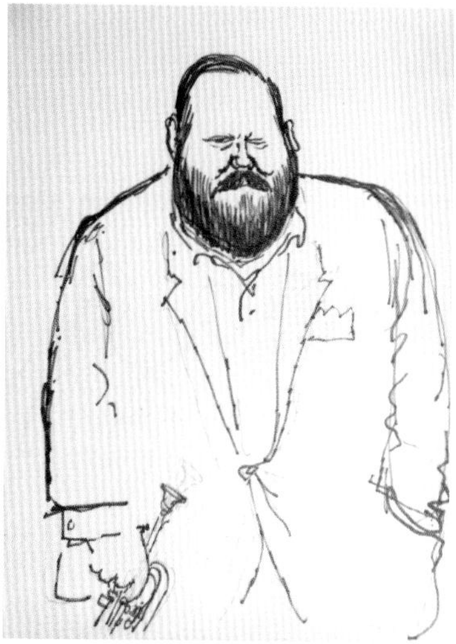

215 AL HIRT (II)
pen and ink
6 x 5 inches

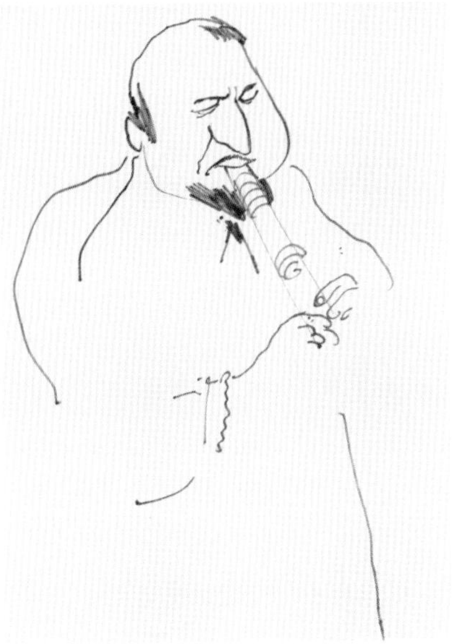

Pete Fountain

Ronald Searle's notes described the clarinettist, Pete Fountain (born 1930), as 'the most popular in New Orleans' and 'maybe even better than Benny Goodman'. After a stint with the Lawrence Welk Orchestra, he returned to New Orleans, where he soon led bands under his own name and owned his own clubs, beginning with the French Quarter Inn, on Bourbon Street, in 1960. From there he developed a friendly rivalry with Al Hirt, later recording several albums with him.

216 PETE FOUNTAIN
pen and ink
11 x 8 ½ inches

Sweet Emma Barrett

New Orleans jazz pianist and singer, Emma Barrett (1897-1983), received the nickname 'Bell Gal' because she wore a red cap and garters with bells that jangled in time to her music. Working first with the Original Tuxedo Orchestra in the 1920s and early 30s, she reached her height in the 1960s as a member of the Preservation Hall Jazz Band, which performed at 726 St Peter Street in the French Quarter as well as undertaking tours.

Ronald Searle heard her at another of her regular venues, the Old Absinthe House on Bourbon Street, where she led a quartet of performers that also comprised trumpeter, Percy Humphrey (1905-1995), his brother the clarinettist, Willie Humphrey (1900-1994), and the drummer, Cy Frazier. Searle noted that she 'would have been one of the greats if she had been what she is forty years ago'.

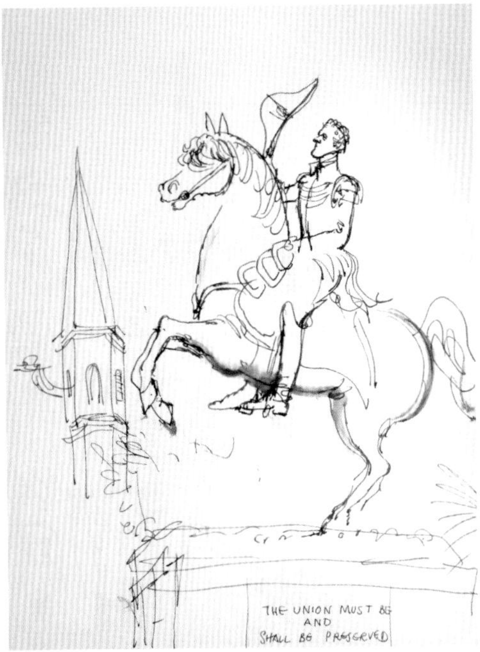

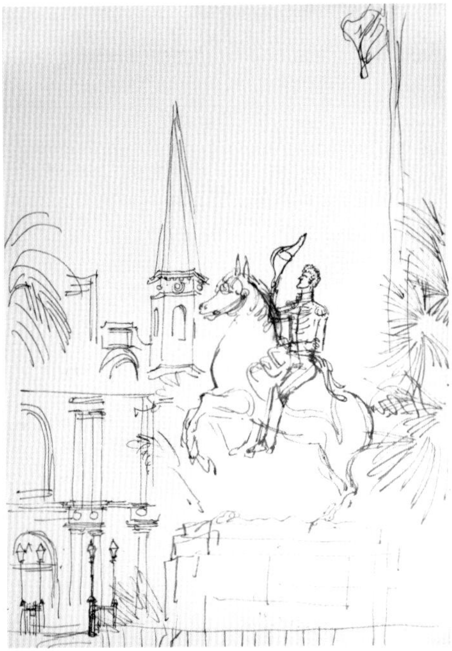

217 EQUESTRIAN STATUE OF ANDREW JACKSON, JACKSON SQUARE
pen and ink drawing of trees and a bench on reverse
pen and ink
11 x 8 ¾ inches

218 SAINT LOUIS CATHEDRAL, JACKSON SQUARE
pen and ink
12 x 8 ¾ inches

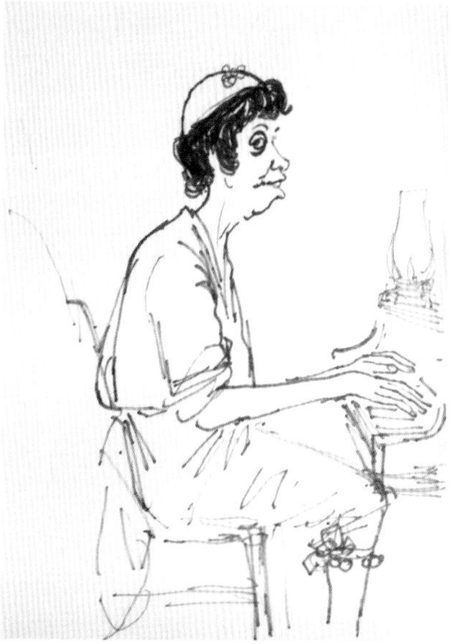

219 SWEET EMMA BARRETT (I)
pen and ink
11 x 8 inches

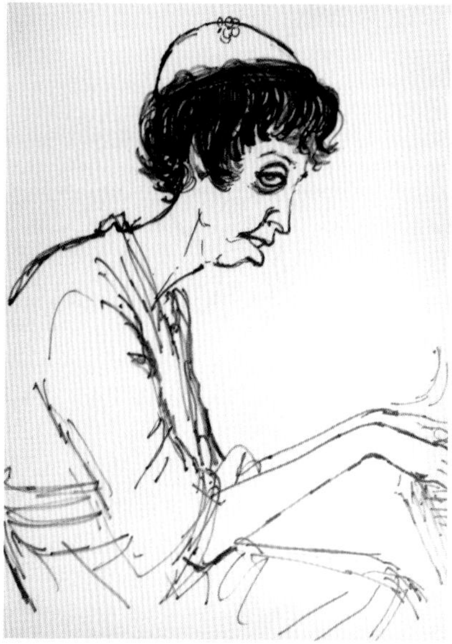

220 SWEET EMMA BARRETT (II)
pen and ink
12 x 8 ¾ inches

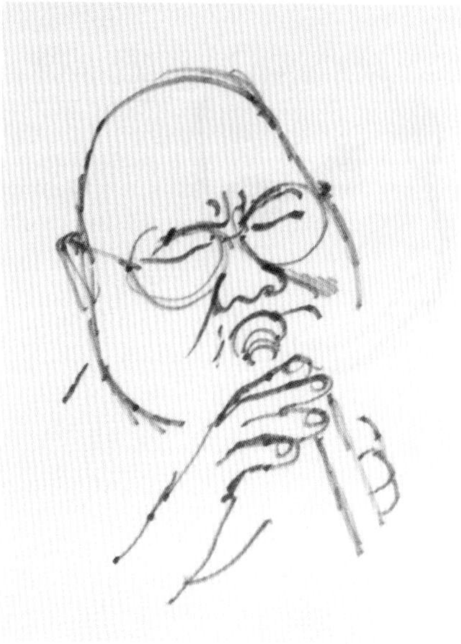

221 PERCY HUMPHREY
pen and ink
6 x 5 inches

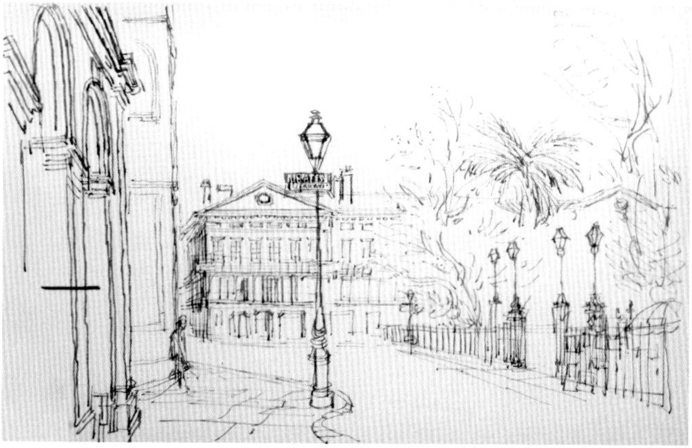

222 ROYAL STREET
pen and ink
8 ¾ x 12 inches

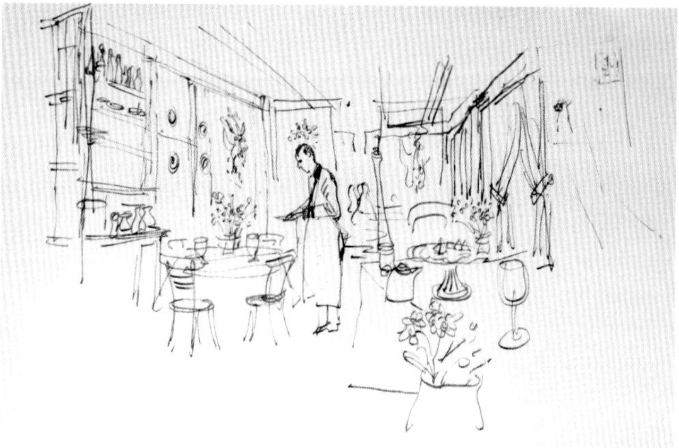

223 RESTAURANT INTERIOR
pen and ink
8 ½ x 11 ½ inches

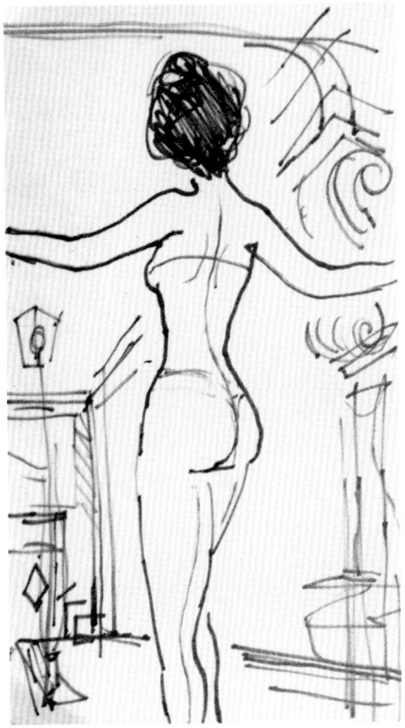

224 ON STAGE
pen and ink
8 x 4 ¾ inches

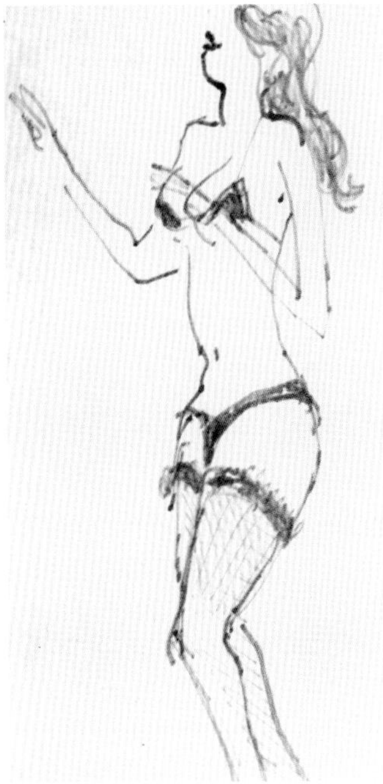

225 DANCING
pen and ink
8 x 4 ¾ inches

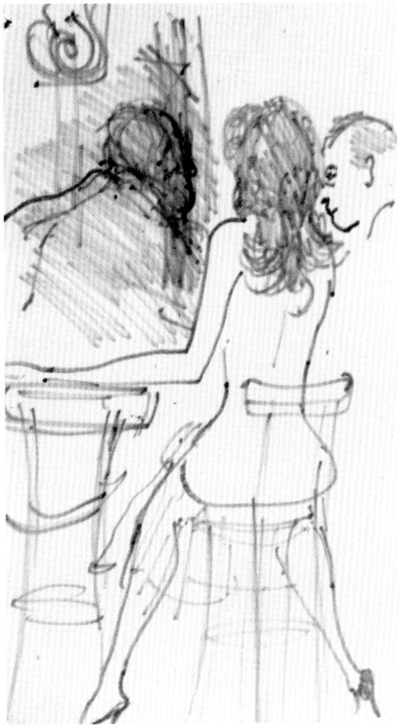

226 AT THE BAR
pen and ink
8 x 4 ¾ inches

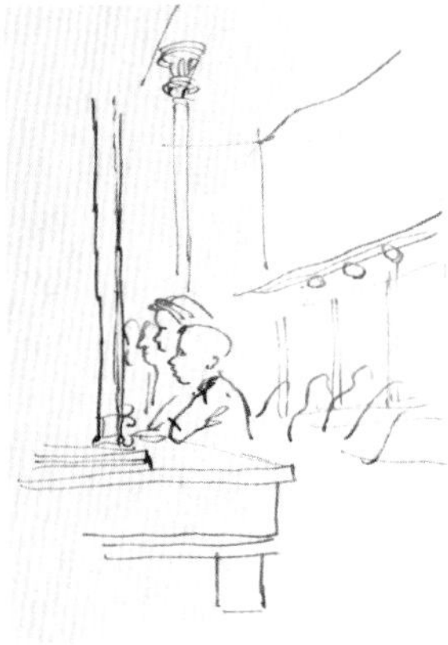

227 CLOSE TO THE STAGE
pen and ink
6 x 4 ½ inches

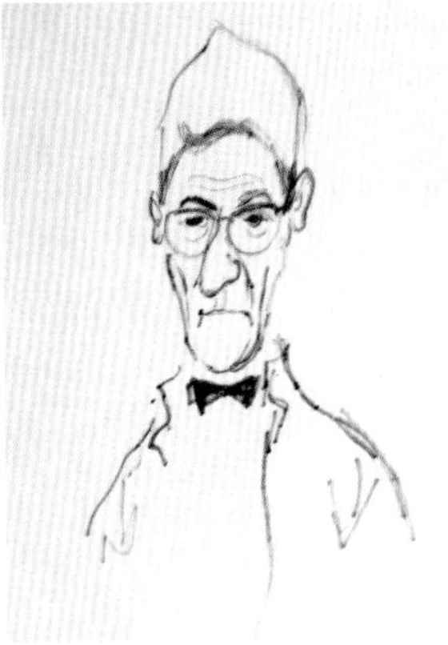

228 BARMAN
pen and ink
5 ½ x 4 ½ inches

'The smaller "clip joints" feature a continuous – a steady shuttle service of "Exotics". The girls operate – hardly dance up and down a strip of stage behind a long bar, frequently backed by a wall of mirror. The dancing is basic and feeble accompanied by a worn out drummer and tired records … she has supplied herself and put onto the record player before she steps out onto the bar stage.'

(Ronald Searle's notes on New Orleans Strip Joints)

1958: Work in Hand

Work in Hand

Always hard working, and increasingly successful, Ronald Searle produced lists of work in progress in order to keep abreast of the many projects that he had in hand at one time. This example shows how meticulous they were, and how beautiful they could be. It also encapsulates a point in his career, about midway through 1958.

The major book projects of the time comprised *The Big City* (with Alex Atkinson, Perpetua) [**185-193**], and *The Compleet Molesworth* [**160**] and *The Dog's Ear Book* (both with Geoffrey Willans, Max Parrish), all of which would be published in the October. However, there are other books on the list that would eventually come to fruition, including *The St Trinian's Story* (with Kaye Webb, Perpetua, 1959) [**49** & **50**, **53** & **54**], Christopher Fry's *A Phoenix Too Frequent* (Oxford University Press, 1959) [**179-181**, **183**] and Robert Graves' translation of Homer's *The Iliad* (Doubleday, 1959). The reference to 'A Christmas Carol' may relate to a feature for *Life* magazine (published in 1960) rather than Searle's edition of Charles Dickens' novel (Perpetua, 1961).

As a magazine illustrator and cartoonist, Searle was working mainly for *Punch* and *Holiday*, but he was also responding to many commercial commissions, including greetings cards for Valentines, a poster for Lemon Hart Rum [see **138-150**] and even a 'notice on throat clearing' for the Royal Festival Hall.

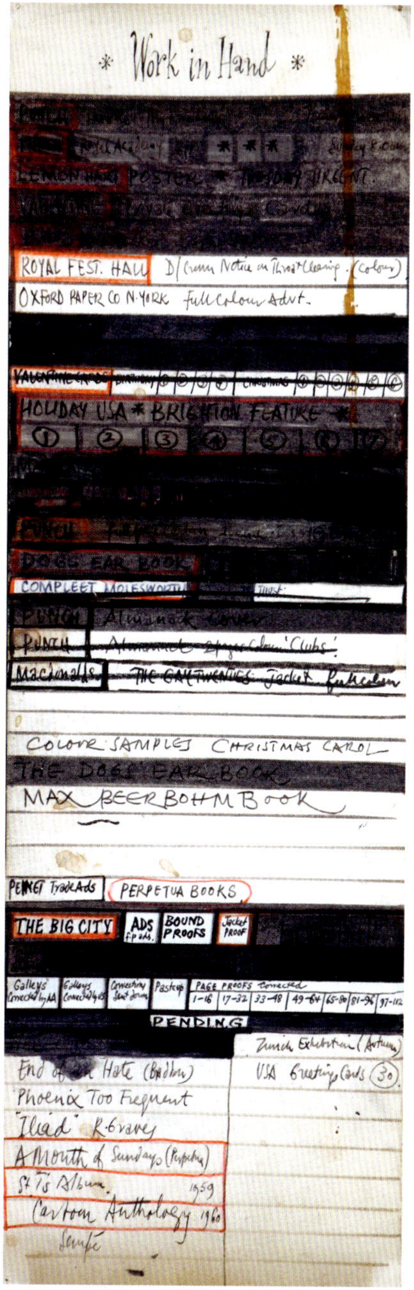

229 WORK IN HAND
extensively inscribed with a list of projects
pen ink, coloured pencil and crayon on board
15 ½ x 4 ¾ inches

1959: Paris sketchbook drawings

230-244 are taken from a sketchbook of Paris, circa 1959

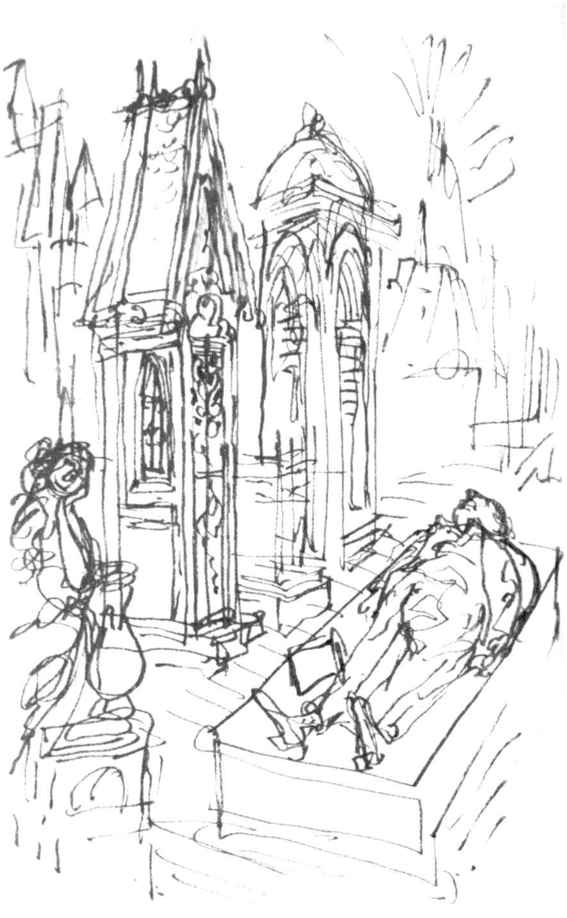

230 THE GRAVE OF VICTOR NOIR,
PERE LACHAISE CEMETERY
pen and ink
6 ½ x 3 ¾ inches

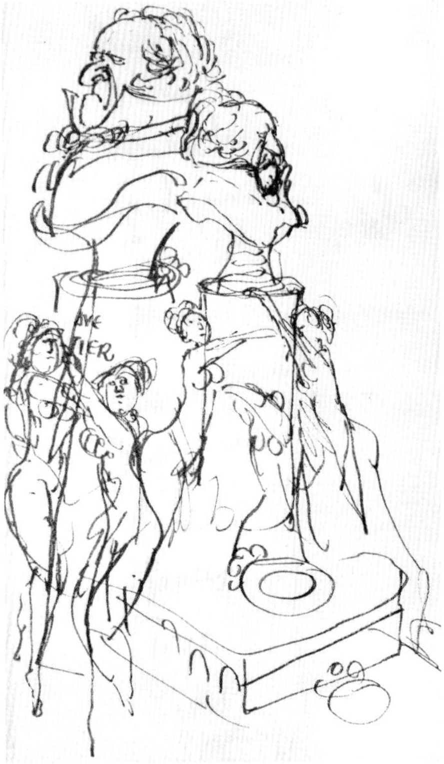

231 MONUMENTS,
PERE LACHAISE
CEMETERY
pen and ink
6 ¾ x 3 ¾ inches

The Grave of Victor Noir, Père Lachaise Cemetery

Yvan Solomon (1848-1870) worked under the name 'Victor Noir', as a journalist for *La Marseillaise*. He is remembered for the manner of his death. He agreed to act as a second in a duel between his editor, Paschal Grousset, and Prince Pierre Bonaparte, cousin to the reigning emperor, Napoleon III. Instead of contacting the Prince's seconds, he and his fellow second visited Bonaparte, who was willing to fight the newspaper's owner, Henri Rochefort, because he was a nobleman, but not an inferior. It is believed that Victor Noir then slapped Bonaparte, who responded by shooting him dead. This led to a public outcry, which was further fuelled by Bonaparte's acquittal. A life-sized, highly realistic bronze statue by Jules Dalou marks Victor Noir's grave. The large bulge in its trousers has since become a popular fertility symbol for women visitors.

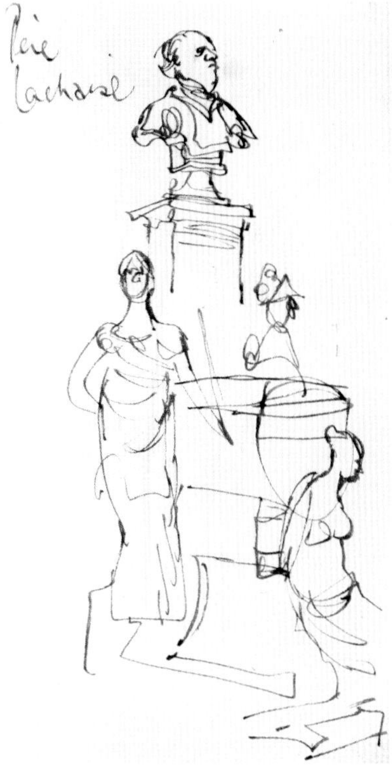

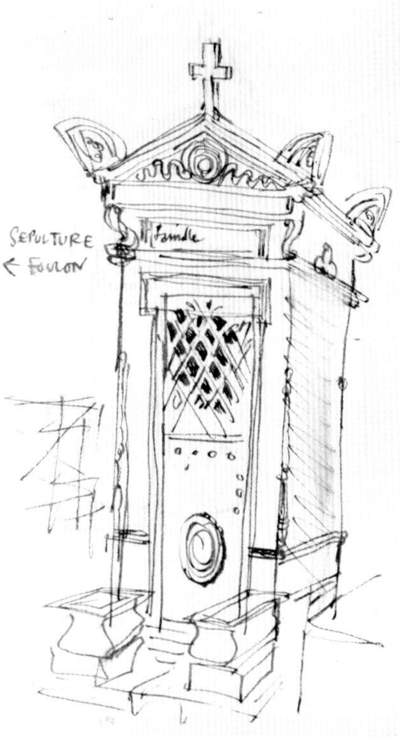

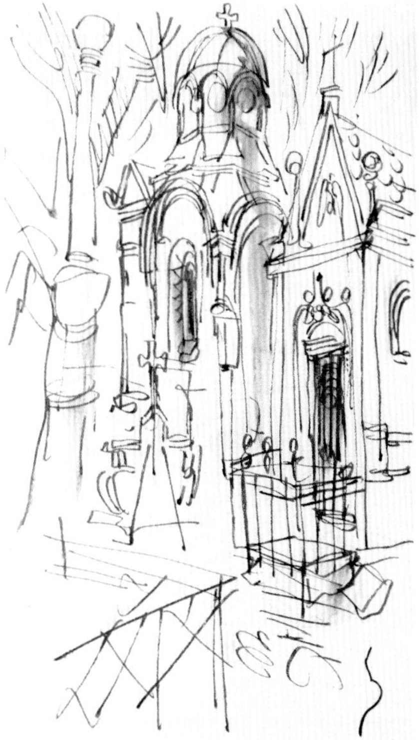

232 PERE LACHAISE
inscribed with title
pen and ink
6 ¾ x 3 ¾ inches

233 FAMILLE FERVRIER, 26TH DIVISION, PERE LACHAISE CEMETERY
inscribed 'Sepulture Foulon'
pen and ink
6 ¾ x 3 ¾ inches

234 TOMBS, PERE LACHAISE CEMETERY
pen and ink
6 ¾ x 4 inches

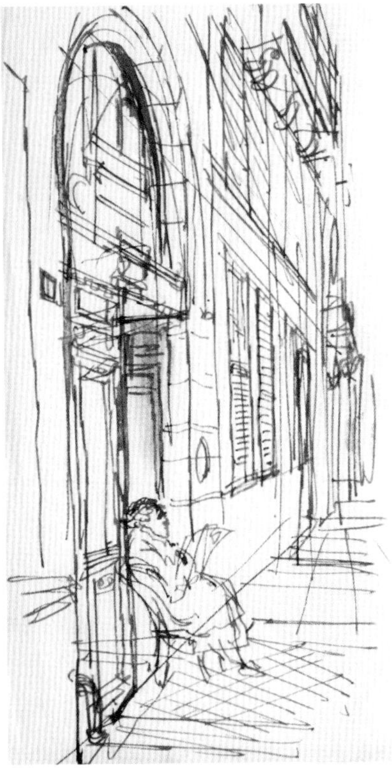

235 CONCIERGE
pen and ink
6 ¾ x 3 ¾ inches

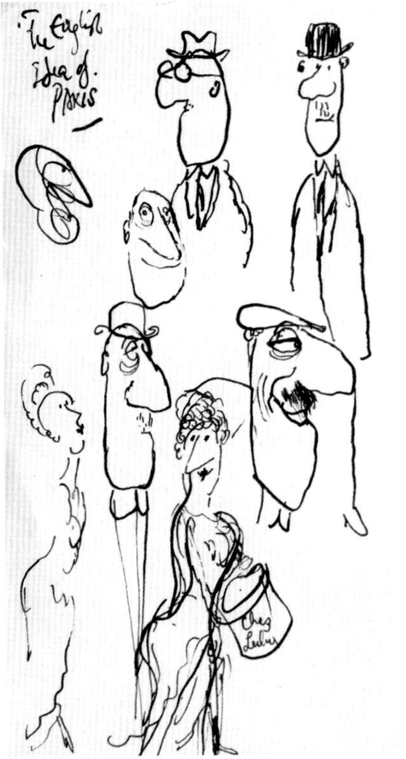

236 THE ENGLISH IDEA OF PARIS
inscribed with title
pen and ink
6 ¾ x 3 ¾ inches

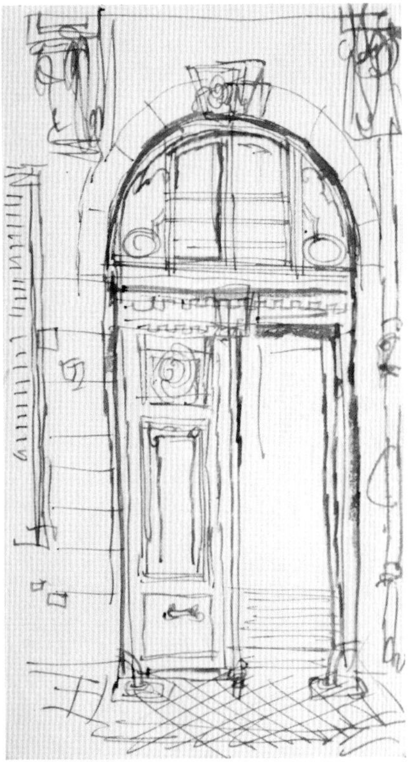

237 DOORWAY
pen and ink
6 ¾ x 3 ¾ inches

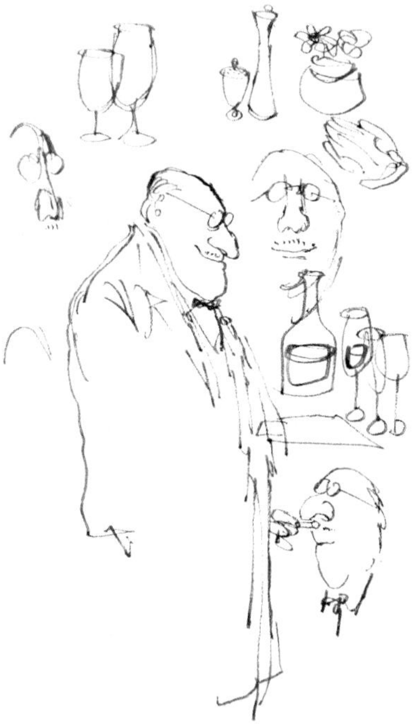

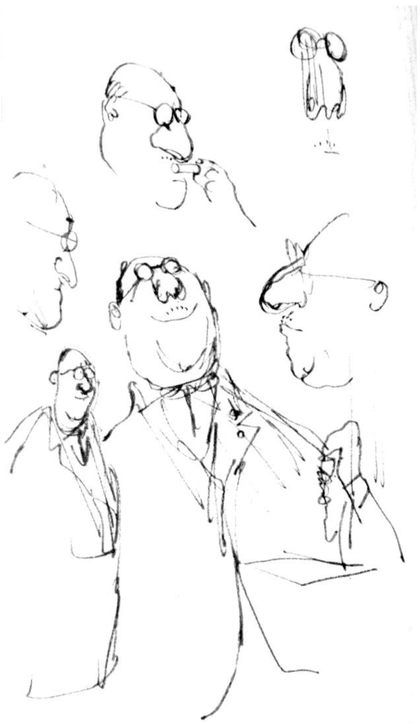

238 SOMMELIER (I)
pen and ink
6 ¾ x 3 ¾ inches

239 SOMMELIER (II)
pen and ink
6 ¾ x 3 ¾ inches

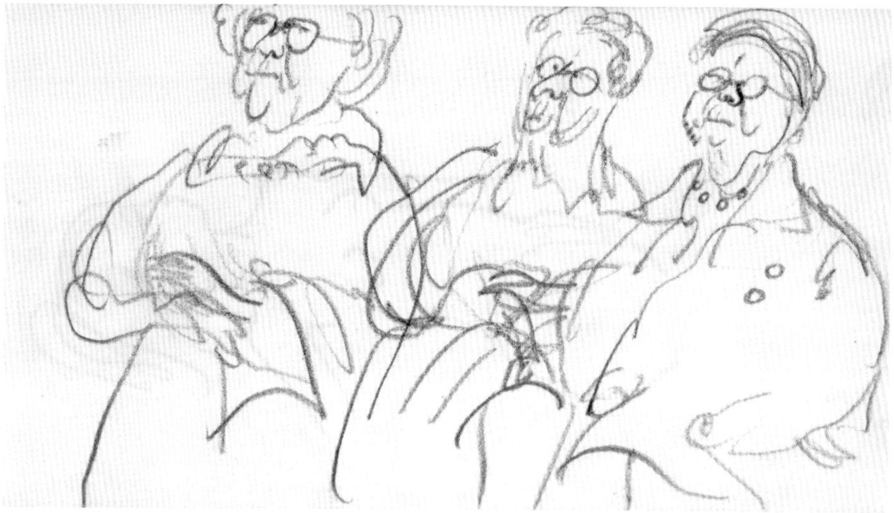

240 TOURISTS AT A LEFT BANK CLUB
pencil
3 ¾ x 6 ¾ inches
Preliminary drawing for *Punch*, 4 May 1960, page 625

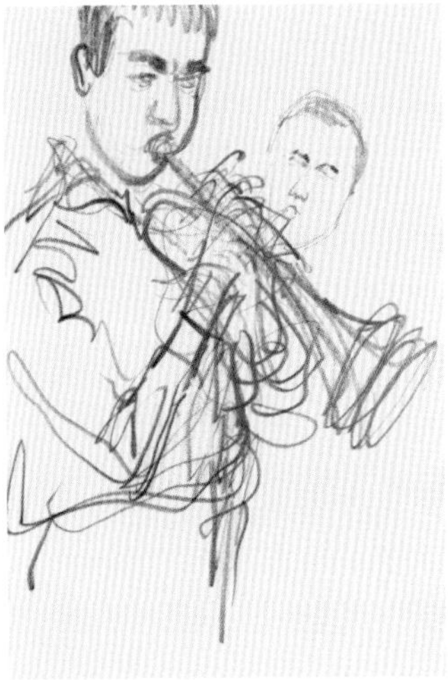

241 TRUMPET
pencil drawing of a trombone player on reverse
pencil
6 ½ x 4 ¾ inches

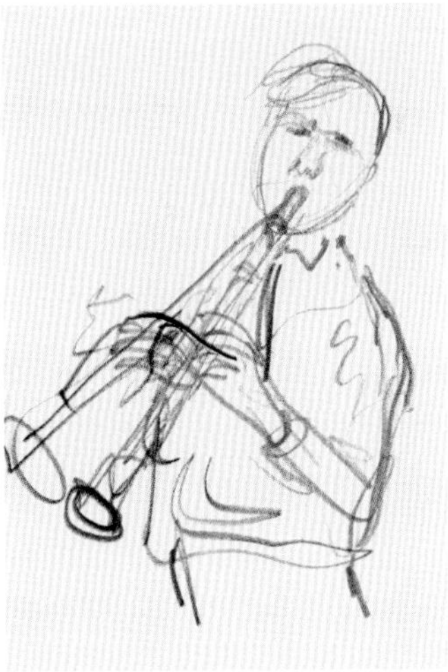

242 CLARINET
pencil drawing of two women in a jazz club on reverse
pencil
5 ½ x 4 ½ inches

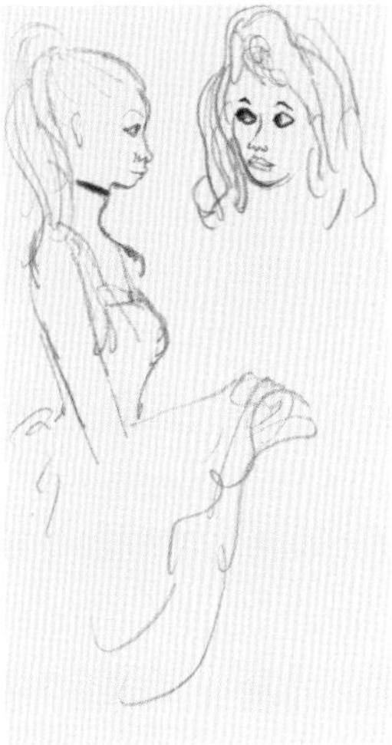

243 DANCERS (I)
pencil
6 ½ x 3 ¾ inches

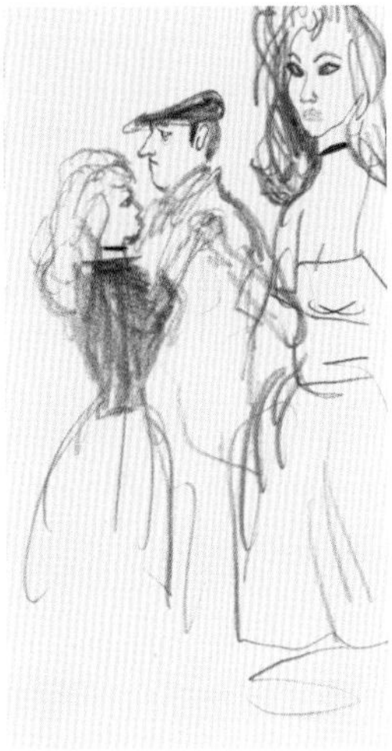

244 DANCERS (II)
pencil
6 ½ x 3 ¾ inches

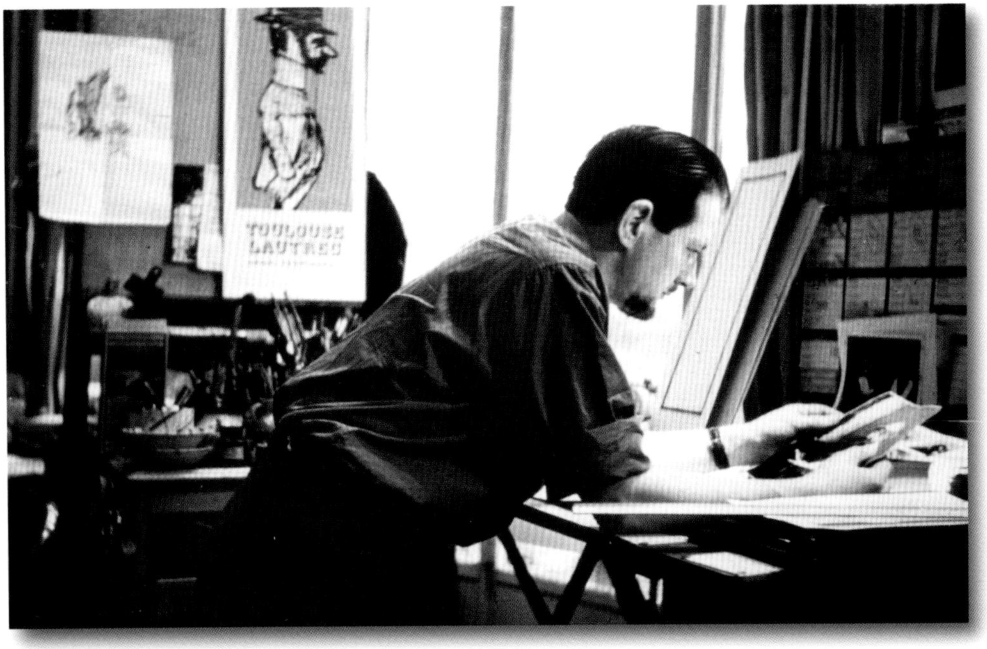

Ronald Searle in his studio, looking at images of Toulouse-Lautrec, 1959

3: LETTERS AND CARDS TO JEAN ELLSMOOR

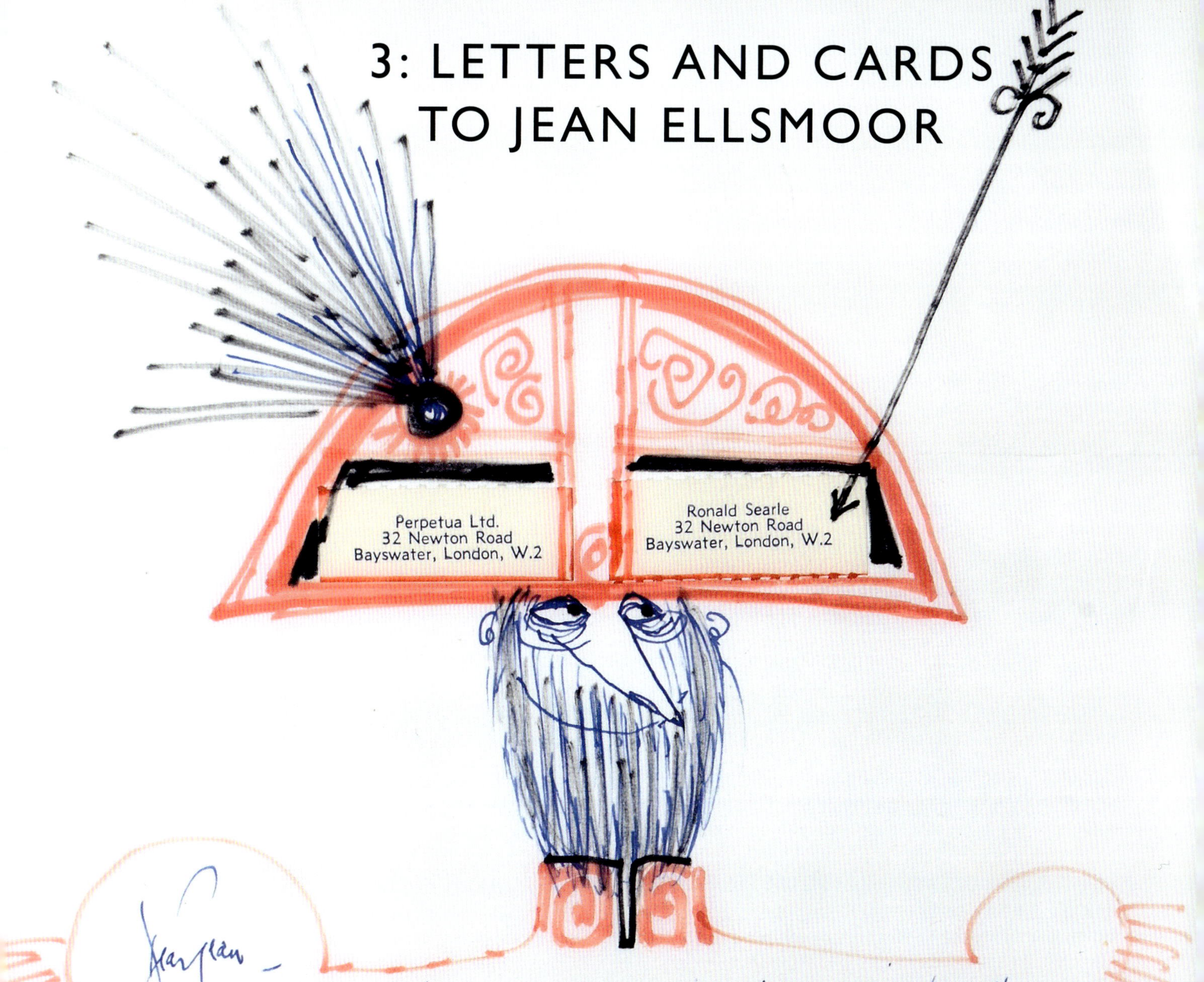

Dear Jean –

I love my stick-ons. What a bright idea – I'll try not to use them excessively – but there is an awful temptation to reach for the little leather cases and slap one on whatever is handy. I was thinking ... my forehead for simple identification. Kaye loved her

Jean Ellsmoor was Ronald Searle's secretary – in one capacity or another – for over 20 years, from 1956 to 1977. As is evidenced by the letters, he shared with her many details of his life, and relied on her to ensure that his work ran smoothly. In addition to a general secretarial role, she was involved in Searle's publishing company, Perpetua Books, and edited two of its publications for the series, 'Art and Destiny': Humphrey Hare's translations of Henri Perruchot's *Manet* (1962) and *La Vie de Gauguin* (1963). After 1977, she continued to work as an editor, and especially of art books.

During her time with Searle, Jean Ellsmoor and her husband, Brian, lived at Noirmont, The Heath, Weybridge, Surrey, and then, from 1961, at 1 Child's Walk, London SW5. Brian was an architect, who studied at the Bartlett School of Architecture, University of London, and worked for three London practices: Elliott Cox and Partners (until 1958), Stewart Hendry & Smith (in the 1970s and 80s) and Lawrence & Wrightson (as a consultant from 1990).

Searle's letters to Jean comprise a remarkable record of the period from his becoming a properly international artist (his first visit to the United States in 1957) to his moving to his final home, in Tourtour, in the Haute-Provence (in 1977). It was her dedication and efficiency that enabled him to travel regularly and widely, and yet maintain his existing commitments at home. For instance, while he was on that first trip to the USA, working on an animated film, Jean was back in London liaising with publishers and other companies, and sending him material for other projects: Lemon Hart, St Trinian's, Longanesi, etcetera.

Jean became all the more indispensable from the autumn of 1961, when Searle left his wife, Kaye, and their children, to begin a new life in France with Monica Koenig. In continuing to run his office, she helped to provide him with an income at a time when money was at its most short, while also rationalising operations: sending on his reference material, and disposing of unfinished artwork and redundant files.

Increasingly, Jean became a friend, both to Ronald and to Mô, who often added her own *post scriptum* to his letters. Their topics of correspondence became more personal, and cards and presents passed between them. Occasionally they met up – both in London and Paris – though this seems to have come to an end even before the Searles settled in Tourtour. Certainly, and inevitably, Ronald became preoccupied by Monica's physical state, following the diagnosis of a combination of cancers late in the 1960s. Then, in 1977, an astronomical rise in the rent on their Paris apartment – at 4 rue Antoine-Dubois – encouraged a permanent move south. However, the last letter to Jean, in this extant correspondence, remains as affectionate as ever.

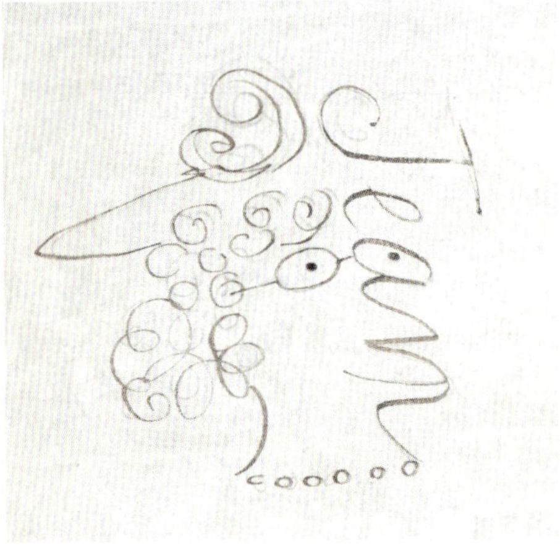

245 JEAN
pen and ink
3 x 3 inches
Provenance: Jean Ellsmoor

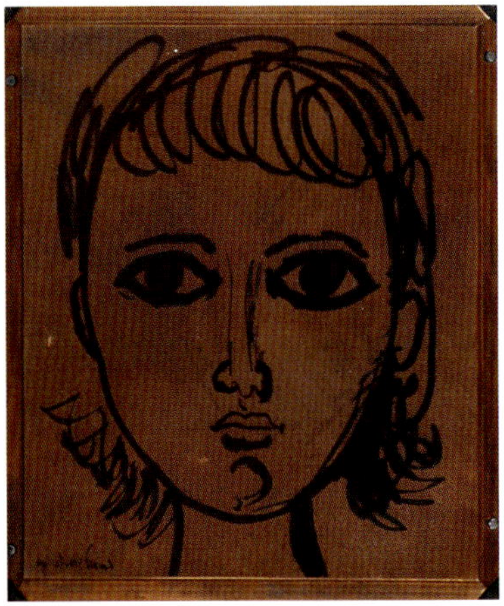

246 JEAN ELLSMOOR
printer's block
4 ¼ x 3 ½ inches

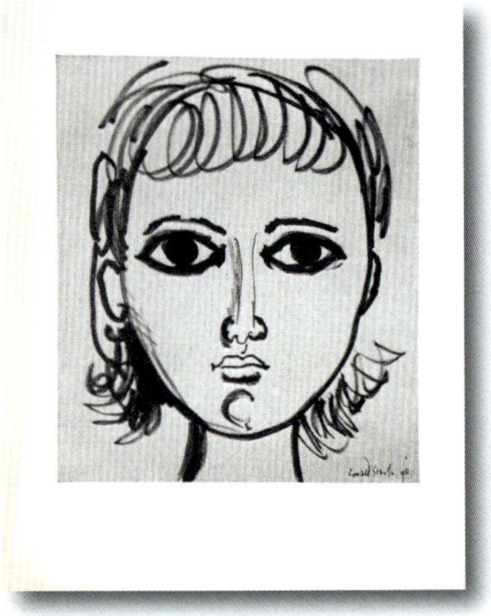

Copy of Brian and Jean Ellsmoor's Christmas card for 1957 with image by Ronald Searle

247 LETTER TO JEAN ELLSMOOR
MONDAY AM, MARCH 1956
(not illustrated)
autographed signed letter
written in pen and ink
on one side of a picture post card
5 ¾ x 4 inches

248 MERRIER THAN THIS I MEAN
inscribed with title and 'Jean and Brian'
pen and ink on printed Christmas card
7 x 8 inches
Provenance: Jean Ellsmoor

For transcriptions of these letters, see pages 161-199

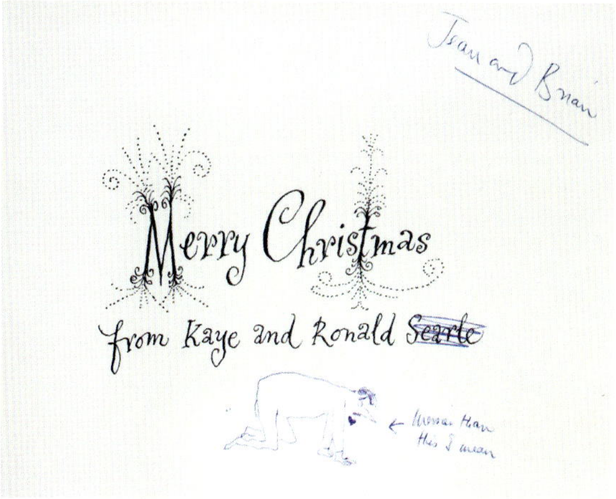

249 LETTER TO JEAN ELLSMOOR
WEDNESDAY, 12 DECEMBER 1956
autographed signed letter
written in pen and ink
on one side of one sheet
10 x 8 inches
includes pen and ink drawings
[with stamped addressed envelope]

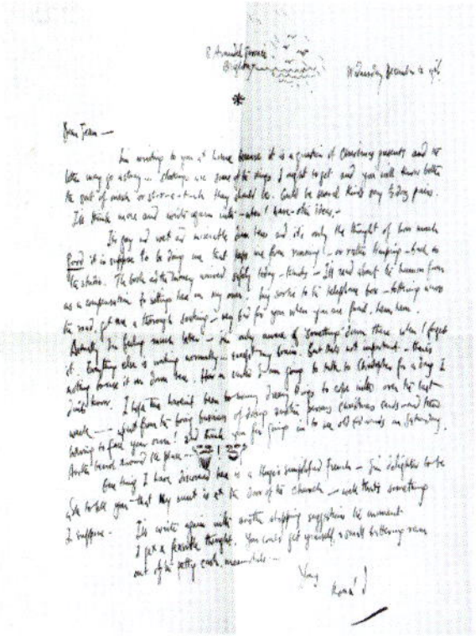

250 LETTER TO JEAN ELLSMOOR
SATURDAY, 15 DECEMBER 1956
autographed signed letter
written in pen and ink
on one side of one sheet
10 x 8 inches
includes a pen and ink drawing

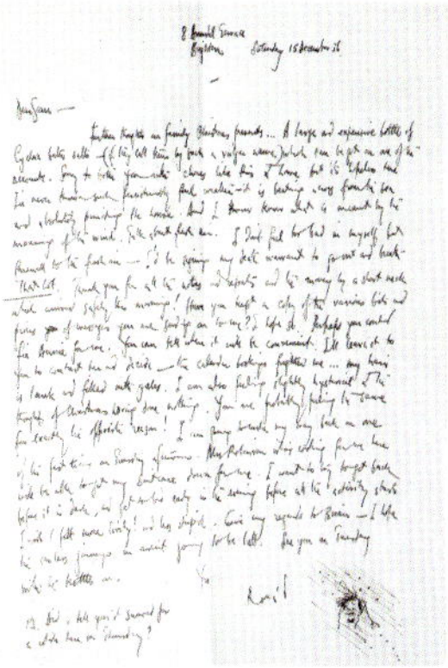

251 LETTER TO JEAN ELLSMOOR
PARIS, WEDNESDAY
JANUARY 1957
(not illustrated)
autographed signed letter
written in pen and ink
on one side of a picture post card
5 ¾ x 4 inches

252 TYPED LETTER TO JEAN ELLSMOOR
SATURDAY NIGHT, 18 MAY 1957
(not illustrated)
signed
typed letter
on four sides of four sheets
9 ½ x 6 inches

253 TYPED LETTER TO JEAN ELLSMOOR
SUNDAY 2 JUNE
(not illustrated)
signed
typed letter
on two sides of two sheets
9 ½ x 6 inches
[with stamped addressed envelope]

254 TYPED LETTER TO JEAN ELLSMOOR
MONDAY 10 JUNE 1957
signed
typed letter
on two sides of one sheet
9 ½ x 6 inches
includes a pen and ink drawing
[with stamped addressed envelope]

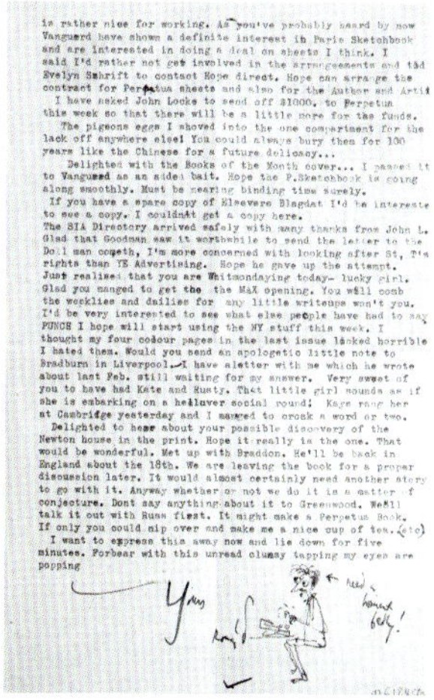

is rather nice for working. As you've probably heard by now Vanguard have shown a definite interest in Paris Sketchbook and are interested in doing a deal on sheets I think. I said I'd rather not get involved in the arrangements and tód Evelyn Shrift to contact Hope direct. Hope can arrange the contract for Perpetua sheets and also for the Author and Artist

I have asked John Locke to send off $1000. to Perpetua this week so that there will be a little more for the funds.

The pigeons eggs I shoved into the one compartment for the lack off anywhere else! You could always bury them for 100 years like the Chinese for a future delicacy...

Delighted with the Books of the Month cover... I passed it to Vanguard as an added bait. Hope the P.Sketchbook is going along smoothly. Must be nearing binding time surely.

If you have a spare copy of Elsevere Blagdat I'd be intereste to see a copy. I couldnAt get a copy here.

The SIA Directory arrived safely with many thanks from John L. Glad that Goodman saw it worthwhile to send the letter to the Doll man cometh, I'm more concerned with looking after St, T's rights than YE Advertising. Hope he gave up the attempt. Just realised that you are Whitmondaying today- lucky girl. Glad you manged to get the the MAX opening. You will comb the weeklies and dailies for any little writeups won't you. I'd be very interested to see what else people have had to say PUNCH I hope will start using the NY stuff this week. I thought my four codour pages in the last issue looked horrible I hated them. Would you send an apologetic little note to Bradburn in Liverpool. I have aletter with me which he wrote about last Feb. still waiting for my answer. Very sweet of you to have had Kate and Rusty. That little girl sounds as if she is embarking on a helluver social round! Kaye rang her at Cambridge yesterday and I manged to croak a word or two.

Delighted to hear about your possible discovery of the Newton house in the print. Hope it really is the one. That would be wonderful. Met up with Braddon. He'll be back in England about the 18th. We are leaving the book for a proper discussion later. It would almost certainly need another story to go with it. Anyway whether or not we do it is a matter of conjecture. Dont say anything about it to Greenwood. We'll talk it out with Russ first. It might make a Perpetua Book. If only you could nip over and make me a nice cup of tea. (etc)

I want to express this away now and lie down for five minutes. Forbear with this unread clumsy tapping my eyes are popping

Yours
Ronald

255 LETTER TO
JEAN ELLSMOOR
DIRLETON, NORTH
BERWICK, MONDAY 1959
(not illustrated)
autographed signed letter
written in pen and ink
on one side of a picture post card
5 ¾ x 3 ¾ inches

256 LETTER TO
JEAN ELLSMOOR
MIDNIGHT MONDAY
(not illustrated)
autographed signed letter
written in pen and ink
on one side of a picture post card
5 ¼ x 3 ¼ inches

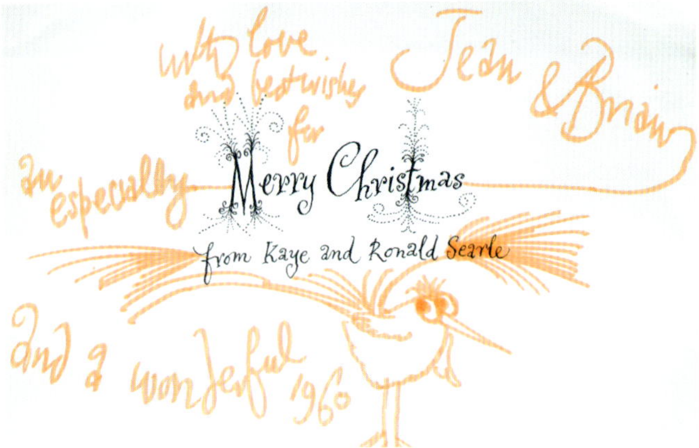

257 CHRISTMAS BIRD
inscribed 'Jean & Brian, with love
and best wishes for, an especially,
and a wonderful 1960'
coloured ink on printed
Christmas card
7 x 10 ¼ inches
Provenance: Jean Ellsmoor

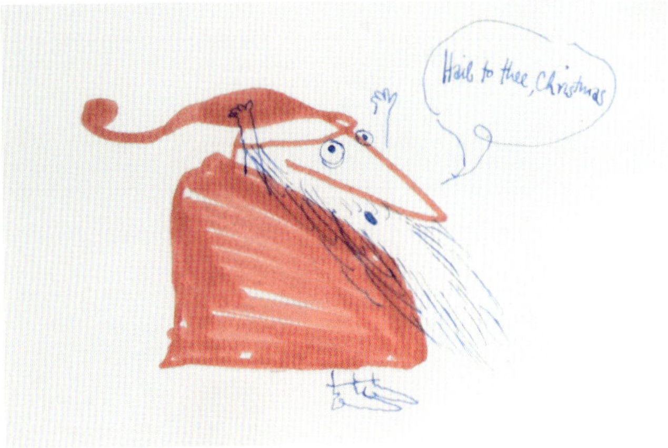

258 HAIL TO THEE,
CHRISTMAS
inscribed 'Hail to thee, Christmas'
inscribed 'Brian & Jean with
Happy Christmas Wishes & Best
Love for a Wonderful 1960,
Kaye, Kate, John & Ronald' on
reverse
pen ink and coloured ink on
printed Christmas card
6 ½ x 8 inches
Provenance: Jean Ellsmoor

259 LETTER TO JEAN
ELLSMOOR
JANUARY 1960
(not illustrated)
autographed signed letter
written in pen and ink
on one side of a picture post card
3 ¾ x 5 ¾ inches
includes a pen and ink drawing

260 LETTER TO
JEAN ELLSMOOR
WEDNESDAY 10 FEBRUARY
[1960]
(not illustrated)
autographed signed letter
written in pen and ink
on one side of a picture post card
5 ¼ x 3 ¼ inches

261 LETTER TO
JEAN ELLSMOOR
NEW YORK, FRIDAY 1960
(not illustrated)
autographed signed letter
written in pen and ink
on one side of a picture post card
3 ½ x 5 ½ inches

262 SALT LAKE CITY,
MONDAY 10 OCTOBER
[1960]
(not illustrated)
autographed signed letter
written in pen and ink
on one side of a picture post card
3 ¼ x 5 ¼ inches

263 TYPED LETTER TO
JEAN ELLSMOOR
FRIDAY 21 OCTOBER 1960
(not illustrated)
signed
typed letter
on two sides of one sheet
6 ¾ x 5 ¼ inches folded
[with stamped addressed envelope]

265 LETTER TO JEAN ELLSMOOR
BEIRUT, WEDNESDAY [1961]
(not illustrated)
autographed signed letter
written in pen and ink
on one side of a picture post card
5 ¼ x 3 ¾ inches

266 LETTER TO JEAN ELLSMOOR
JERUSALEM, SATURDAY [1961]
(not illustrated)
autographed signed letter
written in pen and ink
on one side of a picture post card
5 ¾ x 4 inches

267 LETTER TO JEAN ELLSMOOR
JERUSALEM, TUESDAY 11 APRIL [1961]
(not illustrated)
autographed signed letter
written in pen and ink
on one side of a picture post card
5 ½ x 3 ½ inches

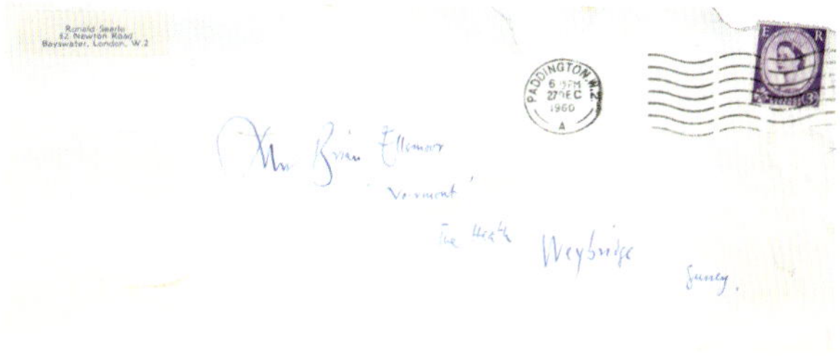

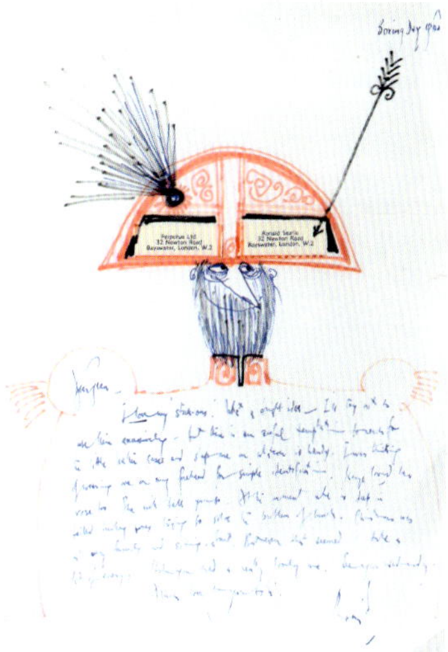

264 LETTER TO JEAN ELLSMOOR
BOXING DAY 1960
signed
autographed signed letter
written in pen and ink
on one side of one sheet
9 ¾ x 7 ¾ inches
includes a pen ink and coloured ink drawing
[with stamped addressed envelope]

269 LETTER TO JEAN ELLSMOOR
LATE THURSDAY NIGHT
(not illustrated)
signed
autographed signed letter
written in pen and ink
on two sides of one sheet
10 ¼ x 7 ¼ inches
[with stamped addressed envelope]

270 TYPED LETTER TO JEAN ELLSMOOR
SATURDAY 3 JUNE 1961
(not illustrated)
signed and inscribed
typed letter
on two sides of one sheet
10 ¼ x 7 ¼ inches
[with stamped addressed envelope]

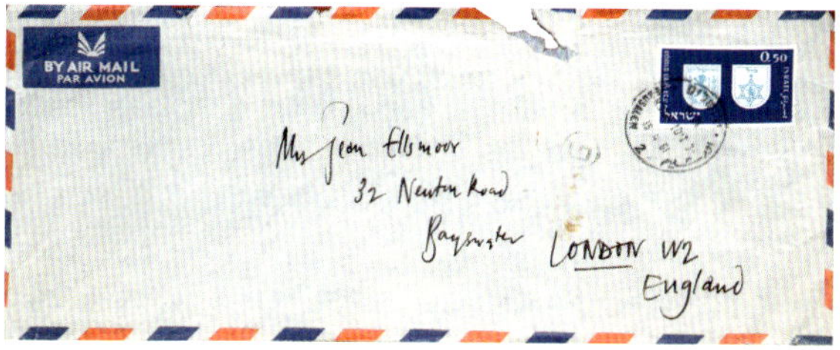

BY AIR MAIL
PAR AVION

Mrs Jean Ellsmoor
32 Newton Road
Bayswater LONDON W2
England

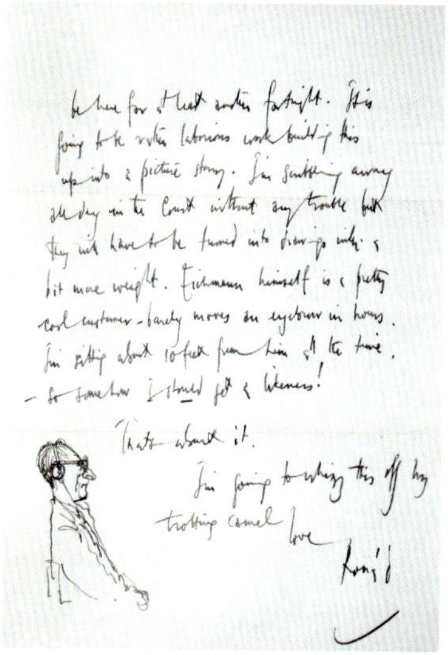

be here for at least another fortnight. It is going to be rather laborious work building this up into a picture story. I'm scribbling away all day in the Court without any trouble but they will have to be turned into drawings with a bit more weight. Eichmann himself is a pretty cool customer - barely moves an eyebrow in hours. I'm sitting about 10 feet from him all the time. - so somehow I should get a likeness!

That's about it.

I'm going to whizz this off by trotting camel

love

Ronald

268 LETTER TO JEAN ELLSMOOR
JERUSALEM, ISRAEL, FRIDAY 14 APRIL
autographed signed letter
written in pen and ink
on two sides of one sheet
9 x 7 inches
Similar to a drawing for *Life*, 30 June 1961, page 30, 'Newsfronts of the World'
includes a pen and ink drawing of Adolf Eichmann
[with stamped addressed envelope]

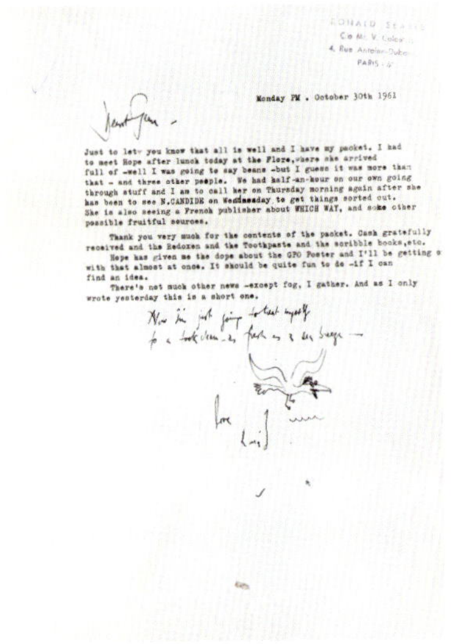
RONALD SEARLE
C/o Mr. V. Coloutsis
4, Rue Antoine-Dubois
PARIS - 6e

Monday PM . October 30th 1961

Just to let you know that all is well and I have my packet. I had to meet Hope after lunch today at the Flore, where she arrived full of -well I was going to say beans -but I guess it was more than that - and three other people. We had half-an-hour on our own going through stuff and I am to call her on Thursday morning again after she has been to see N.CANDIDE on Wednesday to get things sorted out. She is also seeing a French publisher about WHICH WAY, and some other possible fruitful sources.

Thank you very much for the contents of the packet. Cash gratefully received and the Redoxen and the Toothpaste and the scribble books, etc.

Hope has given me the dope about the GPO Poster and I'll be getting on with that almost at once. It should be quite fun to do -if I can find an idea.

There's not much other news -except fog, I gather. And as I only wrote yesterday this is a short one.

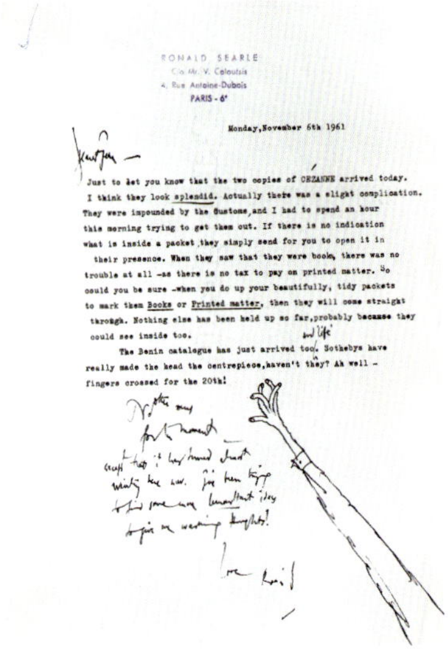
RONALD SEARLE
C/o Mr. V. Coloutsis
4, Rue Antoine-Dubois
PARIS - 6e

Monday, November 6th 1961

Just to let you know that the two copies of CEZANNE arrived today. I think they look splendid. Actually there was a slight complication. They were impounded by the Customs, and I had to spend an hour this morning trying to get them out. If there is no indication what is inside a packet, they simply send for you to open it in their presence. When they saw that they were books, there was no trouble at all -as there is no tax to pay on printed matter. So could you be sure -when you do up your beautifully, tidy packets to mark them Books or Printed matter, then they will come straight through. Nothing else has been held up so far, probably because they could see inside too.

The Benin catalogue has just arrived too. Sothebys have really made the head the centrepiece, haven't they? Ah well - fingers crossed for the 20th!

271 LETTER TO JEAN ELLSMOOR TUESDAY 26 SEPTEMBER 1961 (not illustrated)
signed
autographed signed letter
written in pen and ink
on two sides of one sheet
10 ¼ x 7 ¼ inches
[with stamped addressed envelope]

272 TYPED LETTER TO JEAN ELLSMOOR MONDAY 30 OCTOBER 1961
signed
typed letter
on one side of one sheet
10 ¼ x 8 inches
includes a pen and ink drawing

273 TYPED LETTER TO JEAN ELLSMOOR MONDAY 6 NOVEMBER 1961
signed and inscribed
typed letter
on one side of one sheet
10 ¼ x 8 inches
includes a pen and ink drawing

274 TYPED LETTER TO JEAN ELLSMOOR THURSDAY AFTERNOON, 16 NOVEMBER 1961
(not illustrated)
signed and inscribed
typed letter
on one side of two sheets
10 ¼ x 8 inches

276 NOEL
pen ink, watercolour and bodycolour
7 ½ x 5 inches
Provenance: Jean Ellsmoor
A Christmas card sent to Jean Ellsmoor, Christmas 1961

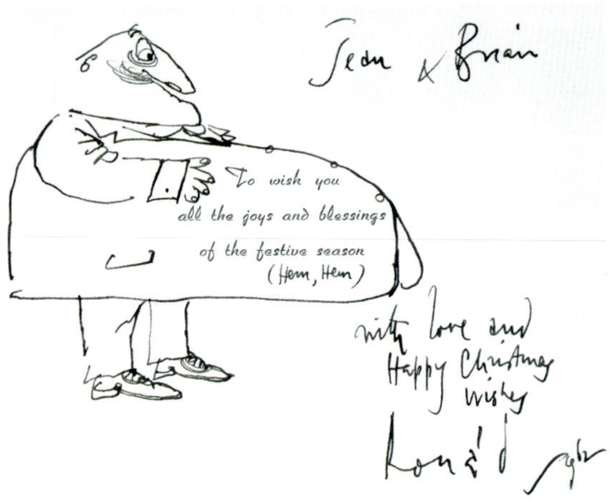

275 HEM, HEM
signed and inscribed 'Jean & Brian, with love and Happy Christmas wishes' and '(Hem, Hem)'
pen and ink on printed Christmas card
4 ¾ x 5 ¾ inches
Provenance: Jean Ellsmoor

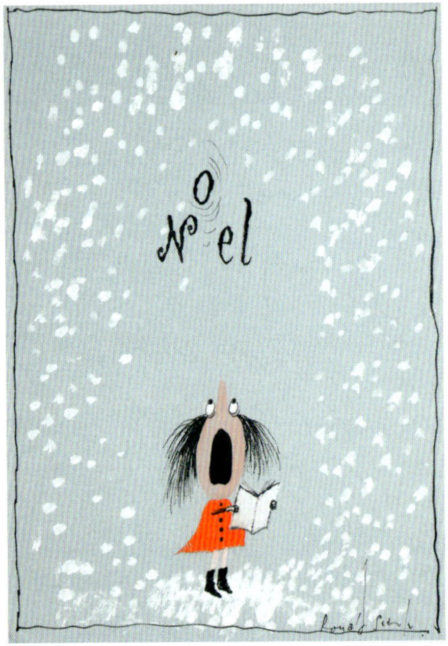

277 TYPED LETTER TO
JEAN ELLSMOOR
WEDNESDAY
27 DECEMBER 1961
(not illustrated)
signed and inscribed
typed letter
on one side of one sheet
10 ¼ x 8 inches

278 TYPED LETTER TO
JEAN ELLSMOOR
WEDNESDAY PM,
9 MAY 1962
(not illustrated)
inscribed
typed letter
on one side of one sheet
10 ¾ x 8 ¼ inches

279 TYPED LETTER TO
JEAN ELLSMOOR
SATURDAY 9 JUNE 1962
signed and inscribed
typed letter
on one side of one sheet
10 ¼ x 8 inches
includes a pen and
ink drawing

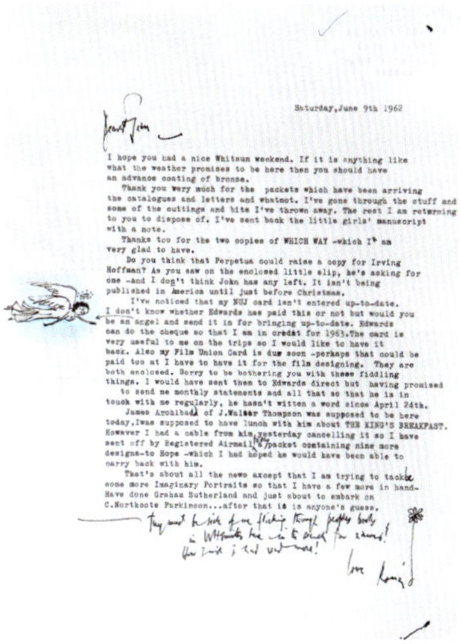

Saturday,June 9th 1962

I hope you had a nice Whitsun weekend. If it is anything like what the weather promises to be here then you should have an advance coating of bronze.

Thank you very much for the packets which have been arriving the catalogues and letters and whatnot. I've gone through the stuff and some of the cuttings and bits I've thrown away. The rest I am returning to you to dispose of. I've sent back the little girls' manuscript with a note.

Thanks too for the two copies of WHICH WAY -which I am very glad to have.

Do you think that Perpetua could raise a copy for Irving Hoffman? As you saw on the enclosed little slip, he's asking for one -and I don't think John has any left. It isn't being published in America until just before Christmas.

I've noticed that my NUJ card isn't entered up-to-date. I don't know whether Edwards has paid this or not but would you be an angel and send it in for bringing up-to-date. Edwards can do the cheque so that I am in credit for 1963.The card is very useful to me on the trips so I would like to have it back. Also my Film Union Card is due soon -perhaps that could be paid too as I have to have it for the film designing. They are both enclosed. Sorry to be bothering you with these fiddling things. I would have sent them to Edwards direct but having promised to send me monthly statements and all that so that he is in touch with me regularly, he hasn't witten a word since April 24th.

James Archibald of J.Walter Thompson was supposed to be here today,Iwas supposed to have lunch with him about THE KING'S BREAKFAST. However I had a cable from him yesterday cancelling it so I have sent off by Registered Airmail a packet containing nine more designs-to Hope -which I had hoped he would have been able to carry back with him.

That's about all the news except that I am trying to tackle some more Imaginary Portraits so that I have a few more in hand-Have done Graham Sutherland and just about to embark on C.Northcote Parkinson...after that it is anyone's guess.

280 TYPED LETTER TO
JEAN ELLSMOOR
FRIDAY PM, 6 JULY 1962
(not illustrated)
signed and inscribed
typed letter
on one side of two sheets
10 ¼ x 8 inches

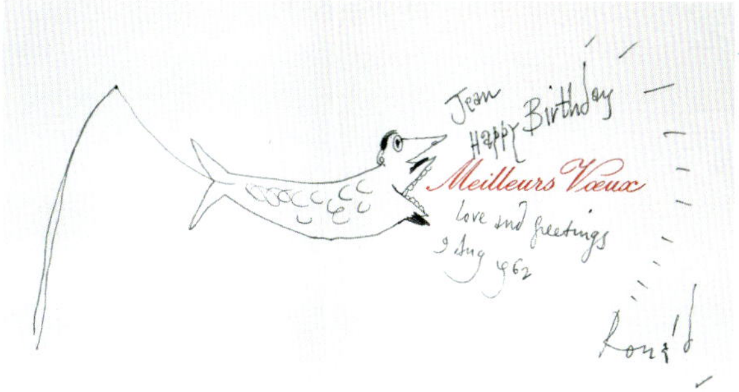

281 BIRTHDAY FISH
signed, inscribed 'Jean, Happy Birthday, love and greetings' and dated '9 Aug 1962'
pen and ink on printer paper
5 ½ x 10 inches
Provenance: Jean Ellsmoor

282 LETTER TO
JEAN ELLSMOOR
BAYREUTH, WEDNESDAY
17 OCTOBER 1962
(not illustrated)
autographed signed letter
written in pen and ink
on one side of a picture post card
5 ¾ x 4 inches

283 A WARM HEARTH
signed, inscribed 'With love to you both for a Happy Move Happy Home a warm Hearth and all nice things' and 'PS just a Symbol of course – Olde Englishe' and dated '19 November 1962'
inscribed 'Jean & Brian' on reverse
pen and ink with coloured pencil
on greetings card
7 x 10 inches
Provenance: Jean Ellsmoor

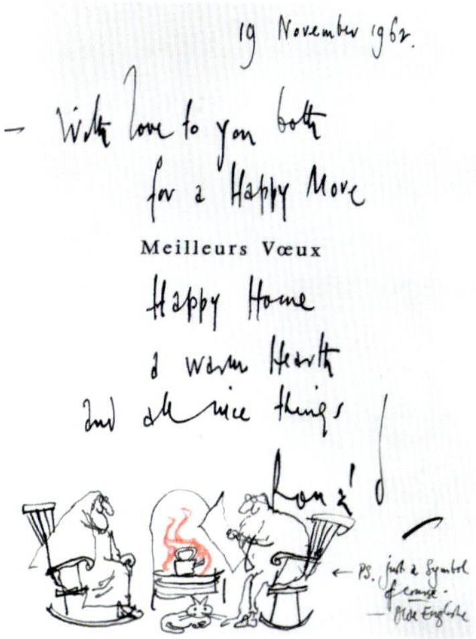

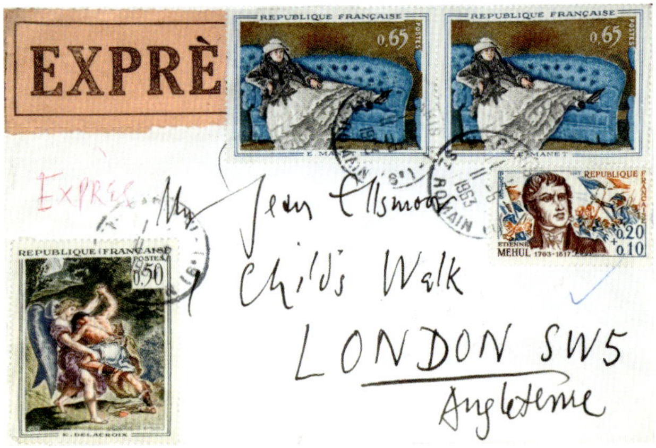

287 LETTER TO
JEAN ELLSMOOR
MONDAY NIGHT,
10 JUNE 1963
signed and inscribed
typed letter
on one side of one sheet
10 ½ x 8 inches
includes a pen and ink drawing
[with stamped addressed envelope]

284-286, 288, 290-308, 310-316 & **318-321** are not illustrated

289 LETTER TO JEAN
ELLSMOOR
TUESDAY, 9 JULY 1963
signed and inscribed
typed letter
on one side of one sheet
10 ¼ x 8 inches
includes a pen and ink drawing
[with stamped addressed
envelope]

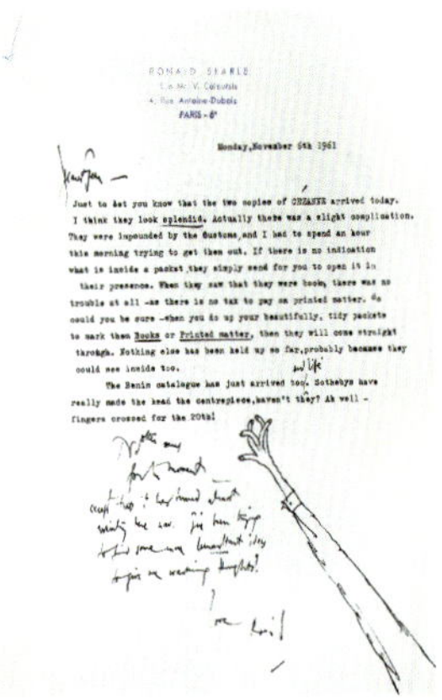
RONALD SEARLE
4, Rue Antoine-Dubois
PARIS - 6e

Monday, November 6th 1961

Just to let you know that the two copies of CEZANNE arrived today. I think they look splendid. Actually there was a slight complication. They were impounded by the Customs, and I had to spend an hour this morning trying to get them out. If there is no indication what is inside a packet, they simply send for you to open it in their presence. When they saw that they were books, there was no trouble at all – as there is no tax to pay on printed matter. So could you be sure – when you do up your beautifully, tidy packets to mark them Books or Printed matter, then they will come straight through. Nothing else has been held up so far, probably because they could see inside too.

The Benin catalogue has just arrived too. Sothebys have really made the head the centrepiece, haven't they? Ah well – fingers crossed for the 20th!

284 LETTER TO
JEAN ELLSMOOR
ASHLEY FALLS, SATURDAY
2 MARCH 1963
autographed signed letter
further signed and inscribed by
Monica Searle
written in pen and ink
on one side of a picture post card
3 ½ x 5 ¼ inches
[with stamped addressed envelope]

285 LETTER TO
JEAN ELLSMOOR
PHOENIX, ARIZONA,
8 MARCH 1963
autographed signed letter
written in pen and ink
on one side of a picture post card
5 ½ x 3 ½ inches

286 LETTER TO
JEAN ELLSMOOR
ULM – DONAU,
SUNDAY 16 JUNE 1963
autographed signed letter
further signed and inscribed by
Monica Searle
inscribed 'Never mind perhaps
ye rain wille stoppe soone'
on reverse
written in pen and ink
on one side of a picture post card
5 ¾ x 4 inches

288 LETTER TO
JEAN ELLSMOOR
COLOGNE, TUESDAY
2 JULY 1963
(not illustrated)
autographed signed letter
inscribed 'Having a lovely time!' on
reverse
on one side of a picture post card
5 ¾ x 4 inches

290 LETTER TO
JEAN ELLSMOOR
MADISON, 7 JANUARY 1964
signed
autographed signed letter
written in pen and ink
on three sides of three sheets
10 ¼ x 8 inches
[with stamped addressed envelope]

291 LETTER TO
JEAN ELLSMOOR
BAYREUTH, THURSDAY
21 MAY 1964
autographed signed letter
further signed and inscribed by
Monica Searle
written in pen and ink
on one side of a picture post card
5 ¾ x 4 inches

292 LETTER TO
JEAN ELLSMOOR
LE CANADEL, SUNDAY 27
SEPTEMBER 1964
autographed signed letter
further signed and inscribed by
Monica Searle
written in pen and ink
on one side of a picture post card
5 ¼ x 3 ¼ inches

293 LETTER TO
JEAN ELLSMOOR
BERLIN, SATURDAY 24
OCTOBER 1964
autographed signed letter
written in pen and ink
on one side of a picture post card
5 ¾ x 3 ¾ inches

294 LETTER TO
JEAN ELLSMOOR
PARIS, SUNDAY
signed and inscribed
typed letter
on one side of a picture post card
5 ½ x 4 inches

295 LETTER TO
JEAN ELLSMOOR
BOXING DAY 1964
signed
autographed signed letter
written in pen and ink
on one side of one sheet
10 ¼ x 8 inches
[with stamped addressed envelope]

296 LETTER TO
JEAN ELLSMOOR
HONOLULU, 17 FEBRUARY
1965
autographed signed letter
further signed and inscribed by
Monica Searle
written in pen and ink
on one side of a picture post card
5 ½ x 3 ¼ inches

297 LETTER TO
JEAN ELLSMOOR
SUNDAY, 25 APRIL 1965
signed and inscribed
further inscribed by Monica Searle
typed letter
on two sides of one sheet
10 ½ x 8 ¼ inches

298 LETTER TO
JEAN ELLSMOOR
TUESDAY, 18 MAY 1965
signed and inscribed
further inscribed by Monica Searle
typed letter
on three sides of three sheets
10 ½ x 8 ¼ inches

299 LETTER TO
JEAN ELLSMOOR
TUESDAY, 8 JUNE 1965
signed and inscribed
typed letter
on one side of 'A La Cheminee de
ma Grand-Mere' greaseproof
wrapping paper
12 ¾ x 8 ½ inches

300 LETTER TO
JEAN ELLSMOOR
THURSDAY, 1 JULY 1965
signed and inscribed
typed letter
on two sides of two sheets
10 ½ x 8 ¼ inches

301 LETTER TO
JEAN ELLSMOOR
SUNDAY AFTERNOON,
24 OCTOBER 1965
signed and inscribed
typed letter
on four sides of four sheets
10 ½ x 8 ¼ inches
[with stamped addressed envelope]

302 LETTER TO
JEAN ELLSMOOR
SATURDAY 19 MARCH 1966
signed and inscribed
typed letter
on two sides of two sheets
10 ¼ x 8 inches

303 LETTER TO
JEAN ELLSMOOR
GOOD FRIDAY, 1966
signed and inscribed
further inscribed by Monica Searle
typed letter
on three sides of three sheets
10 ½ x 8 inches

304 LETTER TO
JEAN ELLSMOOR
NEW YORK, 14 FEBRUARY
1967
autographed signed letter
further signed and inscribed by
Monica Searle
written in pen and ink
on one side of a picture post card
5 ½ x 3 ¼ inches

305 LETTER TO
JEAN ELLSMOOR
SUNDAY NIGHT,
19 FEBRUARY 1967
signed and inscribed
further inscribed by Monica Searle
typed letter
on one side of one sheet
8 x 5 inches
[with stamped addressed envelope]

306 LETTER TO
JEAN ELLSMOOR
THURSDAY 19 JULY 1967
signed and inscribed
typed letter
on two sides of two sheets
10 ¼ x 8 ¼ inches
[with stamped addressed
envelope]

307 LETTER TO
JEAN ELLSMOOR
PARIS, SUNDAY 5
NOVEMBER 1967
autographed signed letter
written in pen and ink
on one side of a picture post card
5 ¾ x 4 inches

308 LETTER TO
JEAN ELLSMOOR
TUESDAY 29 FEBRUARY 1968
autographed signed letter
written in coloured ink
on one side of a picture post card
6 x 4 inches

310 LETTER TO
JEAN ELLSMOOR
PARIS, BOXING DAY 1970
autographed signed letter
written in pen and ink
on one side of a picture post card
5 ¾ x 4 inches

311 LETTER TO
JEAN ELLSMOOR
PARIS, TUESDAY 20 JULY
1971
autographed signed letter
written in pen and ink
on two sides of two picture
post cards
each 4 x 5 ¾ inches

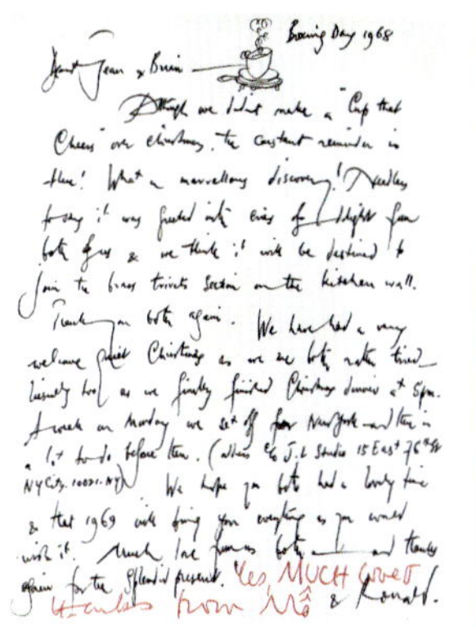

309 LETTER TO
JEAN ELLSMOOR
BOXING DAY 1968
autographed signed letter
further signed and inscribed by
Monica Searle
written in pen and ink
on one side of a picture post card
6 x 4 ¾ inches
includes a pen and ink drawing

312 LETTER TO
JEAN ELLSMOOR
WEDNESDAY, 18 AUGUST
1971
signed and inscribed
typed letter
on one side of one sheet
10 ¼ x 8 ¼ inches

313 LETTER TO
JEAN ELLSMOOR
WEDNESDAY NIGHT,
3 NOVEMBER 1971
signed and inscribed
typed letter
on three sides of three sheets
10 ¼ x 8 inches
[with stamped addressed envelope]

314 LETTER TO JEAN ELLSMOOR
PARIS, SATURDAY AFTERNOON
8 JULY [1972]
signed and inscribed
further signed and inscribed by
Monica Searle
typed letter
on one side of a picture
post card
5 ¾ x 4 inches

315 LETTER TO JEAN ELLSMOOR
MONDAY 6 AUGUST 1973
signed
typed letter
on one side of one sheet
11 ¾ x 8 inches
[with stamped addressed envelope]

316 LETTER TO JEAN ELLSMOOR
TUESDAY, 9 APRIL, 1974
signed and inscribed
typed letter
on two sides of one sheet
11 ½ x 8 ¼ inches
[with stamped addressed envelope]

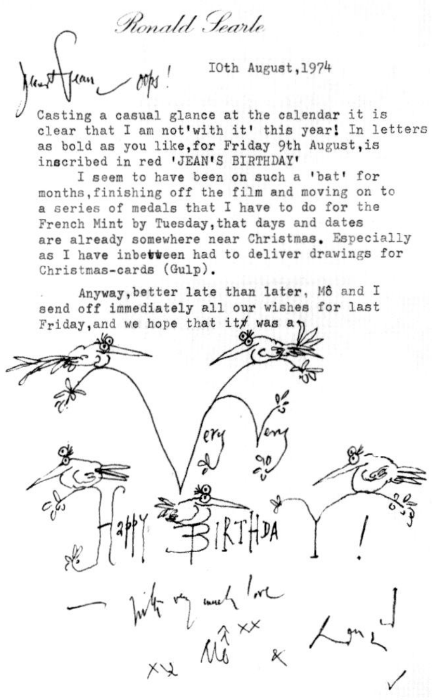
Ronald Searle

10th August,1974

Casting a casual glance at the calendar it is clear that I am not'with it' this year! In letters as bold as you like,for Friday 9th August,is inscribed in red 'JEAN'S BIRTHDAY'

I seem to have been on such a 'bat' for months,finishing off the film and moving on to a series of medals that I have to do for the French Mint by Tuesday,that days and dates are already somewhere near Christmas. Especially as I have inbetween had to deliver drawings for Christmas-cards (Gulp).

Anyway,better late than later, Mô and I send off immediately all our wishes for last Friday,and we hope that it was a

317 LETTER TO JEAN ELLSMOOR
10 AUGUST 1974
signed and inscribed
typed letter
on one side of one sheet
8 ¼ x 5 ½ inches
includes a pen and ink drawing
[with stamped addressed envelope]

318 LETTER TO JEAN ELLSMOOR
SUNDAY, 22 JUNE 1975
signed and inscribed
typed letter
on two sides of two sheets
11 ½ x 8 inches
[with stamped addressed envelope]

319 LETTER TO JEAN ELLSMOOR
SATURDAY 6 MARCH 1976
signed and inscribed
typed letter
on one side of a picture
post card
5 ¼ x 7 inches

320 LETTER TO JEAN ELLSMOOR
27 NOVEMBER 1976
signed and inscribed
typed letter
on one side of one sheet
3 ¾ x 5 ¾ inches
with a Christmas card signed and inscribed 'Jean & Brian, with love for a marvellous Christmas & everything you wish in the New Year 1977' and stamped with new address
further signed by Monica Searle
5 ¾ x 4 ¼ inches

321 LETTER TO JEAN ELLSMOOR
7 AUGUST 1977
signed and inscribed
typed letter
on two sides of two sheets
11 ½ x 8 ¼ inches
[with stamped addressed envelope]

4: 1960s-1980s

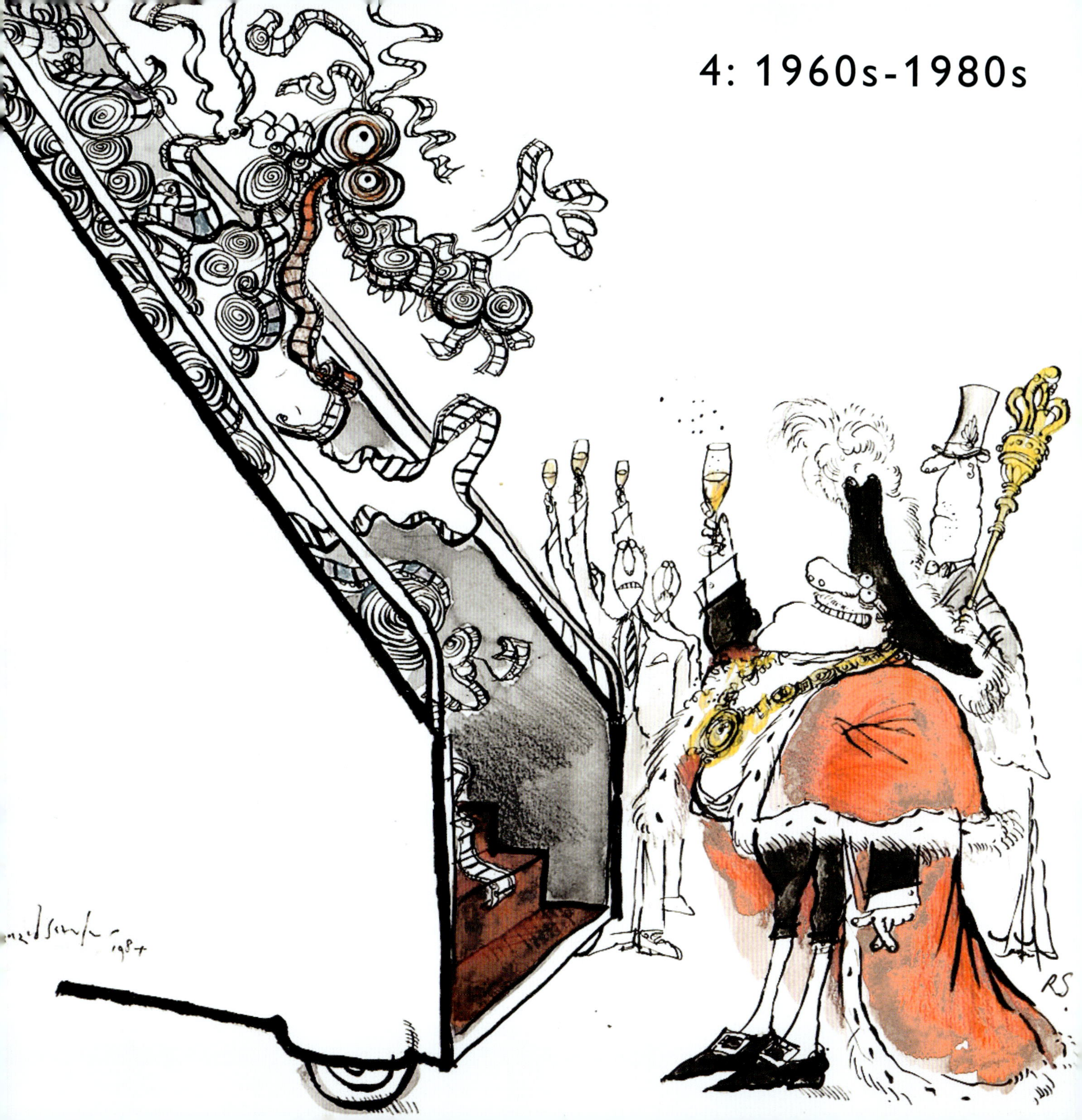

1958-70: Kate Searle's Autograph Book

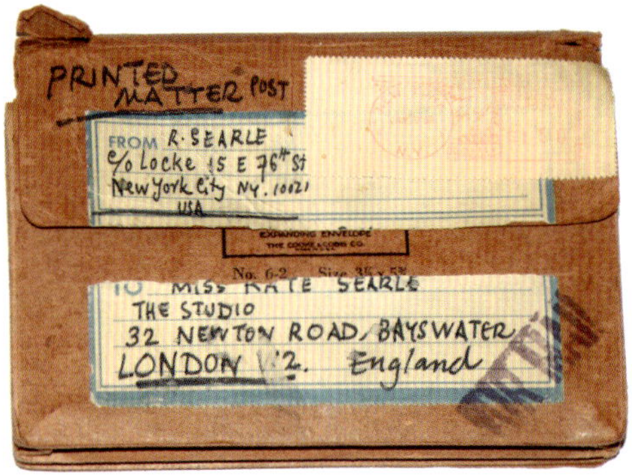

322 KATE SEARLE'S AUTOGRAPH BOOK
inscribed 'Kate Searle' on front cover
inscribed 'Kate Searle, 32 Newton Road, Bayswater, London W2, England' on front endpaper
inscribed 'This book belongs to Kate Searle with love from Daddy' and dated '17 July 1958' on title page
drawing of a St Trinian's girl opposite title page, inscribed 'The Happiest Days of Who's Life?'
3 ¾ x 5 ¼ inches
in an expanding envelope inscribed 'Printed Matter Post, [from] R Searle, c/o Locke 15 E 76th St, New York City NY 10021, USA' [to] 'Miss Kate Searle, The Studio, 32 Newton Road, Bayswater, London W2, England' and stamped 'New York, Jan 10 '69'

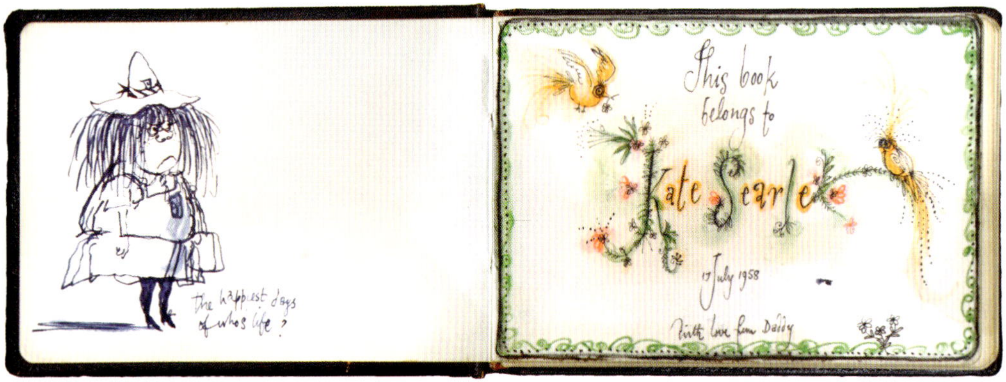

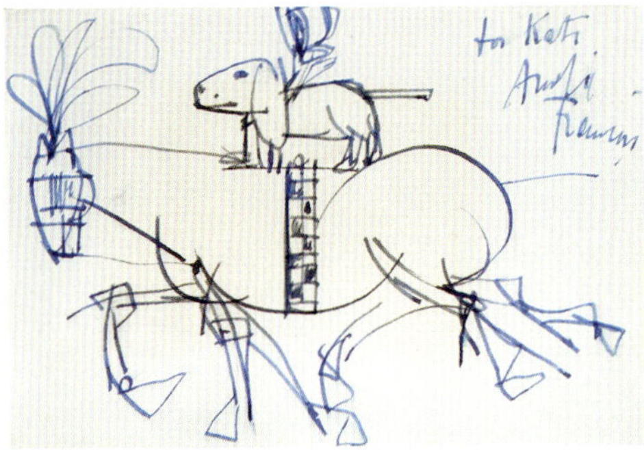

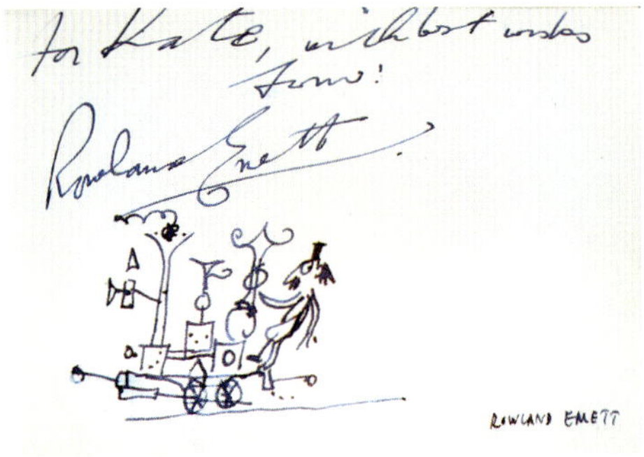

Kate Searle's Autograph Book

In 1958, Ronald Searle presented his 11-year-old daughter, Kate, with this autograph book, probably as a birthday present. Before he gave it to her, he wrote her name on the leather binding and her full address on the front endpaper, and created an elaborate dedication on the following page. At this time, or perhaps, a little later, he added a drawing of a St Trinian's schoolgirl opposite the dedication.

Between 1958 and 1970, Kate then collected autographs, often from members of her father's circle, some of which he annotated. Late in 1968, Searle took the book with him to New York, and returned it to Kate by post, as is evidenced by the accompanying 'expanding envelope', embellished with addresses written in his characteristic hand, and postmarked 'Jan 10 '69'.

The autographs include:

James Thurber (1894-1961), American writer and cartoonist
Searle met Thurber in London on 26 June 1958, when Thurber attended the *Punch* table. Ten days later, he asked for his autograph. In 1962, Searle would illustrate Thurber's *The Thirteen Clocks and The Wonderful O*. In 1983, he would produce a portrait medal of Thurber.
Wendy Toye (1917-2010), actress, dancer and director [see **328**]
André François (1915-2005), Hungarian-born French cartoonist
Searle first met his fellow *Punch* contributor, André François, in 1947. They developed a close friendship and mutual admiration. In 1960, Searle edited and introduced *The Biting Eye of André François* for his own publishing imprint, Perpetua Books. François included a characteristic drawing with his autograph.
Geoffrey Willans (1911-1958), author and journalist
Geoffrey Willans is best known for his collaboration with Searle on the Molesworth books [see **159-161**].
Diana Graves (1915-1975), actress
A niece of the writer, Robert Graves, Diana Graves became an actress. Following her divorce from the actor, Michael Gough, she moved to Rome, at the age of 35, to start a new life. Searle designed the dust jacket for *To My Astonishment* (1958), her account of this new life.
Peter Sellers (1925-1980), actor and comedian
Elizabeth Allan (1908-1990), actress
Frankie Howerd (1917-1992), comedian and actor
Frankie Howerd would appear in Gilliat and Launder's film, *The Great St Trinian's Train Robbery*, in 1966, as 'Alphonse' Askett, hairdresser and member of a criminal gang.
John Robinson, actor
Laurie Lee (1914-1997), poet, novelist and screenwriter
Searle met Laurie Lee through his wife Kaye Webb, who worked with him in her position as an editor for Penguin.
Richard Findlater (1921-1985), theatre critic and historian
John Courtenay Trewin (1908-1990), writer, journalist and theatre critic
The Cornishman, J C Trewin, was the favourite colleague of Eric Keown and Ronald Searle, in their capacities as theatre critic and caricaturist for *Punch*. Searle's caricature of Trewin appears in Christopher Fry's *An Experience of Critics* (1952) [see **74**].
Bernard Miles (1907-1991), actor, director and writer
Searle's caricatures of Bernard Miles in performance appeared in the pages of *Punch*. In 1960, Miles contacted Searle over the matter of microfilming the notebooks of the Modernist theatre practitioner, Edward Gordon Craig, as Searle's wife, Kaye Webb, had attempted to publish Craig's memoirs. In 1961, Miles mounted an exhibition at his Mermaid Theatre, in London, to celebrate Craig's 90th birthday.
Robin Bailey (1919-1999), actor
Searle's caricatures of Robin Bailey in performance appeared in the pages of *Punch*. Bailey's comment that accompanies his autograph – 'the rain in Spain stays mainly away from 32 Newton Road' – alludes to the fact that, in 1959, he played Henry Higgins in the first Australian production of Lerner and Loewe's musical, *My Fair Lady*. 32 Newton Road was the Searles' address.
Bernard Fergusson, Baron Ballantrae (1911-1980), brigadier in the British Army, military historian and Governor-General of New Zealand
In 1956, Searle joined Bernard Fergusson's staff in the Department of Psychological Warfare as part of Britain's response to the Suez Crisis.
Michael Bentine (1922-1996), comedian and comic actor
Keith Michell (born 1928), Australian actor, and his actress wife, Jeanette Sterke (born 1934)
Sir William Watt Leggatt (1894-1968), Australian soldier, lawyer and politician
William Dargie (1912-2003), Australian portrait painter
Jerome Robbins (1918-1998), American choreographer, director and producer
Michael Flanders (1922-1975), actor and singer, and Donald Swann (1923-1994), composer, pianist and linguist
Flanders and Swann's 1951 revue, *Penny Plain*, at St Martin's Theatre, London, included a number entitled 'Surly Girls', featuring three male performers dressed as St Trinian's Schoolgirls, and a backcloth by Searle himself. A caricature by Searle of the comedy duo appeared in *Punch* on 16 January 1957.
Ann Todd (1909-1993), actress and producer
A caricature by Searle of Ann Todd as Lady Macbeth appeared in *Punch* on 1 September 1954.
Rowland Emett (1906-1990), cartoonist and kinetic sculptor
In 1953, Searle and Kaye Webb included Rowland Emett in their *Punch* series, 'People Worth Meeting'. He included a characteristic drawing of a railway engine with his autograph.
Michael Redgrave (1908-1985), actor, director, manager and writer
Stanley Holloway (1890-1982), actor, comedian, singer, poet and monologist
Searle designed the poster for one of Stanley Holloway's most popular films, *The Lavender Hill Mob* (1951), directed by Charles Crichton for Ealing Studios. His caricature of Holloway as Alfred P Doolittle in *My Fair Lady* appeared in *Punch* on 7 May 1958.
Moray Watson (born 1928), actor
Natasha Parry (born 1930), actress
Willoughby Goddard (1926-2008), actor
James Mason (1909-1984), actor, and his daughter, Portland Mason (1948-2004)
Searle became good friends with James Mason and his family. James Mason attempted to accompany his autograph with a self portrait.
Huw Thomas (1926-2009), broadcaster, barrister and Liberal Party politician
Leonard Sachs (1909-1990), South African-born British actor
Ronald Allen (1930-1991), actor
Robert Graves (1895-1985), poet, novelist, scholar and translator
Searle illustrated *The Anger of Achilles* (1959), Robert Graves' translation of Homer's *The Iliad*.
Sybil Thorndike (1882-1976), actress
Sir Laurence Olivier (1907-1989), actor, director and producer
John Gielgud (1904-2000), actor, director and producer
Searle's caricatures of Sybil Thorndike, Laurence Olivier and John Gielgud in performance appeared in the pages of *Punch*.
Julie Andrews (born 1935), actress, singer and writer, and her first husband, the stage designer, Tony Walton (born 1934)
Searle's caricature of Julie Andrews as Eliza Doolittle in *My Fair Lady* appeared in *Punch* on 7 May 1958.
Jack Hedley (born 1930), actor
Jack Hedley had a long relationship with Searle's collaborator, the director, Wendy Toye.
Jerome Lawrence (1915-2004), American playwright
Alec Clunes (1912-1970), actor manager
Frank Launder (1906-1997), writer, director and producer
Frank Launder directed the St Trinian's films in collaboration with Sidney Gilliat (1908-1994).
Johnny Morris (1916-1999), television presenter
Beverley Sisters, female vocal trio: Joy (born 1924), Teddie and Babs (twins born 1927)
Rube Goldberg (1883-1970), American cartoonist, sculptor, writer, engineer and inventor
Rosemary Sutcliff (1920-1992), novelist and writer for children
Lionel Bart (1930-1999), writer and composer of musicals and pop songs
Russell Braddon (1921-1995), Australian novelist, biographer and scriptwriter
Searle was a friend of Russell Braddon from the time that they spent together as Japanese prisoners of war at Changi Gaol, Singapore, during the years 1942-45. He illustrated *The Naked Island* (1952), Braddon's account of his experience as a prisoner of war [**14**].
Kenneth Allsop (1920-1973), broadcaster, writer and naturalist
Christopher Fry (1907-2005), playwright
A friend of Christopher Fry, Searle illustrated his book, *An Experience of Critics* (1952) [**74**], and his play, *A Phoenix Too Frequent* (1959) [**179-183**].
David Arkell (1913-1997), journalist, translator and biographer
Searle and David Arkell became close friends soon after they met in the offices of the magazine, *London Opinion*, in 1945.
William Mayne (1928-2010), writer of children's fiction
Haro Hodson (born 1923), cartoonist and illustrator
John Searle (born 1947)
John Searle is the son of Searle and Kaye Webb, and twin brother of Kate.
Kaye Webb (1914-1996), journalist and publisher
Searle became Kaye Webb's third husband in 1948. He left her in 1961, though did not divorce her until 1967.

1960: Book Illustrations

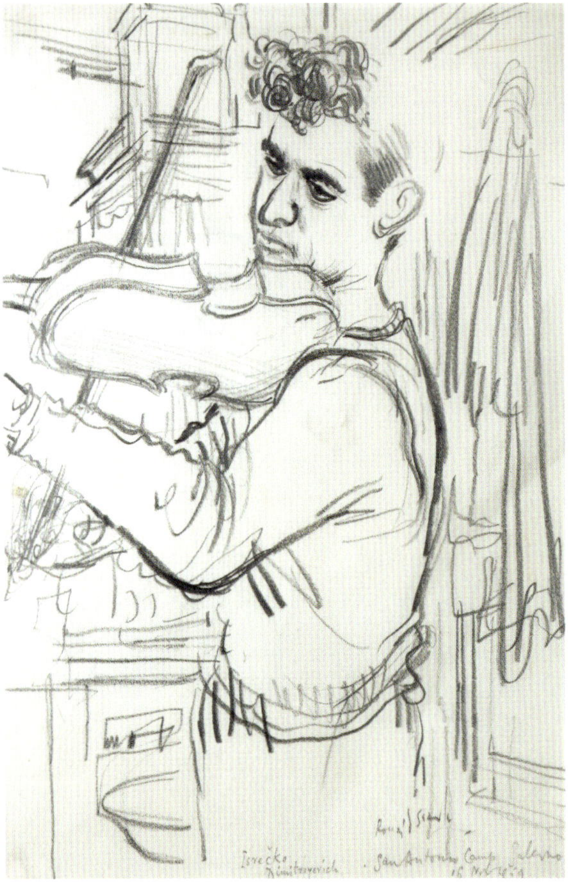

'In the last weeks of 1959, Ronald Searle and Kaye Webb worked on their last collaborative effort, another job from the "unrefusable" category. World Refugee Year was in progress, promoting an appeal on behalf of the "100,000 refugees left in Europe alone". The office of the United Nations High Commissioner for Refugees invited the two observers to visit camps in Austria, Italy and Greece, and bring back a report. The three-week working journey was as arduous as any Searle had undertaken since the war, and was reminiscent of that time in other ways. Nobody in the European camps was starving in the sense that he had known, but to move among people who felt that they had been left behind by history was an unpleasantly familiar feeling. The drawings he made were fanatical in their excavation of a calm beauty from all the desolation.'

(Davies, page 132)

'Isrecko Dimitriyevich has escaped twice. The first time, in 1957, he was sent back as under age and put back in prison. When he was released he escaped again and joined his mother and brother in the San Antonio Camp, Naples. Isrecko's father was a musician killed in the war. He himself works tirelessly, believing that one day he will get to the United States to continue his training.'

(Kaye Webb and Ronald Searle, *Refugees 1960*, Harmondsworth: Penguin Books, 1960, page 35)

324 ISRECKO DIMITRIYEVICH, SAN ANTONIO CAMP, SALERNO
signed, inscribed with title
and dated '16 Nov 1959'
pencil
13 ¾ x 9 ½ inches
Illustrated: Kaye Webb & Ronald Searle, *Refugees 1960*, Harmondsworth: Penguin Books, 1960, page 35
Exhibited: 'Ronald Searle: A Celebration', Ruskin Gallery, Anglia Ruskin University, Cambridge, January-February 2008

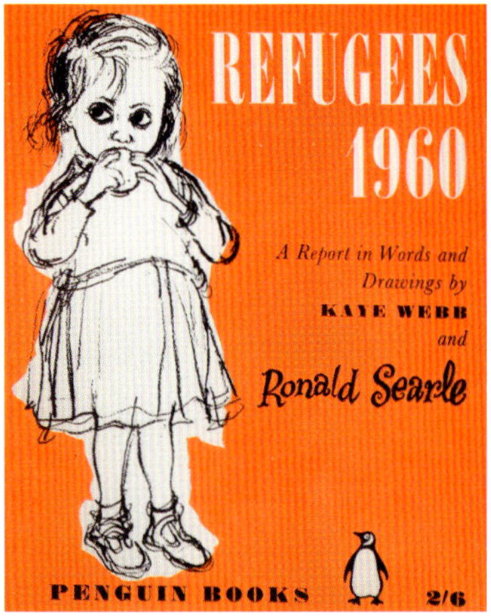

323 REFUGEES 1960
Kaye Webb and Ronald Searle
Refugees 1960
Harmondsworth: Penguin Books
1960
first edition
soft cover
48 pages
8 ¾ x 7 ¼ inches

325 WELCOME HONOURABLE VISITORS (I)
pencil
7 ¼ x 4 ¾ inches
Preliminary drawing for Jean Raspail, *Welcome Honourable Visitors*, London: Hamish Hamilton, 1960, front dust jacket

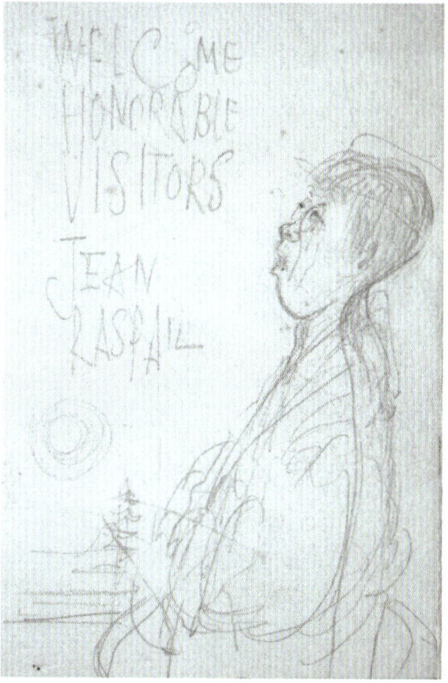

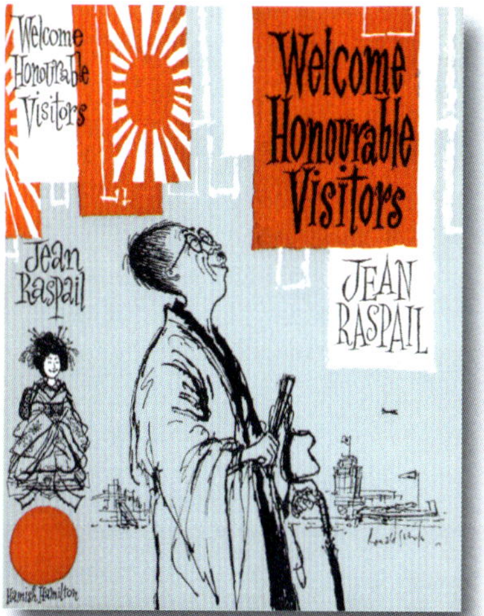

Published dust jacket for *Welcome Honourable Visitors*.

326 WELCOME HONOURABLE VISITORS (II)
pencil
7 ¼ x 4 ¾ inches
Preliminary drawing for Jean Raspail, *Welcome Honourable Visitors*, London: Hamish Hamilton, 1960, front dust jacket

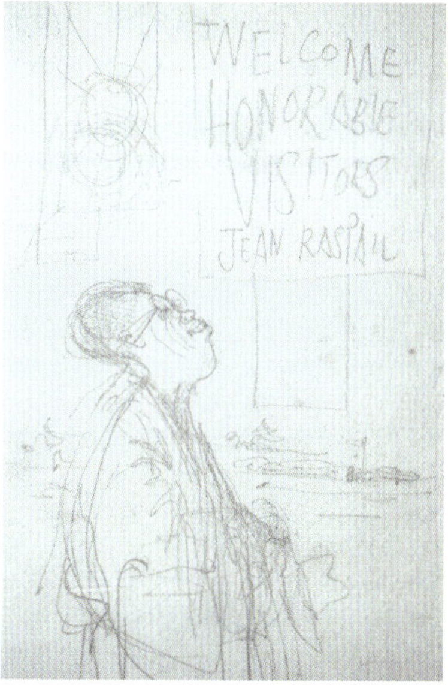

1960: Cote d'Azur

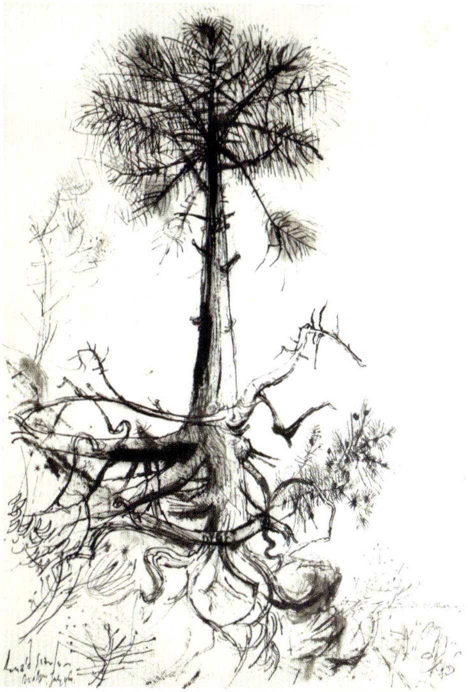

327 COTE D'AZUR
signed, inscribed with title and dated 'July 1960'
pen and ink
14 ½ x 10 inches

The King's Breakfast

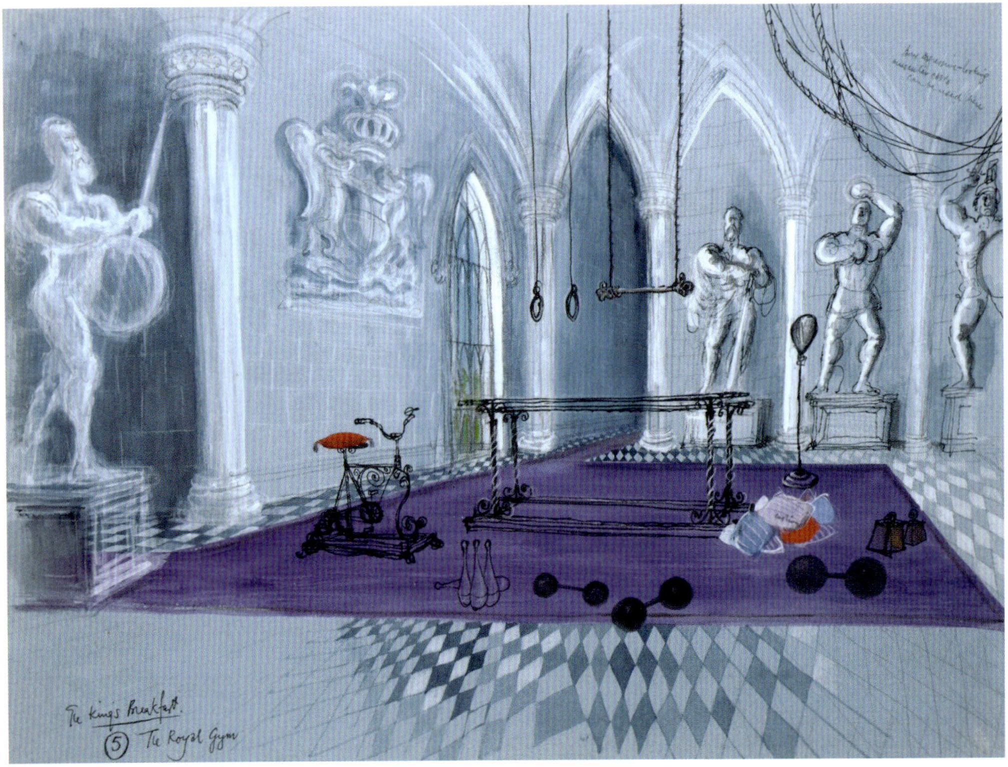

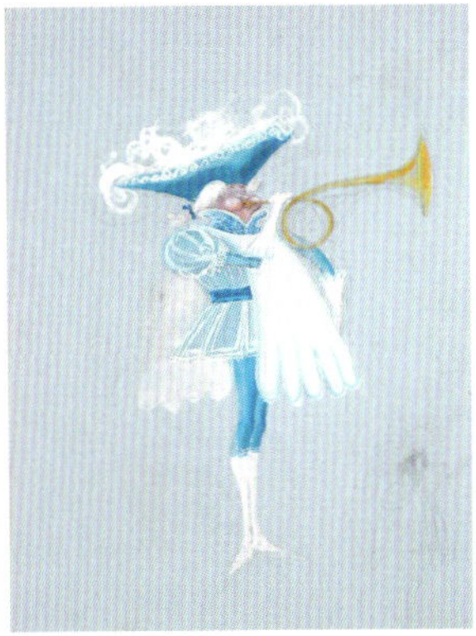

328 THE KING'S BREAKFAST
THE ROYAL GYM
inscribed with title, 'Any aggressive-looking muscular casts can be used here'
pen ink, watercolour and bodycolour with pencil on tinted paper
14 ¾ x 19 inches

reverse:
1ST TRUMPETER
watercolour and bodycolour with pencil
17 ¾ x 14 inches

The King's Breakfast
Ronald Searle first worked as a designer for Wendy Toye (1917-2010) on the short feature film, *On the Twelfth Day …*, which she directed and starred in. It provided a charming comic take on the carol, 'The Twelve Days of Christmas', with designs that 'put a gorgeous sheen of unreal decorative patterning on everything, including the animals' (Davies, page 109).

Made in the years 1952-53, it was only released in 1955. By then, Searle and Toye were collaborating on *Wild Thyme*, a musical revue by Philip Guard and Donald Swann, which began its pre London tour in Bath on 23 May 1955. A review by a local critic mentioned 'some of the most beautiful scenery I have ever seen' (quoted in Davies, page 110).

Though Searle and Toye became lifelong friends, they collaborated only once again, and after a gap of eight years. In 1963, they worked on a second short film, *The King's Breakfast*, a dramatisation in dance and mime, of the A A Milne poem about a king who had no butter for the royal slice of bread. A large cast included Maurice Denham as The King and, most relevantly to the present design, Warren Mitchell as the Gym Instructor and David Warner as the 1st Trumpeter. The film competed at the Cannes Film Festival in the year of its release.

1960-1985: Magazine Illustrations

1960: Junior Miss

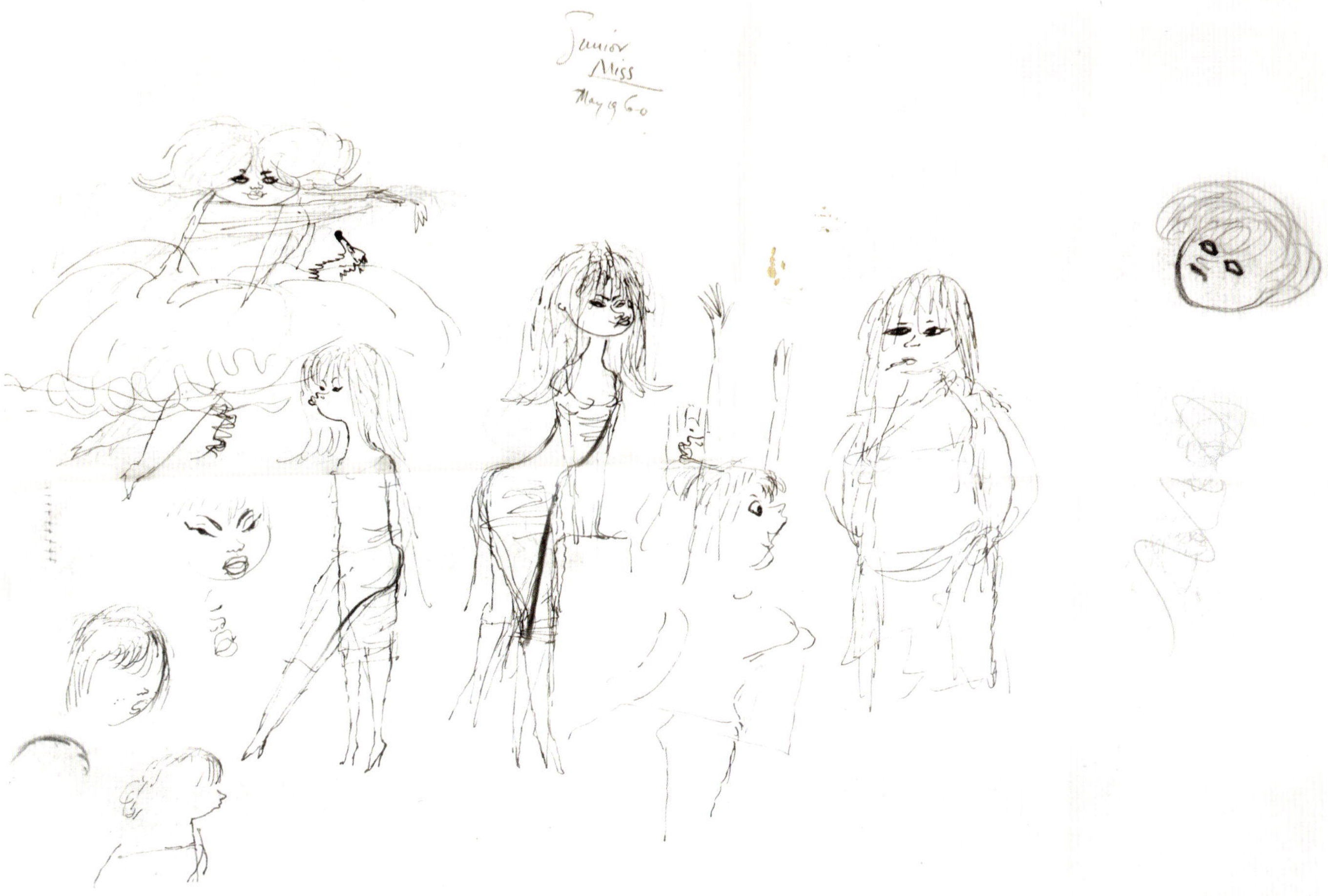

329 TEENAGERIE
inscribed 'Junior Miss' and dated 'May 1960'
pen ink and pencil
15 ½ x 21 inches
Preliminary drawing for Yardley's *Junior Miss*, issue 6, 1960, pages 26-29, 'Teenagerie'; *Daily Mail*, 1960, 'After they left St Trinians'

1960: The New York Times

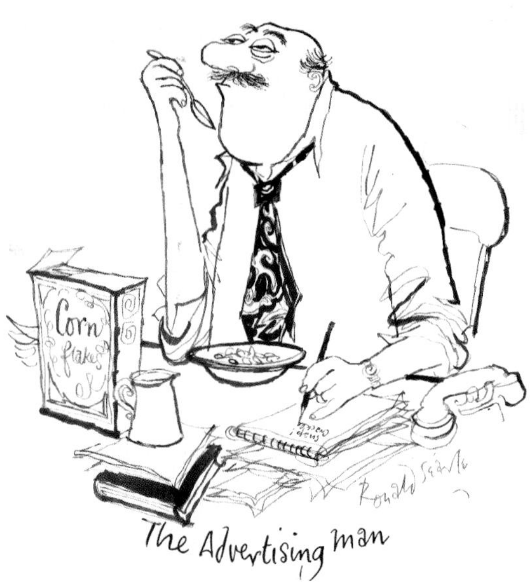

330 THE ADVERTISING MAN
signed and inscribed with title
pen and ink
9 x 8 ½ inches
Design for an oversized match book, commissioned by *The New York Times*, circa 1960 (one in a series of twelve)
Literature: *The Daily Telegraph*, 7 January 2012, News Review & Comment, 'Matt on Ronald Searle'

'With his garish tie and wispy moustache, I think the advertising man's expression as he's eating his bowl of cornflakes is hilarious – you wonder what slogan he's about to come up with. Searle's real talent was capturing not just the type, but a mood and attitude as well.'

(Matt, 'On Ronald Searle', *Daily Telegraph*, 7 January 2012, page 23)

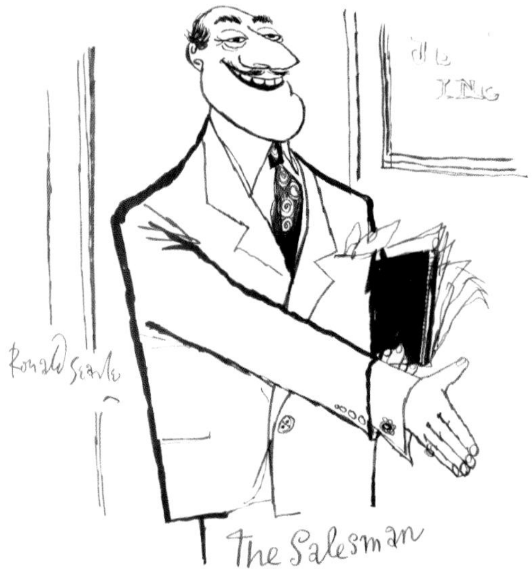

331 THE SALESMAN
signed and inscribed with title
pen and ink
9 x 8 ½ inches
Design for an oversized match book, commissioned by *The New York Times*, circa 1960 (one in a series of twelve)

Circa 1961: Holiday

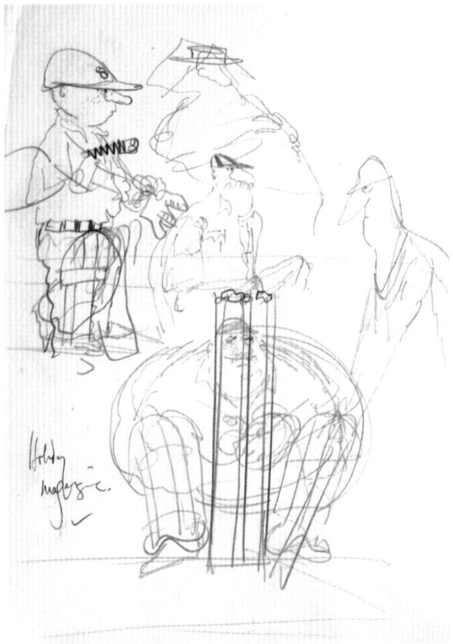

332 CRICKETERS
inscribed 'Holiday Magazine'
inscribed 'Endpapers' on reverse
pencil
9 x 6 ¾ inches

1961: Life

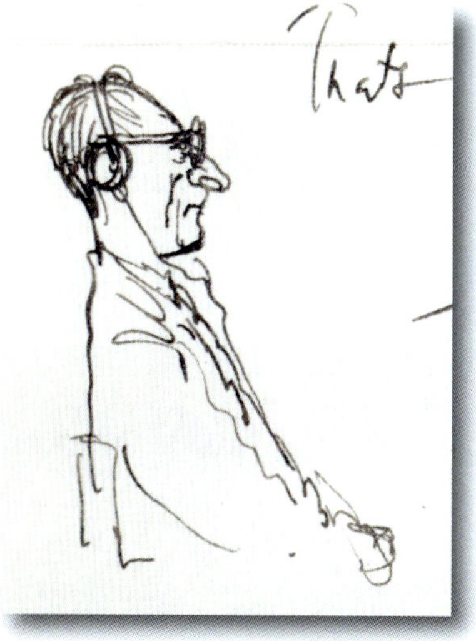

Detail of letter to Jean Ellsmoor, Jerusalem, Israel, Friday 14 April 1961 [328]

'In 1961, he was voted Cartoonist of the Year by the National Cartoonists' Society in New York, but he was naturally not at home when the news arrived. It was only the end of April, but already he was completing his third foreign trip of the year: two to Paris, followed by another Life-sponsored excursion, this time for the trial of the Gestapo chief Adolf Eichmann [in Jerusalem] …

Arrested in May 1960, … Eichmann was put on trial for crimes against the Jewish people, found guilty, and, after appeal, hanged on 31 May 1962. Searle deepened his knowledge of what the court proceedings brought to light by visiting surrounding towns and kibbutzim to meet survivors of the Holocaust. In court, Searle said, Eichmann had the demeanour of a "horrible little functionary"; it was "difficult to associate him completely" with the horrors he had perpetrated.'

(Davies, pages 134-135)

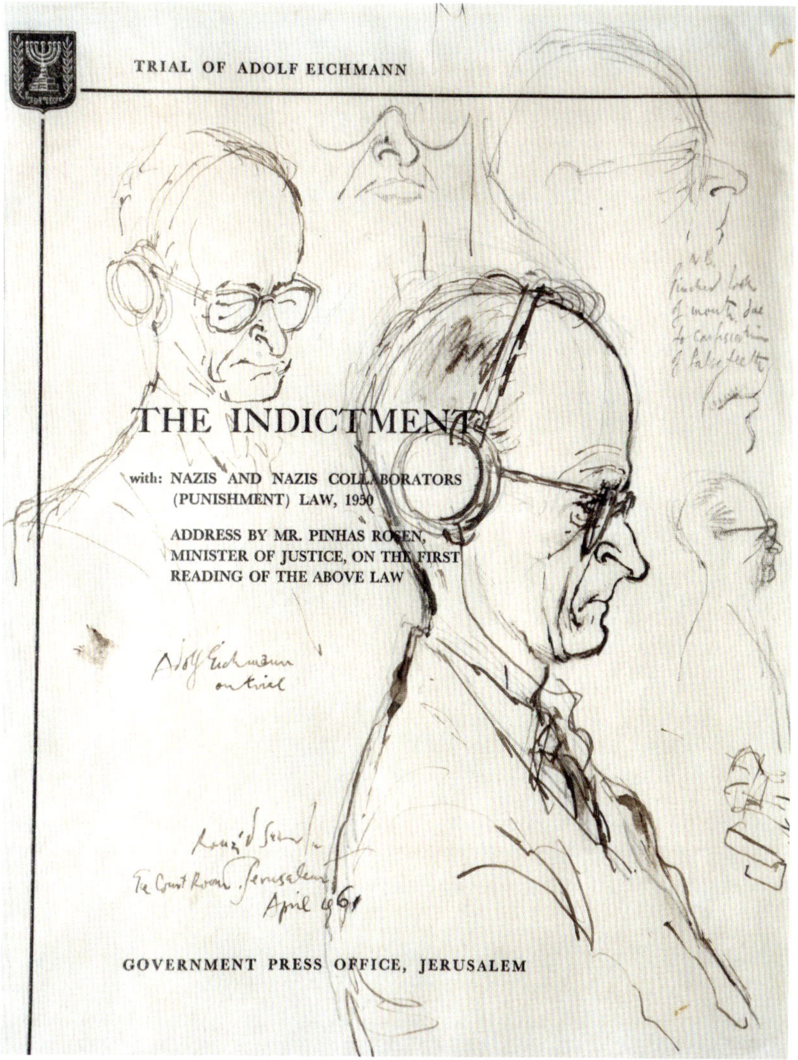

333 ADOLF EICHMANN ON TRIAL
signed, inscribed with title, 'The Court Room. Jerusalem' and 'NB Pinched look of mouth due to confiscation of false teeth', and dated 'April 1961'
pen ink and pencil on front cover of the indictment document, Government Press Office, Jerusalem
10 ½ x 8 ¼ inches
Provenance: Magdalene Street Gallery, Cambridge
Preliminary drawing for *Life*, 30 June 1961, page 30, 'Newsfronts of the World'

1961-62: Punch

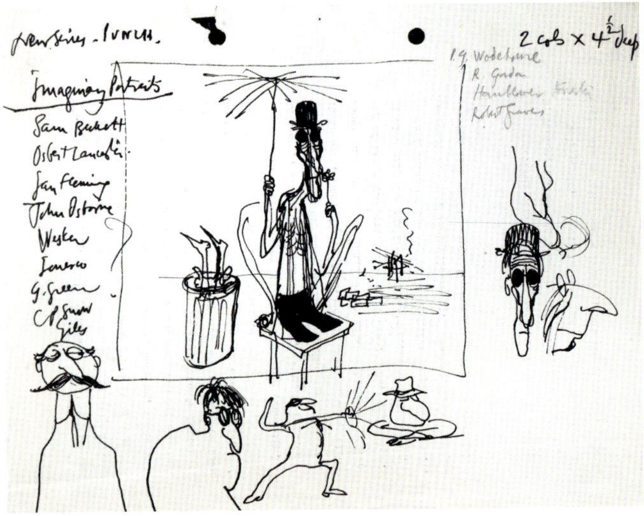

Samuel Beckett

Ronald Searle became a friend of the avant-garde writer, Samuel Beckett (1906-1989), in the 1950s, lunching regularly with him during trips to Paris with the *Punch* theatre critic, Eric Keown. His image for the series, 'Searle's-Eye View', alludes to Beckett's best-known plays: the waste land of *Waiting for Godot* (1953); Hamm, the blind invalid of *Endgame* (1957), whose parents live in dustbins; the bananas from *Krapp's Last Tape* (1958); Winnie's umbrella from *Happy Days* (1961).

334 SEARLE'S EYE VIEW
3 – SAMUEL BECKETT
inscribed 'New Series. Punch, Imaginary Portraits' and inscribed with a list of subjects for the series
pen and ink on reverse of typed manuscript
7 ¾ x 9 ¾ inches
Preliminary drawing for *Punch*, 13 December 1961, page 882, 'Searle's-Eye View'

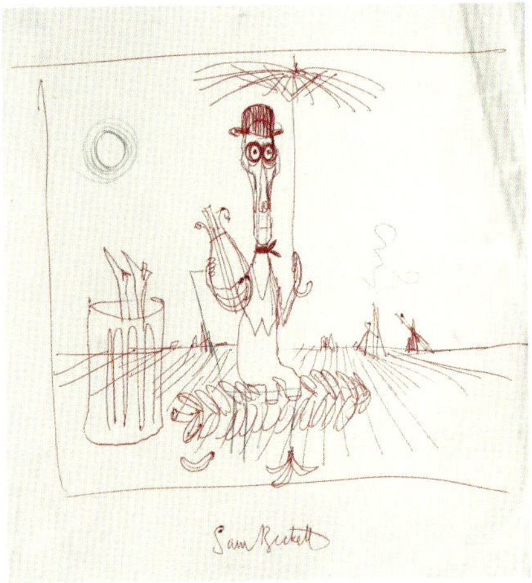

335 SAM BECKETT
inscribed with title and 'Punch, New Series, Imaginary Portraits'
coloured ink with pencil
10 ½ x 8 inches
Preliminary drawing for *Punch*, 13 December 1961, page 882, 'Searle's-Eye View'

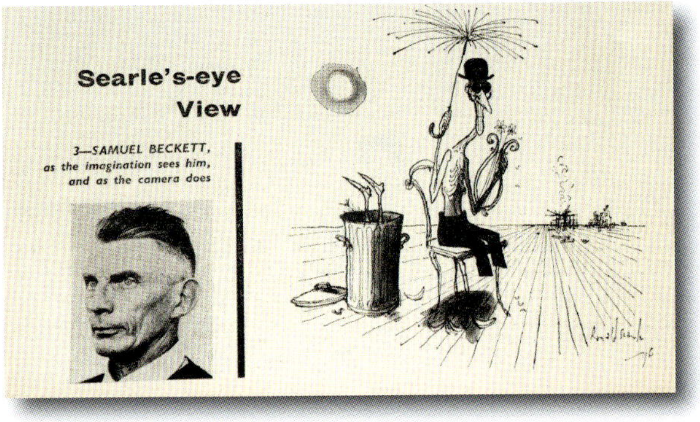

'A series had been devised by which he could keep Punch *supplied while "on the move". The "Imaginary Portraits", as he called them, or "Searle's Eye View", as* Punch *preferred to bill them, presented famous figures as their reputations suggested they ought to look, rather than as they were. They ran on until the following September, scoring several bull's-eyes but never quite convincing their creator.'*

(Davies, page 139)

336 SEARLE'S-EYE VIEW
2 – COLIN WILSON
signed and inscribed 'Imaginary Portraits: Colin Wilson'
inscribed 'Punch', stamped with copyright details and dated '6 Dec 1961' on reverse
pen and ink
13 ½ x 14 ½ inches
Illustrated: *Punch*, 6 December 1961, Page 842, 'Searle's-Eye View'

Colin Wilson

Colin Wilson (born 1931) is a novelist and existentialist philosopher, who made his name with *The Outsider* (1956), 'the seminal work on alienation, creativity and the modern mind-set' (according to the information on its original dust jacket).

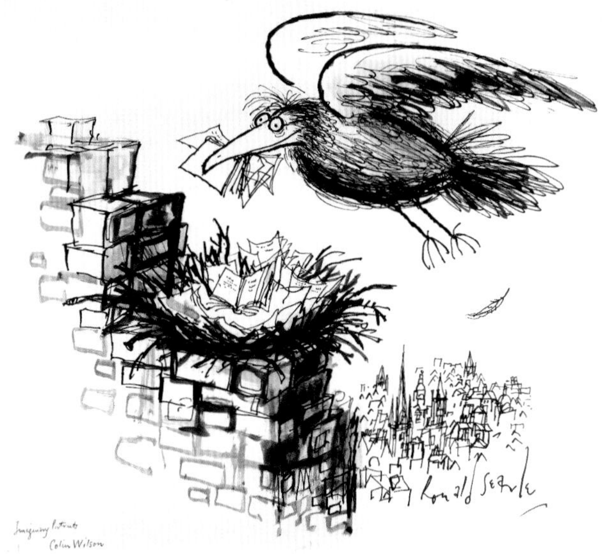

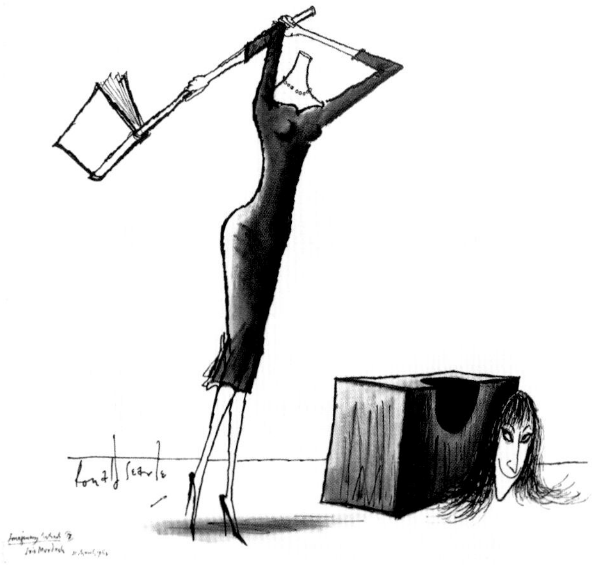

337 SEARLE'S-EYE VIEW
17 – IRIS MURDOCH
signed, inscribed 'Imaginary Portraits 17 Iris Murdoch' and dated '21 March 1962'
inscribed with publishing details and dated 1962 on reverse
pen and ink
16 x 16 inches
Illustrated: *Punch*, 21 March 1962, page 478, 'Searle's-Eye View'; *Searle in the Sixties*, Harmondsworth: Penguin Books, 1964, [unpaginated]

Iris Murdoch

The early successes of Iris Murdoch (1919-1999) – notably *Under the Net* (1954) and *The Bell* (1958) – established her as a writer of philosophical novels that analysed political and social questions with incision and wit.

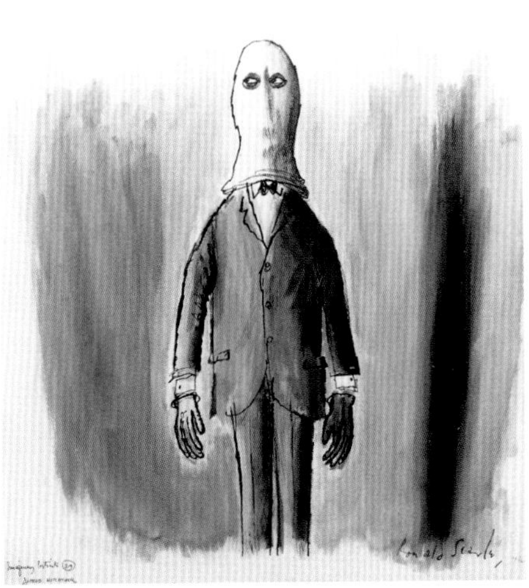

338 SEARLE'S-EYE VIEW
27 – ALFRED HITCHCOCK
signed, inscribed 'Imaginary Portraits 29 Alfred Hitchcock' and dated 1962
inscribed with title and publishing details, and dated 1962 on reverse
pen ink and monochrome watercolour
15 ½ x 13 inches
Illustrated: *Punch*, 6 June 1962, page 882, 'Searle's-Eye View'

Alfred Hitchcock

For long considered the Master of Suspense, Alfred Hitchcock (1899-1980) remained at the height of his career at the time that Ronald Searle produced this caricature. *Vertigo* (1958), *North by Northwest* (1959) and *Psycho* (1960) had all been released in the previous five years.

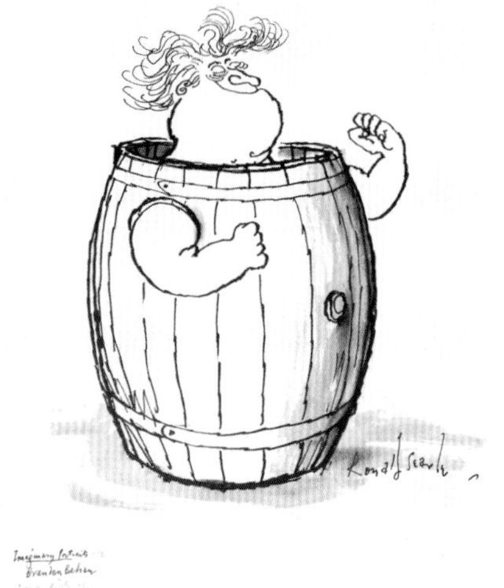

339 SEARLE'S-EYE VIEW
31 – BRENDAN BEHAN
signed and inscribed 'Imaginary Portraits: Brendan Behan'
pen ink and monochrome watercolour
15 ½ x 12 inches
Illustrated: *Punch*, 4 July 1962, page 32, 'Searle's-Eye View'

Brendan Behan

The bohemian Irish writer, Brendan Behan (1923-1964), is best remembered for his plays, *The Quare Fellow* (1954) and *The Hostage* (1958), and for his autobiographical novel, *Borstal Boy* (1958). He would die of the effects of alcoholism only two years after Ronald Searle produced his caricature.

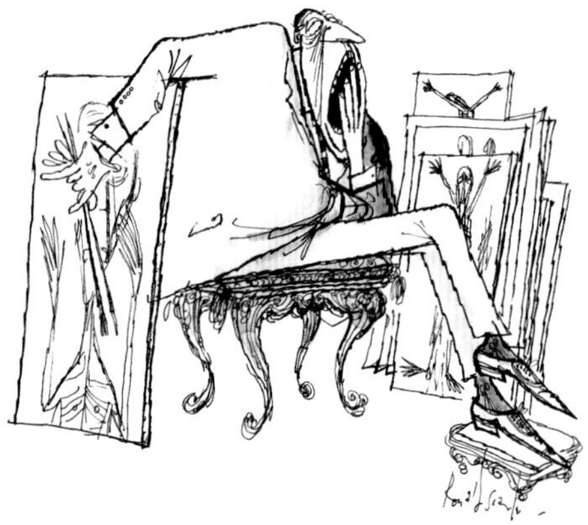

340 SEARLE'S-EYE VIEW
40 – BERNARD BUFFET
signed and inscribed 'Imaginary Portraits 40 Bernard Buffet' and with publishing details
inscribed with publishing details and artist's agent's address, stamped with copyright details and dated '5 Sept 1962' on reverse
pen and ink
14 ½ x 14 inches
Illustrated: *Punch*, 5 September 1962, page 356, 'Searle's-Eye View'

Bernard Buffet

Ronald Searle's caricature suggests that the Expressionist painter, Bernard Buffet (1928-1999), was prolific and repetitive. In later life, both Searle and Buffet lived in Tourtour, Provence, Buffet committing suicide there following the onset of Parkinson's Disease. In 2010, a square in Tourtour was named after Buffet and his wife, Annabel.

1967-84: TV Guide USA

341 WHO KILLED HOLLYWOOD SOCIETY?
signed and inscribed with title
pen ink and watercolour
11 x 13 ¾ inches
Illustrated: *TV Guide, USA*, 25 November 1967

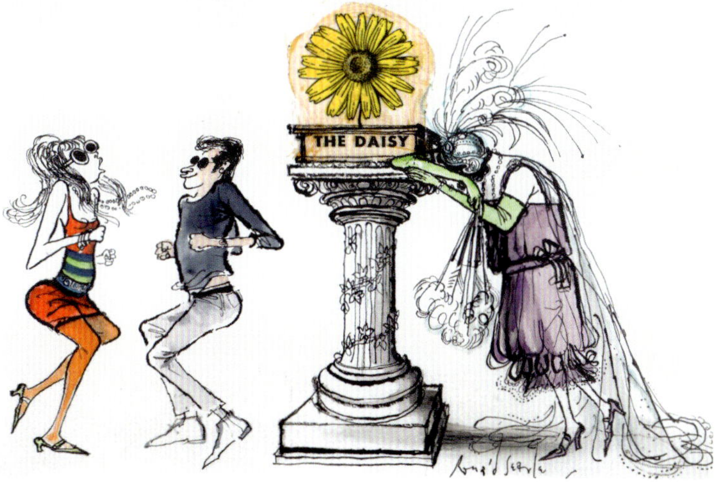

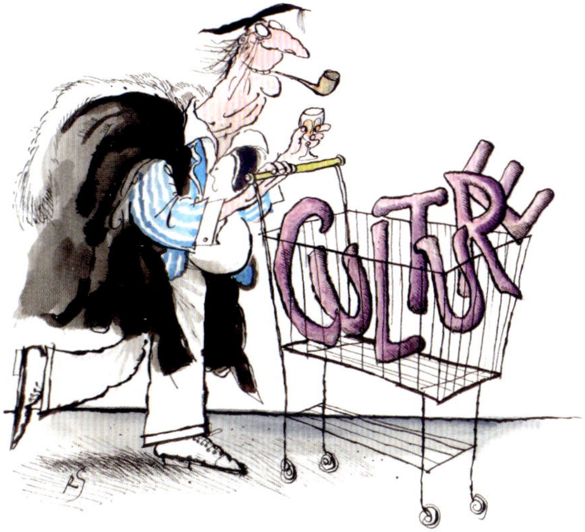

342 SUPERMARKET CULTURE
signed with initials
inscribed with publication details and stamped with agent John Locke's studio address on reverse
pen ink and watercolour
11 x 9 inches
Illustrated: *TV Guide, USA*, 1975, 'The Saga of Culture'

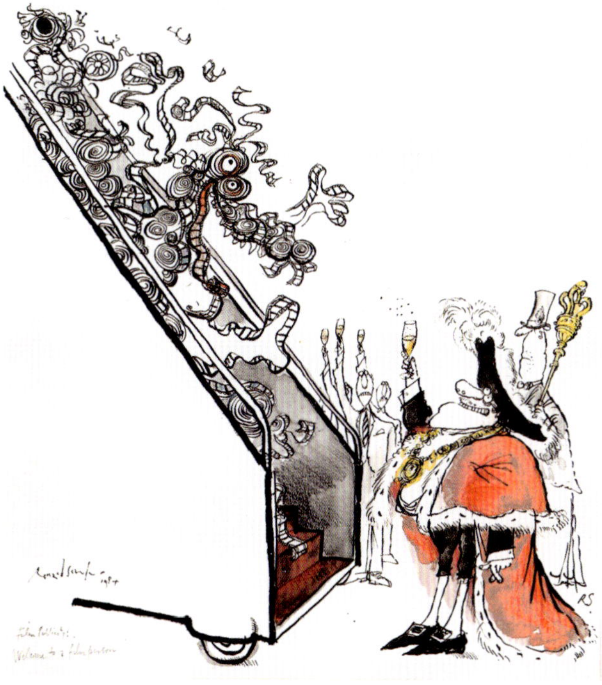

343 FILM PUBLICITY: WELCOME TO A FILM PERSON
signed, inscribed with title and dated 1984
inscribed with title, medium, size and publishing details, stamped with artist's studio stamp and copyright details,
and dated 1984 on reverse
pen ink and watercolour with crayon
14 x 12 ¼ inches
Illustrated: *TV Guide, USA*, 1984

Circa 1985

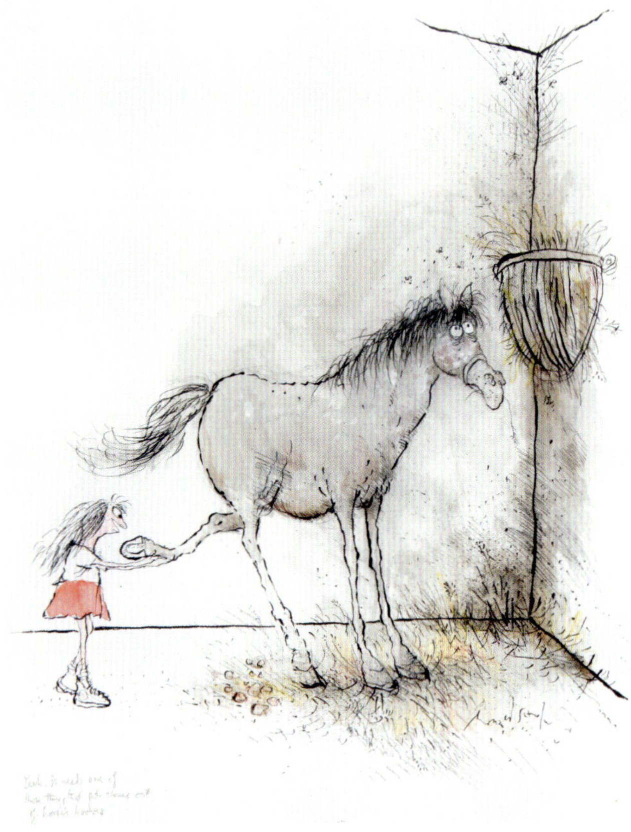

344 YEAH, IT NEEDS ONE OF THOSE THINGS THAT GETS STONES OUT OF HORSES' HOOVES
signed and inscribed with title
stamped with artist's name on reverse
pen ink and watercolour with bodycolour
14 ¾ x 12 ½ inches

reverse:
THE TANK (not illustrated)
stamped with artist's name
pen ink and pencil
12 x 12 inches

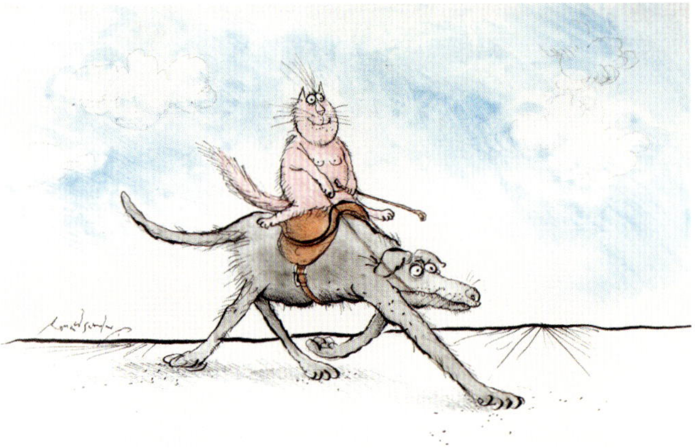

345 GODIVA RIDES AGAIN
signed and inscribed with title
inscribed 'Godiva Rides Again' and stamped with artist's name on reverse
pen ink and watercolour with pencil
9 ½ x 12 ¼ inches

reverse:
AN AMOROUS CAT
pencil
9 x 12 inches

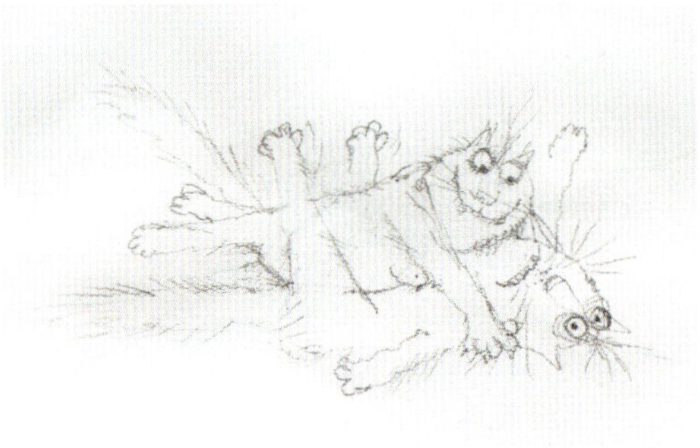

1982-83: Lloyds Bank

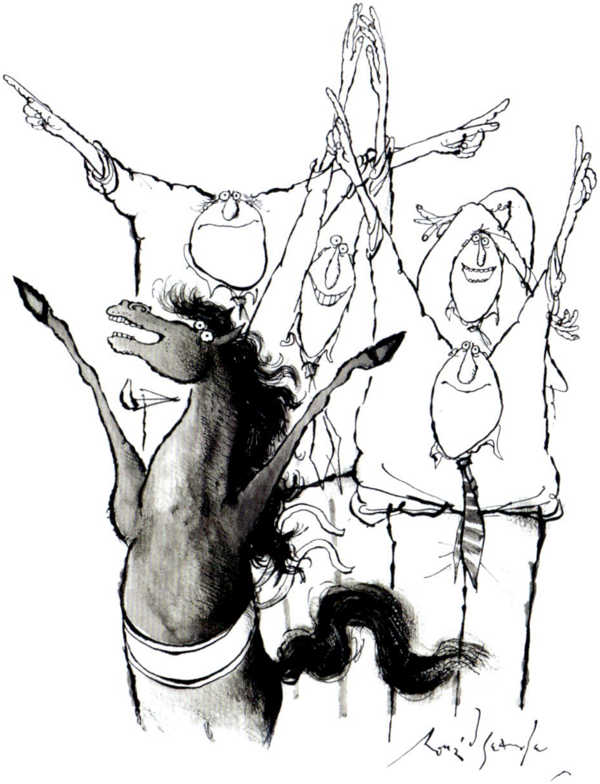

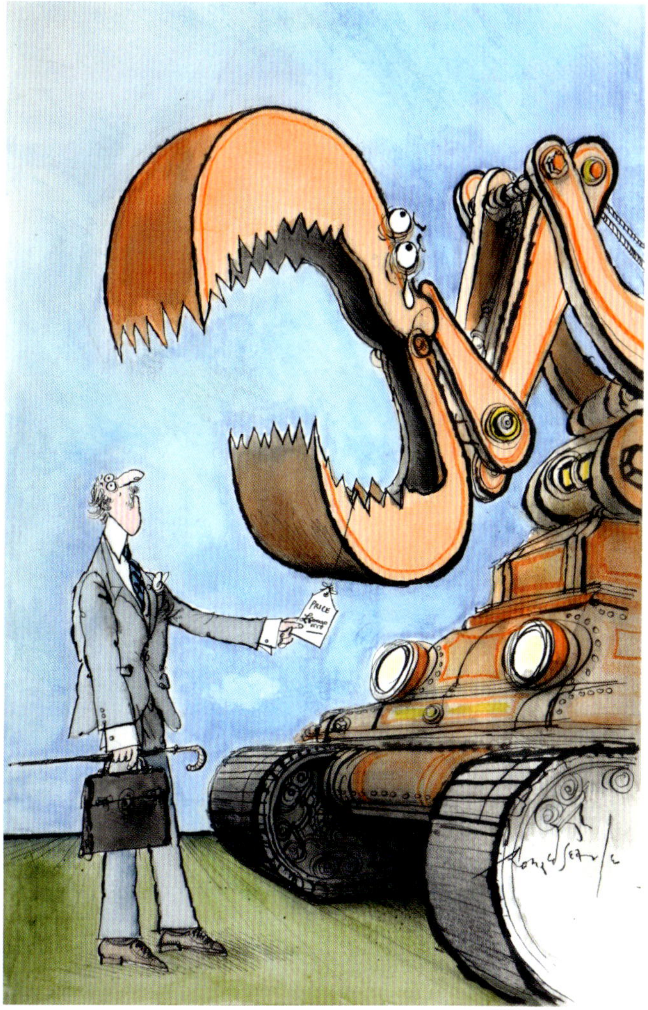

346 TIC-TAC
signed and inscribed with title
inscribed 'Lloyds Bank, B&W Press Advertising, Open Outcry' below mount
inscribed 'Financial Tic-Tak, for a Lloyds Bank brochure', stamped with artist's agent's address and copyright details, and dated 1983 on reverse
pen and ink with monochrome watercolour
14 x 10 ¼ inches
Drawn for a brochure for Lloyds Bank

347 STARTING YOUR OWN BUSINESS: CHOOSE YOUR EQUIPMENT CAREFULLY
signed
inscribed with title and 'Lloyds Bank brochure', stamped with artist's agent's address and copyright details, and dated 1982 on reverse
pen ink and watercolour
15 ¾ x 10 ½ inches
Drawn for a brochure for Lloyds Bank

1983: Design for a Lithograph

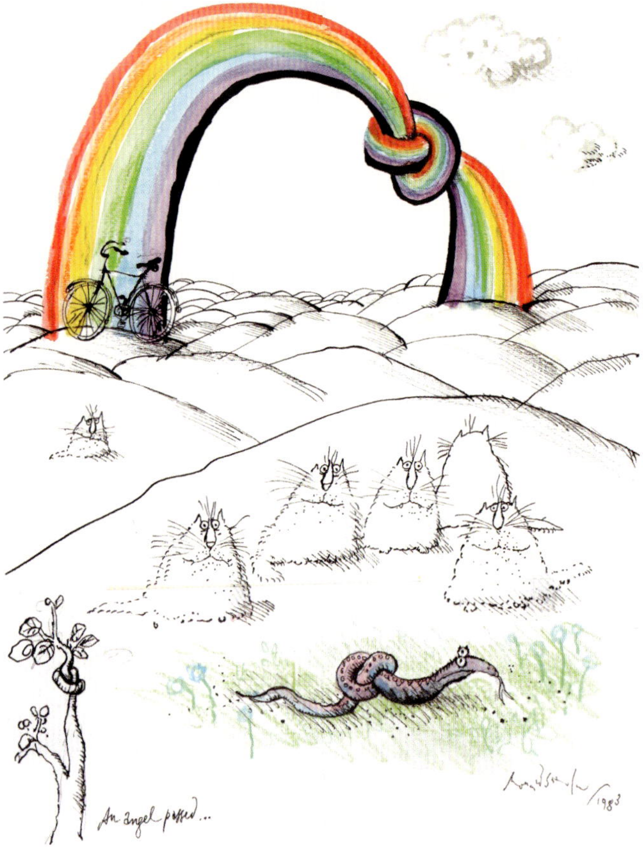

348 AN ANGEL PASSED ...
signed, inscribed with title and dated 1983
inscribed 'Preparatory drawing for the lithograph', stamped with artist's address and dated 1983 on reverse
pen ink and watercolour with coloured pencil
10 x 7 inches
Preliminary drawing for a lithograph, reproduced in *Ronald Searle in Perspective*, Sevenoaks: New English Library, 1984, page 202

1989: Slightly Foxed – But Still Desirable

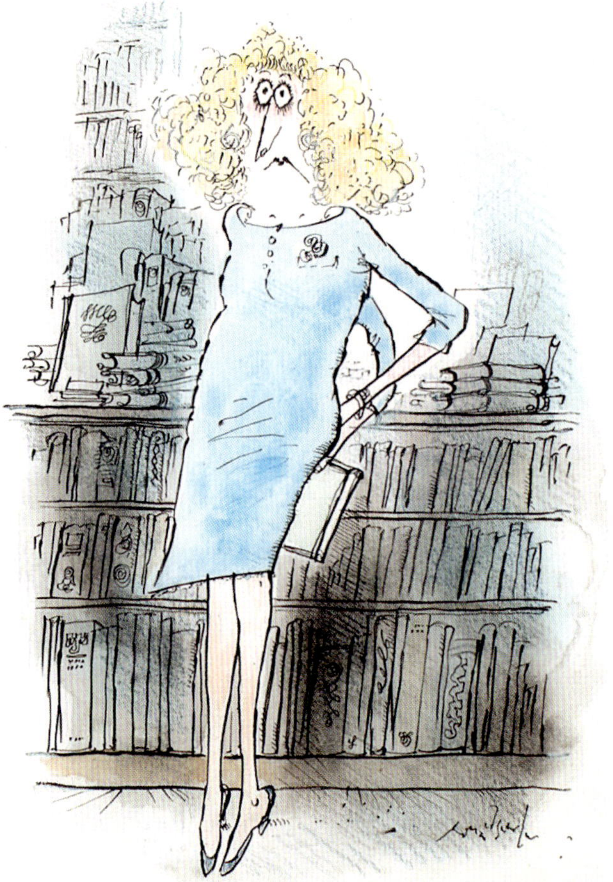

349 SLIGHT SPLITTING OF PASTE-DOWNS
signed and inscribed with book title
pen ink and watercolour
12 x 9 inches
Illustrated: *Slightly Foxed – But Still Desirable. Ronald Searle's Wicked World of Book Collecting*, London: Souvenir Press, 1989, page 63
Exhibited: 'Ronald Searle: A Celebration' Ruskin Gallery, Anglia Ruskin University, Cambridge, January-February 2008

5: 1990s-2000s

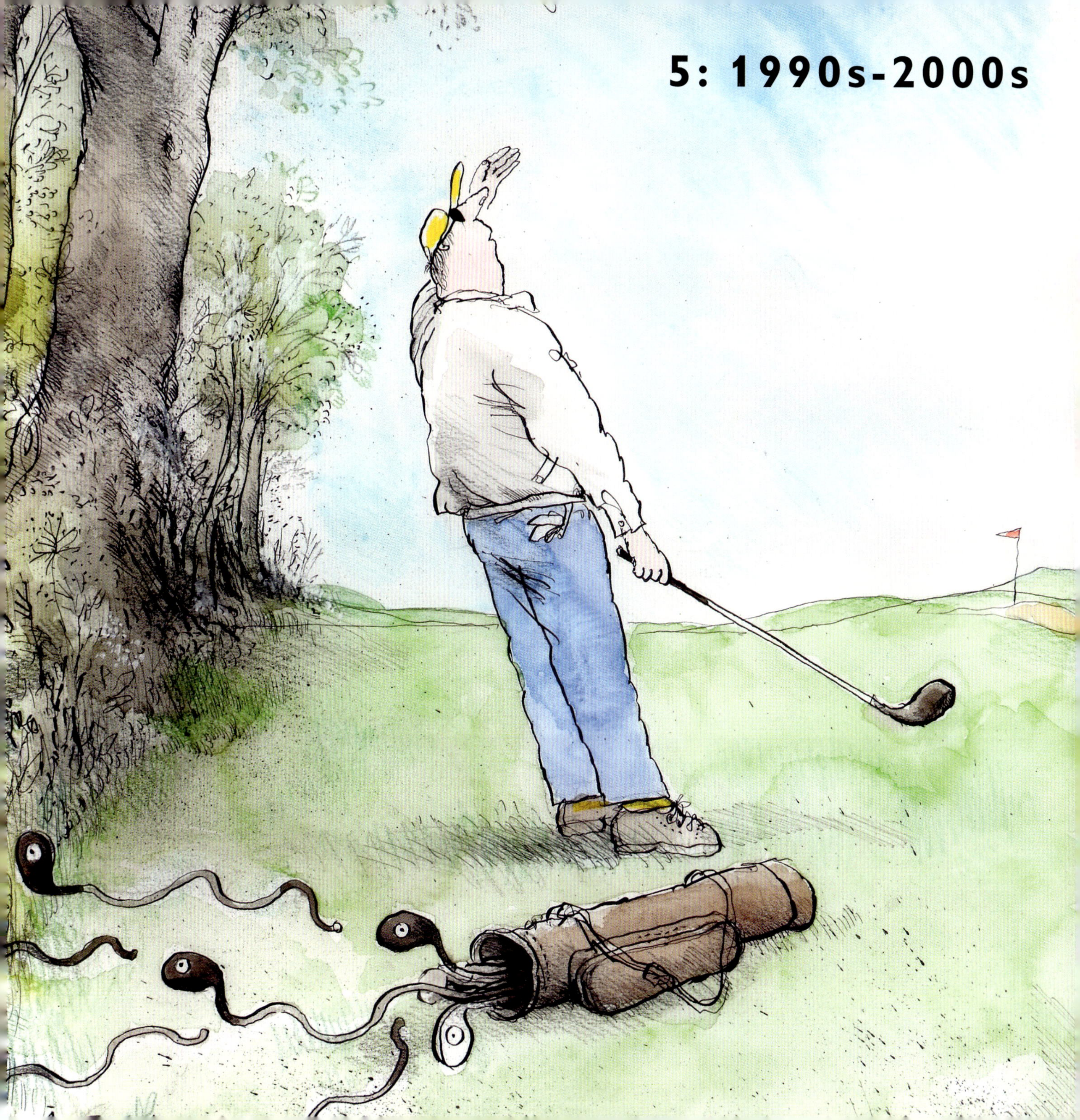

1992-1995: Magazine Illustrations

1992: Forbes FYI Magazine

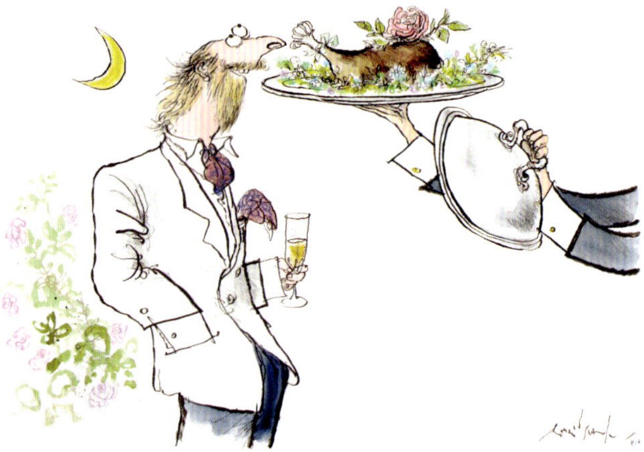

350 GOURMET
signed, inscribed with title and dated 1992
pen ink, watercolour and coloured crayon
11 ¾ x 15 ¼ inches
Illustrated: *Forbes FYI Magazine*, New York, 1992

1994: The New York Times

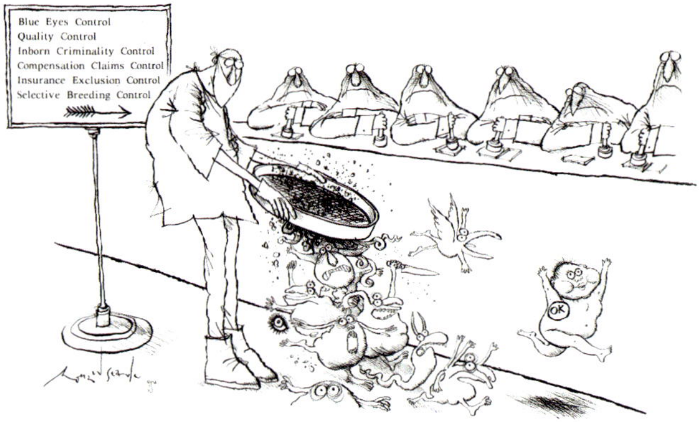

351 CLONING
signed, inscribed with title and dated 1994
inscribed with title and publishing details, stamped with copyright details and dated '4 February 1994' on reverse
pen and ink with coloured pencil and collage
13 x 18 ¾ inches
Illustrated: *The New York Times*, 4 February 1994

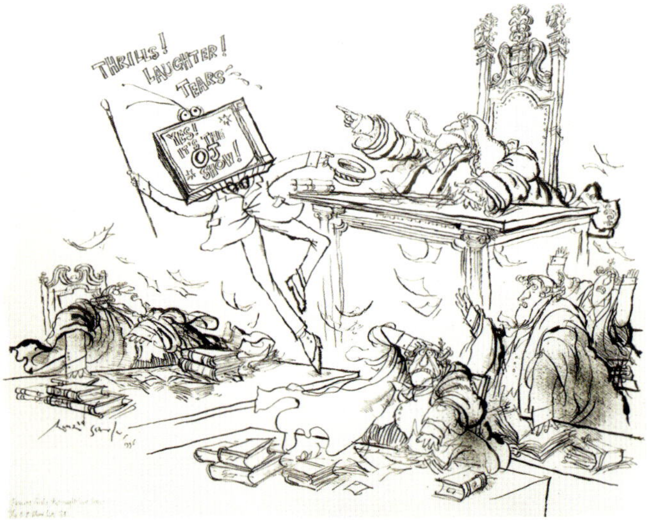

352 FAMOUS TRIALS THAT MIGHT HAVE BEEN
THE OJ SHOW HITS GB
signed, inscribed with title and dated 1995
inscribed 'Famous trials that might have been: the OJ Simpson Show hits GB' and with publishing details, stamped with artist's agent's address and copyright details, and dated '2 May 1995' on reverse
pen and ink
16 ½ x 19 ½ inches
Illustrated: *The New York Times*, 2 May 1995, 'Trial of The Vanities' by Frances Fyfield
Exhibited: 'Ronald Searle', Chris Beetles, 2003, no 129; 'Ronald Searle: A Celebration', Ruskin Gallery, Anglia Ruskin University, Cambridge, January-February 2008; 'Happy Birthday Ronald Searle!', March-April 2010

Circa 1995

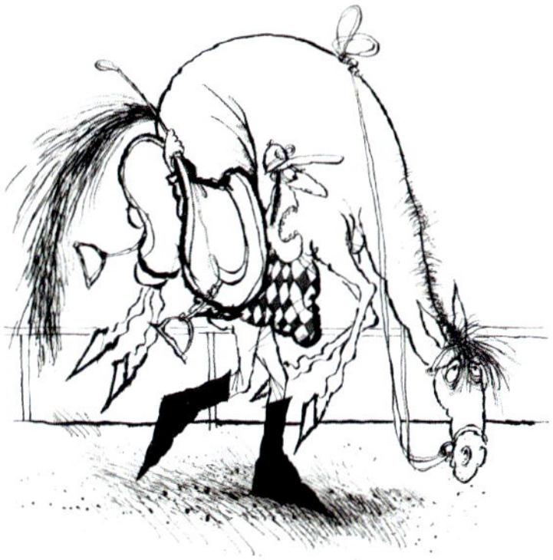

353 NAG NAG
stamped with agent John Locke's studio address on reverse
pen and ink
12 x 9 inches

'Searle was very good at drawing animals as well as people; he captured their characters perfectly. Here the horse's facial expression is just as funny as the angry jockey's. The gloomy-looking steed to be being ticked off for performing poorly in a race.'

(Matt, 'On Ronald Searle', *Daily Telegraph*, 7 January 2012, page 23)

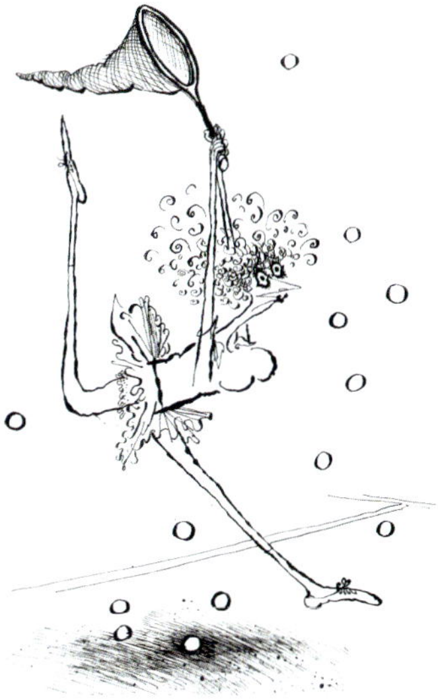

354 NOVICE
stamped with agent John Locke's studio address on reverse
pen and ink
11 ½ x 7 ¾ inches

2000: Into the Rough

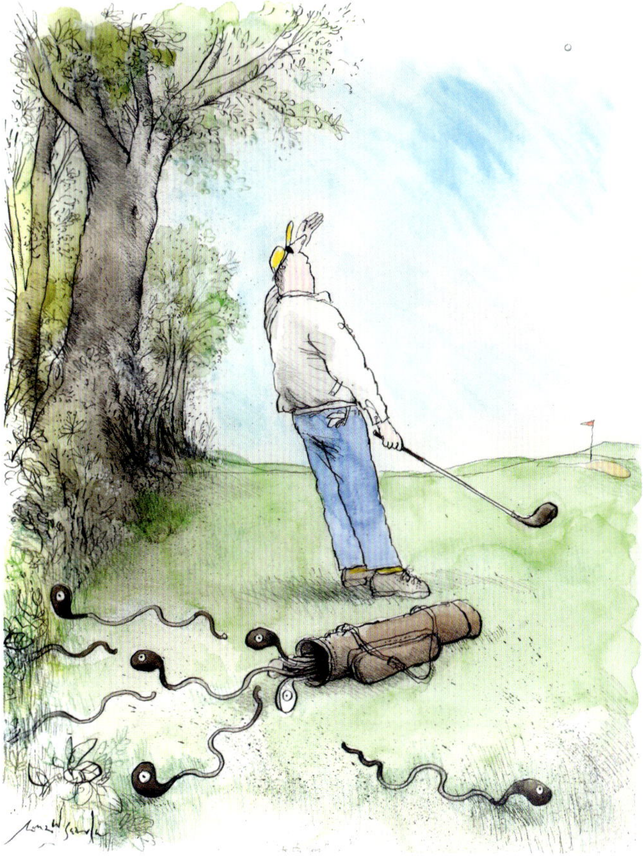

355 INTO THE ROUGH
signed and inscribed with title
pen ink and watercolour
19 ½ x 16 inches
Drawn in 2000 for the unpublished book, *Into the Rough*
Exhibited: 'Ronald Searle: A Celebration', Ruskin Gallery, Anglia Ruskin University, Cambridge, January-February 2008

2006: Cat O'Nine Tails

356-373 are all illustrated in Jeffrey Archer, *Cat O'Nine Tales*, London: Macmillan, 2006

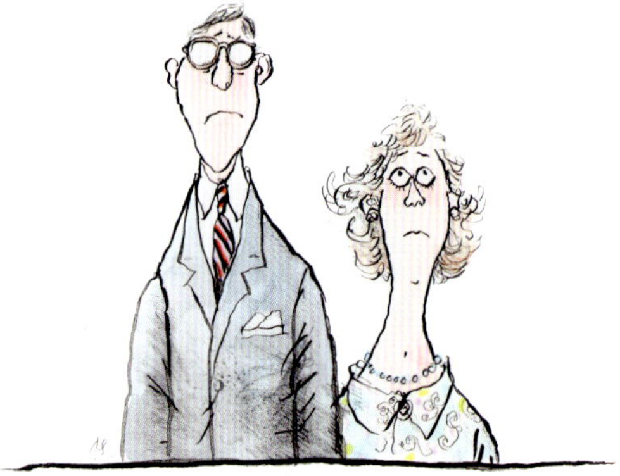

356 NO CHOICE BUT TO SEND YOU BOTH TO PRISON
signed with initials and inscribed with title, chapter title and '24'
pen ink, watercolour and crayon
11 ¾ x 9 ½ inches
Illustrated: page 5, 'The Man who robbed his own Post Office'
Exhibited: Ronald Searle, Cat O'Nine Tales & Other Artwork, October 2006, no 127

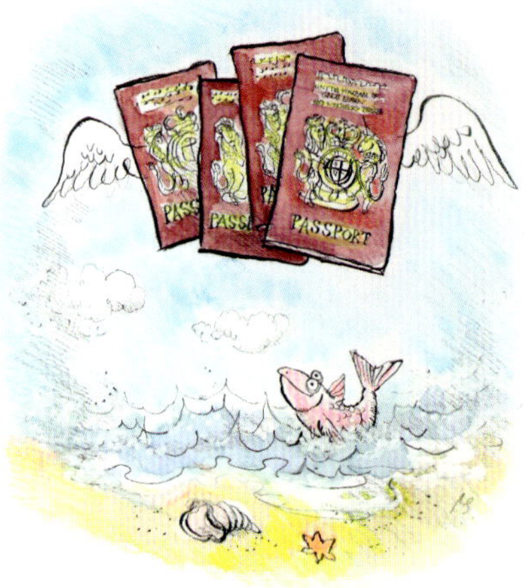

357 FOUR PASSPORTS
signed with initials, inscribed with title, chapter title and '26'
stamped with artist's agent's address and copyright details and dated 2006 on reverse
pen ink, watercolour and crayon
11 x 9 ½ inches
Illustrated: page 27, 'The Man who robbed his own Post Office'

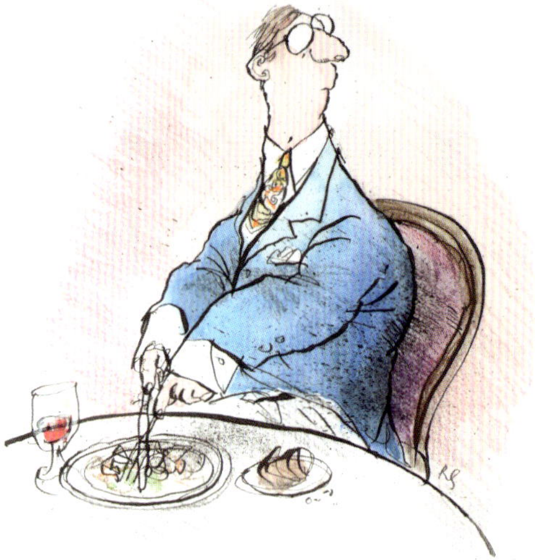

358 MR CARTWRIGHT WAS COMMITTING TO MEMORY
signed with initials, inscribed with title, chapter title and '16'
stamped with artist's agent's address and copyright details and dated 2006 on reverse
pen ink, watercolour and crayon
11 ¼ x 9 ½ inches
Illustrated: page 46, 'Maestro'

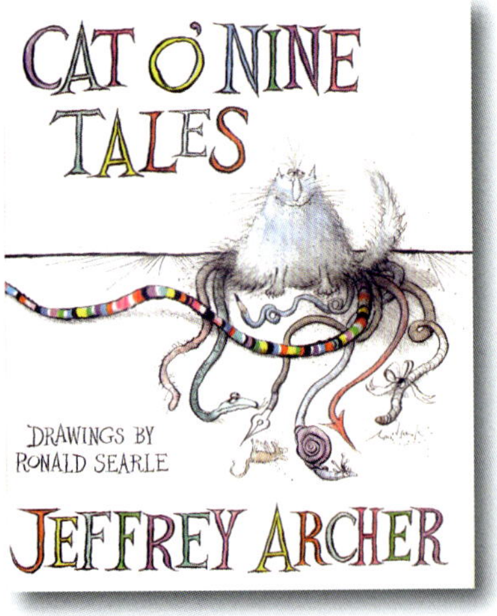

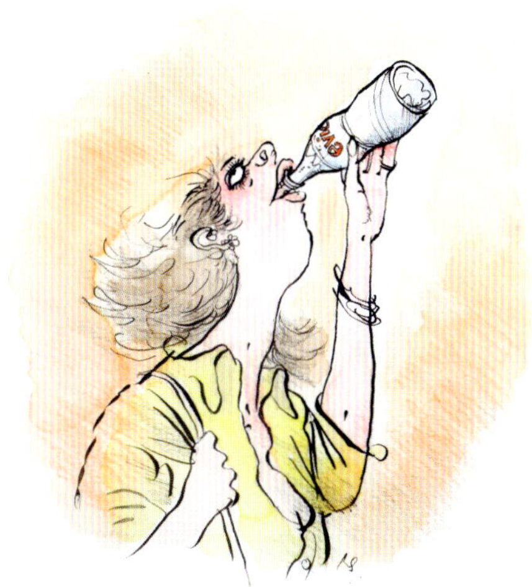

359 REGULAR GULPS
signed with initials and inscribed with title, chapter title and '20'
pen ink, watercolour and crayon
11 x 9 inches
Illustrated: page 78,
'Don't drink the water'

360 THE WINDOW SHATTERED
signed with initials
inscribed with title, chapter title and '9' below mount
pen ink, watercolour and crayon
11 ½ x 9 ½ inches
Illustrated: page 90,
'It can't be October already'

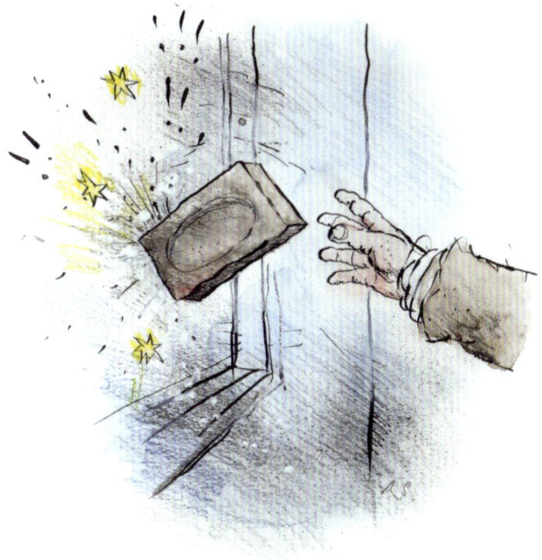

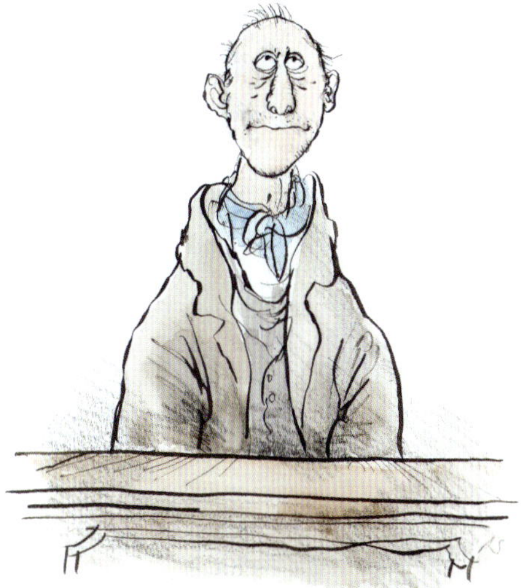

361 PAT IN THE DOCK
signed with initials and inscribed with title, chapter title and '10'
stamped with artist's agent's address and copyright details, dated 2006 and sketches of elaborate letters on reverse
pen ink, watercolour and crayon
11 ½ x 9 ½ inches
Illustrated: page 97,
'It can't be October already'

362 IN THE SWEATBOX
signed with initials
inscribed with title and chapter title, and '11' below mount
pen ink, watercolour and crayon
11 ½ x 9 ½ inches
Illustrated: page 100,
'It can't be October already'

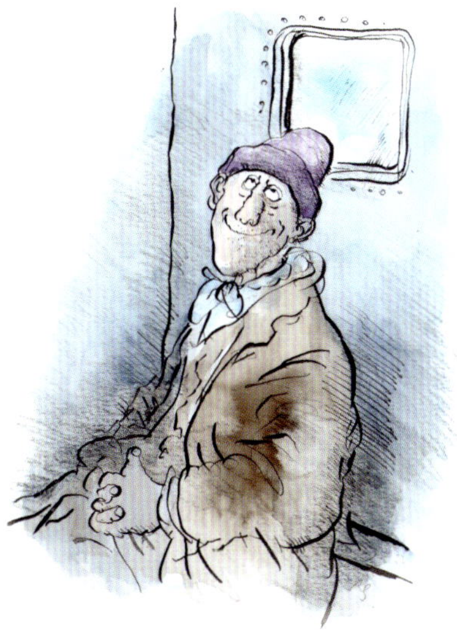

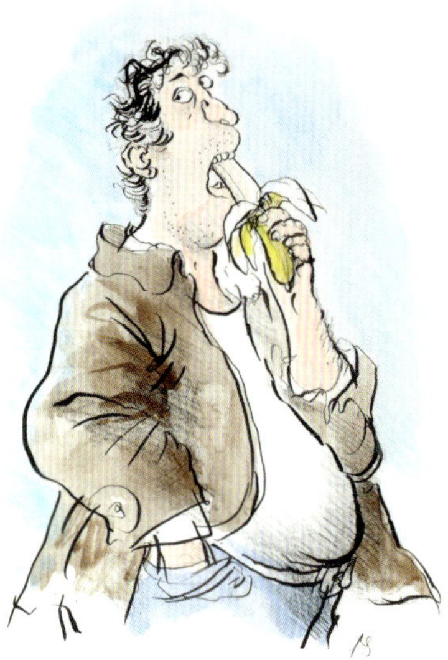

363 DOUG
signed with initials, inscribed with title,
'You know what I mean?' and '27'
stamped with artist's agent's address and
copyright details, dated 2006 and pencil sketch
of hand holding arrow on reverse
pen ink, watercolour
and crayon
11 ¼ x 9 inches
Illustrated: page 154, 'Know what I mean?'

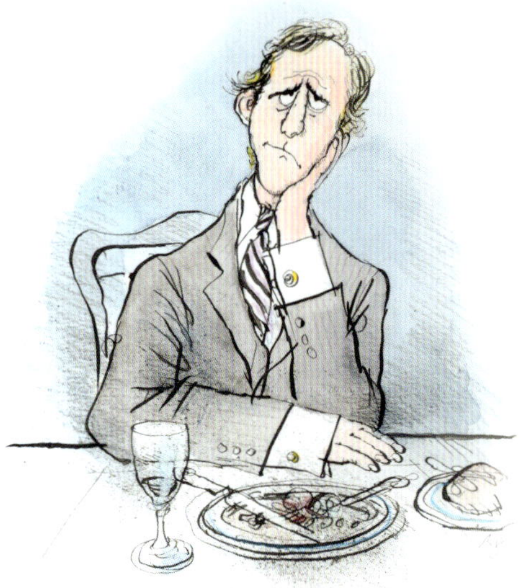

364 BOB – A WEED
signed with initials, inscribed with title,
chapter title and '8'
stamped with artist's agent's address and
copyright details and dated 2006 on reverse
pen ink, watercolour and crayon
11 ½ x 9 inches
Illustrated: page 143, 'The Wisdom
of Solomon'

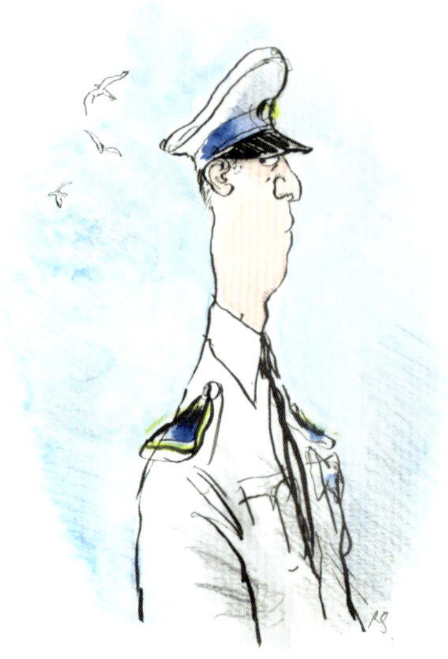

365 BILL TALBOT – SUSPICIOUS
signed with initials and inscribed with title,
'You know what I mean?' and '28'
stamped with artist's agent's address and
copyright details and dated 2006 on reverse
pen ink, watercolour and crayon
11 ½ x 9 inches
Illustrated: page 156, 'Know what I mean?'

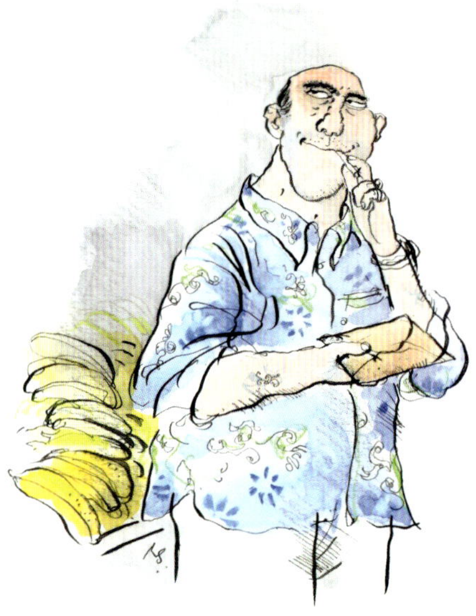

366 THE MAN FROM MARSEILLE
signed with initials, inscribed with title, 'You
know what I mean?' and '29'
stamped with artist's agent's address and
copyright details and dated 2006 on reverse
pen ink, watercolour and crayon
11 ½ x 9 inches
Illustrated: page 163, 'Know what I mean?'

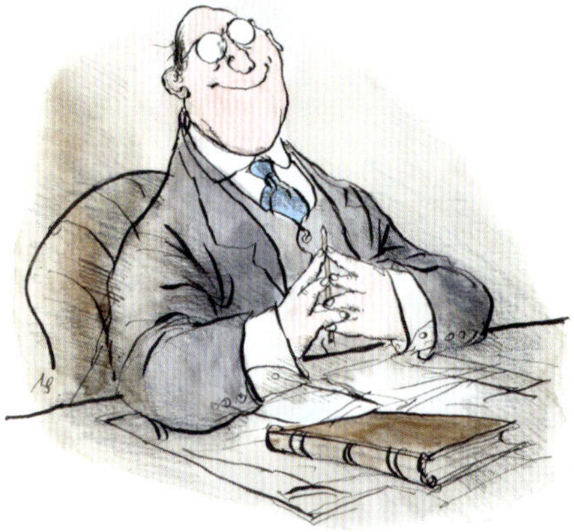

367 YOUR ACCOUNTS ARE IN APPLE PIE ORDER
signed with initials, inscribed with title, 'A safe pair of hands' and '30'
stamped with artist's agent's address and copyright details and dated 2006 on reverse
pen ink, watercolour and crayon
11 ½ x 9 ¼ inches
Illustrated: page 174, 'Charity begins at home'

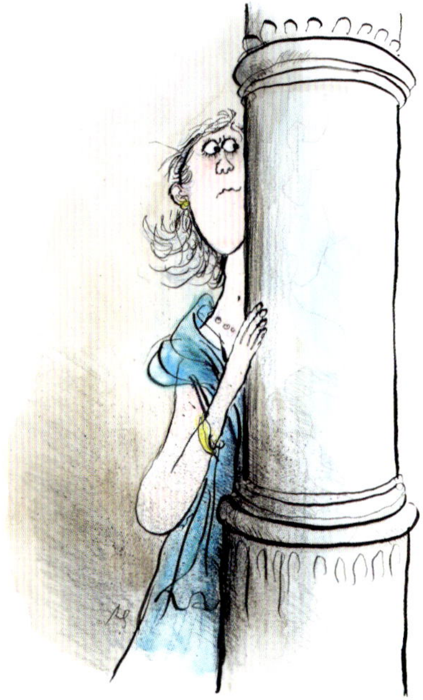

368 THE DETECTIVE SLIPPED BEHIND A MARBLE PILLAR
signed with initials
inscribed with title, 'A safe pair of hands' and '33'
pen ink, watercolour and crayon
11 ½ x 9 inches
Illustrated: page 190, 'Charity begins at home'

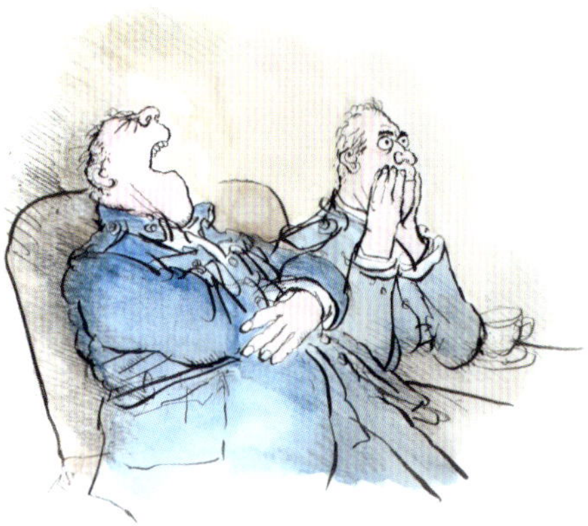

369 BOTH ON DUTY THE SAME NIGHT
signed with initials, inscribed with title, 'The perfect murder' and '13'
stamped with artist's agent's address and copyright details and dated 2006 on reverse
pen ink, watercolour and crayon
11 x 9 ½ inches
Illustrated: page 205, 'The Alibi'

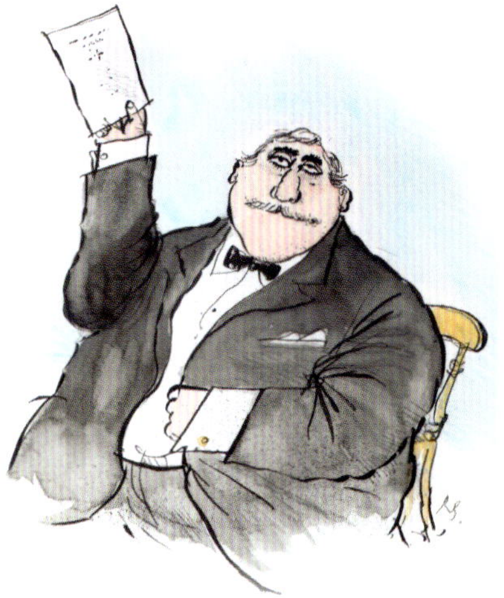

370 SOLD FOR FIVE THOUSAND TO MR GEORGE TSAKIRIS
signed with initials, inscribed with title, chapter title and '21'
stamped with artist's agent's address and copyright details and dated 2006 on reverse
pen ink, watercolour and crayon
11 ½ x 9 inches
Illustrated: page 212, 'A Greek Tragedy'

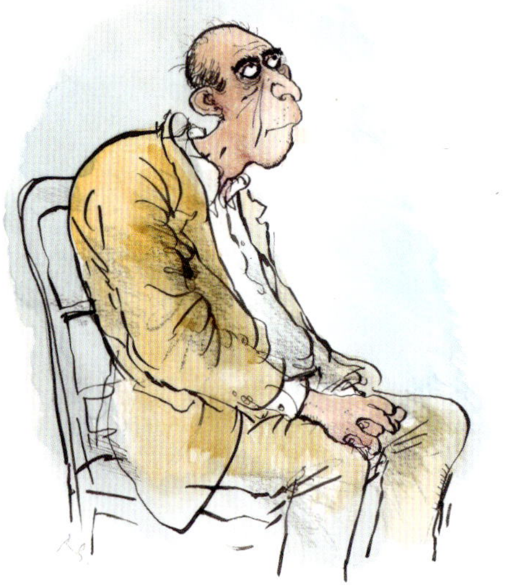

371 MALIK
signed with initials
inscribed with title, chapter title and '4' below mount
pen ink, watercolour and crayon
11 ½ x 8 ½ inches
Illustrated: page 226, 'The Commissioner'

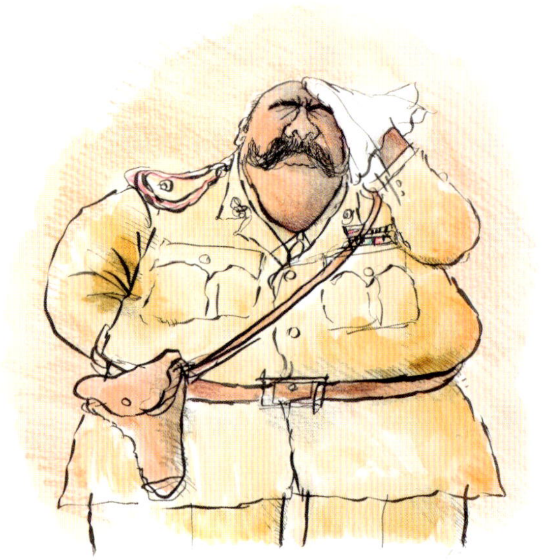

372 THE COMMISSIONER
signed with initials and inscribed with chapter title and '5'
pen ink, watercolour and crayon
11 x 9 ½ inches
Illustrated: page 224, 'The Commissioner'

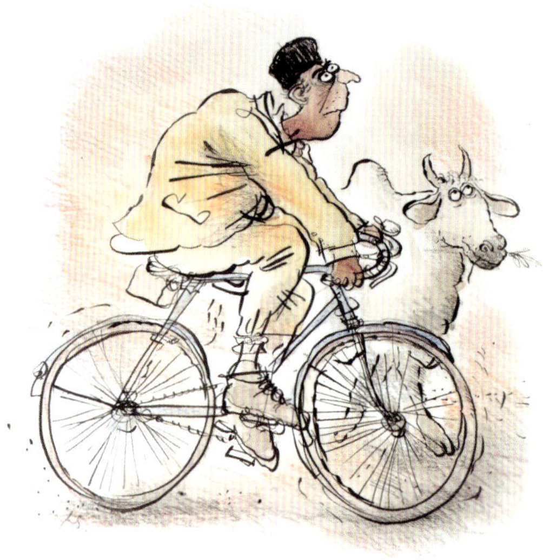

373 MALIK AVOIDS A COW
signed with initials, inscribed with title, chapter title and '6'
inscribed with title, chapter title and '6', stamped with artist's agent's address and copyright details, and dated 2006 on reverse
pen ink, watercolour and crayon
11 ½ x 9 ½ inches
Illustrated: page 236, 'The Commissioner'

APPENDIX

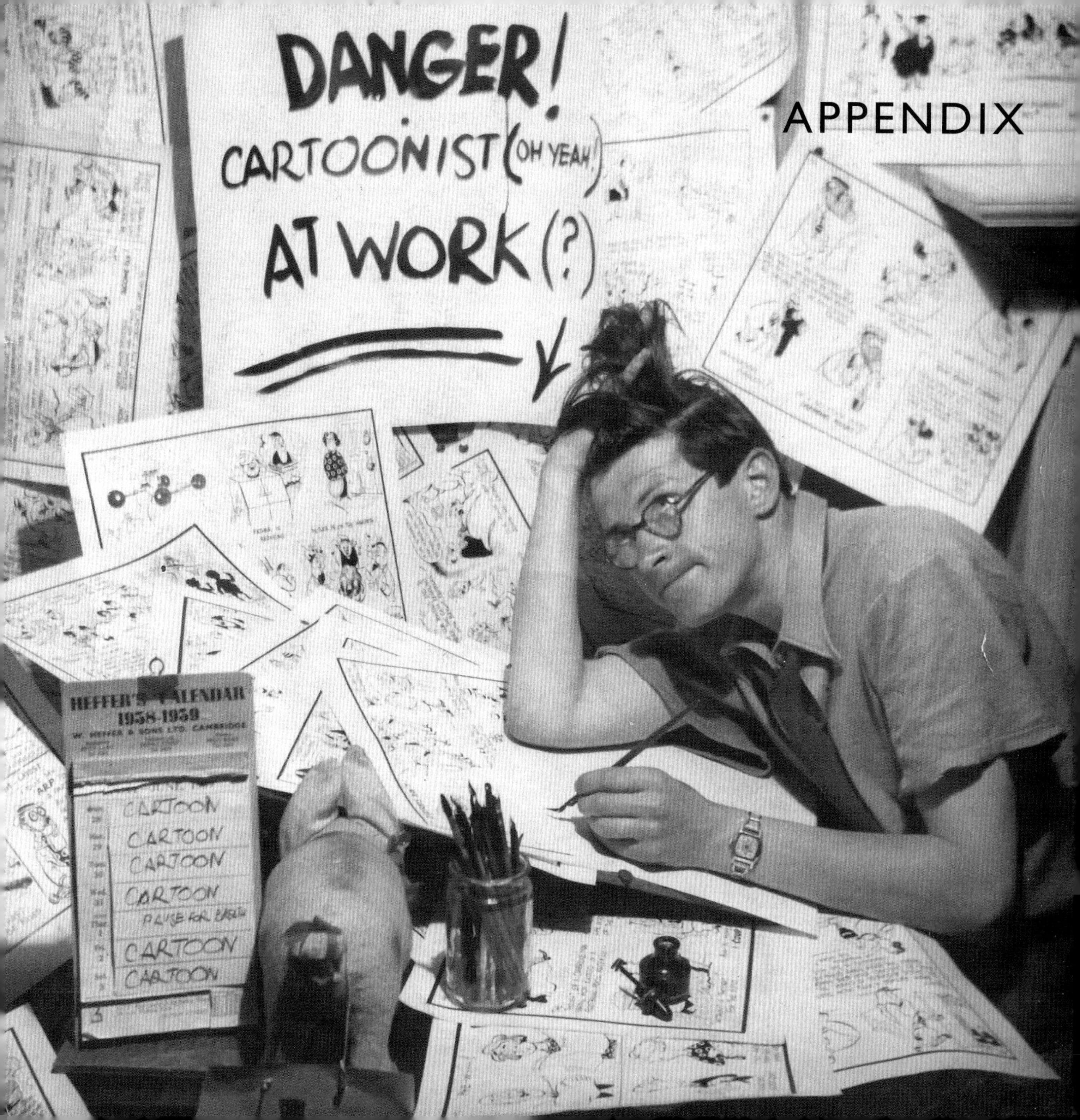
DANGER!
CARTOONIST (OH YEAH!)
AT WORK (?)
HEFFER'S CALENDAR
1958-1959
W. HEFFER & SONS LTD. CAMBRIDGE
CARTOON
CARTOON
CARTOON
CARTOON
CARTOON
CARTOON

17 CHANGI GAOL, SINGAPORE, SATURDAY 21 SEPTEMBER 1945
Handwritten on airmail letter card

EX – PW
MR MORLEY STUART
EDITOR
'CAMBRIDGE DAILY NEWS'
CAMBRIDGE
ENGLAND
VIA AUSTRALIA

Ronald Searle RE 2072249
Changi Gaol, Singapore Sept 21 1945. Saturday

Dear Mr Stuart
A little more scribble for you – I find writing the only thing to keep my mind off the terrible drag of these days. A (natural, I suppose) reaction has set in now and everyone is despondent and bored after the first excitement of our release. Nothing seems to be happening, the remains of the 18 Div are about the only prisoners left here – we feel nobodies baby and quite forgotten. Every day seems to have at least 96 lon–g hours, and home seems further away than ever. The drawings on the back of this are the first I've done for days – I feel much too depressed – I thought that these few little 'high spots' might amuse you – they've whiled away the time anyway. Really, though, the best high spot of all was quite a scoop a fantastic affair. Tom Driberg ('Hickey' of the Express) came here with Mountbattens entourage as a press attaché or something anyway he introduced me to the Supremo and Lady Louis and they took myself and two other friends down to the Government house where we had dinner with them and their red tabbed, gold braided, beribboned chiefs of staff
– about 40 altogether – This is me trying to convince myself that it wasn't a dream
(you must remember that a few hours before I was in my cell) –
Incidentally, I was dress like this
An old cardigan, 1 piece of blue silk as a scarf ancient shorts and a pair of cut-down Jap boots! –
my entire wardrobe at that moment (Sept 14).
Supreme-Commander-Southern-East Asia-Admiral-Lord-Louis-Mountbatten sent us off with a chit (at midnight) back to the gaol!
It is a gem – RONALD SEARLE, PAUL MILLER, JACK WOOD
The above mentioned personnel have been guests of the Supreme Allied Commander South East Asia Command, at Government house Singapore
Signed B H Kimmins
Major General
Army Chief of Staff. 14 Sept 45
Show <u>that</u> to your Sergeant major said the general – that should fix it alright if he wants to know why you are out late.
Fantastic wasn't it? The Colonels here are furious.

I'm going off to hitchhike into the city – I will try to get this off at the same time.
Incidentally it was exciting to see the CDN again after all this time – a copy turned up here date July 26 '45 with all the election results. Feel homesick now! If you do see Mrs Livingstone, or Annely of the old school will you let him know how I am. Incidentally I <u>am</u> very well indeed! I have written home again, but I send them all my love in this letter as well!
For the moment, goodbye
Yours
Ronald

18 HMT SOBIESKI, MONDAY 1 OCTOBER 1945
Handwritten on airmail letter card

EX – POW MAIL
MORLEY STUART ESQ
'CAMBRIDGE DAILY NEWS'
ST ANDREWS STREET
CAMBRIDGE
<u>ENGLAND</u>

with drawings on reverse

'HMT Sobieski' Monday Oct 1 1945

Dear Mr Stuart –

The impossible has come true and we <u>are</u> on the way. Leaving Singapore last Thursday we are due to arrive at Colombo tonight. Perhaps a little shore leave and shopping and then Aden, Port Said, Alexandria and England about October 25. The journey has been fairly calm so far – nevertheless my stomach feels <u>most</u> peculiar!

Would you be kind enough to let either Mr Annely or Mr Livingstone know, that as far as I know out of our old Class 4a, Turkentine and myself are OK and that Stuart Ludman and Cyril Cattermole are dead, Stuart died, of Cerebral malaria, at Changi Prison and Cyril in a railway camp in Burma.
Light is fading – I must get my hammock down, they are impossible things to handle in the dark!

Yrs

Ronald

19 MONDAY NIGHT [1946]
Handwritten letter

34 Tite Street
Chelsea SW3

Monday night

Dear Mr Stuart

I am glad you are about again. Isn't this being – confined-to-bed business depressing? I got up yesterday for the first time after several gloomy days of malaria – (I can't seem to get rid of it) – It reoccurs so frequently that I am looking upon it as a monthly accumulated punishment for any misdeeds during that period! Before I go any further – Thank You for the Kind note in Saturdays 'TT' – mother sent it on to me. The broadcast this evening was quite good fun – I do hope you managed to 'listen in' and that it was bearable.

Before I 'went sick' I had been spending some interesting hours at UNO – I was sent as a press representative – in reality – to do sketches, but I found I spent far more time following the proceedings than sketching! The blue and gold décor in Westminster
Hall had a cheerful dignity and freshness that set off the rich red plush of the presidents' chairs and the (apparently) gold plated microphones – lined up on the rostrum. It was like a game standing in the 'lobby' crowd trying to guess which countries this and that face represented. The Saudi Arabian delegation provided the glamour – their natural bearing and timeless, placid manner made the rest of the assembly look rather 'utility'. Two other people stick out in my memory – are the rather pathetic figure in black of Mrs Roosevelt and the other, Bevin – oozing personality.

[over page]

I took one of the delegates, an American girl, to see Hermione Gingold in 'Sweeter and Lower', which included a wonderfully satirical tableau with Henry Kendall as a rather full busted Brittania singing 'there's life in the old girl yet' She was enthralled. 'Gee', she said 'thats what I like about the English – they don't only take cracks at their weak spots – they Boast about'em!'

Between times I am spending some happy hours at Vera Volkova's ballet studio – watching Margot Fonteyn and some of the other brilliant Sadlers Wells ballet lights – (to say nothing of a dozen or so up and coming protegés) – go through their paces in preparation for the opening of the ballet season at Covent Garden. It is providing fascinating material for some new pictures I'm planning.

Chelsea I like – I'm quite content to feed myself on two gasrings – between bouts of drawing. There are no mice, and the soot comes in from the Lots Road power station – but then so does the sun! Still in the army – still getting extensions of leave; my one uniform is beginning to look a little battered!

I get most of the CDN's from home, so I'm not completely out of touch whilst I am up here
I hope no more
germs pass your way!

Yours

Ronald

20 WEDNESDAY
Handwritten letter

[Printed image of a cancan dancer, address crossed through]
34 Tite Street
Chelsea SW3

Wednesday

Dear Mr Stuart –

How are you? – I saw from TT that mother sent me that you are 'indisposed' – I hope you are better now.
I am sending you today's 'illustrated' which contains those 'serious' sketches I told you about months ago – it has been a long time awaiting publication but I think the wait was worth while! If you are interested at all – I am broadcasting next Monday (11th) at 6.30 in the light programme. – a short talk in the 'World and His Wife Series' – they were rather intrigued with the magazine Exile which we produced :– Changi and so I have to talk mainly about publishing that. As you can see I have a studio up here now so that I really can get down to things on the

[over page]

doorsteps of the publishing houses – I Do come back to Cambridge most weekends so I haven't entirely deserted my 'first love'!

Yours

Ronald

21 25 SEPTEMBER 1947
Handwritten letter

[Printed Address with image of woman]
RONALD SEARLE
M.S.I.A
Studio Two, 77 Bedford Gardens
Park 9519 London W.8

September 25 1947

Dear Mr Stuart

Macdonalds the publishers are going to produce
a book of my cartoons – at their own suggestion. This will cover the best of the work I have done over the last few years together with an introduction – by DD Wyndham Lewis possibly. The book won't be out until next Easter due to the usual production difficulties but stuff is already going to the bookmakers and the first dummy will soon be taking shape.

I want to include a dedication and my mind immediately went to you for had it not been for your encouragement and for publishing that first cartoon way back in 1935 who knows what would have happened to my 'funny' drawings! I know that the old CDN days did everything for me in developing my ideas and drawing and I want to make this little acknowledgement,

[over page]

would you mind if I put something like this:

FOR MORLEY STUART,
? YEARS EDITOR OF THE
CAMBRIDGE DAILY NEWS,
WHO STARTED ME ON THIS.

– I hope not.

Yours

Ronald

22 18 APRIL 1948
Handwritten letter

[Printed address with image of a woman]

RONALD SEARLE
M.S.I.A
Studio Two, 77 Bedford Gardens
Park 9519 London W.8

April 18 1948

Dear Mr Stuart

I am so glad you like the book – I am glad it has turned out to be a good backing for the dedication. I managed to slip down to Cambridge for the day last Saturday to see mother. It was the first time I had been back for some months to spend a moment in the bosom of the family for I have new responsibilities now. I am a married man! My wife, Kaye Webb, was assistant editor of 'Lilliput' for several years and now writes a weekly 'show business' article for the 'Leader' – consequently we spend a great many of our evenings at the theatre! We are extremely happy – especially as we are both in the same field of business – and working very hard.

<u>Of course</u> I shall be able to do you

[over page]

a cartoon for your Diamond Jubilee number. I shall either send it – or bring it in myself in a fortnight or so. It will be nice drawing for you again.

I see the CDN regularly. Mother sends me them each week.

Thanks for the very generous amount of space you devoted to the review of 'St Trinians' – I am sure it has already made a difference to the sales in Cambridge. Mother tells me that Heffers have sold out their first quota. The BBC are going to broadcast a review of it on May 1 in their New Books and Old Books programme. Arthur Marshall is the speaker, which should be rather amusing. I hope to be in to see you one day – meanwhile all power to the pen …

Yours
Ronald

23 17 SEPTEMBER 1945
Copy of typed letter

Ronald Searle. 2072249. Changi Gaol.
Singapore.
Sept. 17th 1945

Dear Mrs Ludman,

May I offer my very deepest sympathy to Mr Ludman and yourself for the tragic loss you have suffered with the death of Stuart, The great gap left in my life with the Loss of him as my closest friend, is but a trifle compared with that left by him as your son. The lives of everyone who knew him will be poorer by his death, his personallity is irreplaceable. After leaving England we first met again in a rubber plantation at a little Singapore village called Bukit Arong, about 10th Feb 1942. I had come back from fighting in Malaya and Stuart, happily spared that wretched business, had arrived from India. We had a good reunion and parted again to meet up in the Changi Prison Camp shortly after capitulation. During the next year we saw each other quite often although we were in different parts of the Camp. And then in the Spring of 1943 we were sent up into the Jungle to work on the Siam-Burma Railway. We were split up for a year – stuart going upon 'F' Force to Burma and myself on 'H' force to Siam. Start's typing abilities spared him the gruelling work with the labour gangs and he worked as clerk to an interpreter under the Japanese. It was up there his attacks of malaria began.

At the end of the year we were evacuated from the jungle to a place in Siam called Kamburai. I was unfortunately sent to the hospital camp several kilometres away, but Stuart sent me messages from the 'fit' camp. The Japs took us back to Singapore where we spent a great deal of ourtime together and this continued in the big Asiatic Prison, Changi Gaol,
Where we were transferred in May 1944, and where we managed to live together for quite a while. Apart from his Malaria, Stuart kept as fit as could be expected. We had all lost weight, food was short and prison conditions of overcrowding and depression didn't help things at all. But Stuart's spirits were high always. He read a lot and kept up his studies of Music, and we talked together many many times about our homes and letters. You were always in his thoughts.

He was taken ill with a very bad attack of Cerebral Malaria and rushed to Hospital but despite every possible attention from some of the best Medical Men, he died after a very short time at 10 15pm March 2nd 1945, Padre Duckworth was with him at the end.

Paul Miller, myself and some of Stuart's friends from HQ acted as bearers and he was buried with full service in a little cemetery amoung the Coconut trees at Wing Loon, Changi. His grave has had every attention.

I know words can sound hollow and meaningless but from the bottom of my heart I send you my utmost sympathy in this your time of great grief. You have lost a fine son.

Very sincerely
Ronald.

24 CHANGI GAOL, SINGAPORE, 17 SEPTEMBER 1945

Handwritten airmail letter

EX – PW

MISS ANNE DEWING
11 RIVERSIDE ROAD
NORWICH
NORFOLK
ENGLAND

Ronald Searle RE. 2072249
Changi Gaol. Singapore
September 17 1945.

Dearest Anne –

Writing this letter is perhaps the saddest moment of my life. Think of me as being with you in your misery.

As you may already know, Stuart died on March 2 1945 of an attack of cerebral malaria after a very short illness, at this prison.

I can still hardly believe it, although I helped to carry him to thelittle Wing Loon Cemetery at Changi, among the coconut palms.

We spent a lot of time together and it made life so much easier. so often we talked into the night about our plans for the future, after the long weary years of imprisonment and misery had dragged themselves out. He talked and thought about you constantly and often as we lay in prison he would tell me how excited he was about the things of the future, how he would marry you, and how you would work together in an exciting future. His spirit was wonderful under dreadful conditions and apart from loss of weight and recurrent malaria which affect us all, he kept quite well. Happily his typing ability and office knowledge kept him out of much of the labour gang work. Apart from one gap of a year when Stuart was in Burma and I was in Siam we were always in the same camps or prison. I won't bother you with details here, it is just a list of skittling from bad to bad.

The thing that seemed so tragic to me was the fact that Stuart got through all the worst business so wonderfully well, kept his spirits through all the brutality and the impossible 'never-ending' atmosphere and then – so close to the end, was snatched away in a moment

[Over page]

He kept your photographs with him all the time and was always reading your letters. You did so much to bring him through the worst moments, Anne, although so many thousands of miles separated you from him.

Chin up, Anne dear – now all this misery of war has finished hardships will be but a trifle after this. So many have to make a fresh start in what may be a hard but wonderful future. I know Stuart will be behind you in whatever you decide to do.

God bless, Anne, take care of yourself, remember me to your mother and friends and I will write to you again as soon as I can

Love
Ronald

25 HMT SOBIESKI, MONDAY 1 OCTOBER 1945

Handwritten airmail letter card

Advanced Base Post Office 4 OCT 45

EX – PW MAIL

MISS ANNE DEWING
11 RIVERSIDE ROAD
NORWICH
NORFOLK
ENGLAND

Aboard 'HMT. Sobieski'
October 1 1945 Monday

Dearest Anne –

Just a hastily scribbled note to send off at Colombo – we are due to arrive there tonight.

We left Singapore on Thursday but I still shant believe it is true until we strike Colombo – I keep feeling that Malaya is just over the horizon. Our other stops are Aden, Port Said – maybe Alexandria and then England about October 25.

The journey so far has been quite uneventful and reasonably

[other side of page]

calm. To tell you the truth I have been asleep most of the time – the sea air is so invigorating!

Forgive all this drivel, Anne dear, won't you? It's idle chatter to cover the misery I feel in coming back alone leaving all my friends back there somewhere in Malaya. To tell you the truth I feel almost afraid to come back to civilisation again the very thought of dodging traffic and meeting people is an appalling prospect I think I shall stay in hiding most of the winter and let the effect break gradually

[over page]

Already the happenings of those years are beginning to fade – perhaps by the end of a month when this voyage is over I may feel a little better. I needed air badly – it was difficult to breath – the stuff that filtered through the prison grills.

I want to write you lots more but the crowded atmosphere of this ship doesnt help. You understand don't you, Anne?

Take care of yourself, remember me to your mother and wish me a safe trip home.

Lots of love
Ron

26 HMT SOBIESKI, RED SEA, WEDNESDAY 10 OCTOBER 1945
Handwritten airmail letter card

FIELD POST OFFICE 174 12 OC 45

EX – POW MAIL

MISS ANNE DEWING
11 RIVERSIDE ROAD
NORWICH
NORKOLK

ENGLAND

Ronald Searle
RE 2072249
EX – POW Singapore RAPWI

HMT Sobieski. Red Sea. Oct 10 1945 Wednesday

Dearest Anne –
Time does pass slowly – how impatient I am to get home – We are three days ahead of schedule already but still we seem to crawl … through the heat. The heat leaves me gasping, rather like the suffocating heat that comes out of the jungle after a storm. Strangely enough, though, as we came into the gulf of Aden we passed about a dozen small whales! They wallowed around the ship rather like submerging submarines and spouted around the place. Of course there are dolphins and sharks and flying fish in profusion – sometimes leaving an impression rather like this –>
I feel that the sea air is doing me all the good in the world – I feel less morbid, I feel I can breath now without choking and I am beginning to get rid of that prison outlook. I think I do feel fine now! I'm disappointed not to have had any mail since 2 written in Aug. before we were

[new page alongside]

released. I'm so anxious to know how everything is at home now, and whether they've got my letters and know that I am free and well and on the way – they should do I've sent stacks of letters and things. Perhaps there will be something for me at Port Said, where this will fly off to you. It's agony still being cut off. Still I suppose I must be patient and eat and sleep and take my vitamin pills and mepacrine – what a life! I have done a little drawing during the last day or so. I saw some rather striking types of Indian females at Colombo and I've been trying to get them onto paper. I'm almost satisfied with one of them – but I can't seem to settle down to anything seriously yet – perhaps it is the general rather unsettled atmosphere of the entire ship – I expect it will go when I can get somewhere quiet and restful again. Cambridge will do! –
How are you, Anne? I often wonder what you might be doing. Perhaps trying to make a new flight of Angel Road 'angels' experience themselves, perhaps Maddermarketing perhaps looking out of the front room across the river …

[over page]

I hope you've been able to keep well and keep above a lot of the irritations and boredom of all the war business. When I get back I must take a flat somewhere (if there's a hope) in Cambridge or London and work like hell to make up for all this time I have lost.
I've got so much to do, so much to catch up on, such a heluva lot to improve on that I don't think I shall have time to breath until I am ninety.
I wonder if you'll see much of a change in me when I come up to show myself to you. My skin is yellow, I've more hair on my chest and the remains of my Thailand mustache. I've got a few scars, I've lost a little weight my face may be a little harder, but my hands are alright! I don't think I'm a great deal different – just got rid of my 'puppy fat'!
Anyway, Anne, after I've made the required overtures to the family I will come up to see you – then we can go somewhere quiet, and sit, and have a talk. Love to your mother, take care of yourself. Next letter from England!

My love

Ron

27 SUNDAY NIGHT OCTOBER 1945

Handwritten letter with envelope

Postmark – 12.15 PM – 29 October 1945 – Cambridge

MISS ANNE DEWING
11 RIVERSIDE ROAD
NORWICH
Norfolk

29 Collier Road
Cambridge

Sunday night

Anne, dearest –

At last I have time! God, this last few days has been exciting and tiring. Continual visiting – duty visits to relations and the like has left me fagged out. I tore myself away from supper out tonight because I was determined to get a letter off by tomorrow to you. I didn't want to scribble off a hasty little note, so forgive me, won't you?

Thank you for your lovely letter – that was all I wanted. We didn't dock until Tuesday. Wednesday night I got home from the transit camp. Thursday, Friday and Saturday have dashed by before I could turn round, so you see just how difficult it would have been to try and dash up – I don't want to make an unsatisfactory, fleeting appearance I want to come and have a good long weekend with you and sit quietly and talk – or perhaps walk. The quieter side is more in my line now! I don't know why but I get tired very easily. I went out for a drink with Dad on Friday – but after 10 minutes in a smoky crowd I broke

2

out in a cold sweat and had to be taken home! Silly isn't it? I enjoy shutting myself up in my pokey little room here and just gazing at everything again – do you think it's the gaol complex?! Everyone tells me I look just the same, perhaps fitter than I did when I left four years ago – that's good, so perhaps I haven't changed after all; the sea voyage did me such a lot of good. It was good to get some clean air inside my lungs again. I'm settling down again now, mustn't eat much but I enjoy the tasty bits! Everything that happens now seems just a dream so long, long ago – I almost wonder if it did happen. Olive of course has brought me down to normal and after my four years of celibacy I can now face a girl quite normally! I think you will find me just the same, Anne.

I went round to see Mr & Mrs Ludman last night – I was almost afraid to go but I'm so glad I went quickly I feel I have eased their minds a little more telling them all the little things they wanted to know. Poor dears they are terribly upset. I felt that when I came to the door they hoped it was Stuart

3

who had really come back. I felt so unhappy. And now I want to come to you Anne, just quietly – and I want to take you into my arms and give you a long kiss to take away a little of that pain you must have suffered – to give you a little of that love you have lost – to thank you for all those lovely little moments we had together and which did make existence a little easier. You do understand, don't you?

When shall I come up? I think perhaps Friday afternoon Nov 9 would be alright, don't you? That would give an evening and two clear days wouldn't it – and I could go back Monday morning when you go back to school. I've got to go up to London this week some time for a few days – 'Lilliput' and 'London Opinion' have written – and on top of that I have to report to the M of I regarding the publishing of a magazine produced at Changi. When that's done I shall be free – and it should be finished by then. So as far as I know then shall we fix Friday the 9th for a long weekend? – that is if your mother will tolerate me! Give her my love.

4

I've started already sending stuff away – lots of cartoons and prison drawings that I brought back with me. I shall bring some up – with me for you to see and I shall also try to carry your picture of the soldier back to it's rightful home! I am so anxious to make a start again – to make up for that time I've lost. I think I shall definitely go back to the Art School for 6 months, or a year for a 'refresher' course – I believe the government will pay for it anyway! Anyway I shall be putting in classes before I am demobbed – I've been given free run of the school. I've got six weeks leave – and then I believe they throw me out – God, I hope so, I've had all of the army I want! I bought myself a pair of corduroys yesterday – that's the first step!

You've got to tell me all you find wrong with me – and make me straighten the kinks out! You are my critic.

5

I shall probably talk you hoarse and squeeze you to death – but it will be a nice few hours together. And this time there will be no sailing – I shall often be able come up and see you – (I think it is home for good now for me) – quite often But still I mustn't hold too high hopes about the future – everything is so indefinite at the moment I'll just go on taking life as it comes for a while, until something hits me! I've had Ramsey & Muspratt photograph me, I'm having notepaper printed I'm buying drawing stuff at extortionate prices, I'm still sorting out papers – but I'm gradually straightening the studio out. I can almost get in the door now! Do you remember this
peculiar animal? It still sits by my bed
– it has been there all the time
contemplating it's young! – even as I
write this! – well it will be able
to produce more offspring now because the Red Cross issued me with a kangaroo (of all

[over page]

things) when we reached Suez – that shows you how young I look! Good lord, it is almost 1. o'clock I must stuff some vitamin tablets and quinine into me. These multi-vit tablets are marvellous but strangely enough the only vitamin not included is vit. E! – Now I wonder why? Perhaps they want to sterilise us! Enough of this, I'm very sleepy and I've got to be up and out again early to visit the old school and take Olive shopping.

Write soon Anne, love to your mother and a big kiss from me to you

As ever
Ron

PS. licks back to Scottie – I still have the moustache and I'm still yellow!

28 FRIDAY
Handwritten letter

[Printed address in red with image of cancan dancer and bottles of wine]

RONALD SEARLE
TWENTY-NINE
COLLIER ROAD
CAMBRIDGE

Friday

Dearest Anne

Thank you so very much for that beautiful little volume of verse – I couldn't have wished for anything better. Something nice and comfortable to sink myself into when I get depressed! I'm in a dreadful turmoil à ca moment. I'm moving – or rather waiting for the van to come and take away my junk. Tomorrow I follow and from then on my home will be on the first floor – 34 Tite Street Chelsea SW3. I'm sorry in a way to leave this den of mine here but perhaps I can make the other place as nice and comfortable. You will come and visit me in it sometime – won't you? What sort of Christmas did you have? – Not too depressing I hope. Mine was rather ruined – I managed to get a spot of malaria on Christmas Eve and spent most of the time either in bed or in a daze! Flora and her niece came

[over page]

down for a couple of days – we didn't do much – it was all pleasantly quiet. I don't feel too badly now – but I wish this moving business was over. I don't know whether you will like this book – although I don't feel completely in sympathy with the artists technique he has definitely got the atmosphere – from experience I can feel some of those incidents. It was the only thing in Heffers I could find that I felt worth sending – and I got the last copy of that.

How are you? – Despite this stinking letter, write to me won't you. When the muddle is over I really <u>will</u> get down to a long one.

I went out to get coffee this morning but the filthy weather soon drove me in again – shivering!

Did the 24th turn out to be alright?

Goodbye for the moment, Anne.
Much to love to you
Ron

29 WEDNESDAY 7 NOVEMBER 1945
Handwritten letter

7B Edith Grove
Chelsea SW10

Wednesday
Nov 7 1945

My dear Anne –
I'm afraid I've got myself into an awful muddle up here with interviews and work wanted – making it impossible to get to Cambridge or Norwich until at least next week. I came up here to see the magazines and things in reply to their telegrams and I landed myself right in the middle of everything. Everyone seems very enthusiastic about the stuff I've brought back. Illustrated grabbed some of my sketchbook studies, had me photographed and are doing a blurb with a doublepage feature in a December number. Lilliput, London Opinion Men Only and the rest are after me and – (god knows why) – they wail that they are short of humorous artists. Well, as you can imagine, I've dived into the thick of it

[over page]

while the going is good, I didn't expect such a lift up as quickly as all this – so I daren't risk losing it. So you can see, Anne, that the weekend has gone to pot for the moment, Olive is upset because she's got tickets for the Arts on Thursday and I can't get, mother hasn't seen me for more than a night in a week – so I am very unpopular!
But we will have a moment to ourselves as soon as I can do it without having to dash off. This will be only a short note, but tubes and busses have haunted me lately and I am feeling completely fagged out. I'll write a much more reasonable letter as soon as I can and thank you for your last, lovely long one!
My love and don't be too angry,
Wearily,
Ron

31 WARD A, PRINCESS BEATRICE HOSPITAL, TUESDAY 5 MARCH 1946
Handwritten letter

Ward A
Princess Beatrice Hospital
Earls Court SW5
Tuesday 5.3.46

Dearest Anne,
The birthday telegram was a pleasant surprise. Thank you! I suppose you won't be very surprised to see the address above – I've been heading for it for some time I know. Every fever and malaria attack I've had at regular intervals since I've been up here has pulled me down and I just couldn't pick up in between times. Maybe it will do me some good – resting, but they are a bit heavy on the drugs. I've been in just over a week and with luck I may be out in another week when I may go down to the seaside or somewhere to convalesce.
I have just written to Mrs Ludman sending her a photograph & negative of Stuart's grave, which I wrote and asked someone to take at Singapore – and which arrived by airmail today. I took a chance that they might like to have it – although I was rather afraid to send it in case it upset them again. I do hope it doesn't. Unfortunately on the cross it gives the wrong age. I don't know who's fault that could have been. There isn't very much to tell you – I've being carrying on with my drawing as best I could but a lot of it I just had to drop because it became too much for me. I did concentrate the best stuff on to Lilliput and left enough surplus energy to do life drawing and some watercolour. I've been demobbed (praise God) at last – may my uniform rot in the cupboard!
Strangely enough I find bed somewhat tiring – probably because the days are so long when one is called at 5.0am! – about all I can remember about them is a long chain of cigarettes! Visiting days are far and few between but happily I do get a welcome gathering for the few moments allowed so that helps to break the monotony. Are you keeping alright, Anne? – write sometime and tell me what you are up to won't you?
Now I must rest
'bye 'bye for now
Love
Ron

30 COLLIER ROAD, 5 DECEMBER 1945
Handwritten on reverse of exhibition invitation card

Dec 5 1945
Collier Rd
Anne, darling –
Can you come down Saturday morning and stay until Sunday afternoon or evening? I've got to go back to London early Monday and I do want to show you my stuff so that you can tell me whether I've improved or not. Two of the kids from school who I've been staying with in Chelsea will be in for tea on Saturday – they are coming down to see the stuff but apart from that we shall [have] the whole time to ourselves. Do try and make it, won't you?
Love Ron

32 CAMBRIDGE, SUNDAY 24 MARCH 1946
Handwritten letter

[printed address]
RONALD SEARLE,
34, TITE STREET,
CHELSEA, S.W.3

Sunday – Cambridge.
March 24 '46

Dearest Anne –

I'm out of hospital and have come home for a short weekend. The first time I have been home for a month. I thought of trying to slip up to see you today but it was difficult really. Apart from the fact that mother wanted me to stay and talk to her I had to go over to see John Hookham (the ginger headed art master from the school) and take him some of the recent stuff I had done. It's quite exciting, you see, Anne, because the Cambridge University Press are going to publish a book of my drawings – a selection of about 40 from the exhibition. The best part of it all is that it is to be presented as a book of my drawings and NOT as a collection of Japanese sketches or anything morbid. I don't think they will be even in chronological order. So perhaps they can stand for the first time on their artistic interest. It will be about quarto size, published, I hope, in the Autumn at about 5/- or 6/-. It won't be particularly pretentious or elaborately bound, to keep the price within popular reach (which I think is a very good thing) – I believe it will have an introduction by someone – I don't know who or what – the CUP are doing that themselves. and if there is room they may include a couple of recent drawings too. Anyway I am not worrying what they are going to do with the stuff because the CUP only turn out presentable books and I feel it is something of a distinction to be printed by them – don't you? I'm terribly excited about the whole thing. I do want my serious stuff to get a foundation and I think this may be it. They are paying me a Royalty – but I don't think it will amount to much – it doesn't matter really, the drawings are the important thing.

[over page]

I'm having to stay in London for a while because I'm under treatment now with my own Doctor. Although the treatment at the hospital may have helped the malaria my general condition was pulled down more – so I'm getting liver injections, homogenised spinach, tonic, ferosulphate, multivite tablets and I expect to blow up any moment! I've had to get on with some work as well – stuff that was waiting for me otherwise I should lose the contacts and the boy must live! I shall have to postpone thoughts of a holiday until later. Anne dear. I don't think I shall be able to get home for at least three weeks. I'm so glad the broadcast went over alright, I had wondered what it was like – I was more than nervous – I was shaking. Kaye Webb clutched my arm and that alone saved me from falling out of my chair.

Officially it was liked and I may get more in the Autumn. Eileen Malory the director of the programme wants me to spend three weeks with her in September travelling around with Gipsies (it's being arranged officially) and we may do something together on it. Even if it is only a book it will be fun, but it may be broadcasts.

Let me see – what else … I may be appearing in New Yorker soon I had to send them a batch of stuff last week, that'll be fun, won't it? 'Punch' published one this week for the first time & Men Only want me to do colour stuff for them in future.

I've been to the ballet at Covent Garden twice lately, first to see The Sleeping Beauty and last week Rake's Progress Nocturne, & Miracle in The Gorbals. I was afraid that my senses might have been dulled over the last years but there was no cause for fears of that sort. I just sat and lapped it up. And it was all just as exciting as ever.

2

[printed address crossed out]

I had lunch with Margot Fonteyn and Vera Volcova on Thursday and I want to get back to sketching at rehearsals next week again if I can.

I'm glad you've been able to tell me some reactions you've heard about my stuff. I get one or two opinions from people I know but mainly the others come from friends, and on the whole I find it difficult to get an unbiased opinion – as you know yourself people who know me often find it safer not to be critical – unfortunately. I didn't go to the Picasso Matisse exhibition mainly because the place was always eight deep – but I gather that there was nothing there that advanced on the work they had done over the last 15 years. All that fuss was rather silly – I suppose it is because The majority of people who swarmed had only just found out that the two painters existed. No, I don't get a great deal of response from the latest 'period' of Picasso – I prefer the blue & green periods purely because I feel more in that direction myself, and not in the more remote; but I don't deplore his personal advances. If he <u>feels</u> that way about things – if his personal vision <u>is</u> remote, let him express it but it doesn't necessarily follow that it is significant, or an advance, he is covering ground that has to be covered by someone, so it isn't a waste of effort; I don't think it can ever be appreciated generally because the expression <u>is</u> so personal – and naturally obscure. I don't think it can do any harm. If there are people who are weak enough to be swayed by it as an easy way out, without a great deal of basic work and thought, it doesn't matter, because they are the sort of people who would be too weak to push forward on their own legs anyway.

Others will draw the good from it and use it in their own way to express their own individual visions and that I think is where the advance comes in – transfusing life blood when the body that

[over page]

contained it is becoming decadent. I find myself that feeling for people and things is too strong to be dismissed in the abstract or formalized. I don't mean that one must be realistic but I do mean that there is a personality in things that is destroyed when approaches are too remotely scientific – and besides I like people to get some response from my work! (or should it be some people to get response…)

I quite expect that I shall be influenced here and there by influences that have any thing to offer, but I don't think it will overwhelm me. I think it is good to absorb and convert – one can never expect to search out all the problems on ones own and every painter must be expected to be influenced by someone at some time or other. After all, Picasso was influenced by Toulouse Lautrec for some years himself & then his blue period followed!

Heavens, you do sound busy with your little theatre – lucky kids! I <u>shall</u> see it sometime.

I'm going to take mother to the cinema now so I must tear myself away, Anne – I shall go to bed as soon as I get in. I like to behave myself and get to sleep about 9.30 these days.

I hope to tell you more about the serious stuff soon – if you can stand it – I want to start school soon, probably the LCC the Chelsea Polytechnic is a little crowded I think at the moment.

Look after yourself and give my love to your mother

My love, as ever,

Ron

33 GOOD THURSDAY 1946
Handwritten letter

[Typed address]
RONALD SEARLE,
34, TITE STREET
CHELSEA, S.W.3 Thursday 1946!

Dearest Anne,
I've only just had a chance to reply to your letter
because I have been cramming time in on what work I could before
I went away for Easter – I'm going today down to Westgate,
I am feeling a great deal better compared with the state I was in
probably because I am just finishing the course of liver injections
and have been out into the sun a bit. I shall be thoroughly
disappointed if it rains over Easter – (it has started already) but I
don't think that will keep me in. I expect to be back about
Tuesday night. Yes! I must see you before you go back Anne –
and you must come and look at this place. I'm afraid
there is little or nothing new in the way of work to show you.
most of my recent stuff is at the framers and won't be back
for a couple of weeks – but anyway I can dig up
enough to prove that I am not slacking! I don't know
what work I shall drop in for when I get
back until I get back, but wouldn't the best thing be for me either
to
ring you at your London address or, if there isn't a 'phone
(like this place) give me the address and let me wire you on Wedy
morning when I find out how I am fixed? That will
be alright won't it? I daren't fix up a definite date
now because my time is so inconsistent and I wouldn't
want to have to break a date – because I hate it, and am
so disappointed when it is done to me!

[over page]

By the way – I've been granted a pension on my malaria.
The magnificent sum of 8/6 a week! – only for seventy weeks
though. Apparently it's not their concern what happens after that.
Anyway it will pay some of the rent! Really I'm a little
bitter about being thrown out in the condition I was – especially
as it has taken a great deal of my pocket money to get myself
fairly well again – but still, who should I be to grumble ….
I'm very lucky, really, aren't I?
I won't try and write any more now because I
must pack my bag – but when we meet we can
talk about all the things we want to – much better
than just scribbling them down.
I hope you have a nice Easter in Cambridge.
Give my kindest regards to Mr & Mrs Ludman, and tell
me all about it when you come.

My love – and take care of yourself.

Ron.

34 CAMBRIDGE, SUNDAY 5PM MAY 1946
Handwritten letter with envelope

Chelsea 1 – pm 27 May 1946 S.W.3

Miss Anne Dewing
11 Riverside Road
NORWICH
Norfolk

[Printed address crossed out]
RONALD SEARLE
34, TITE STREET
CHELSEA S.W.3

Cambridge
Sunday. 5.0 pm.

Dearest Anne -
At last I've got a chance to write. I've been
just as hectically busy as ever since I saw you and
this weekend I made a determined effort to get home
not that it has been much of a weekend off because
just before I left Chelsea an order came for a cheap edition
book jacket for a stupid Ethel Mannin book. As the roughs
had to be in at the beginning of the week I've been doing
that here. I am catching the 7.5 back tonight. I'm feeling
a lot better now. Still a little tired – but infinitely better.
My doctor told me the results of the pathological examination.
– no sign of malaria (altho' it is not usually found unless active)
and no anaemia. Mentally I've felt fairly normal – a few
fits of depression, a few flusters when I got a bit upset dashing
about – but really quite successful. I had an interesting week
last week. I had dinner with Tom Driberg at the H of C and spent
the evening drinking and having a good conflab – about
10.0 I went in and listened to the debate

[writing upside down right hand corner]

PS
Sorry I haven't
your letter with
me. So I may not
have replied to
things I should
have replied
to!

[over page]

for the first time and was amazed at the casual atmosphere
of the whole proceedings. Nothing particularly significant was being
discussed but Wednesday was much better. Tom got me in for
question time in the afternoon – and later Bevin made a statement
on the Polish forces' rehabilitation. Churchill was there – in fact
I believe most people were excepting the PM – And then the
long business began on the Pensions Bill. Thursday Kaye Webb
and myself went to the ITMA broadcast – an ambition of mine!
I met Topolski earlier in the evening – very briefly.
Friday I went to the New to see OUR TOWN (Thornton Wilder)
before it comes off. It is a great pity that the play hasn't
been supported. It is good, unconventional and sincere. A
cross section of American life in a little town. Without
scenery and with Walter Connolly as the stage manager
narrator. I suppose because it is unconventional
and slight it is not considered good value
for money. Well thats rather a dull preamble of my
recent hours off and if my writing is getting

ever more illegible it is because I am writing
this on the train now, halfway to Liverpool Street.
School is going quite solidly – although I've missed quite a lot of attendances in one way and another – my life there turns out very stodgily – pudding like

2

[printed address crossed out]

and unless it improves considerably by the end of the term I think I shall finish again and fight on by myself. There is no doubt about it – there is a certain atmosphere that one feels almost bound too in art school life classes – and for me it still seems to be rather 'heavy-going' life for exam standard. I'm sure much of my quicker stuff from my own model here earlier on is more useful – but nevertheless – rubbing up the groundwork won't do any harm as long as I know where to hold it. Colour is proceeding – still doing exercises. (pencil is enforced I'm afraid – my pen is empty).
I got 'London Opinion' to go through the Exile and type out the obituary for you. It is slightly inaccurate but forgivable – written by Alan Roberts (who had a story in [I believe] April 'Lilliput') – I pass it on to you, Anne – and leave it for you to decide whether it should go any further.

[over page]

I am still going to Volkova's ballet class on Wednesdays – making dozens and dozens of quick scribbles – shorthand records of poses and positions it is wonderful practice time for me from the point of view of rapid notetaking because I should imagine that nothing could be more difficult to capture than split second ballet movements And, of course, my models couldnt be better to provide the authentic positions and technique, for instance, Last Wednesday morning they consisted of Margot Fonteyn June Brae, Pamela May, Violetta Prokhorova, Ashton, Henry Danton, and supporters. That was an especially interesting session because Mdme Karsavina came in for a few moments to look round – a very sweet person, I should say.
Oh dear, almost Liverpool St I must end.
Love and 'bye for the moment
Ronald

35 SATURDAY NIGHT
Handwritten letter

34 Tite Street
Chelsea SW3

Saturday night

Dearest Anne –
Well I am firmly in now! I think I can really say I have settled down now in my one large room. I like it here – the room is pleasant – plenty of built in cupboards, tall, well lit – quite enough for me. I had it decorated bookshelves and a gas fire built in – washbasin fixed – lino put down – and that with the sticks from my room at Cambridge make the place quite habitable. I felt rather unhappy about leaving Cambridge and my room there behind, it all had so much to hold me – but I feel that now maybe I've come back to begin some sort of life again I have been wise in putting the old associations behind. And now I like the room up here as much as my old one. I'm enjoying London life – especially as I am still at the stage where I find it exciting. I do my own cooking on a couple of

2

gas rings – which is a bind sometime. And there is no hot water in the place but I am lucky to get a studio of any sort so I'm not grumbling. (You must forgive the scrawl but it is 2.0 in the morning and I am feeling a little tired – but determined to write to you whilst I can.) I've been working hard on straight stuff – apart from regular life drawing – I've been pounding away on two new pictures – fairly large ones – which I feel (or like to feel) are the most significant things I have produced up to date. Watercolour and line – but I don't think they have lost anything by it. My main work other than this has been illustration – I've hardly done more than a couple of cartoons since December – the illustrations are mainly for Lilliput – and not completely commercial. In fact one I have been working on

3

over the last week for April Lilliput is a straight one on Asquith, I did some interesting research on that reading contemporary reports of the 1911 year in the commons – down in Reynolds news office. I have some others which promise to be interesting – illustrations on the ballet which means I sketch when I want at a ballet school. I went to UNO last night with the press and had an interesting half hour watching the involved business of electing the secretary general. I saw Bevin, Eleanor, Roosevelt, the Russians in fact most of them for the first time, it was intensely interesting. But I think it was the Saudi Arabian delegation that held my attention most. Topolski was there sketching. I am trying to get a regular sketching pass so that I can go in when I want – whether I use the

4

notes or not they'll be interesting to
do – and keep. I've got to make a
short interest broadcast on the light
programme at 6.30 Feb 11 (I think) –
and if it goes alright I may do casual
broadcasting. I felt a little nervous about
it all – but now that I have bashed out
my script I feel a little easier. Try and
listen won't you – and weep for me
if I make mistakes. Watch for next
week's 'Illustrated' too – (on Wednesday) – I think
it will feature some of my 'straight stuff'.
If you want the list of people publishing
my stuff, Anne, – here it is – vaguely –
Lilliput (regularly), London Opinion (regularly)
Men Only (occasionally) Punch (occasionally)
Tatler (published 2-3 a week for 2 months but
I haven't sent them anymore) Everybodys had
some and have used it up – so they've had 'it'

5

Woman & Beauty (illustrations each month)
Womans' Journal (occasionally),
Strand (occasionally) Illustrated (Feb 6) –
and the New Yorker (I hope!)
But it is hopeless trying to get hold of
copies of magazines – the 'pockets' are
about the only things that can be
bought casually. I like to think though
that my best stuff goes into Lilliput.
– that's my pet! I'm meeting some
quite interesting people – and am
getting to know my editors better,
I'm still in the army – they are sending
me leave extensions every 2 weeks
without comment – and so I go on.
I'm keeping fairly well – tired usually,
bouts of depression and elation.
The doctor has put me on priority milk

6

and I am getting treatment for
my beri beri as well as prophylactic
malaria stuff – I've lost a little weight
but I can't grumble. I don't know
whether you will like the photograph
or not – if not you can file it away!
Your 'soldier' is still hanging in
Cambridge – ready for you when you
want it – delivered to you. What are
you doing, Anne – still Maddermarketing?
How are the puppets going – and the theatre,
How are you keeping? – although I don't
deserve to hear at all for holding out so long
– but I wanted to write and send your
photograph at the same time.
I must go to bed now – I can
hardly keep my eyes open!
Goodnight, Anne, dear, love
Ron.

[reverse of 6]

Hope there
aren't too many
mistakes – I haven't –
read it back!

36 SATURDAY
Handwritten letter

[Printed address with image of a woman]
RONALD SEARLE
M.S.I.A
Studio Two, 77 Bedford Gardens
Park 9519 London W.8

Saturday.

Hello! Anne, dear –
I am resuscitated! Back from the gloam.
I suppose you have wondered why I have kept
such an unearthly silence over the last week or so. The
answer is simply – depression, complete and absolute.
I suppose it was the aftermath of 'flu and
bronchitis and then coming back to a turmoil of
uncompleted and accumulated work – all pressing!
Consequently I put in some solid overtime and
my temper was somewhat frayed – certainly I was
no fit companion for a hospital patient. You have
been spared the pain of having me sitting on the
end of your bed huddled and blinking like a sick
bear. A sure recipe for keeping you on your

[over page]

bed an extra week! Anyway it has
passed and I am feeling almost my sub normal
self again!
All being well I shall be
in either Tuesday or Friday evening to tender
my apologies in person.
Meanwhile here is a little piece
of frippery to keep you occupied for five
minutes and as that Oliver person says –
'I hope you like it'
I hope they are treating you
well this time – but you can tell me
all about it on Tuesday … Or Friday
Till then, then!
Yours
Ronald

37 THURSDAY NIGHT

Handwritten letter

[Printed Address with image of a woman]
RONALD SEARLE
M.S.I.A
Studio Two, 77 Bedford Gardens
Park 9519 London W.8

Thursday night

My dear Anne –
My silence and absence has been due to being bedridden myself! I went down to Westgate for a couple of days holiday last week and developed 'flu' and bronchitis on arrival. Since then I have been buried under the bedding – disgusted with the world. I staggered back to London this morning to deliver my 'Punch' drawing – then back into bed. I am going down to Cambridge tomorrow because I can't face any more of my cooking and at the same time see mother who hasn't been too well and celebrate a double birthday with

[over page]

Dad. I hope to be back next week and fit enough to pop in and cheer you up.

At the moment it would be unfair to breath germs over you and turn you suicidal with my air of depression.

My ballet book has arrived from Paris and looks quite well. I shall bring you a copy to look at and tell you what I have been painting when I come up.

Dizzily yours

Ronald

38 WEDNESDAY

Handwritten letter

[Printed Address with image of a woman]
RONALD SEARLE
M.S.I.A
Studio Two, 77 Bedford Gardens
Park 9519 London W.8

Wednesday

Dear Anne –
Just a very hurried note to send off a few things to read.

Things have been very upset since I saw you last.

Mother was taken away in an emergency ambulance and was hanging between life and death for several days – altho' she doesn't know it. She is still very ill but over the crisis and is being pumped full of adrenaline

[over page]

penicillin and oxygen. Asthma with complications is the trouble and it practically drove me silly watching the poor darling trying to breath.

Anyway the main thing now for her is complete relaxation and rest and now she is fully conscious her old spirit is back. But on top of this! The morning after she was taken to hospital her mother died.

We shan't tell her until she is really better again. Of course I had to go rushing up to Leicester to see about the funeral and arrived back in London this afternoon. I must try and cram in a couple of days work & then go back to Cambridge. I expect I shall be in Cambridge more than London for a while so I can be contacted there!

Sorry to depress you with all

[written on side of back page]

– this, Anne but it has been quite impossible to visit. I do hope the final stages of the treatment are getting things moving. You should be out soon, eh?

Must go now – forgive the scrawl and confusion wont you

Ron

[written across top of back page]

P.S don't tell Mrs L about grandma's death.
In case it gets to mum by roundabout means, will you.
Sorry to fuss.

39 CAMBRIDGE, SUNDAY

Handwritten letter

As from –
Studio 2
77 Bedford Gardens
W8

Park 9519

Cambridge
Sunday

Hello, Anne!

I'm taking a short weekend away from work and determined not to repeat my past (depressed) performance I am staying in this evening to write you – exactly one year to the night since I arrived home again. It still seems impossible that it is a year already – so much has happened, flashing through like an age in four reels of celluloid. A two hour performance – and it only seems that since I saw you in the spring, under a cloud of post malarial depression. A lot has happened since then – and I hardly know where to begin. I think perhaps the best way is to take your questions in order!

Yes – Things are well with me. I've been keeping (I almost dare to say 'very') well; Still a little pale to look upon and like an xylophone about the ribs, but nothing that can't be overcome in time. I think I look a little less miserable and I have a beard of sorts – not because I want to look 'arty' (in fact I'm dressing extremely conservatively I'm told) but because I have an affection for it; I used to like fingering it in the jungle. I am sending you a couple of photographs so that you can get over the shock and at the same time letting you see the studio. Which brings me to the next question! I love my new place. If ever there was a room in which I enjoyed working it is this one. It is really quite large (there are four corners like the one in photograph – tho' not as untidy!) with a huge window and plenty of light. Built as a studio and one of several, it is just what I wanted – with a bathroom cum passageway – and kitchen, so I can have a bath now and cook without stooping, and if I want to get out of the room I don't have to go out in the street as I did in Chelsea – some of the main reasons why it became intolerable. Of course the real reason why I moved was because I've coveted this place ever since I came up to dinner with Cluysenaar the Belgian painter, last Christmas. He promised me first option if he left – and when he did – I got it in July.

[over page]

2

Work is progressing well – and I hope soon it will be as I want it to be. I swore that I'd take almost anything for the first year and to try and accumulate a little money – I still haven't any money but it's almost time to cut out a great deal of the commercial stuff. I think the book will be a turning point and then serious work will get the majority of time. The book should be out by Christmas. It has already been advertised in the Times Lit. Sup and is in the C.U.P. autumn catalogue. I can hardly wait for it to appear … It will cost about 6/- and will be quite large (about 12″ x 9″) and thin. Most of the drawings are reproduced the same size and it is called just 'Fourty Drawings'. I have been doing some serious stuff. You can see one of my recent paintings on the easel in the studio photograph. I am trying to get enough for an exhibition in the Spring. There is already a chance of it being at the Leicester Galleries. I do hope it comes off.

Last week I was in Paris. I have been approached by a French publisher who wants me to do a book of drawings of the English ballet by me to coincide with the Covent Garden B visit in November – which means I've got to get on with it. It will be a limited edition – not very big, with a short review of English ballet in French. It will be good fun to do – especially as it is one of a series of six by European artists on different themes. There is too much to see in Paris and my stay was too short but I enjoyed every second of it.

As far as commercial work goes I've never had so much. Apart from the usual stuff I joined the Daily Herald in June and am drawing for them a couple of times a week, unless there are lots of T.U.C. reports – as there were last week – when I was squeezed out! Lots of other magazines have asked me for stuff – consequently doing a cover for Our Time and straight illustrations for Woman's Journal, decorations for The Strand and book jackets for someone else. I change my method of approach so many times that I almost forget what my basic one is! Anyway it is experience and it is not doing me harm artistically as long as I can retain a sense of proportion. I think I am holding my own with other people if one can judge on commissions and increase in rates.

My gipsy holiday was wrecked partly by the 'Herald' who made me appear regularly and mainly because the girl responsible got engaged and her fiancée didn't approve!

I have been asked to do another broadcast – but I haven't thought of anything worth saying – that no one else couldn't do. At one time there was even a chance of my getting the introducers job on the 3rd Programmes Visual Arts thing – Oh, well.

3

What interesting folk have I met? Well – several for a fleeting moment. Topolski, Geoffrey Grigson, Gerald Kersh, Stephen Potter, V-S. Pritchett, Maurice Richardson, Bill Naughton – some at dinner some at other peoples houses. Brassai and Andre Francois I spent an evening with in Paris and H Morrison and Dalton I had for an hour or two at the Bournemouth conference of the Labour Party Morris Richardson I found charming, we ate a sandwich in a Fleet street pub and it seemed difficult to believe that he wrote crazy surrealist dwarf stories. Elliot Mason I enjoyed with her stream of stories. But three people I've got to know over the period are Tom Driberg who has become a good friend. We've had several jobs to do together such as the week at Bournemouth – Hangmans rope makers in the Old Kent Road. D B Wyndham Lewis lives nearby and demands that I illustrate his work when editors raise the question. Last time he and his wife came to dinner he ate 2 ½ helpings of my casserole (my cooking is improving) which made me proud! The third is James Mason who, liking my drawing asked Kaye Webb to bring me to dinner. He wants to improve his drawings and so … He is intelligent and not a bit the arrogant sadist publicity might lead one to believe. And now – my affairs. Very few people know them but I can give you them in confidence!

I am all but married, but the situation is a little complex. We are living together – (but god forbid that it should be known). She is at the moment divorcing her husband from whom she was parting when I met her – parents approve and life is wonderful although we have to keep it quiet for the time. We have more than a lot in common and we can work together perfectly. Although we've had business contacts since 1940 I didn't really meet her until this year and the rest just came – and – well, I love her. She is Kaye – Kaye Webb, the assistant editor of Lilliput – but that doesn't matter. It is the nicest thing that ever happened to me.

I know it is stupid of me to ask, Anne but please don't mention anything about this – even when you write – in case by slight mischance is goes astray and complicates things. I couldn't bear that. But I know you well enough to feel that I am insulting you by saying such a thing.

You do understand don't you?

[over page]

4

The cat just did this!
Heavens! you do sound energetic. Knowing how incapable I am of trying to dance I don't think I could ever cope with anything as complicated as golf!

I am very glad Stuart's personal belongings have turned up at last. I was worried in case they had been stolen although I knew they had been packed officially. I do hope Mr & Mrs Ludman are getting over it now. I haven't been to Cambridge very often in the last six or seven months but when I did come I felt somehow that it would be better not to go round to Warkworth Street. I don't think they would have wanted me to see them and bring back memories by just appearing. I think I was right don't you?

Yes, do come round when you are in Cambridge I don't expect I shall be back for a while but mother knows you will be coming for your picture and which one it is. I shall be glad to know it is with you again. By the way – we are on the 'phone here now. (Cambridge 55739).

Mother is fairly well. She had several operations on her nose and felt much better but now the cold weather has turned up the old trouble has begun all over again. I don't think she will ever get rid of it now – but she takes it well.

Well, I suppose I had better hie me to bed if I am to put in an appearance tomorrow in London. I keep on propping my eyes open!

Give my love to your mother. I don't think because my further delay in replying has any real excuse – but I can say it helped me a lot and I don't forget you, Anne

Take care and write or ring sometime, won't you?

As ever

247 MONDAY AM, MARCH 1956

Handwritten on post card

Paris 27 March 1956

Mrs Brian Ellsmoor
Noirmont
The Heath
Weybridge
Surrey
ANGLETERRE

Monday am.

Dear Jean –

This is the turning point for me I've already put on several pounds – Hope I have enough money for excess poundage when I fly back! The plane I believe is due back about 5.0pm on Thursday. The sun has truly arrived here today and a few spring hats are creeping out. I haven't had time to get near a tree yet but I'm told you can hear the buds popping. Hope there have been no emergencies there.

Yours Ronald

249 WEDNESDAY 12 DECEMBER 1956

Handwritten letter with envelope

13 Dec 1956

Mrs Jean Ellsmore
'Noirmont'
The Heath
Weybridge
Surrey

8 Arundel Terrace [drawing of seagulls over the sea with rain]
Brighton
Wednesday December 12 1956

Dear Jean –

I'm writing to you at home because it is a question of Christmas presents and the letter may go astray … stockings are some of the things I ought to get and you will know better the sort of mesh or st-r-e-t-ch they should be. Could be several Kinds say ½ doz pairs. I'll think more and write again with – when I have – other ideas. –

Its grey and wet and miserable down here and it's only the thought of how much good it is supposed to be doing me that keeps me from running – or rather limping – back to the studio. The book and the money arrived safely today – thanks – I'll read about the human form as a compensation to sitting here on my own. My sortie to the telephone box – tottering across the road, got me a thorough soaking – very bad for you when you are frail, hem hem. Actually I'm feeling much better – I'm only aware of 'something' down there when I forget it. Everything else is working normally … except my brain. But that's not important, there's nothing to use it on down here. How on earth I am going to talk to Christopher for a day I don't know.

I hope there haven't been too many dreary things to cope with over the last week – apart from the boring business of doing another persons Christmas cards – and then having to face your own! and thank you for going in to see old Edwards on Saturday. Another beard around the place … [drawing of Edwards and a self-portrait]

One thing I have discovered here is a Hugo's simplified French – I'm delighted to be able to tell you that My aunt is at the door of the church – well that's something I suppose.

I'll write again with another shopping suggestion the moment I get a feasible thought. You could get yourself a small battering ram out of the petty cash, meanwhile …

Yours

Ronald

250 SATURDAY 15 DECEMBER 1956
Handwritten letter

8 Arundel Terrace
Brighton Saturday 15 December 56

Dear Jean –

Further thoughts on family Christmas presents … A Large and expensive bottle of Cyclax bath salts – (if they call them by such a vulgar name) which can be got on one of the accounts. Sorry to bother you with chores like this at home but it is hopeless here I've never known such persistently foul weather – it is beating across from the sea and absolutely punishing the house. And I now know what is meant by the moaning of the wind. Talk about fresh air.

I don't feel too bad in myself but farewell to the fresh air – I'd be signing my death warrant to go out and breath – That lot. Thank you for all the notes and reports and the money by a short neck which arrived safely this morning! Have you kept a copy of the various bits and pieces of messages you are sending on to me? I hope so. Perhaps you could fix Annie for me. You can tell when it will be convenient. I'll leave it to you to contact her and decide – the calendar bookings frighten me … my hair is lank and filled with gales. I am also feeling slightly hysterical at the thought of Christmas having done nothing. You are probably feeling the same for exactly the opposite reason!

I am going to make my way back on one of the fast trains on Tuesday afternoon. Mrs Robinson who's cooking for me here will be able to get my suitcase down for me. I want to try to get back before it is dark and get to bed early in the evening before all the activity starts I wish I felt more lively! and less stupid. Give my regards to Brian – I hope the carless journeys in aren't going to be hell. See you on Tuesday with the kettle on.

Yrs
Ronald

P.S. Did I tell you it snowed for a while here on Thursday? [drawing of self-portrait in sleet storm]

251 PARIS, WEDNESDAY JANUARY 1957
Handwritten on post card

Paris 24 Jan 1957

Mrs Brian Ellsmoor
Noirmont
The Heath
Weybridge
Surrey
Angleterre

Paris. Weds pm

Dear Jean

I would say that this is skiing weather – sunny and crisp and frost on the pavements. So you will probably get winter-sporting deluxe. Armoured by my Christmas string vest I am coping with garages, fuel ministers, girls schools and other exciting material. My nose is blue and my fingers nipped. but I am getting the stuff. Up to this moment I've only had time for one meal since Tuesday night so I am doing my duty. Judith et Irwin send their love. They have a nice little flat up above the Pigalle and it looks like being a success. My Picasso – Vollard is signed – so it should be worth more. Don't expect to be back until Sunday. The stuff doesnt go off until Saturday. Back to the board. Regards to Brian.

Yrs Ronald.

252 SATURDAY NIGHT, 18 MAY 1957
Typed letter

Saturday Night
18 May 1957

Dear Jean …

Well at last, the first few minutes break since I've arrived. New York is utterly fantastic; quite unlike anything I've seen in pictures of it. It is a sort of fairyland in almost every sense an extraordinary beauty mixed with potty incongruousness. I haven't had a chance to see much of it yet. In the first two days after docking in a cloudburst at 10 at night I had to attend about fifteen conferences an meetings on a scale that made the scenes in FUNNY FACE small time stuff. All rather dreamlike in their décor and ponderousness – everything marble and icedwater. My contract still is not signed although it had last reached the stage of being handled between lawyer and lawyer. They have drawn up contracts that make British Lion contracts casual little notes. Anyway I've started work and I think Locke will get pretty well everything else he asks for as I'm here and the job is already behind. He's sticking out for another $5000.oo with all expenses and travelling paid outside New York, to cover the West Coast trip. Which is a godsend (assuming that it will be accepted!) as it is layed down in the contract that I HAVE to stay at work for them exclusively for ten weeks until July 24 – and no question of reducing the time. Any additional work that aris arises after that will have to be done in England. But if I work hard – and it looks as if there is hardly going to be much time off – I shall get it all done. As far as I can find out I shall be in New York until about 17th June and then go to Hollywood but that may be changed at anytime depending on the speed of production. They are flying peop people the 3000 miles in to see the drawings in about a fortnight. Locke is being terribly nice and quite unlike what I expected. Smallish middle aged slim and slightly round shouldered asthmatic with a very sweet wife. They have picked the most beautiful view for his apartment – two rooms up on the 23rd floor overlooking in one sweep the the UNO building and the full width of the river and all the skyscrapers a panorama that I imagine couldn't be bettered anywhere in New York. It has been very hot on and off but not unpleasant. More like and English Summer but more humid. I work in a quiet studio with Hilbermann which like everything else is airconditioned and pasturised. Thanks for the letters steadily pouring in. I must sift them through as I go along with this letter. I'm doing all day sessions and what with meetings and one thing and another these are my first words on paper since I got here. Fortunately I feel pretty well so I think I can keep up with the pace but god only knows how I am to gather and do any PUNCH stuff. I am writing to Russell next tomorrow. Letter sifting …

Don't send anymore weeklies. I see that they arrive here without too much delay. The Statesman that is and the others about a fortnight late. But it is not worth spending all that money to airmail them. Just send me PUNCH each week airmail and keep the rest there. Don't bother to save The TIMES that Locke had ordered for me and I get it just two days late. As I havent had a chance to read any of them yet I shall hardly keep level. Last Wednesdays PUNCH arrived safely this morning with your letter of Wednesday. So the post is quite swift. When the bound copies of PARIS SKETCHBOOK are ready would you speed about six copies over here by the speediest possible route – other than airmail.

Pay Digby Morton's bill – it was only a credit note figure subject to what Kaye ordered. They can make skirt.

I am arranging Insurance coverage on the drawings over here together with personal accident additional coverage to guard

against anything happening to me that would make me liable to reemburse the film people for the cost of a film that I might stop through any misadventure. But I think you would be safe to insure the drawings return for 3 months from say July 1st.
When the coffers look as if they might be getting low I will arrange to have some money cable to PERPETUA but I don't want to do that until it is about to get necessary. Unbelievably expensive here. Paris is cheap compared with this. I've only taken two taxis since I came. I walk.
I'm glad that things sound as if they are going smoothly I feel terribly apprehensive about having to be away so long I'll cope with what I can here with the jobs I have to do in addition. Lemon Hart, ST TRINIANS, Longanesi, and quite obviously I must see the Brockbank jacket completed by about the first week in June. There's no sense in having it sent to me in Hollywood. Too risky. Anyway I'll face that one when I come to it. But when Russ has it ready you will have to pack it well and airmail it to me here, and his dummy when it is done.
Valentines: Don't promise anything but just let him send you their roughs for the Valentine cards. Say that youll send them to me incase there is a long shot that I might be able to squeeze them in. But there is always the possibility that he is unlikely to get anything before September. Apologies and all that. And send me their roughs and I'll see what

2

I can manage. I might be able to do them. Don't do anything about the Calendar yet. I dont want to use those photos on my board as they stand. They are too unbalanced as a selection I must get the styles to balance. I forgot to bring a copy of Souls in Torment with me. Perhaps you had better rip out the whole St. T's sections from a proof copy for me two sort over and see what it makes. I might be able to shuffle them into some sort of order. I think it would be wise too to rip out all the St T's sections in the smaller books too. Even the cruder early stuff just so that I know what I am eliminating. Buy copies of the Macdonald books to tear up if we haven't got them spare. Any old prints will do just so that I can be reminded what they are. Better airmail that – I'll try and send you the choice then when the time comes you can let Morgan have the best and clearest photos we have.
Kaye will be answering the bit about the Granada TV but offhand I would say that it was quite out of the question. I'd loathe the idea myself.
KNOPF: Well at least they have agreed to something! It is a relief to know that they will work from the positives and that we don't have to send over all those photocopies. It's a pity that they aren't going to replace the ones that wont click with the Americans but anyway they are doing the book so what the … All their questions seem so technical that we shall have to leave it all to Victor to solve but I thought that their last paragraph about their 10%s and their eight percents ruddy cheeky. Still Victor no doubt will see that Hope gets convin-cing information. I haven't contacted them yet. Or indeed Bach or anyone else. I'm glad to have it off my hands!
As I believe Kaye has already mentioned. Sometime I'll send over to Cole of Knopf a proof of PARIS SKETCHBOOK to save Hope sending one over. She can go ahead when she feels like it and write to them about it. I'll not commit anything. I'll just deliver and xxxxxxxx say that there is a letter following from Hope and that they deal with her about it.
Well – that is about all … except that if any parcels arrive marked personal gift etc … <u>dont</u> open them ! Kaye is

shopping a little and getting things sent back to save luggage. If I get a chance to buy some books or things or unload back any bits and pieces you can unpack those and let me know what has arrived.
I met John Thorne accidentally in a restaurant and Have seen David Hales for a drink and got the Book Centre straightened out.
Its now about 2.0 in the morning and I suppose you are on the verge of waking up. I cant adapt myself to the time lag seems very odd these changes in hours. The tugs are hooting on the river outside and there is a cobweb of lights as far as I can see up in the sky and away to the distance. So beautiful I hope I have a chance to get some of it on paper.
Sent as many bulletins as you can Im a long way from the studio …

[handwritten]

Yours

Ronald.

253 SUNDAY 2 JUNE
Typed letter with envelope

Searle 2310

BEEKMAN TOWER HOTEL
3 MITCHELL PLACE
New York 17, N. Y.

Grand Central Station
June 3 1957

Mrs Jean Ellsmoor
32 Newton Road
Bayswater
LONDON W.2
England

[Contains a match book from WAH KEE Chinese Restaurant, inscribed by Ronald Searle 'why not come for lunch?']

Sunday June 2

Dear Jean … Still scratching away at ninety to the dozen and at last it is beginning to look as if there is something to show for it. There have been several revisions in the story which meant at one point that about a third of what I had alrea sorted out had to be reshuffled. The biggest problem is altering everything that anyone else suggests to keep it my way! With luck in the end the film should look as if I at least drew it. The stickiest day is on Thursday when there is a full scale pan-American conference of client, agency, film company, script writers, animators, imitators, organisers, supervisors, backers, scratchers, and all that goes into making their commission justified. All come to look. I've got to have about ¾ of the visuals ready for that, tremble tremble.

As you can gather it is still going on solidly and only because I went to the office and couldn't get the door open today am I not working there. In between times which means in between dusk and dawn I am out gathering stuff for Punch. I gather that tye first batch arrived safely and that they are going to start off with one big drawing as a double-spread and follow it each week or so with single pages or d/s's. I'm expecting to get off tomorrow another packet … Central Park, Chinatown, Harlem, perhaps even the Bowery. – I may have to go back there for a bit more material. It's exhausting I must confess but I still enjoy drawing Manhattan almost as much as Paris. You'll see what I mean when the first big drawing appears – even though it was the first and I was only just g etting the feeling of it. (I'm trying this so that I can get a lot more in!).

All the St. Trinian pages have arrived safely in their various packets together with the mags and Punch and your last letter of Tuesday. I'll sort over the St. T's pages and if nothing else eliminate those that I don't want using again. I am seeing the US Customs lawyers and General lawyers next week to get my position straightened out regarding sending stuff from England for publication here and also to get my tax position straightened out. I shan't be sending any money back home until I get clear just how much I am going to be allowed to keep. Delicate situation. The contract was signed at last on Wednesday! so I am now officially doing the film! there is very little other news. I had a letter from Arthur wolley to say that he was looking forward to seeing the next LH Poster! Letter from Eric K by sea and a happy letter from PUNCH.

I had a call to see Blanche Knopf – more like an ultimatum. So I saw her for 15minutes last week at lunchtime She showed me the carbon of the letter she had sent to England talked about not being able to take her poodle to Europe – she left here on xxxxxx Thursday and then said that Knopfs thought that Paris Sketchbook wasn't quite their sort of thing. I didn't press to ask why although she pressed to keep the proof for herself … I cabled Hope and I have still another proof here which I can have sent over to whoever she decides to let see it next. I think Kaye may have already mention something about this – I don't know.

Meeting Evelyn Shrift of Vanguard at John Locke's on Tuesday pm. She is a friend of his and its just a drink. Locke has turned out trumps. I like him enormously. Relaxed kind, sort of quietly assured. Couldn't be luckier really to be in his hands. It might have been Stephen Lion …

Kaye bumped into G, Brest in the street … they made polite conversation and parted. We also bumped into Russ B! This place is like a village. Did I tell you that I got into the lift here and found myself going up with Hugh Casson. And so on … Everyone is being extreemly hospitable and it is sort of snowballing but I'm being rather ruthless and only usin the advantage of being conducted to certain areas of drawable material. Otherwise one would be lost I've only had about thre three alcoholic drinks since I arrived. I order a schweppes and the barman or host just looks sympathetic. The general understanding is that you have been 'beating it up' and that a lull is necessary and understandable. Very convenient. It is muggy here. bursts of being frightfully hot and then cloudy and thundery. Have a good view here of the Empire State building beeing struck by lightening. very exciting I've tried to take some pictures of it. I hope they come out.

I found one or two books as I was passing a shop last week. Mostly cartoons and things. they The shop is posting them back. I've addressed them to you so open them when they arrived in a week or so. I'll tuck them away when I come back. Rather sad I haven't had a chance of really looking into the shops yet. I'm dying to have a go, they look very crammed with all sorts of interesting things.

I feel as if I have been here for years … and yet in a way I feel only just round the corner. Your letters come so swiftly that I really <u>don't</u> feel detached …

[handwritten]
Yours
Ronald

254 MONDAY 10 JUNE 1957

Typed letter with envelope

Saturday May 25 TV schedule
11.30 HE-MAN THEATRE – Film
'Belles of St Trinian's'

[With a page from the New York Herald Tribune]

Mrs Jean Ellsmoor
32 Newton Road
Bayswater
LONDON W.2
ENGLAND

BEEKMAN TOWER HOTEL
3 MITCHELL PLACE
New York 17, N. Y.

Monday 10th June 1957
Dear Jean …

Pheew I have just this minute finished a threeday stretch battling through the St. Trinian's film stuff – five maps, credit drawing and the extra smalls. I have put these in a packet with the Brockbank Omnibus jacket which I have managed to get through as well. This lot will be Air-Expressed this afternoon, I'll get it off with this lette Afraid the Brockbank jacket got delayed in the customs – on the declaration form you wrote 'contents one brown paper package'! So they opened it *to see what was inside* [handwritten] and made me pay the duty.

The jacket I think should look OK. You will see that I have left xxxxxxxxxxxx a space for the name of whoever is going to write the foreword. This can be typeset and stripped in in reverse so that it is white on the blue. The blue is to match my sample (enclosed) which is slightly greener than that used by Russell. You had better let him know when it arrives in case he wants to see it before it goes to Victor.

Frank Launder I have written to as well, just to let him know that the drawings are done. Perhaps if you ring his office as soon as they reach you he could collect them.

Gosh what a sweat! I have lost my voice. Bronchitis or something. Thank God I have got through this lot. Things are slightly confused here. The trip to Hollywood is post-poned for at least another week so I shan't be going over ther until after the 24th. So much has to be done to the script still and I am trying to change it more my way which means that there is a delay while the writers sort themselves out. I'm taking four days off to get better and to clear up my own stuff. I'm trying to raise enough energy to tackle Lemon Hart …

Things are not so bad really – its just that having anyt anything else on top of what I am doing here means that I have to put in more hours than I do at home … with social obligations that is. Everyone is so kind that it is tricky to get out of evening engagements when I am working all day. I'm dy ng to get out properly with my sketchbook but so far I've only done skirmishes the total of which went to PUNCH At least the weather isn't too hot and exhausting which is rather nice for working. As you've probably heard by now Vanguard have shown a definite interest in Paris Sketchbook and are interested in doing a deal on sheets I think. I said I'd rather not get involved in the arrangements and told Evelyn Shrift to contact Hope direct. Hope can arrange the contract for Perpetua sheets and also for the Author and Artist

I have asked John Locke to send off $1000. to Perpetua this week so that there will be a little more for the funds.

The pigeons eggs I shoved into the one compartment for the lack of anywhere else! You could always bury them for 100 years like the Chinese for a future delicacy …

Delighted with the books of the Month cover … I passed it to Vanguard as an added bait. Hope the P.Sketchbook is going along smoothly. Must be nearing binding time surely.

If you have a spare copy of Elsevere Blagdat I'd be interested to see a copy. I couldn't get a copy here.

The SIA Directory arrived safely with many thanks from John L.

Glad that Goodman saw it worthwhile to send the letter to the Doll man cometh, I'm more concerned with looking after St, T's rights than YE Advertising. Hope he gave up the attempt.

Just realised that you are Whitmondaying today – lucky girl.

Glad you managed to get to the MAX opening. You will comb the weeklies and dailies for any little writeups won't you. I'd be very interested to see what else people have had to say

PUNCH I hope will start using the NY stuff this week. I thought my four colour pages in the last issue looked horrible I hated them. Would you send an apologetic little note to Bradburn in Liverpool – I have a letter with me which he wrote about last Feb. still waiting for my answer. Very sweet of you to have had Kate and Rusty. That little girl sounds as if she is embarking on a helluver social round! Kaye rang her at Cambridge yesterday and I managed to croak a word or two.

Delighted to hear about your possible discovery of the Newton house in the print. Hope it really is the one. That would be wonderful. Met up with Braddon. He'll be back in England about the 18th. We are leaving the book for a proper discussion later. It would almost certainly need another story to go with it. Anyway whether or not we do it is a matter of conjecture. Don't say anything about it to Greenwood. We'll talk it out with Russ first. It might make a Perpetua Book. If only you could nip over and make me a nice cup of tea. (etc).

I want to express this away now and lie down for five minutes. Forbear with this unread clumsy tapping my eyes are popping

Yours [drawing of a self-portrait typing] Need a haircut badly !
Ronald

255 DIRLETON, NORTH BERWICK, MONDAY 1959
Handwritten on post card

31 August 1959

Mr & Mrs Brian Ellsmoor
'Noirmont'
The Heath
WEYBRIDGE
Surrey

Dirleton. Monday

This seemed a slightly more cheerful idea than sending you a sepia photograph of Dirleton Green deserted by the natives. The Festival feels very dull this year or perhaps it is just me fed up at having to trail up here for the eleventh year in succession. I can't wait to get back on Thursday, even if only to repack. Actually I enjoyed The Congreve – (Old Vic) The Double Dealer worth seeing if you get a chance. Opens in London on the 7th.

Yrs Ronald

256 MIDNIGHT MONDAY
Handwritten on post card

Postmark NEW YORK, N.Y. Sept 29 1959

Mrs Brian Ellsmoor
'Noirmont'
The Heath
Weybridge
Surrey
England

Midnight Monday
Dear Jean I hope the roof isn't too off and that this scrappy card arrives safely under it. I've been on the trot almost constantly since I got here – (you know what it is) – and I fly across to Las Vegas tomorrow. The Exhibition went off very well indeed despite the 85% humidity etc etc etc sold several pictures and talked myself hoarse. All the buddies turned up – about 100 of 'em. So it was like a party – without drink though. – not even icewater Thanks for the nice letter of good wishes which arrived as I left for the gallery. Back in New York Sunday night I hope if I don't get my fingers trapped in a fruit machine

Yours
Ronald

259 JANUARY 1960
Handwritten on post card

9 Jan 1960

Mrs Brian Ellsmoor
Hotel Sonne
SOLDEN
Oetzal Valley
AUSTRIA

– and have a Gei Holiday
I hope your battered typing fingers aren't too numb to hold those stick things whatever they are called. [sketch of ski poles] and that the journey was finally smooth. It's just started to snow here but I don't mind. Life 'have just OK'd the Refugee and the Christmas Carol features. Hooray! Best wishes to the whole party. Tell them to bring you back unfractured.

Yrs Ronald

260 WEDNESDAY 10 FEBRUARY [1960]
Handwritten on post card

Postmark 11 Feb [1960]

Mr &Mrs Brian Ellsmoor
'Noirmont'
The Heath
Weybridge
Surrey
ENGLAND

Wednesday 10th Feb.

Well – I made it and almost caught up with Spring. Apart from a damp day today it has been gorgeously crisp & sunny I've had most of my interviews – 'flue' injections and start the actual drawing tomorrow. Dave is in hospital John is recovering from pneumonia Arthur Kinoy has his neck in a brace – That makes me almost horribly healthy. At least I'm catching up on sleep. World want T-Lautrec. But you may have heard by now via P Hebdan. More news later. Yrs

Ronald

261 NEW YORK, FRIDAY 1960
Handwritten on post card

Posted New York
Feb 12 1960

Mr & Mrs Brian Ellsmoor
'Noirmont'
The Heath
Weybridge
Surrey
ENGLAND

N.Y. Friday

Couldn't resist sending you this picture. Although the weather hasn't been quite like this it was 63° yesterday. Things have been slightly complicated with work – but for the better I think. You'll hear about it next week. I expect to be here in NY until at least next Thursday. Your plaster should be off soon, eh? Well nearly. I'm fine. Just muddled.
Yrs Ronald

262 SALT LAKE CITY, MONDAY 10 OCTOBER [1960]
Handwritten on post card

Salt Lake City
October 10th
Monday

Still doing about 2000 miles a day and desperately trying to draw. Never had such a battle on any job both to work & get sleep. I'm certainly seeing America in the oddest circumstances. Hope all is well. Albuquerque & San Diego tomorrow – and so on … Should be back in New York by next Monday.
Yrs
Ronald

263 FRIDAY 21 OCTOBER 1960
Typed letter with envelope

Mrs Brian Ellsmore,
'Noirmont'
The Heath,
Weybridge,
Surrey.
ENGLAND

The Westbury MADISON AVENUE at SIXTY-NINTH STREET
NEW YORK 21, NEW YORK

21st October, Friday

Dear Jean –

Thank you very much for your bulletins and background bits which I had hoped to have sai 'thank you for' before. Really this has been the most hectic and fantastic trip and I think today will finally see the LIFE job to press. They are running six pages of drawings and it makes quite a strong feature – although most of the time – right up to the moment I had delivered it, I didn't think I should be able to get through. It is the toughest job I have ever had and it wasn't exactly helped by the fact that I caught a dose of bronchitis – or something the moment I got to the Nixon party and since I got back to New York I have had to go for daily jabs of penicillin. However I feel a good deal better now and beginning to unwind after my 11,000 miles of flying in the fortnight.

I have picked up several more jobs to get on with, so I have plenty to keep me busy. After I have finished a spread for Sport Illustrated – which I have to deliver of all things – on Sunday – I get on with a port rait of Khrushchev for Holiday – a full page – which should be fun

2

I'm glad your holiday worked out so successful ly. Sicily certainly has some delights and I think I remember it with more affection than most parts of Italy. And if I try to remember why – I think it was mainly for the lovely view from my window from Taormina to Etna, combined with the smell of hot – damp undergrowth and tile floors.

As you may have gathered my trip whisked me everywhere from the freezing Canadian border to the desert – and always from one extreme to the other within a matter of hours. I spent more time in the air than I did on it. Practi cally an Airhost.

I'm passing on to Alex all the quotes about Russia. They seem very encouraging. Of course – André being here – we are all waiting with our tongues out for the BITING EYE to arrive.

I go up to the LIFE office in a minute to finish off my work on the feature. They had the idea that I should write the opening of every caption in my own fair hand. So it has meant trotting back and forth as they

move on page by page. It finally finished up
as six pages – out next Wednesday. Although
LIFE are supporting Nixon, the ersatz man,
they have let me be critical of both candidates
so, as they said, it is perfect fair as a
feature – both candidates will hate it! So
whoever gets in, I shall probably be banned
from the States in future! Tynan's report
of his being called up in front of the
UnAmerican Activities committee, in the
October issue of HARPERS Magazine, it is causi
some interest here. It mostly arose
through a programme he did for ATV called
'We Dissent'. After his appearance before t
the committee they found a 'technical fault'
in his visa. And that is why he is back in
England. Touchy, arn't they?

Well, I had better stop at this point.
I have to gather my wits and my junk to-
gether and get over to the Time-Life
glasshouse.

Thanks again for all the bits and
encouraging pieces. My regards to
Brian. I hope you don't both feel that
the holiday is already too far behind
you!

[handwritten]

Yours Ronald

[Upside down, handwritten]
Now how did this happen ? PTUP.

264 BOXING DAY 1960

Handwritten letter with envelope

Sticker
Ronald Searle
32 Newton Road
Bayswater, London, W.2.

Mrs Brian Ellsmore
'Noirmont'
The Heath
Weybridge
Surrey

Boxing Day 1960

[large sketch of an admiral with stickers on his hat]

Dear Jean-

I love my 'stick-ons'. What a bright idea – I'll try not to
use them excessively – but there is an awful temptation to reach for
the little leather cases and slap one on whatever is handy. I was thinking
of wearing one on my forehead for simple identification. Kaye loved her
rose too. She will tell you so. At the moment she is deep in
boiled turkey bones trying to solve the problem of lunch. Christmas was
all very family and sitting-about. But even that seemed to take a
lot of energy. Hope you had a really lovely one. See you Wednesday.
Much love to you both.

Ronald
-----

265 BEIRUT, WEDNESDAY [1961]

Handwritten on post card

Mr & Mrs B. Ellsmoor
'Noirmont'
The Heath
WEYBRIDGE
Surrey
England

AIRMAIL

Beirut. Wednesday

Had a perfect flight out here and ever since
I arrived the weather has turned from rain
to bright sun, cool breezes and air smelling
of flowers. It's like stepping into the Bible
when you get out toward the mountains.
There are the camels and the shepherds. From
my window I can see Sidon (but not
quite Tyre!) across the water. Already
I'm feeling lazy but having to fight back the
desire to draw when I want to look. Looking
has won! More news when I get down
to Jerusalem. Love
Ronald

266 JERUSALEM, SATURDAY [1961]

Handwritten on post card

Mr & Mrs Brian Ellsmoor
'Noirmont'
The Heath
Weybridge
Surrey
ENGLAND

AIRMAIL

Jerusalem. Saturday

I've had a really fascinating journey down through
Syria, via Damascus, and Jordan and got here
last night. Have been out sightseeing all day today
in a tremendous burst to see all the Biblical bits
before I go into battle tomorrow and cut myself off
from these parts. The colour and contrasts are
difficult to describe but in parts it is almost
as if things were exactly
the same as they were
1961 years ago.
I doubt if I'll ever remember it all – I've
crammed so much in. But it was very worth
while coming to these parts first. Hope all is well
I'll look forward to news.
Love Ronald

267 JERUSALEM, TUESDAY 11 APRIL [1961]
Handwritten on post card

AIRMAIL

Mr &Mrs Brian Ellsmoor
'Noirmont'
The Heath
Weybridge
Surrey
England

Jerusalem – Tuesday 11th

A brief scribble before setting off for the grand opening at 9.0 am. Thank you for the Friday letter which I got yesterday morning. Glad everything is going allright. I'll try to write sensibly sometime this week but the sessions are going to be fairly long – from 9.0am – 6.0pm So I'll be working nights too! Apart from my usual commencing nerves I'm anxious to get started. But its not going to be easy. Lots of sun and a bit strange here. Love

Ronald.

268 JERUSALEM, ISRAEL, FRIDAY 14 APRIL
Handwritten letter with envelope

Mrs Jean Ellsmore
32 Newton Road
Bayswater LONDON W2
England

P.O.Box 3000
Jerusalem, Israel
Friday 14th April

Dear Jean –

I've just written a note to Peter in answer to his saying OK. If they feel they have got the best possible results then I'll leave it to him to OK and go ahead with the printing. I agree we mustn't miss the shipping dates. I'm posting off the two letters together but you had better ring to check that the message got there. I must say these are strange parts and I find the whole business – both the trial and this half of the city slightly haunting. It's not the most enjoyable of jobs – or places. Thanks for your first letter. I expect there'll be another on its way by now. I feel as if I have been away ten years instead of ten days. All this side of Jerusalem is pretty new of course but consequently pretty dull. I'm very glad I took advantage of the first week of travelling. I wouldn't have missed it for anything – certainly would have missed the best part. This is more like a slightly oriental Notting Hill gate.

I hope everything has been going along alright and not too many pointless things popping up for you. I reckon I'll

[over page]

be here for at least another fortnight. It is going to be rather laborious work building this up into a picture story. I'm scribbling away all day in the Court without any trouble but they will have to be turned into drawings with a bit more weight. Eichmann himself is a pretty cool customer – barely moves an eyebrow in hours. I'm sitting about 10 feet from him all the time. – so somehow I should get a likeness!

That's about it.

[drawing of Adolf Eichmann]

I'm going to whizz this off by trotting camel

love

Ronald

269 LATE THURSDAY NIGHT
Handwritten letter on Gladstone headed paper

Late Thursday night

Dear Jean –
I thought it was about time I scribbled a phrase more than the usual boring postcard. I've just about worked myself silly today and now I am going to pack up until tomorrow I'm on my last feature now – The State Department and it is going slowly but once that is done I am through. So far I reckon I have delivered almost a full page Holiday illustration a day since I came – almost a battery hen. eh? I must say I've had just about enough but it has been harder work this time – delivering more quantity for the money! I'm going up to the country – Cornwall – for this weekend to try and rest for a couple of days with John & Midge and to try and find some more State Dept ideas. I have to treat it like the Establishment Feature. I feel as if I have been away for Years now Sitting at the old board counting the grain in the wood. I haven't had much time to do much else really, except get a change of scene out on the other features. I tossed in a note to you in a letter to Kaye earlier in the week so you could see that I did still exist – but there was nothing to reply to even in a buisinesslike way, really – it sounds as if it has been pretty quiet in the studio. But that's probably just an illusion! Anyway I hope it hasn't been to utterly boring stuck up there in the heat – although I see from the paper that it has cooled off a bit. I've been here much longer than I originally expected but it has simply been a matter of bulldozing through the stuff until I come out the other side. I don't know quite when I shall be back but I shall do something about my ticket next week. I expect I shall get away next weekend. I have several people to see when I have stopped work. Friede, Helmer, Karnblee Tudor etc etc. I had my hair cut yesterday for the first time since I left London – ghastly! It looked as if I were wearing an artistic wig. I feel a bit cleaner now! Delighted to hear about the house and the successful hunting. You must be relieved. I wonder where it is. Well that's about it. I'm going off to bed before this pen falls out of my hand and my writing gets completely illegible!
I expect I'll hear

[on side]

from you before the weekend. If not I'll be back in NY at dawn on Monday morning with a little fresh air inside me. Regards to Brian. See you in about a week

Love Ronald

270 SATURDAY 3 JUNE 1961
Typed letter with envelope

Hotel Gladstone, 114 East 52nd Street, New York 22, N.Y.

Searle 1507

Mrs Jean Ellsmoor
32 Newton Road
Bayswater
LONDON W2
England

June 3 rd 1961 Saturday

Dear Jean:
Thanks for this morning's letter. I was hoping to hear from you before I set off up to Cape Cod – Provincetown area tomorrow. We are going up to John's in Cornwall tomorrow afternoon and staying the night there and then all four of us drive off early on Monday morning. It takes about 7 hours to get there. As far as I can tell we shall be back at the Gladstone here on the following Monday night. Kaye has a flight booked back on the 15th. Flying by day and getting into London at night.

Friede produced a copy of Carol when Kaye went up to World office yesterday to talk to their children's book dept. and I have it here in front of me. I think the colour is even worse than I imagined it might be. It looks so dead and dull but the worse spread of all is the appearance of Marley's ghost (with the mouse in the corner) where some misguided genius has linked in lines that don't exist on the figure. I could kill them/him, whoever it was. It looks like a feeble rough sketch but more than that they chose to draw in lines in quite the wrong place. And having decided to draw Marley's spectacles they didn't bother with the earpiece. And the Fezziwig Ball is indescribable. Where the hell they found those muddy colours I can't guess. It looks just plain dirty. The black and white is all right but for the rest I couldn't be more disappointed.

I delivered my first feature – Washington tourists – to HOLIDAY yesterday and it went down well. 10 drawings – all pretty elaborate for a 6page feature. Now I am trying to make a start on the Atlantic City stuff before it goes out of my head. I can't get that finished before I leave but at least I can shape it.

It looks as if I had better think about the Prisunic poster here. I'd forgotten that they wanted roughs by the end of JUne. Anyway it is nice that they have agreed to pay such a good fee. I'll have to attend to the roughs when I get back to NY.
Nice about Thackeray. I think I payed about £20 for it.

I don't know what the Capital Punishment Memorial is. First I've heard of it. Anyway forget about it for the moment.

I sent off another $1,000 on Thursday for RS Ltd which should help and as more comes in I'll filter more over.

I think that is about it.

[handwritten]
There isn't much news from this end really as I seem to have been stuck at the board as usual – Rather stickily Yesterday – as the Temperature went up to 90°! Better today though, thank goodness. The weather has been strangely mixed The 'Life' Eichmann feature is still held by – what with Trujillo's assassination and Kennedy in Paris and Vienna. They are going to wait until the Trial gets back on the front page. But It looks good the way they've laid it out.

Oh well – Back to the board …

Love

Ronald

271 TUESDAY 26 SEPTEMBER 1961
Handwritten letter with envelope

Mrs Jean Ellsmore
'Noirmont'
The Heath
Weybridge
Surrey
ENGLAND

Tuesday 26 September 1961

Dearest Jean –

It was very very sweet of you to write to me – and more than thoughtful for you to think of sending the cash which was gratefully received – and all safely received. Owing to a stupid muddle in a French post-office no mail reached me until yesterday. Apparently some temporary post office clerk let me fill in a card and then threw it aside for two weeks. Anyway I made enough fuss for it not to happen again – but I hope to have a reliable forwarding on address soon when I get my plans soted out a bit. I've been moving about a bit in a sort of unsettled way and I've been making use of the few US travellers cheques I had left. I feel all right and have had the chance of relaxing a bit in the sun, which has been pretty constant and consoling. I've decided to move on to Germany and Berlin, to try and get something of use there that will help to bring some money into the coffers. I enjoyed your long letter as you headed off into the highlands. I do hope it turned out to be a real holiday for you especially as you were on unexplored territory - and that the gloomy gales didn't wreck everything. To say the least the countryside and the mountain tops must have looked dramatic. Now I expect you have arrived back again – and I hope by the time this gets to you the benefits won't be too far behind you.

I'm so glad – and grateful that you feel you can see things through for me. I hardly knew what I wrote when I left that note for you on my pad. But I was in such a state of upset and misery and gloom – mixed with panic and relief at having finally made the decision to change my whole life – trying to do it with the minimum of hurt to anyone else. I could kill the French post-office for delaying the post as I have been in a state of agony incase anything awful had happened through what I have done. It was just marvellous of you to have been there to cope and I'm really painfully aware of the trouble I must have caused. I hope Kaye will resign herself to the situation as time goes by. I suppose I shall come back to England from time to time, but I'm pretty certain I shall make a new life for myself abroad – I'll manage if I can build up the continental side. Then the money will come into the companies just the same through Hope & John and maybe I could draw a little from Lloyds on RS Ltd and siphon a few expenses off a job here and there.

You know what to arrange if queries come up with Hope – and she'll just have to make the best arrangement she can with Candide.

Bless you and thank you again for saying such sweet things in your letter. I'll write again as I move along

Love

Ronald

272 MONDAY 30 OCTOBER 1961
Typed letter

Rubber address stamp:

RONALD SEARLE
C/o Mr. V Caloutsis
4, Rue Antoine-Dubois
PARIS – 6e

Monday PM. October 30th 1961

Dearest Jean –

Just to let you know that all is well and I have my packet. I had to meet Hope after lunch today at the Flore, where she arrived full of – well I was going to say beans – but I guess it was more than that – and three other people. We had half – an-hour on our own going through stuff and I am to call her on Thursday morning again after she has been to see N. CANDIDE on Wednesday, to get things sorted out. She is also seeing a French publisher about WHICH WAY, and some other possible fruitful sources.

Thank you very much for the contents of the packet. Cash gratefully received and the Redoxon and the Toothpaste and the scribble books, etc.

Hope has given me the dope about the GPO Poster and I'll be getting on with that almost at once. It should be quite fun to do – if I can find an idea.

There's not much other news – except fog, I gather. And as I only wrote yesterday this is a short one.

[handwritten]

Now I am just going to treat myself
to a tooth clean – as fresh as a sea breeze ––

[self-portrait drawing as a seagull]

love

Ronald

273 MONDAY 6 NOVEMBER 1961
Typed letter

Rubber address stamp:

RONALD SEARLE
C/o Mr. V Caloutsis
4, Rue Antoine-Dubois
PARIS – 6e

Monday, November 6th 1961

Dearest Jean –

Just to let you know that the two copies of CÉZANNE arrived today. I think they look <u>splendid</u>. Actually there was a slight complication. They were impounded by the Customs, and I had to spend an hour this morning trying to get them out. If there is no indication what is inside a packet, they simply send for you to open it in their presence. When they saw that they were books, there was no trouble at all – as there is no tax to pay on printed matter. So could you be sure – when you do up your beautifully, tidy packets to mark them <u>Books</u> or <u>Printed matter</u>, then they will come straight through. Nothing else has been held up so far, probably because they could see inside too.

The Benin catalogue has just arrived too and 'life' Sothebys have really made the head the centrepiece, haven't they? Ah well – fingers crossed for the 20th!

[hand written] [drawing of an arm and hand with crossed fingers]

No other news
for the moment
except that it has turned almost
wintery here now. I've been trying
to find some more <u>Lemon Hart</u> ideas
To give me warming thoughts!
Love
Ronald

274 THURSDAY AFTERNOON, 16 NOVEMBER 1961
Typed Letter

Rubber address stamp:

RONALD SEARLE
C/o Mr. V Caloutsis
4, Rue Antoine-Dubois
PARIS – 6e

Dearest Jean

Thursday afternoon, November 16th 1961

Thanks very much for the latest bulletin and the cuttings and the forwarded on Graphis, and so on –all of which have been gently trickling
in. Of course the only thing that I'm dying to see – WHICH WAY – still hasn't arrived! But I expect it will be here any minute now.

Well, be it on your own head – <u>if</u> you feel like sending over drawing card and some note books I'd be infinitely grateful. As you know all that sort of stuff is much more expensive than it is in England and I've been buying the bits as I went along. It would save a lot of money to have the drawing card, because it is nice quality – but
check the maximum size of the packet allowed in the post. It would be awful if you had to bring it back and trim it down. Whatever you can manage I'd be glad to have.

Glad to hear that Whibley can use some pictures. Good idea – although I don't think I would want to have an exhibition at his Gallery. If I can get one at the Leicester when the time comes, I couldn't do better than that. There would be no point in going down the scale to a smaller gallery, would there?

Thanks for the news about the books. I hope something will move on Sempé. If I had to wait until August for publication he'd have every reason to feel fed-up. CÉZANNE sounds slow. But then at 42/- I expect it will be a very gentle seller. Nice news about CAROL and the NBL.

Thanks for turning down A.M Gardner Sewart's idea.
I <u>would</u> like to keep the HOLIDAY index you made. There is an American xx library here, and even if they didn't have back issues for reference I could at least be able to track down a specific number. But all the mags are finished with as far as I am concerned.

PRISUNIC sent me a batch of bags and posters, so you'll have the extra ones for there - and if you want copies – take 'em.

Sotheby's subscription can lapse. I think it would be an unnecessary luxury to renew it.

Hope might be able to get a token franc for the reproduction from Medisances. I don't mind if anybody wants to use it. You could tell her that.

I'm glad you think WHICH WAY looks so good. I can hardly believe it is out at last. Pant, pant – come on postman.

Now – what you say about the time and dwindling days at the studio.
<u>If</u> it is financially possible I would like you to hang on as long as you can. With the odds and ends of queries and enquiries I would have thought that there was a small flow of things to be done. xxxxx As far as the files and things go, it would be nice to have them finished. Perhaps the letter files could be weeded down to the bone so that there are only the essentials there. And I think for example that the majority of the theatre reference file can be slung out. Most of the stuff is years out of date and it would clear out almost two drawers. I would say sling out whatever can be slung out in the way of loose paper in the files and boxes. Any bits and pieces of notes and scribbles which might do for Bradburn can go to him. Any interesting bits that you see which you might like to keep, please take them. I'd like you to have what

2.

you fancy –if there is anything.
If you want to work on the two books at home –well I'll leave that to you. I can only leave it to you in all these things to use your discretion. In time I expect I shall need my reference stuff. And as most of these things have taken a long time to build up it would be a pity not to finish 'em off. Talk with Kaye and see whether the arrangement seems satisfactory to both of you. I only wish there were thousands of ponds for us all to wallow in!
However – it is not to be.

I hate the idea of coming to it – even in the distant future, but you shall have the reference of references. Is there\any special paper you would like it done on? Headed paper I mean. Just tell me anything you want incorporated, and it shall be done.

Well – I finished my FORTUNE job and delivered it last night rather like a yacht in full sail as the thing was so big. It should be on it's way to NY by now. Thank goodness that's done. I'm awaiting the arrival of another ad. to do for John – meanwhile I'm trying to make a start on the Thurber Puffin.
I saw a poster for Arroyo's exhibition – which opened yesterday. The invitation has arrived here from either you or Kaye but I haven't ha had a chance to get in yet. I shall do before it closes.
Yes, I had heard that there was a lot of theatre drawing activity on. I'm glad you had a pick before it all began …
I'm sending back the cutting – although I have kept the Evening News one. Maybe you have a duplicate of that for the file.
Everything you seem to have sent off seems to have arrived OK - as I told you in my last letter. The only thing that is still to arrive is the Copydex. I'll let you know when they turn up. probably in my next letter.

Well that's enough of this patter

[handwritten]

& Thanks for all the help and packing and packaging and what not. I do hope things work out the way you want them to go. But I can only leave it for you to decide. it has been and is very warming to know that you are still nearby.

Love
Ronald

277 WEDNESDAY 27 DECEMBER 1961
Typed letter

Rubber address stamp:

RONALD SEARLE
C/O Mr. V Caloutsis
4, Rue Antoine-Dubois
PARIS – 6e

Dearest Jean
Wednesday, December 27th 1961
Here I am back at the typewriter with a vague idea in my head that I must start drawing again.
But first of all I thought I'd pop this little note into the post to let you know that the second £ envelope has arrived safely, thank you very much, and that I sent you back at once the signed option (I didn't read it I'm afraid) for you to witness and return to Bill O'Bryen, and also posted the Bookers alterations.
I was glad to hear that the $450 had arrived from John Locke. I have written to him to acknowledge it.

I hope you had a lovely Christmas and that everything went as you hoped it might. I expect I shall be hearing from you about it, so I won't speculate.

I forgot to say 'thank you' for your elegant little Christmas card – the handpainted one on silk. Very pretty. And I hope you will already have got my burst of thanks for my golden wallet … I'm still getting over my surprise!

It turned very cold here for Christmas – the coldest the papers said, since 1879. At first I thought it was going to snow – but it was too icy for that but it seemed very appropriate to have that sort of Bob Cratchit nip on your ears. I had a quiet and nicely relaxed time – spent the afternoon with the Bo's and one with Judith and had nice Christmas meals with other friends and ate turkey that Caloutsis had cooked at the bakers. Last night I went to the circus – which was rather
curious as there was hardly anyone there and it seemed as if thex performers were almost outnumbering the audience – if you, include the horses!
Christmas here, of course only lastexd the one day and everything was as usual on Tuesday. Nevertheless I was determined not to do anything on Boxing Day, just to keep the flag flying and all that!
And now I must get my thoughts onto a higher plane than my stomach and tackle a few more Imaginary Portraits. I don't know how I'll do it, I feel quite stupefied!

I'll write a less obtuse letter when my brain starts working again. Meanwhile this letter has a second intention and that is to wish you a really

Happy New Year! [Handwritten]

Love
Ronald

278 WEDNESDAY PM, 9 MAY 1962
Typed Letter

c/o John Locke
56 East 66th Street,
NEW YORK 21. NY, USA

Dearest Jean —

Wednesday pm, May 9th 1962

Well, here I am, just about back from the Arctic Wastes and it was really quite a journey. Talk about heading for the North Pole! I went about 200 miles up beyond the Arctic circle – just about as far as I could get this time of year, travelling up the coast Nome, Kotzebue, Cape Thompson, Point Hope, Cape Lisburne (look it up on the map!) all of it roadless and virtually inaccessible except by dog team or bush plane on skis – both of which I hired! The bush planes were pretty well held up with string and one of them had a door which flew open every time the plane went more than about 50mph. But fortunately I had my belt fastened so I didn't fall out onto the frozen Arctic ocean and the pilot simply leaned over me and pulled it shut at intervals!

And then me muffled up on a sled being whisked off through a blizzard which finally snowed me in for three days at one village, with the Eskimo driver balancing on behind and fifteen dogs pounding on for all they were worth. Quite a sight. The temperature was about 5° and ink frozen in pen!

The Eskimos I found fascinating and friendly, almost child-like – and lovely to sketch. They really are as one reads, Living on hunting and still catch whales from walrus skin boats. I really fell for Alaska and the Arctic. There is something really strange & wonderful coming onto a village in the wilderness of ice and snow with no trees within hundreds of miles and nothing but existence to concentrate on. It was the most extraordinary feeling to get to one community at Point Hope, which had been cut off for a week by snow storms and to land in a tiny little plane on skis and see the whole village come out of their little shacks and melt towards the plane pulling sleds and peering out of their wolverine furs and showing up incredibly vividly in bright reds and blues of calico over-dresses against the snow.

I got a good feature and took it up to Philadelphia today. HOLIDAy are very happy about it. Altogether I did about 10,000 miles. And I am still in a bit of a muddle as to time and one thing and another. There was another six hours time change from here to there.

I found your letter of the 16th waiting for me and realised that it is just about a fortnight since I scribbled even a card to anyone but the difficulty of getting the drawings and the almost insurmountable task of getting a letter posted from up there – it became apparent that it would be quicker to start from here again!

Which I am doing.

I have come back to a heavy run of work again but with luck I am hoping to clear out of America by the 21st May, providing the planes aren't too booked up. All being well I should be back in Paris on the 22nd – then I shall try to get away for a few days rest Anyway, unless you hear from me to the contrary, take the 21st as the leaving date. Quite long enough.

I'll try to answer your letter sensibly but it will be a bit cryptic now as I am still pretty tired.

279 SATURDAY 9 JUNE 1962
Typed letter

address rubber stamped RONALD SEARLE

C/O Mr. V Caloutsis
4, Rue Antoine-Dubois
PARIS – 6e
Saturday, June 9th 1962

Dearest Jean –

I hope you had a nice Whitsun weekend. If it is anything like what the weather promises to be here then you should have an advance coating of bronze.

Thank you very much for the packets which have been arriving the catalogues letters and whatnot. I've gone through the stuff and some of the cuttings and bits I've thrown away. The rest I am returning to you to dispose of. I've sent back the little girls' manuscript with a note.

Thanks too for the two copies of WHICH WAY – which I am very glad to have.

Do you think that Perpetua could raise a copy for Irving Hoffman? As you saw on the enclosed little slip, he's asking for one – and I don't think John has any left. It isn't being published in America until just before Christmas.

I've noticed that my NUJ card isn't entered up-to-date. I don't know whether Edwards has paid this or not but would you be an angel and send it in for bringing it up-to-date. Edwards can do the cheque so that I am in credit for 1963.The card is very useful to me on the trips so I would like to have it back. Also my Film Union Card is due soon – perhaps that could be paid too at I have to have it for film designing. They are both enclosed. Sorry to be bothering you with all these fiddling things. I would have sent them to Edwards direct but having promised to send me monthly statements and all that so that he is in touch with me regularly, he hasn't written a word since April 24th. James Archibald of J. Walter Thompson was supposed to be here today, I was supposed to have lunch with him about THE KING'S BREAKFAST. However I had a cable from him yesterday cancelling it so I have today sent off by Registered Airmail a packet containing nine more designs – to Hope – which I had hoped he would have been able to carry back with him.

That's about all the news except that I am trying to tackle some more Imaginary Portraits so that I have a few more in hand – Have done Graham Sutherland and just abut to embark on C. Northcote Parkinson… after that it is anyone's guess.

[Hand written]

– They must be sick of me flicking through peoples books in WHSmiths here in the search for a dwng! How I wish I had read more!

[drawing of a flower]

Love
Ronald –

280 FRIDAY PM, 6 JULY 1962
Typed letter with envelope

Mrs Jean Ellsmoor
'Noirmont'
The Heath
WEYBRIDGE
Surrey
ANGLETERRE

c/o Mr. V. Caloutsis
4 rue Antoine-Dubois
PARIS 6e
France.

Dearest Jean – Friday pm, July 6th 1962

Many thanks for the letter and the packet of bits and pieces – and Sotheby's catalogues.

Thank you for making a fuss too about the caricature exhibition xxx caption and the biographical note. How curious that they should have left the compilation to an Amateur – and an American one at that. I'm looking forward to getting your report on the opening – and the catalogue. I hope they have done it well, as it will probably be a long time before another exhibition of that sort is brought together.

I hadn't paid the German Film fee. I asked them at the time I think (or else you did –) to send the bill to Perpetua. I paid 11,000 Francs for transport and customs duty after it's month in bond, but that was to the shipping agents here, not to the TV people.

Thanks too for getting me the African catalogue from Sotheby's very interesting to have – even without the prices.

So Gauguin goes to Hare again. That's what happened before. Peter put up the idea of some girl doing the translation, and then said – never mind, the devil we know, etc.

Let's hope he works well at the Saville.

The two Japanese cartoon books are nothing to bother about. I'll keep them here unless they are wanted – which I doubt.

Funny cutting about the Philistine in Newcastle who preferred Searle and Thurber to the Mona Lisa! Perhaps I should send a cartoon up there for the South Shields Education Committee to set up a fund of its own!

I heard about the Mason split last week. Cutting enclosed. The Lolita embellishment I suppose was inevitable when the warped imaginations got going.

I've seen the Japanese version of Singapore – and it is fascinating.
I had no idea that there were so few of them up until now. Seems that their planning was a little less worse than ours – but it is also nice to think they were surprised at their speed of advance. We were!

Borrow as many books as you like as long as you keep a note of them as I shall want them one day. But I shouldn't take them out too obviously – otherwise your borrowing might get complicated.

Sorry to hear about the slasher and the coat. What a bloody street that is for petty thievery. But it is such a bore to have to lose a coat when you can't get it on the insurance. Shame …

My French certainly isn't fluent. I have the odd phrase and a good deal of English. In fact it is not much better than it was. Silly isn't it?

I'm going to leave this letter open until after the post tomorrow, incase there is any last thing to mention – and then I'll give it a good lick and pop it off to you.
Paris has been rather overcast and really quite cool this last few days and surprisingly quite. On the whole there don't seem to

2.

be many tourists around and with the hoards of French having poured out of Paris with the start of the school hols the place is half deserted. But it is rather nice like that. I have been working away doing a bit of sorting out and planning. (sounds like an excuse to be lazy) but do you know it has taken me until about now to get over all that travelling. I'll have to get down to things a bit more seriously next week. I've taken on that American book illustration job A TALE OF TWO CITIES, which means a bit of combing and reading – and I have had a query from the Film company here as to whether I would be interested in another film job. I said 'Yes'. So they are putting it to the client. That's about all really. Except that Caloutsis is back and posting off stacks of copies of the STUDIO all over the world.

Enough chatter for now …

……………………

Saturday

Could you order me as soon as poss (Jean: groans, groans) ible a dozen copies of my passport photo taken I think at – was it – Dorothy Gray studio in Westbourne Grove. The reference number is U.A.72 taken in I think 1960. Merci, mille fois.

[handwritten]

No post today
So I'll pop this off.

Love
Ronald

282 BAYREUTH, WEDNESDAY 17 OCTOBER 1962
Handwritten on post card

Mrs Brian Ellsmoor
c/o J. G. Francis
P.O. Box 3561
NAIROBI
KENYA
East Africa

Bayreuth Weds
17 October 1962

Got here Tuesday night – out of Berlin and through a couple of hundred miles of Russian Germany. Apart from filling in a ton of paper and being checked by a Russian guard and ten E. German controls all went smoothly! Saw this enchanting little theatre yesterday, and a schloss and whatnot. gobbled a bit of local Venison and will be heading for Nurenburg and further south today. Cold, sunny, blue sky and all that. Hope all goes well – and fascinatinglywise, as they say. Regards to Brian

Love R.

284 ASHLEY FALLS, SATURDAY 2 MARCH 1963
Handwritten on post card with envelope

– Searle c/o Locke
56 East 66th Street NY21 NY. USA

Mrs Jean Ellsmore
1 Child's Walk
LONDON SW5
England

[handwritten on back of envelope]

W. F. Astley-Jones
180, Broughten Ave
Aylesbury, Bucks
Aylesbury 5040

[Printed]
TWIN LAKES CONNECTICUT
BETWEEN SALISBURY AND CANAAN

[handwritten]
Arrow pointing to printing
Near the new farm Ashley Falls Saturday
2 March 1963

come back – we
miss you – John
& Midge

(Monica Searle's handwriting)
Hello, many greetings! How are
you? This time I am enjoying
myself very much – except
that it would be lovely if
you were here with us.
Much love Mô.

[Ronald Searle's handwriting]

All Just to let you know that one and
all have a soft spot for you.
and are having nice thoughts about you love R.

285 PHOENIX, ARIZONA, 8 MARCH 1963
Handwritten on post card

Phoenix Arizona March 8 1963.

Dearest Jean – I don't know whether or
not you got here – anyway I have
reached it feeling rather as if I am
in a slightly unreal cowboy setting.
It is all very wild and prickly outside
the town and have explored a bit of
it. Lovely and hot and blue skies
and perfect for working out of doors
despite the dullness of the subject.
Anyway I feel well and am working
nobly and should be back in N. York
sometime next week when I've got all
my notes. Thanks for your lovely
Birthday card which came just before I
left. Trés gai! Very pretty & funny.
Will write properly when I am back in
NY. There never seems to by time on a job
M sends all greetings too. Much love
R.

286 ULM – DONAU, SUNDAY 16 JUNE 1963
Handwritten on post card

Never mind
perhaps ye rain
wille stoppe
soone

Ulm – Donau Sunday 16 June 63

Dearest Jean – I'm at the
starting post and it is a bit damp
Hasn't stopped raining since
I crossed the German border –
good thing some of the pictures
are to be in watercolour.
Heading down to Bavaria
tomorrow to tackle the beery
side and the Alps
Would you watch out for any
Beckett reviews can't get
the papers here. The Observer is
supposed to be doing something
– and TIME. Cheers and
another card soon Love R.

[along side of card]

and from M 2

287 MONDAY NIGHT, 10 JUNE 1963
Typed letter with envelope

@ 4, Rue Antoine-Dubois,
PARIS 6e, France.
Monday night. June 10 1963

Dearest Jean (that should be written actually) [drawing of flower in red biro]

This is just a quick note to let you know that your Express letter came here during the morning, and then the Cable asking for Malingue to be phoned arrived at 6.00pm.

diplomatically but firmly
I got Mo to phone him at once / and she told him that you were desperate about the pictures as you have to have them in to the publisher by the end of this week.

He said he would send them off right away and that you should xx have them in time. So … I hope it has had some effect and that he does get them away in the morning.

Rather desperate rush here to get through in time to get off again. Hope by Wednesday.

Working hard on Dutch stuff. Subject was of all dull things Natural Gas wells (Pipes sticking out of the ground) for an ESSO Magazine. Hamburg was simply getting a bit of Germany out of the way early and seeing KRISTALL which seems very OK.

Will try to write properly tomorrow, want to catch the post with this …

[handwritten]

– Haste – and much love

R.

and from M who hopes
the call has had
some effect

288 COLOGNE, TUESDAY 2 JULY 1963
Handwritten on post card

Cologne Tuesday July 2 1963

Dearest Jean –
Just to let you know that by
the time you get this I'll be back
in Paris. I'm about a week behind
due to the rotten wet weather, but I
have enough to finish the work off in
Paris from what I have from
earlier trips. Was hoping to get to Berlin
amongst other places – but I'm leaving it all
here – especially as the expenses have run out!
All well otherwise – Look forward
to hearing from you.
Much love R
& from M.

289 TUESDAY, 9 JULY 1963
Typed Letter

[drawing of a head with tongue stretched out]

4, Rue Antoine-Dubois, Paris 6e

Dearest Jean Tuesday, July 9th 1963

Thanks for all the packages which were here when I got back – books and whatnot. And for the other two packages. Yesterdays formidable pile of lists which is tremendously useful – and this morning's packet of printed and letters.

And thank you too for my Birthday Stickers! I'm sure they will be tremendously useful and I've started with this envelope. What a nice idea.

I'm returning one or two annotated bits including the GRAPHIS form. The rest I have disposed of or am answering.

I seem to have been typing letters almost ever since I got back. There were a lot of little bits that had to be attended to. So I have still not started to get on with the rest of Germany.

By the way – Alaska is in the current (July) HOLIDAY. Doesn't look bad at all. Ten pages of it.

I heard from Edwards – his letter crossed with mine. Said he'd sprained his ankle and got a puncture. And that he forgot about the increased monthly allowance and is sending me an extra £100 – £60 for June & July increase and £40 expenses. Which is a great relief. Germany took care of a lot of expenses,which I shall get back of course, but I have to wait.

Edwards says he is coming to Paris from August 5th – 9th. Parked on a boat near the Pont des Invalides somewhere! So I'll have to see him when the children are here. [handwritten] Bad timing

I feel very much in a muddle at the moment. I can't get over the fact that I'm not travelling this week, so I can't settle, It has been so long on the move!

This is only a short one because I expect that I shall be hearing from you any moment now … I mean other than in packages!

By the way – how is ESCAPE FROM THE AMAZON getting on? Any idea when Victor is likely to be turning up proofs. And – between you and me – has John Trewin started Cruikshank? Or is that for 1964. I only wondered when I saw the Perpetua section in MJ's catalogue. Which looked quite attractive, I thought.

So did the Moulin de la Galette in 1900 (see enclosed)

I remember going to see a verse play in it by A.Dumas the Less with Eric and until 15 minutes after the start of the play – (which had been recommended by the Harold Hobson of the French Critics) – we were outnumbered by the cast. Two other people came in and balanced things up!

[handwritten]

Sun is shining beautifully here
hope Child's Walk has some.
Love
R

PS. M & Valerios
send their cheers.

290 MADISON, 7 JANUARY 1964

Handwritten letter with envelope

Mrs Jean Ellsmoor
1 Child's Walk
LONDON SW5
Angleterre

As from: 4, rue Antoine - Dubois
PARIS 6e France

Madison. 7th Jan 64 pm

Dearest Jean –
I'm afraid this letter won't be as long as yours! Partly due to no settling period being long.
Walking being tiring and pen instead of typewriter.
Thanks for the word about the Belsky's. I haven't had a word from them for ages it seems, apart I think for a note when you were here? and then a bottle of whisky with a card which was delivered into Valerios' hands by I expect the chap you and Cooee stayed with that night you missed the plane. So I've had no indication of them coming here at all. Meanwhile I sent a P.C. today to F & C saying that I was having a jolly week with the children before going off to Germany and then N York within three weeks. So I didn't know whether their next card would come from the Bundesrepublic or USA. I still don't know exactly when I am going to Hamburg. KRISTALL wrote yesterday saying OK come and talk. So presumably they are interested in the Foreigners Eye View or something like. If I don't go next week then I'll just have to stay in hiding while the Belsky's are here and if they turn up at Valerios' door he'll say I'm in Germany. I agree with you. I don't want them to have added munition for their chatter. As I said before – and I wish they would get it into their heads. I don't care a damn who knows my affairs except for one thing and the only reason I'm being secretive about them – The Children.

By the way are you sure the Belskys are coming January or February? Jan 15th is a Wednesday and the 17th a Friday. February 15th is a Saturday and the 17th a Monday. Only you mention it as a weekend …

Your New Years Eve sounded a wow. I mean the table too! Hope it didn't pall for you in the end. And thanks for the T & H geography and background colour so I can visualise you up there and I'm glad that the job has proved less formidable than it seemed. Good. By the way thanks for the copy of the T&H. South America book which arrived yesterday – whats a small imperfection? This is fine. I've had no time to even glimpse at it & I don't suppose I shall till the kids go back –

2

But copies like this are marvellous to have.
I'm having a nice time with the kids. We haven't been particularly enterprising. but at least the weather is walkable about in. And I hope they are enjoying it.
They go back midday Friday train
There haven't been any cheques to send you to post because I haven't had word from Edwards since 16 Dec or bills to pay. I hear from Kaye that Goodman has said that his Accountants are able to take me on and that they advise me to be taxed in France. That he is writing to me. So I am awaiting news.

Meanwhile I can't think of any other suggestion to change the cheque signing business short of causing a flow of documents at the moment. I've just revised the RS Ltd business by having Edwards name taken off. It meant a 'Board Meeting' to pass a minute and Edwards having to approve it as secretary and so on. and then relodging it at Lloyds. To get your signature accepted now would mean scrapping that lot and starting the round again. My only suggestion for safety would be for me to sign a cheque book – you lodge it at Lloyds Bayswater – or your local Lloyds if there is one round the corner – and then xxxx go in on the odd Saturday morning to write out any necessary cheques which Edwards will have sent you. How's that? It won't be every week. I may be only once a month. depending on the urgency of anything that has to be paid.

I've hardly had time to really sort out things and I guess now I'll have to abandon any hope of finally getting straight until after America. I've got a couple of rush jobs to do and I must get back to work as soon as I can.

I hope you picked a nice nude. Delighted to have it displayed!

Hewison wrote the other day – first time since last August – about doing a

3

couple of serious drawings for an Elspeth Huxley series. I said I couldn't – which I can't because of going away – but they offer me such dreary stuff anyway.

Your Christmas Card – not the one in the briefcase but the other – the little man playing a flute or something on a blue background. arrived I think the day I thanked you for it. After Christmas.

Mo's sister went back to London on Monday so you should get your official little present in the post this week.

'Fanny Hill' – you won't have any trouble getting her here. The American paperback is on sale at Brentano's – and every where else I should imagine. The copy I read Mo brought with her sister and is going the rounds. Her sister was taking hers back to England – so she may never be heard of again – locked up in a customs shed with her copy somewhere!

Thats it for now until I get back to the typewriter at the end of the week – Love from one and all. And I'll let you know about travel & Germany and dates as soon as they are fixed.

Love
R
----

291 BAYREUTH, THURSDAY 21 MAY 1964
Handwritten on post card

Bayreuth Thursday 21 May 1964

Dearest Jean: I hope you had a glorious holiday and are back – if reluctantly – at least refreshed and bronzed.
This trip is going slowly – partly because of the weather – (chased by rain most of the way) and the quantity of work. By Monday morning when we leave here I hope to have 12 spreads completed. 28 or so drawings. From here, on Monday morning, we head down and West to tackle Rothenberg, a village in the Odenwald, and Heidelberg – which will take 5 or 6 days – then back to Paris on the fastest or most direct train possible. The latest we should be back in Paris is Saturday May 30, which is tighter on time than I had intended. This will still give me a few days to get straight and complete the spreads on the places I've managed to get to, before coming to London. Which will be just over half the work. The second half will have to be done here in October, alas. It looks as if we shall be in London on June 9.
Mô has to have her front teeth replaced, or recrowned, rather urgently & much to her misery, and her sister has got her an appointment starting at dawn on June 10th for about 10 days. This fits in with 20th Cent Fox business and I shall also take advantage of being able to dash down to Cambridge to see my mother and father. I'm not telling anyone that I'm coming over otherwise it will lead to the complication of having to see The Lot and as I shall be at the film studio most of the time I'll be keeping out of the way. I'll write when back in Paris – with positive bookings and all that – but perhaps you could have a note there waiting for me so that I know how things are generally – although after this lot I hardly feel I have the strength to face problems. Would much prefer a session in the sun doing nothing! I've decided that basically I'm idle! Love R

[In Monica Searle's handwriting]

I do hope you are beautifully brown, relaxed – blissful after your brief rest. As for us only a frog could survive this climate. If you see us in London, looking [?] green & leaping nervously to and fro you'll know we transformed – the end Love Mô

[In Ronald Searle's handwritting]
World have a nice Perruchot splash
in TIME. See enclosed

292 LE CANADEL, SUNDAY 27 SEPTEMBER 1964
Handwritten on post card

Le Canadel Sunday 27 Sept 1964

Dearest Jean – the holiday is passing all too quickly but we have been terribly lucky with the weather – hot, sunny, if limpid I think they call it, which has aided the unwinding no end. Today it has poured cats and dogs non stop, however, but we have been able to recruit drivers & get lifts here and there along the coast and at least to the Sunday Newspaper stalls. I hope your holiday was a great success and wasn't too soon over – or too Frozen North Will be back in Paris on the night of October 6th - a week on Tuesday when I must get down rapidly to the rest of the 20th Cent Fox publicity. Which will mean a scant 2 weeks in Paris and then Berlin and other German stopovers … No news really – except the rest seems to be working alright Difficult to do nothing, though! Love R.

[In Monica Searle's handwriting]

Yes, we cd. do with another two months! No desire to return at all. Much love
Mô

293 BERLIN, SATURDAY 24 OCTOBER 1964
Handwritten on post card

Saturday October 24 1964. Berlin

Dearest Jean – Got here on Thursday night after a rather fogbound series of flights. Finally reached Hamburg 3 hours late and had the Kristall meeting at the airport! Then leapt on the BEA to Berlin through the fog and drizzle and tottered into the destination. The weather has been miserable up to today so there has been a chance of working out of doors. Had to do the East Zone for the most of today and it is still very bleak and deserted over there with the wind whistling through Karl-Marx Allee which is no cosy Oxford Street although three times as wide. Finally ended with tea in Moscow house where hoards of people were gloomily listening to a sort of Palm Court orchestra
It will take until about Monday to get the material here on East & West Berlin so I expect we'll be flying off to Dusseldorf on Tuesday and then doing the rest down to the south by road – finally flying back from Stuttgart. Determined – despite the slow start – to try and be back within 2 weeks. Over in the East a short taxi trip cost about 11/-. That's why everyone is on foot. It's pretty cold – but not intolerable as I finally bought a warmer overcoat before leaving Paris, which fits! Monica – doing stalwart translation and sends much love. You'll be getting another card en route. Sorry missed hearing from you before taking off. Hope all is OK.
Much love R.

294 PARIS, SUNDAY [1964]
Typed post card

4 rue Antoine – Dubois, Paris 6e, Sunday.

Dearest Jean ———

[typed – brackets written in red biro]
Finally got my bag unpacked and about to embark on the second half of Germany hoping that some of those stomachs will improve in perspective! Must say the prospect of not having to leave again for a month is almost too good to be true. I got to the point where I wanted to kick my case.
I came back with half the material – mostly in colour and I think it is quite funny in the Dublinstrain. It will take me about another ten days to complete now. Then I can get it off to America and charge them for it.
I hope the American money arrived all right

There was no word from Edwards. And my July money has come through – despite three requests to fix the increase (in May) – at £50.still. Maddening. (to be kept so short.)
I hope all is well. I look forward to hearing what has been doing and whether you have grown webbed feet.
Thank goodness after a pelting Germany, Paris is warm and sunny.

[Handwritten]
Love
R.

PTO An earlier Jean
collecting her
breakfast stout.

295 BOXING DAY 1964
Handwritten letter with envelope

4, rue Antoine-Dubois, Paris 6e

Mrs Jean Ellsmoor
1 Child's Walk
LONDON SW5
Angleterre

Boxing Day 1964
Dearest Jean –

Only with great effort were those pretty packages untouched until Christmas! And when the time was ripe no time was lost! The candle is now burning in the window for you. And I was thrilled with my sweater – right colour fit – hole for pinhead and everything. It's going to be terribly useful – especially for trips. Great success! I haven't tasted the Swedish (?) rock yet but we're all so blown out it isn't difficult to say why!
Mô will no doubt write later as she is deep in getting supper ready for more animals to tackle the turkey carcass – but she was exclaiming all over the shop about her scarf. It's been a nice Christmas. Every one very relaxed. Nothing burnt and the right shaped hats in the crackers. Even a snow shower yesterday as we ate Christmas Dinner. I hope yours has been as nice and that you had some lovely surprises. Now I must write some 'Thank You' letters – this is a thank you, thank you, one!

Much love
R

296 HONOLULU, 17 FEBRUARY 1965
Handwritten post card

Honolulu 17 February 1965

Dearest Jean – About the only place you'll find the romance of the Sandwich Islands is on postcards like this. It is really rather like Los Angeles and an awfully long way to come for the same sort of material. However the people are nice and the climate is sunny and steadily in the 70's it has taken us just about a week to acclimatise and drag ourselves about. this enervating air I suppose geared to flopping on the beach and not moving. One thing they do have here is flowers and flowers and flowers
I expect we shall be leaving here at the end of the month to go to Los Angeles where I have a weeks job to do.
So we should be back in New York after the first week in March. I hope Hope had some good news about the American publication of 'Magnificent Men' book I had to leave it in Malcolm Reiss's hands. Apart from not having started to draw yet – all is going wellish
Hope you are fully revived and unflued now.
– Much love R.

[In Monica Searle's handwriting]

Greetings from the most
commercial paradise so far
& much love Mo>>>>>

297 SUNDAY, 25 APRIL 1965
Typed letter

4, rue Antoine-Dubois, Paris 6e

Dearest Jean – Sunday, April 25th, 1965

As you can see I häave ä neü typewriter $£1;"=%&( )_ §§§§/+ßßßß::
´^`üüÜÜÄä?!£!!-' which seämßß to häv§ a lot of rathür odd thingß

on it + that's the result of going to Germany. I took the plunge as the machines were so cheap there and bought myself this Olympia model which is really rather handsome and which was quickly made into an English keyboard by transposing one key and which then left me with German and French accents. Or at least enough to add confusion to most of my letters.

The French let it through without duty yesterday afternoon, although I declared it! A reward for my incredible honesty, I feel.

The German trip was successful and all went according to plan. KRISTALL, although they have dropped the series (so far) this year, are continuing at once under their new editor, who arrived last Tuesday. And we agreed, mutually, to wash out the extra journey to Germany in July, up to the North. They may have some detective stories for me to illustrate later on – amusingly they stressed.

The exhibition looked excellent and rather magnificent. I thought you would like to know about it as you had such a hand in gathering stuff for it.

The gallery itself , which looks rather like a small Parthenon, was well plastered with posters outside and a banner across the temple door bearing a not unpleasant 'Searle' about six feet long!

Inside all was guarded by uniformed German gents ready to fend off any attempt by International gangs to smuggle out any of my work, to sell on the closed market. Through the magnificent marble hall of the permanent collection one came on the gallery about as big as the Duke of Yorks Theatre where everything was handsomely and simply framed and mounted. It really looked rather good. Screens took in the surplus and the occasional old rejection was hung on a tastefully draped black silk hanging. The books were reverently placed in glass cases and in some, twice removed, were lying framed pictures – including Molesworth. Some of the finger marks on the sample books looked rather intriguing under glass. Ix tell you I felt as if I was looking at something from another artist, from some other time. I certainly didn't feel it had anything to do with me. As one of the directors of the museum unfortunately said: " I hope you like the memorial exhibition". It felt rather like that. Anyway it lived up to the catalogue and I was really very pleased.

We went onto Hanover to see the director of the Wilhelm Busch museum, where the show goes in July. He has tried to persuade me to go for the opening. But I haven't committed myself at this stage. It might be better for me to be absent and mysterious!

The exhibition has been extended in Bremen for another week. So instead of closing today it closes next Sunday.

I hope Hope passed you the message of thanks for the coffee pot

[over page]

which I passed over to her when I was speaking about Huber before leaving on Thursday.

The pot was fine, but two cups too small. As I mentioned on my card. They had got a 6 cup pot in a 8 cup box. It was marked (8 on the box and 6 on the bottom of the pot) but that will carry us over until Valerios comes back. But after that it won't go round so Mô will get the bigger one later in the year. The main thing is to say thank you for dashing out to get this in your last moments before going of to Amsterdam,and delivering it to the Suttons, who carried it safely across. Very sweet of you, and I hope that Amsterdam proved as pleasant as it looked the one day I had there, with Arthur Woolley. Although I am afraid it must have been a bit chilly judging from the Easter weather in Paris. Snow and all that. Frankly it isn't much warmer now.

All our front windows are blocked with an enormous fence and scaffolding whilst an enthusiastic lot of characters tear off the roof. So we can only see the sky from the almost total darkness indoors. Hope to God they take it away before the decent weather comes. But it looks so permanent I am afraid it is for a month or more.

Tomorrow I must get my nose into the Shell book on London, as the jacket is being demanded. But before I get going I thought you'd be amused to hear about the exhibition.

That's all for now and you must admit the letter looks a bit préttier§ßäÜ=+!

[handwritten]

———— Much Love
Ronald
and from Mô too, who is deep in —
cooking herrings. Very tasty judging
by the smell.

[In Monica Searle's handwriting]

They weren't bad actually, considering I tried them fat-free. Interesting ….. Thank you VERY much from me too for all the trouble you took *vis á vis* the cafetière. It's saving my life I can tell you. I had been reduced to making extra-extra strong coffee in a teeny pot (the one I bought whilst in London). it was entirely inadequate for early morning Searle,

[on side]

let alone early morning eyes glued shut
Stirling. Thank you again.
Much love & many kisses from Mô
P.S. The typewriter model is called Monica.
such a nice thought !!

298 TUESDAY, 18 MAY 1965
Typed letter

4, rue Antoine-Dubois, Paris 6e

Dearest Jean – Tuesday, May 18th, 1965

Now the men have stopped banging for the day I can sit down and concentrate for a moment. Boy, shall I be glad when they get this roof finished. Still, only a few days and then we can get out of the way and they can bang to their hearts content.

Thank you for your long letter and all your news. I hope you didn't lose too much of the Production Course producing that! How did the exam go. Did you get extra impositions?

I slogged away and got the SHELL Children's Guide to London illustrated, and to Hope, and then arrived my Cousin Molly and her husband whom I'd never met before and, until they went back on Sunday, nothing much was done except take advantage of the fabulous weather and roam the streets and museums. As they went the sun went in and now it is warm, grey and showery.

It had better clear up in time for Monday when we are going to drive off into – well, simply into France and see what happens and where the roads take us. We shall be away about a week and avoiding the weekends will probably get back on Monday or Tuesday June 1st.

I am ready for a break now, especially as it is so difficult getting any work done through the noise.

I shall be away when the Telegraph come out with their three pages on the MAGMEN book. Friday 28th May, isn't it? In any case come to/ think of it, I can't get it here. So perhaps you could get your Vasser girl to go out and snap up a few extra copies. The MAGMEN book looks very pretty, I think. I haven't tried to read it again, since I read it in MS. If only Alex had been alive he would have made something of the subject. However …

I hope the film gets favourable reviews so that the book doesn't have too much of a battle. Hope tells me that advance orders are around 4000 copies.But you probably know all this already. I spoke to her on the phone last night because I had had a long panic cable from Norton in New York who are publishing the book over there. They have just discovered that there is a pocket-book about to be distributed with the same title by arrangement with Fox.

Did you get a copy of the book all right. I only have four here, but I have asked Hope to ask Dobson's to sent me a few more.

Glad to hear that you have drawn out what I owed you. I am waiting on answers to various things from Peat, Marwick so that I know what to do about the account. It must be almost empty now. If it gets really stuck perhaps Hope could feed some in as I am waiting for Peat, Marwick before I can complete my Tax Exemption
certificate. Meanwhile there is another little bill enclosed which I'd like you to pay while the checkbook still applies. What did Diner's Club say about switching? I shall be glad when the final unravelling is done so that I know where I am with money.

2.

Yes, this is an Olympia portable. Would you like to see what there is on it? You would. Good.

; " = % & ( ) _ § / : `
1 2 3 4 5 6 7 8 9 + ß ´

Q W E R T Y U I O P Ü
q w e r t y u i o p ü

A S D F G H J K L £ Ä
a s d f g h j k l $ ä

Z X C V B N M ? ! '
z x c v b n m , . –

I didn't realise that the German keyboard is the same as the English one. Except that the Y and Z are transposed. I had that changed and the £$ key added in place of those O's with two dots on the top. ß I gather is for Straße. But § I guess will have to wait until I write $unday.

No, I didn't take any pictures of the German opening. Next opening is Dusseldorf mid-June. The reviews so far have been excellent, and have come from all over the place in Germany. It would appear that my work is completely unknown in Germany judging by the surprise expressed in some of the reviews. So all this may help to pick up the books and the KRISTALL readership. After a gap of four months KRISTALL have started again this current issue, with Bonn.

There is a letter in this issue resenting the critical smears of Searle. Gentle criticism is always welcome, it says, but not this sort of dirty rudeness. Signed A TEACHER.

I wrote a letter to the Belsky's and with it sent a catalogue of Bremen, before your letter came. So that may have smoothed the path. Oh dear … I said in the letter that I had passed through Lon London on the way to get to/my father in Cambridge for a week of staying with him and getting my mother away, and that it was all rather worrying as a trip.

If Hope isn't about when I come over then I might make it for a coffee with C & Franta. But I am not saying anything to them about it until the last minute. Perhaps from the airport.

I am booked on the AF flight getting to London at 10.10am June 4 as before. Let me know about lunch. That would be very nice and I would prefer to be indoors than/(out) in a restaurant in London.

Then I shall dash straight to Liverpool Street and catch the fastest train away before the Whitsun crowds get going. I am hoping that Katie will be able to come to Cambridge on Saturday and Sunday and perhaps Johnny on Sunday to take her back. However, I am awaiting news on that. I shall leave Cambridge early Monday morning to go straight to London airport to catch the 3.0pm plane back. Thanks for getting me my train ticket. There might be large queues at Liverpool Street.

§ § § § 3. § § § §

============
++++++++++++

h'm

Monica is thrilled that the shoes were such a great success She is very wrapped up in driving at the moment. Well, not exactly at this moment as she is getting the dinner. Marlis will be back starving in a moment and I'm starving and it is nearly 7.0pm.

The driving lessons are every afternoon this week, followed by an hour of back treatment by the Ex-Champion Middleweight Boxer of France. So by the \time we go off on Monday I'll have to ring a bell to get her in and out of the driving seat and stand by the car with a bucket and sponge.

There is no other absorbing news really. Signor GEC is, I gather, hard at work on the Searle Monograph for the Tolentino festival. Pamphlet enclosed. He says they are awaiting the arrival of the pictures with great expectancy. Judith has been to dinner for a couple of/ weeks on the run. I mean twice in two weeks. She seems fine, although in a bit of a panic about getting working contacts again. Still, things seem to be trickling in gently to just keep her going. She painted her studio out from top to bottom and even got going on some of the furniture. It looks charming (that was before the children came back from Majorca – when we went for dinner one evening) and she feels she has finally painted Irwin out with it. I gather that all he has sent her since he left for the States is $150. Anyway, there is no doubt she would rather remain here worrying than go back there.

We went to the 20th-Anniversary-of-the-Capitulation-of-Germany celebrations a couple of Saturdays back and there was the most fabulous firework display at the Palais de Chaillot. We stood and got it framed by the arch of the Eiffel Tower. Something like a quarter of a million people turned out for it the papers said. It felt a bit like that when we walked home!

Dinner's ready! So I shall leave you here …
------------------------------ With much love
R.

[In Monica Searle's handwriting]

Dearest Jean,
After that graphic description, what more can I add, except that on Monday I drove a large 4C4 Peugeot for the 1st time (steering wheel gears, ecstasy for broken backs). But for the holiday I'm sticking to the R8. Talking of broken backs, I discovered yesterday that the boxers brother (who was treating me that time) is a Judo Black Belt. A talented family, no? I ought to end in fine fettle – or not at all.
much love& how I wish I were seeing you Whitsun Mô

299 TUESDAY, 8 JUNE 1965

Typed letter on 'A la Cheminee de ma Grand-Mere' greaseproof wrapping paper

Branch Office
4 rue Antoine-Dubois, Paris 6e

Tuesday, 8th June, 1965

Dearest Jean –

Just a little note now that I'm back again and about to face up to getting some drawing done!

I hope you had a lovely weekend and refreshed yourself nicely. Mine was full, but a great success. Kate came on Saturday morning and we had a lovely day drifting around the market and the river then Johnny and Kate's friend Peter turned up on Sunday morning as planned and they all – including Rusty – drove back on Sunday teatime. I Got away early on Monday, had a sandwich with Wendy and got off as planned at 3.opm. No travel complications at all.

It was LOVELY seeing you even for such a short time. Thank you for that delicious lunch on the terrace which set me up nicely for the train – which I caught! And thanks too for the Primitive Art volume. Fascinating. I dipped deep into that at Cambridge. Gillray I haven't done more than glimpse through. At first glance it seems rather dull.

That's all for now!

[handwritten]

– Much love
pp. Grandma's Chimney

– and from Mô too

300 THURSDAY, 1 JULY 1965
Typed letter

4, rue Antoine-Dubois, Paris 6e

Dearest Jean — Thursday, 1 July,1965

How the days trot by! Here everything has been rather submerged under the Huber translation problems with 4 rue A-D acting as a sort of clearing station and inbetween I'm still battling to get rid of the TVGUIDE stuff I committed myself to in the USA and would prefer to forget about! Specially when it is as hot as it was yesterday.
Hope you are getting some nice rays of warmth to spread over your terrace, too!

Yesterday there came here a very nice young chap — (about 22) Anthony d'Offay (38 Devonshire Place, W.1. (Welbeck 7566) who recently put out a marvellous catalogue of drawings and mss including letters from Gauguin with sketches on 'em and a lot of Schuffenecker drawings which he got from the family you met. etc, etc, including Lautrec, Signac, Cezanne sketches. He has obviously a marvellous nose for digging up stuff. Anyway — Betram Rota of Vigo Street is moving to better premises in Saville Row and this chap has taken part of those premises to open a gallery specialising in drawings, in September, and he wanted to konw whether I would let him have things of mine to sell in the gallery. I said certainly I was happy to sell but that there wasn't a tremendous selection of framable stuff, as so much was travelling about. But I said that you took care of everything of mine there was available and also had an idea of the sort of prices they had fetched, and that he should get in touch with you and arranged what he liked with you.
I think you'll like him very much as a person and of course he is deep in the areas you covered with Manet and Gauguin.

Also instead of cash-if any of my things sell there — he offered possible exchanges for drawings I might want, which might be very interesting when I want (for example!!!) Forain Berard, Lautrec, Daumier, C.Guys, Leonardo …

Anyway, this seems a very useful contact and a horribly tempting one! So you'll let me know what it is about when he gets in touch with you. I'm all for getting rid of some of the bulk of the drawings in the portfolios. I bet you are too!

The application form has arrived from the French Diners' Club so I assume this will go through. So you could send back my English card now to the GB Diner's Club and get it off your hands.

There was a pleasurable session here on Tuesday evening when André and Margaret François came to dinner. Topor came too whom they hadn't met and everyone got on well. Hadn't seen André more than once briefly since New Year's eve. Not that it was his fault. He brought me back the cover drawing of BITING EYE which he had on loan for an exhibition at Keels ages ago. Nice to see it again. It is a very pretty drawing.

2

Lou Glessman the new HOLIDAY art editor (who was Frank's assistant) arrives on Saturday for three days and will need attention. Huber is coming to Paris to meet here with Roland Gant to go over the second half of the translation July 9-10-11th. It is a marvellous text. A great success. I hope Huber isn't drummed out of Germany after publication!
Apart from the no plans — except that Johnny has decided not to try to go to Australia this summer and wants to wander off around Europe again. He has suggested starting in Paris at the end of July. So what I\think I shall try to do is to coincide with him and Kate and I'll take them off on holiday somewhere at the end of the month instead of simply taking Kate away in August as I thought. Then Johnny can go on and Kate come back to London. However, I have yet to organise that — find somewhere to take them — and try to coincide them. I forsee complications. However …

August — apart from Monica's sister arriving for her summer holiday at the end of the month — looks quite bare. Unless Glessman turns up with some feature to be done, there is no plan for travelling anywhere on work until America next year. A very rare situation.

Are you still toying with the idea of coming over for a little shopping??? You only have to say the word — but not before July 15th (Bastille celebrations) because there was great difficulty in getting Huber boo ked into a hotel before that date.
I hope your eyes are visible over your work desk … busy girl.

Monica has given up smoking — apart from one a day after dinner - and is now crocheting like a demon to keep her mind off it and her hands busy. I think she is making a sort of angora sock in which to cover the house — if not the street! She sends much love.
The Belskys (or rather Cooee) wrote — sometime back, I am afraid and I haven't got round to replying — to say that they has given my address to Sergin and Joanna Celibidache. She said that Joanna C. knows me although I don't know her, whatever that means ad that they have a flat in Paris. I seem to know that name — Celibidache. But my mind is a total blank as to who or where. Do you know?
[hand written]

— Read any good shop windows lately?

Much Love
R.

301 SUNDAY AFTERNOON, 24 OCTOBER 1965

Typed letter with envelope [an unfranked postage stamp is contained inside]

Mrs Jean Ellsmoor
1 Child's Walk
LONDON S.W.5
Angleterre

4 rue Antoine-Dubois, Paris 6e

Sunday afternoon, 24th October, 1965

Dearest Jean –

Does Delphi seem far away? Has the golden tan departed? As you say on your post-card, why do holidays have to end!

How are you over there in that foggy bowl?

We got back with just about enough time to unpack the bags and shake the sand out, when my sister and her husband arrived for their week. It was John's first Paris trip and he managed to out-eat Valerios all the way. It was quite a week of feeding them and 'doing' Paris. They left last Saturday and it wasn't until Sunday that we were able to say that we were back here again – and had to get down to some work.

This week has been quite a week of doing this and that. A big adv. to promote the use of plaster (of all things) which is to appear as a full-page in FIGARO. Then the start of a new once-a-month cartoon for FIGARO LITTERAIRE. First came out on Thursday, and several other bits and pieces. Now, at last I am able to sit and tap before Monday springs up again!

I have just Expressed a letter to Hope telling her that I hope to come over on Thursday, Nov.4th – until Monday 8th. With luck she will be able to fix a meeting for me with British Lion about the ST. TRINIAN'S TRAIN ROBBERY film publicity, and get any other discussions out of the way. I shan't be staying in London overnight or anything. So when my usefulness has expired in London I shall go straight onto Cambridge. My father has to go into hospital again they tell me. I have asked Hope to phone you and tell you I should be coming. I haven't gotx my ticket yet, but I don't anticipate any complications, except weather, of course! But I shall confirm anyway, when I have the ticket in my grasp. If you could keep in touch with Hope to see what she books me for we might at least split a coffee and biscuit at some point before I go to Liverpool St.

I expect to be over again later in the month to go to Cambridge, so that Mô can take advantage of whisking over too with her sack to collect the Christmas goodies! Actually with the sun we are getting here, and have been getting for the last two weeks, (1 rainy day) Christmas couldn't seem further off. Yet it is only

eight weeks tomorrow. That makes our time rather short as I have had it confirmed by John that we are expected over there in [handwritten] NYork by January 4th. Advancing the usual trip by a month. This has been rather unavoidable because the TV GUIDE want to get going on another set of features about TV shows which are running now, and they wanted me there in December. John held out the temptation of having Christmas over there with them – but I have shied off that one! So we go immediate after, and a few days after getting there, go on\to Los Angeles.

Offhand it will be two months as usual – unless it is essential for me to stay xx to get this new pattern of TVGUIDE and VENTURE established in place of HOLIDAY. Actually we are waiting now to hear from Arnold Ehrlich (that friend of Alex's on HOLIDAY – who left to join VENTURE as articles editor)- and who was supposed to have arrived in Paris last night. They have asked me to do a 12page feature on the Americanisation of Europe (without moving) and he is xxxxxxxx to talk to me about it, so that I can start.

The Americanisation of Saint-Germain des Près is a good start. The DRUGstore opened opposite the Deux Magots on Wednesday. Couldn't be less American, really. Rather like the one in Champs Elysées but outdoing it in glamour and sculpture. Something for you to check on when you come back here! Their sundaes are supposed to be the new Paris experience. There is a cinema embodied (in it) too, which has opened with the Fellini – "Juliet of the Spirits". Queues all round the corner into the Rue de Rennes.

André telephoned the other day – He's deep in his steel paintings – if that is possible. One he says is three metres long. His exhibition opens at Delpire's Gallery, behind the church of Saint-Germain-des-Près, on Wednesday week. I haven't seen him since before you were here, but I haven't forgotten about that little drawing you want.

Valerios is drilling and hammering and plastering away upstairs, whilst Marlis looks on delicately from her chaise-long. She was operated on the day we got back from holiday – 16 stitches in her tummy – and has to have a months convalescence. Valerios, now that they have got the little room in order and sleeping in there, is tackling the studio, to capture all the space he has suddenly revealed by moving out the bed. He goes back\to Athens on Nov. 3rd

3.

to prepare his exhibition which opens in the Athens Hilton about mid-November. He has show us the photos of the 30 pictures he has done. Some of his best work to date I think. So he won't be back until just before Christmas.

Mô is deep in her second Crochet Marathon. She has promised (rashly, she says) a large cot – cover for a baby due about Christmas – -day to her ex-driving instructor and his Indo-Chinese wife. It is based on the sugar icing of Playbox Biscuits, and looks really edible! * [in margin handwritten * hope the baby doesn't take it too literally] What with that, and cooking for the hungry wolves on these two floors and drying bouquets for the winter and coping with visitors she has finally finished her week's wash and sunk deeply into the sofa with a Penguin thriller …

I have just written a note to the Belsky's, to keep them quiet. I had one from them (some time back) telling me that they took a trip with your friend with the private plane, and\that Franta circled over Fontainbleau. They mentioned that work (for him) has stopped with the credit squeeze. Has this affected architects very much? I hope that Brian hasn't been affected.

What other news? Peat, Marwick write to tell me that Edwards has been discharged from hospital and is now able to get on with RSLtd accounts. Johnny has gone to Trinity Dublin (last Monday). Kate is well away at the Central School of Arts & C's. I hear from the Tolentino Italians that there is a gold medal there for me, and they hope to deliver it one day. I am just about over a stinking cold I caught just as I arrived on holiday and which stopped me from bathing (infuriating!). MAGNIFICENT MEN is on at three cinemas here. The posters look dreadful around Paris. Some in reverse, some with figures I didn't do, horribly done. But at least my name doesn't appear on 'em.

I am waiting to hear news of the German book as it must start on the layout stage soon. Meanwhile the lawyer in America is being bombarded with demands for compensation by Norton's over the MAGMEN book there. The French edition doesn't look bad at all.

There can't be much missing out of the chatter here, to bring you up-to-date, so I think I had better leave you in peace – HERE!

[handwritten]
So -------------- That's all for now. Much love from us both

R.

[In Monica Searle's handwriting]

Dearest Jean,
A word from the lazy one – not reading that thriller actually but cooking a duck & pancakes petit poises while all the waifs stand around sniffing hungrily. I do wish you were there too. It's ????????????????? So will we be in a short time … The boss has given all news so I have only my love left to send & here it is – lots of it

From
Mô

302 SATURDAY, 19 MARCH 1966
Typed Letter

4 rue Antoine-Dubois, Paris 6e

Dearest Jean -------- Saturday, 19th March, 1966

Lovely book! thank you very much. It arrived safely yesterday together with that fascinating packet of Alice in Wonderland cards. Where/ever did you get those? Anyway, late or not, it was a lovely Birthday parcel.

Judith said she has seen you the other day. She came round to dinner on Thursday evening and chatted away until Midnight, with Mô, whilst Valerios and I watched TV. Did I tell you that we have invested in a set since I thought I had better see a screen now and then whilst TVGUIDE is going strong. Small set. SONY actually, with a 7" screen and all the works – including an earplug for personal listening and an indoor antenna. Quite a toy.

I have been slogging away on the HUNCHBACK OF NOTRE DAME, occasionally going to look out of the window to make sure that Quasimodo is up there. That's pretty well finished how and is ready to go off/and be photograph by Chadefaux before I put it into the post to Reader's Digest Condensed books (Ugh!)

We are going to Germany for a few days – Stuttgart actually – on Monday week(28th). Seeing Huber and spending some time in the TV studios there, also with Deryk Mendel from next door and Sam Beckett, as Huber's company are filming Deryk doing a Beckett. We shall be back April 1st.

Have fixed to go to Cambridge after Easter. Mô will be coming too and staying with some people in Bury St.Edmunds, and with her sister. I am meeting Katy and giving her a weeks holiday chez my Mum and D. Leaving here on 14th April (Thursday) and we'll whizz straight through to Liverpool Street and talk to you on the phone when I am down there, with Kate.

I had a letter from xxxx Ioana de Duca Celibidache asking me to ring her (which I didn't) and then an invitation to her exhibition which opened on Thursday in the Blvd St.Germain. (didn't go). I don't feel particularly anxious to get involved with Franta and Cooee's friends living here – especially as the letter seemed to be from a rather steam-rolling type.

Let's see, what else is there – oh, yes. About five months ago

2

we saw a very lovely little Regency armchair, cane seat and all, which matched our other chairs. Finally managed to get the shop to drop the price 200 Frs ! and bought it. So we now have a choice of six chairs for you!

Since seeing you most of the time has been spent trying to sort out and get going again. Of course Robert's funeral set everyone back a bit and it is taking time to get Marcelle back to normal again. At least she has the restaurant to keep her busy. I caught a cold at the funeral which went on from 2.0pm until 6.3opm. It was quite a day one way and another.

We saw in the Sunday Times last week that there is a place called GAFF opening this week in the Boulevard St.Germain selling sausages and mash – sausages flown in daily from GB. We intend to try to find that in the near future … Everything is going so English here!

Have you been to the Antiques Fair? Been tempted?

Jock Whittet is supposed to be arriving Chez Valerios any moment – wants to see him about a new London gallery. Sounds interesting. So I expect we shall be going up to have a drink with them any moment. He is no longer with the STUDIO. It has changed hands once more and Jock seems to be organiser of exhibitions or something now. She be interested to learn more.

I had a birthday card from the Belskys the other day and a letter from the Board of Trade saying that they have agreed to finally knock Perpetua Films off the records without putting me in jail.

And that is about it … Thanks again for my book and the Lewis Carroll cards – and the delicious birthday card!
Mô – sewing full steam ahead (patchwork covers for the Regency chairs) sends much love …

(Handwritten with stamped pointing finger)

Me too – much love

R.

[typed]

PS: If you come across the Daily Telegraph Colour Supplement on Friday, it should have an article by me in it on the Americanisation of Europe. I can't get it here.

PSST: Judith says that the St. Trinian's posters look AWFUL. I haven't seen them yet, but B.Lion say some are on the way.

303 GOOD FRIDAY, 1966
Typed Letter

4 rue Antoine-Dubois, Paris 6e
Good Friday, 1966

Dearest Jean

Thanks for that enormously long letter which arrived last night. I have just tried to ring you but no reply – so I guess you have slid off to the country for the weekend. Jolly good idea!

Thanks for the copy of the TELEGRAPH supplement the other day. It didn't look bad, did it? A bit of a layout muddle, but not too shaming. The TELEGRAPH wrote to say they were pleased, anyway.

I have had a lot of enjoyment looking through the DADA book. I haven't got down to reading it yet but I am delighted to have this subject matter gap filled in the 'library'. Thanks again.

Since I saw you last there hasn't been a lot of news to pass on and what little there is I think I've told you. A great deal of the time has been spent helping to keep up Marcelle Methlin's morale. She has been very good, but it is beginning to flag a bit now. I designed her a menu to put into the window, all decorated and written out by hand, and we got her a (much needed) clock for the restaurant as the old one had packed up after she shifted it to hang a picture of mine on the walls.

[handwritten in margin]
and I've been feeling rather guilty about it although it was a rotten clock!

And we are helping her to make plans with the restaurant, so she has been digging about in the cave – which I've never seen – to bring up odds and ends dumped down there over the last 40years – including the old coffee machine all wheels and pipes which will look lovely in/her window, and an enormous old hand grinder for coffee. She also discovered a bottle of prune liqueur which she said must have been down there for at least 35 years. I have drunk half of it already. Very potent! Everytime I go near the restaurant she plonks it in front of me. Very dangerous to strike matches within ten feet of it!

Abu Abraham of the OBSERVER turned up one day and we took him out for a meal and had a nice evening as you know, Hope came in for an hour on her way to Greece. Very tired she looked and rather worn out – but chatting as usual. Pity about Greece being so remote. Still, I expect when you go that way again you ' ll be able to unfold your tent on the land!
Judith we saw just after she saw you and then she came round last night for a cold collation. We haven't seen her for a couple of weeks before that because Ivan had mumps. She was a bit down last night with a sore throat and a touch of the despondencies. Said she might be going back to America again in the summer. Other – wise nothing much happening. We had a brief supper because Mô was in bed after the Doc had been, having had a rather violent upset all the night before. Must have been a bug or something which struck home rather nastily and today she is still rather limp and mostly in bed. The only consolation she feels about it is that she lost over a kilo in one night – perspiring it off.

B. Larsson far from being a possible proud mum is utterly furious and horrified and views the whole business as a disaster. We heard from her several times briefly but not often now as she says she feels too ill to put pen to paper. What makes her particularly

2

furious is that everyone else at home and away are thrilled! She is apparently coming to England at the end of April and staying there for the rest of the year. Presumably to have the baby at her mother's.

We have got a folly in the house now. We had been looking for a cupboard (discreet) to put into the hall in which to unload some of the bottle and pots and bits. We looked around without much success as we needed something narrow and not very big. I dreamed about hunting for this dammed thing and wasn't all that keen to have anything blocking the hall anyway.

So I dreamed that the hunt was still on and in my dreams went to the Place des Vosges and into an antiquaire and found the thing there. I forget now what I saw.

Anyway next day after breakfast I suggested an outing to the Place des Vosges. Took a taxi and it stopped in the square – (no particular place) – just stopped where we arrived. We got out, paid the taxi and found ourselves right outside an antique shop. Went in saw a piece of furniture, fell in love with it, walked all round the square trying to make up our minds about it. Came back before he closed at 12,30 and bought it. At 5.30pm last Wednesday week it arrived.

It is about 7 feet tall about 6feet long and fills the whole wall between the kitchen door and the passage. Difficult to describe it really. Its a dresser in pine, about mid 18th Century – a sort of Welsh dresser with wiggles on. Apparently it is Canadian-French. It is really rather magnificent, bags of character, very simple – and I am still startled by it. Well, you'll see ……… when you come. When are you coming?

I had always rather longed after a grandfather clock but that dream I think has gone forever now. Unless we do what my grandfather the clockmaker used to do, that is to dig a hole in the floor of any cottage that was too low to take one and set the clock down into it. Could always stick the clock down into the apartment below and make our bit look like a floor level clock.

Thanks for all the bits and pieces of news in your letter.

INSURANCE: You find a separate page about that attached to this.

OXFAM: If you've got anything there which might do I don't mind if you send it to them.

EDWARD JARVIS: I think we've forgotten about him already, haven't we?

JAMES HALL TOMSON: as it is a fellow artist why don't you write back and say that you think you could find something for him at about £5.

GALLERY IN BASLE: I'll write to them and tell/them to get in touch with Bremen. Maybe they could take the German show which is just heading for Austria. The catalogue is in German which might work nicely for Switzerland.

LOCARNO GALLERY: I have had a letter from them too about presenting a drawing so I'll write from here.

[handwritten] Came a long time ago and I'd forgotten about it.

MICHAEL BATEMAN: OK. I'll think about his idea and the pictures and so on when I hear from him. It is going to be a slight problem finding something which will make a very good display. I may have to get 'em from America.

COLLECTORS CORNER: If you are collecting their next catalogue would you get one for me too. Sounds fascinating

3

The map of China sounds quite a find.

The sausage and mash place we decided not to bother with. Apparently it is a sort of bleak dancehall attached to a cinema where one can presumably get snacks on the side – which I suppose include sausages.

I didn't know there were two Atterburys so I don't know which one I met now I see both names. Perhaps it was Roland Atterbury – I met once at J. D. Scott's. Anyway maybe you'll find out before I remember as he is a near neighbour. The postcard makes the cottages look dreamlike and I imagine they must look even prettier than that.

Child's Walk should look pretty too set off against the white next door. I shall look forward to seeing it.

I think going to Cambridge I shall whizz straight through as I am supposed to be meeting Katie there. We should be arriving about 11.0am as it is a flight (AF9o6) which leaves here at 9.55am. Mô's sister is here at the moment for Easter and she will also be going over with us on the same flight. As there is no gain in time now I don't get that hour in hand for getting to the station which means I can't get to Cambridge until mid-afternoon. However we'll be in touch and I'll talk to you on the phone when I get to Cambridge. I have booked back on flight AF815,13.00hrs take off, on Friday 22nd April … and Mô has got your message about having a good gobble somewhere!

Will Express this off now

Oh, by the way I received a long (for Franta) somewhat emotional letter about the 'Self-Service! drawing of mine which Cooeee gave him for his birthday. Quite/carried away he was. I've told Cooee that this is a transaction as it is a birthday present from her and not from me. So now I shall have to think of something nice and expensive I need which she can get in payment. I think I told you that she wanted the original (which is in USA) and so I made a quick copy of it

[handwritten]

That's all for now ---------- will be talking to you next week. Much love

R.

[In Monica Searle's handwriting]

Dearest Jean,

I never seem to thank you in writing for square & egg-shaped eggs & better late than never, thank you VERY much. I have been fiendishly groggy & haven't decided yet whether or not I shall be coming to London. But if yes, I do hope you will drug all your bosses & totter out for a nice long lunch with me. For once R. has underestimated. I lost 3 kilos in that one night. No doubt I shall soon gain them

[up side of page]

again, Hélas! When are you coming to Paris?
I hope I see you very soon.
Easter kisses & love from Mô

304 NEW YORK, 14 FEBRUARY 1967
Handwritten on post card

New York 14 Feb 1967
Dearest Jean : Well, the trip is almost at an
end and will be returning to Paris in 10
days time (Friday 24th). It has been quiet
here. Nothing sensational in the way of
work just a couple of TVGUIDE things and
some odds and ends. However have consolidated
things with the "New Yorker" and Bryan Holme
has taken the cat book and so on, so it
was worth while just for the talks. But
alas I think we return as broke as we
came – Just coming out of an icy
blast in New York. final digging out
going on now. The place was really tangled up
with snow and bitter cold. In the country
this weekend it was 52 below freezing – 20°!
Wow! Hope you have been springlike over there.
& that all is well with you. Everything is more
or less the same here – except for the addition of
an inherited daughter by John and Midge which
has changed their living quite a bit. All well with
us & we're looking forward to getting home again
– Much love R . –

(In Monica Searle's handwriting)

& lots of love from me too
& kisses – Mô >

305 SUNDAY NIGHT, 19 FEBRUARY 1967
Typed letter

[handwritten]
c/o Locke 56 E 66th Street
NY City 10021 NY.
Sunday night. 19 Feb 1967
Dearest Jean –
[Typed]
Came back from the country tonight to
find your letter awaiting … T.V. Much!
We go to Philadelphia in the morning
for the opening of the exhibition and
back/again in the afternoon. Then it is
clearing and packing.
No, I hasn't really been a success, the
trip. However, there have been some
useful discussions and the NEW YORKER is
wide open for me, they tell me.
Enclosed is a letter from A.D'Offay
which I thought you had better have,
as he is likely to ring you and ask to
see the Cruikshank stuff. Offhand I
am rather against breaking it up unless
there is a remarkably good price in the
offing …
My father's birthday is on March 6th and
I shall probably aim at coming over for
that so perhaps I could go through the
albums then prepare your toothache!

Delighted to see in cold print in the
TIMES of Friday that the divorce went xxxx
through without too much attention. The
Main thing is that it has AT LAST been
achieved. Now perhaps I shall be able
to get myself straight! What a relief!
Regards to the 'Au Pair' – but I had better
let her guardian deal with that!
Hastily –and I'll write again when
I'm back and the coming – over date is
fixed.
[handwritten] V. Much love R.

[In Monica Searle's handwriting]

So glad you are keeping an eye on
mademoiselle – greetings to her, but
much love & kisses to you – Mô
(along side of page) P.S. When is your Paris week-end?

306 THURSDAY 19 JULY 1967

Typed letter with envelope

[Handwritten, with a cutting from Time Magazine dated July 14 1967]

Mrs Jean Ellsmoor
1 Child's Walk
LONDON S.W 5
Angleterre

4, rue Antoine-Dubois, Paris 6e

Dearest Jean –

Thursday pm,
19th July, 1967

Thanks for your nice letter yesterday. Brought a refreshing breeze into this sweltering city. Seems to be stuck at around 90° and not at all good for working! The important thing was the sugar sifter and not the plastic bag. Far less attraction-drawing for the customs. As it was there was no bother at all and it was greeted with great excitement as you may already have heard from Mô. She wrote to you and Brian today and I add my renewed thanks for such a lovely present.

You asked me to let you know what the silver marks were when interpreted. I've looked them up and they turn out to be Birmingham 1964. (see enclosed card on which I have copied them for you).

I am aiming at coming to Cambridge next – (all being well with the ticket and fitting-in with my mother) – on August 9th (how about that for a day?) and I shall come back to Paris on the Saturday (12th). When I have got my booking, which I hope will be early morning (say arriving 9.40ish) I'll let you know positively. Then you can tell me how that fits in. I could stop by the office on the way to the station for a break.

When I was on the plane to Paris last week I was idling through TIME Magazine and nearly jumped out of my seat when I saw the enclosed cutting …… quite by chance. I wrote a rude letter to TIME, an extract of which appears in this week's issue. Can you imagine that a month after the event they print that, and without checking with either party concerned! So the confusion continues – the forewarning of which was the arrival of that letter from George Fearon which I haven't had the heart to answer yet!

Did I tell you that Frank Zachary is back as Art Director of HOLIDAY again. They have brought him in to try to save it. When I got in on Thursday he phoned and gave me a fast job. So perhaps we are back to square one again … who knows.

Tell Brian I think it is very sweet of him to help Katie solve her plan-chest problem. I think the one she has chosen is ideal for her, and if it is possible for him to order it professionally then that would be marvellous. I will deal with the payment promptly either here or there, if the order can go through. And if it can't, well thanks for trying. This plan chest is Katie's request for her 21st Birthday present a year in advance.

Did you see my GRAPHIS cover on the current issue? No:129. Very prettily reproduced.

Judith came round to dinner the other evening – Saturday – before going off to Majorca on Sunday with the children until first week in September. Same as ever she was. First time I have

2.

seen her since we all ate together at the Coupole when you were here.

By the way, instead of closing my personal bank account at Lloyds Bayswater, which is now all clear of transfers and such, and £5 in credit (put there by Peat, Marwick to keep it alive!) I have had it transferred to Lloyds, Cambridge. Then when I am clear of my debts this year I might be able to transfer something over to it and use it for the odd bills and things.

Peat, Marwick feel now that things are almost wound-up. Everything has been settled with them up to May now. So I expect they will wind up the odd things they have in hand and then perhaps just keep an eye on things for a nominal sum each year.

It is too hot to write any more. I'm dripping all over my keyboard! …

[handwritten in blue ink]

– & I'll write again when I have positively fixed the Cambridge trip

Much love

R.

307 PARIS, SUNDAY 5 NOVEMBER 1967

Handwritten on post card

4me Antoine-Dubois
75 – Paris 6e
Sunday 5th November 67

Dearest Jean –

Did you get back alright? We had your exotic card from the Middle East while we were in the process of cancelling our holiday. It has been all very hectic here finishing the new litho's & getting them printed & all the extras for the exhibition which opens at LA POCHADE on Thursday. This is supposed to be in invitation card for you. They have done 8 different ones, but when I turned this over there was nothing on the back! – nor on the others. So I seemed to have picked up a dud batch & have to wait until the gallery opens tonight to get you one! The exhibition will be the 20 originals – the book. Lithographs & the postcards This time they are for sales (Hopefully). Shall be in Cambridge from 14th & going back 17th . I am waiting to hear from Katie so that I know whether I'll be seeing her in London, or whether she'll come on to Cambridge with me, as I gather Kaye will be away for a month from the 12th & Katie will be alone. Perhaps we could have a coffee or something going or coming. Anyway I'm due to arrive 10am on Tuesday 14th. Have just got rid of H. Huber who came here to discuss the Comic Art History for 4 days and all is behind! Look forward to a word from you. Meanwhile much love from Mô & from me. Love R.

308 TUESDAY 29 FEBRUARY 1968
Handwritten on post card

Thursday 29 Feb 1968,

Dearest Jean
Just a word to let you know I have
fixed for Monday — (leaving Thursday),
I have a seat on the 8.o'clock flight
getting into London 9.0am'ish, So I'll
Come on direct to you. from there.
I told Hope I could phone her from yours
& join her at her office during the morning
with the dummy and maybe have a
sandwich with her. Anyway see how it
goes. Love from Mô & to all including Valerios!
from me too.
See you Mondaymuch love
R.

309 BOXING DAY 1968
Handwritten on post card

Boxing Day 1968
Dearest Jean & Brian – [drawing of a cup and saucer]

Although we didn't make a "Cup that
Cheers" over Christmas, the constant reminder is
there! What a marvellous discovery! Needless
to say it was greeted with cries of delight from
both of us & we think it will be destined to
join the brass trivets section on the kitchen wall.
Thank you both again.
We have had a very
welcome quiet Christmas as we are both rather tired —
leisurely too as we finally finished Christmas dinner at 5pm.
A week on Monday we set off for New York and there is
a lot to do before then. (address c/o J. L Studio 15 East 76th St
NYCity. 10021. NY). We hope you both had a lovely time
& that 1969 will bring you everything as you would
wish it. Much love from us both – and thanks
again for the splendid present.

[In Monica Searle's handwriting]
Yes, MUCH love it
thanks from Mô
[In Ronald Searle's handwriting]
& Ronald

310 PARIS, BOXING DAY 1970
Handwritten on post card

Paris. Boxing Day 1970.

Dearest Jean –
There is no doubt about it. Trying to write
on Boxing Day. after a 'blow up' on Christmas Day
is not exactly going to bed to sparkling results.
I spent yesterday evening in a sort of hoggish sleepiness,
leafing through 'African Art". I must say it is a very
good addition to the A. A. shelf. It has a lot of illustrations
I've not seen before, and the colour is rather good
isn't it
Anyway thank you – but also thank you
from us both for the fascinating little..... (well,
when I used to play with the family, we called it
"Put & Take"..). but this is far more exotic, this
"Je m'aime – passionnement " (as it is lying before me
at present) I think Mô has decided to wear it on
a bracelet. I'm thanking you from both of us –(for
the Virgo matches too) – as Mô is deep in bed with
a stinking cold; she caught it from the doctor of
all people. Nevertheless we had a lovely Christmas
& now we are heading for a thoroughly lazy.

311 PARIS, TUESDAY 20 JULY 1971
Handwritten on two post cards

(1)

<u>Paris – Tuesday</u> 20.7 71

Dearest Jean – Brought this postcard down South
to send peacefully to you during the week &
as you can see – it never got sent ! For various
reasons. Social ones & the heat. It was about
90° all the time, and impossible to do <u>anything</u>
The main reason for being down there at the
Festival d'Avignon was that they decided to present
me with the Prix du Festival (large lump of silver)
But on top of that (Surprise) The mayor presented
me with the medal of the Ville d'Avignon (a large
lump of bronze) All this at the Marie, and
in suit and tie. I MELTED all over the place.
However it was all very enjoyable – but <u>very</u>
dignified with handshaking
& speeches. We all drank a
lot after. On top of this

we had to attend receptions and the exhibition
opening, etc etc etc. & finally climbed
on to the 'Mistral' Saturday evening after
six days of dripping, in a state of
<u>total</u> collapse. I didn't wake up until
Sunday afternoon. Mô had her
treatment last night – (They have told her
to expect it every fortnight until at least
Jan 1973) – so we have to expect plans to
be cramped until some time to come ...
They are letting her off the needle for 3 weeks in
September so that we can get our Le Canadel

holiday in as usual.
Friday afternoon I am flying to Birmingham.
Haven't seen my mother since last December
& it is about time. Flying back direct on Tuesday
morning again. Time has flown. I've just
realised that the last time I paused in London
was when we had a drink together last
June 29th. (Katie picked me up at the airport
& drove me to the station last December- but
that doesn't count) ----- >

(2)

-> One of the main problems about going up
to Olive's is that there is no room for me in
the house, So I have to stay with a
neighbour. However – although I miss Cambridge –
the arrangement is much better & proving a
great success. I had expected to be working on
another film or something in England
this spring but nothing materialised in that
direction. So there has been no work of any sort
from GB to bring me over as it did last
year and pay the expenses. Valerios told me
yesterday that you had phoned whilst we were
away. I was stricken with remorse as I never
even thanked you for your holiday postcard.
Now August is rapidly approaching & you
have to tell me
what you would like, to mark to 9th Aug.
Then we will arrange to get someone to
bring it over to you, as there is no indication
at the moment that I shall be coming to
carry it over myself. You could always
phone me at Olives (CBromwich 2529) one
day. (Not Saturday evening as I am taking
them all out to dinner).
Hope everything is going along marvellously
for you. I seem very out of touch.
Anyway – may be talking to you over the
weekend. Meanwhile very much love
to you & Brian from Mô & me.
That's all for the moment – and I hope
it is legible!.
Love R.

-----

312 WEDNESDAY, 18 AUGUST 1971
Typed Letter

4, rue Antoine – Dubois, Paris 6e
Wednesday, 18th August, 1971

Dearest Jean –
Many thanks for the fascinating book … BLUNTED SIGHT. Have
you read it? I should have written immediately. However I
got into the book immediately instead! Marion left
yesterday, and also left behind the book for Mô's birthday.
Which I must give her on the day, down in Le Canadel.
I must say we can hardly wait to get away. Paris is very
heavy and stormy, and there is a sort of August inertia
which doesn't either help work or thought.
We leave on the 6th September and get back on the 29th
for Mô's treatment on the 30th. However she still has two scheduled
before we go. One on Monday, and another just before
we leave. However, she said she would rather lie in bed
down south and feel awful, than to lie in bed here feeling
awful and waiting to go down south.
Nothing very exciting happening here. Various projects which
need a lot of crystalising, and several things which are
much less interesting since the dollar collapsed.
Hope told me before she left that she leaves Greece on the
15th. So I guess you will be down there long before that if
you are coming back on the 22nd.
From the photos Hope showed me it should be gorgeous
down there on the Greek coast.
My sister is coming to the end of her fortnight in
Yugoslavia (Adriatic coast). Sounds a great success, thank
goodness, as it is the first real holiday the family have
had together. My mother has been in Cambridge for ten days
with neighbours and moves on to her brother's tomorrow in
Bromley. She sounded full of beans when I spoke to her
yesterday. A great burden off my mind that this is all working
out so well in Birmingham.
Once we are back in Paris after the holiday there may be
odd duty trips, but otherwise I don't think we shall be far
away. We will be speaking when things have settled down
again and we can tackle the question of your birthday present.
Hope you had a nice birthday day. We thought of you on the 9th.
In case the pace warms up between now and packing I hope
you have a lovely holiday, and will expect a glamorous card
either to Paris or to: Hotel de la Plage,
LE RAYOL/CANADEL-sur-Mer,
83-(Var) France.

[Handwritten]
– Meanwhile much love from us both
R.

313 WEDNESDAY NIGHT, 3 NOVEMBER 1971
Typed letter with envelope

[Handwritten]

Mrs Jean Ellsmoor
1 Child's Walk
LONDON S.W 5
Angleterre

4, rue Antoine – Dubois, Paris 6e
Wednesday night, 3rd Nov. 1971

Dearest Jean –
Oof! Sorry I am a little behind in answering your letter. I have had Mô in bed for nearly three weeks with a chest infection – and the treatment on top of it. She got up yesterday and put a foot out today, and we go for X-Rays on Friday, to see what it was all about.
Consequently I have got somewhat behind with everything. Pity this happened. But it did, right after our return from holiday – which seems far, far away now! and not simply 3 weeks.
Of all things, as far as work goes, I am closeted with Gilbert & Sullivan! A freebooting Canadian liquor king has had the idea of going into films, after having made a mint of money he doesn't really need by putting on 'Sleuth' far and wide. He wants to do a cartoon film based on the characters and songs of G&S. Anything from half-an-hour to an hour-and-a-half. I am being a little wary of it until I see where it goes. But for the time being I have contracted to work from Oct 1st to Nov. 30 creating the characters. I finally got round to starting them at the weekend! which means doing two months in one … hence also another Oof! Apart from that there have been scattered things. Work in America has picked up a little. I'm doing fairly frequent things for the 'New York Times' Sunday edition; More for BOAC; and slipping cover ideas off to NEW YORKER when I get the inspiration. They have bought me for their coming Christmas cover, which is nice, as it will still be freshish in the air by the time we get there. All being well, the first week in January again. At least we are trying to arrange Mô's treatments that way, to get three weeks skirmishing there.

Germany anyway has become quite a 'hot' market for exhibitions. They have been going well. But this last one – (the one you have a catalogue of) – all prints, sold about 100 things, and the gallery are finally glowing. Although I must say they have never grumbled when things went slow. They are arranging other shows again for me next year in Switzerland and, I think Austria. Which is always a good second fiddle when Magazines start limping as they are in America at the moment. As you probably know first 'Venture' then 'Look' – both Cowles publications – died this summer. 'Holiday' has more or less faded away to a staff of five working out of two rooms in the Waldorf. I guess 'Life' will be next … TV is bound to strike other countries the same way in the not too distant future. So I think it wise to keep a firm eye on the TV and the gallery business. All in all things haven't changed much, have they? It is a constant change.
I am supposed to have a little book: "The Addict" out for Christmas (at the modest price of 50p!) but Dobson was let-down by the colour printers and I haven't yet seen a copy. Just a rough pull – which depressed me. Anyway, I hope you will be getting a copy before Noël strikes.

2

Other book news. The snail book (French edition) was awarded the Grand Prix de l'Humour Noir last Tuesday. Which doesn't mean a thing beyond the announcement, and the right to put a black band round the jacket in the hope of whipping-up a few more sales. They showed the book on the TV News here that night, which, I am sure, pleased J.J.Pauvert, who hasn't yet covered his costs on it!

Our holiday down south was not much of a rest until the last (and extra) week. We were supposed to have gone back after 3 weeks then Mô's prof. had to speak at a cancer conference in Holland and postponed our return. By that time pretty well everyone had returned home and to school, and at last the Côte was silentish. Up until then – apart from rather disturbed weather – I have never known the coast so noisy with people and traffic all hours of the day and night. Everywhere was crowded long after the normal end of season and it was really no fun. Especially as the little hotel we are more or less forced to go to, is very simple. xxx Finally because of the thin walls, I was forced to rent the adjoining room so as not to have to listen to the conversation of the couples behind the bedhead who added up their pocket-money until the early hours before talking about the food. It wasn't even interesting!
The last week was superb. The sun shone all the time and the sea simply lapped. Which made up for all the rest.

Ah, that was a long time ago!

Don't bother about Regency chairs for the moment, Thanks. Mostly due to having to cut down on expenses, a bit due to the medical problems, and this and that … (Mother, Sister and their holidays, and odds and ends) … But it was nice of you to suggest it.

The Hogarth exhibition. I heard there was one coming. If you get to it I would be grateful for a catalogue. The Hogarth prints I did have I have lost sight of a long time ago. I don't remember seeing them here ever.

I was hoping to have come over my first free weekend, at the end of November, via London and up to Birmingham. It is well over a year, isn't it since I came to London? However that has been effectively squashed, as there is a film meeting coincided here with the Canadian coming from Los Angeles, and Hope putting a protective padding between us, He is coming to go over the work I have been doing for him – and carry it all back to USA, and bringing his cheque book too, I hope! It is then we reflect whether there is a future (which means 9 months to a year and a bit more) in the project.

How I shall get to Birmingham now before Christmas I don't know. I have to be in Berlin the following weekend, until 11th December, for things to do with G. Gurlitt. I may simply have to try a dash the weekend before Christmas, or abandon the idea until after USA. A great deal of this planning complication is having to arrange everything around the Transfusions. Mô gets completely knocked out for four or five days each time – and she really dreads it. Miserable for her, but that is the pattern. And when she is feeling ready to get on her feet we cram in what we can. But even when she is feeling better she can't really get up until lunchtime.
I must stop typing as it is 10'00pm and the neighbours have the right to complain at 10.01! continued by hand …

[Handwritten]

3

— which I hope won't be too painful. The law is the law in these parts! I have been combing the calendar up and down and I really think it would be silly to attempt to suggest a safe moment for you to nip over for 48 hours, because if I can get myself disentangled one weekend I'm going to have to come over there. Why don't you save up 84 hours & come in the spring, when the sun is shining & the birds are singing &

the shops are open....! and make a leisurely excursion it would be much nicer than having you scramble here to go away the next day ...

I'm sorry it is so bunged up. but if you come we would prefer to have you here free of film magnets or doctors & unable to budge. If things work out I may catch sight of you in London before USA. Only if the worst comes to the worst will I have to do Birmingham direct from Paris.

Anyway I'll let you know if I am able to fix anything – but it will be in December I'm sure, not this month which is impossible now.

A good chat would cover at least a dozen more pages – but better not in this writing.

So I'll leave this now with very much love. Mô sends hers – love & kisses that is ----

me too

Ronald

PS: The 'Comics' book you mention must be a re issue. I had this from Penguins in 1967.

314 PARIS, SATURDAY AFTERNOON 8 JULY [1972]

Typed post card

4 rue Antoine-Dubois, 75 – Paris 6e
Saturday aft. 8th July.

Dearest Jean –

By the time you get this I shall be in Cambridge. I'm leaving in the morning to be there for lunch. Shall stay until Thursday am. and flying off after lunch as usual. Katie is coming down to join me on Wednesday and coming back on the train with me on Thursday morning; (July 13)

Shall we communicate telephonically before Thursday? (OCA-3-55739)
Hope Brian's back is normal now and that you can round off work for holidays. It is soon, isn't it?
Look forward to chats ...
(handwritten)
– V. Much love R.

[In Monica Searle's handwriting]

& much love from me too Mô X X
X X

315 MONDAY 6 AUGUST 1973

Typed letter with envelope

Mrs. Jean Ellsmoor,
1 Child's Walk,
LONDON S.W.5 Angleterre
(printed on flap)
Exp: Searle, 4 rue Antoine-Dubois, 75006 Paris
(printed address)
4, rue Antoine-Dubois, Paris 6e

Monday, 6th August, 1973

Dearest Jean

Oh yes, where were we?

Do you know I still have a third of my Christmas Cards unsent on the desk. You don't. But I do. So far this year has been a series of scrambles. It took months to recover from the vast BN exhibition. Then I was already behind with the Gilbert and Sullivan film, which is moving along at a pace to be ready for the cinemas next year – in the autumn; plus various sinister complications with Mô's treatment, all of which are behind us now.

Since we cut the phone bell off some weeks ago as a protectionx (it works well) and fight merrily along to keep even with what comes in, and has to go out, the pace has begun to slacken a little. Apart from correspondence, which shames me everytime I look at the pile now turning yellow at the edges, I am more or less even with the work.

The film has me under contract until next spring, and as I am feeding about 40 people with their daily work in London and Los Angeles, I feel a certain responsibility weighing on me! Especially as we are now thinking of getting away for hols, (from which we go on to Munich for my next show), and will not be back until late October. As you can imagine there is a certain amount of getting-ahead to be done ...

At the moment there has been no sign of needing to come to London for the film work, as it has been a question of creating on the drawing-board, and people coming to carry it away. Later in the year there may be results to see and discuss over there. Come to think of it, apart from an hour on the way through to Birmingham in the spring of 1972, it must be over 3 years now since I stayed in London. How flies time.

Meanwhile you seem to be leaping hither and thither. Thank you for your New York card in June, and thank you for my Birthday card in March. I must think what would appeal to me ...

But mine is behind and yours is imminent. The 9th is creeping up,and as this intends to be a Birthday letter, I must say right away I HOPE YOU HAVE A VERY HAPPY BIRTHDAY, and, of course Mô and I would like to know what you would like as a present to add to all the presents I am sure we owe you know and have not yet had. I have a careful list of them somewhere, so they are NOT forgotten.
When you have decided, let us know and I will add it and then do something about it and then attend to the question of delivery. If it does not come before I shall attempt to deliver it personally later
in the year if I am to be brought over.

Very much love from Mô and me, and, once again

HAPPY HAPPY BIRTHDAY

Love

Ronald

316 TUESDAY, 9 APRIL 1974

Typed letter, with envelope

Mrs. Jean Ellsmoor,
1 Child's Walk.
LONDON S.W.5
Angleterre

4, rue Antoine-Dubois, Paris 6e

Dearest Jean – Tuesday,9th April, 1972?73?74?

Lovely to have your letter and all the news. So T&H is now in the past. But Phaidon should be a lovely change if only because you can walk there! Get the 2 vols of CARRACCI bound! I have been battling to get this title since the end of last year through Heywood Hill, who chase it everywhere for me without success. But the result is always the same – 'binding'.

I have to do a series of medals for the French Mint this year – starting with Carracci. One of the big Carracci experts in Berlin tells me that the only book is the Phaidon one, for its self-portraits of Annibale.

This medal thing is interesting. The French Mint are doing a lot of medals on every conceivable subject. They are doing one of me sometime this year for those who wish a bronze paperweight weighing about a pound. Because of that the subject came up and I am to do a series of 'daddies' of caricature: Carracci, A.; Ghezzi, Hogarth, Rowlandson, Gillray, Cruikshank. An interesting new departure for me.

Meanwhile, as Hope told you I imagine, I have spent a year on the Gilbert and Sullivan film which is now well on the way after delays due to the three-day week and complications with filming. It won't be screened now until spring 1975. But the book is coming out for Christmas published by Cape. My contract ended in January so I am more or less out of it now. But I think it is going to be entertaining and worth doing once in a life-time.

Apart from the film work which seems to have eaten up my life for over a year, I have been scratching away at lithographs and trying to continue with the rest of the output. The NEW YORKER ran five covers of mine last year – which was good, out of 52. They have changed art director now, so I am easing myself back in again. They have taken three more over the last six months so I am hopeful of holding that shop-window into the USA.

Did you see my cover on the current GRAPHIS? (NO169). It is nicely reproduced. That was a NEW YORKER reject and now I see it I think it is better on GRAPHIS.

We have had a lot of ups and downs over the last six months especially with Mô's health. It is four years now since the treatments began. We had it broken to us last month that she is going to be on treatment for the rest of her days. Apparently, and this was news to us,

she is the sole long survivor in the world at present, from this particular and bizarre combination of cancers. Up until they began to experiment on Mô, the limit was 12 months. As she agreed to be a guinea-pig for the development of a new drug by the Swiss for the Ville Juif cancer research unit, no-one has survived on what was available. Now after three years of this drug they apply it to others and already two other people have xxxxxx gone over the limit. One for 14 months and one for a bit longer. Needless to say we were somewhat shocked by the revel- -ation. But as we know that the professor is very given to keeping his mouth shut unless he is sure, we assume he told us all this as there were to be no surprises to come in the future – unless it is the development of more sophisticated drugs.

What is consists of is a replacement of all the tubes and drips and injections of acid into the veins. Now there is this special pill that unravels itself over 24 hours and does the same thing. There are two days of this pill.

2

to kill cells, and then two to three days of injections to batter down what is left. After a month, if the blood balance gets back xxxxxx over the danger level, they start again. The effect is pretty tough on Mô but much less so than the five days of injections she was having. So far as we can divine the treatment can be no worse and can only get better, depending on the discoveries in the years to come. Although Mô says she is not sure she likes being 'N°1' …

The trouble with the medical bombardment is the occasional cycle of depression that comes with it and plunges her into the depths. I suppose it is like recovering from 10,000 doses of flu, added to the fact that the heavy doses of radiation have withered away most of her shoulder muscles on the left, and restrict her arm movements badly. Being left-handed it doesn't help. Anyway, there you are. You ask for details and those are they to date.

Because of this and also because we prefer more and more to cut out the socialising, we keep as quiet as possible and cut our encounters to the minimum. Which means more time to get on with things and it is certainly more peaceful.

We go off to Germany again in 10 days for a round of various calls, as Germany is such an interesting market these days. More interesting on the whole than America. I am in the process of arranging with the gallery in Munich a big travelling museum show for the end of 1975 and all 1976 throughout Germany & perhaps Switzerland, starting off in the Prussian Nationale Gallery in Dahlem/Berlin.

The last exhibition in Munich in October went very well and I am getting about half-a-dozen exhibitions a year in Germany and Austria which Gurlitt arrange. So the gallery side moves along very nicely, and prices for a rich Germany hover between £350 and £550 a drawing now, as people begin to collect satirical scribbles.

The lithographs are continuing steadily. I produce about 10 a year to be sure that one covers another, printing being so expensive. But we have managed to hold the price down to £35 a piece whilst everyone else pushes the prices up. Paris must be heading for the prize as the most expensive city in the world. Not that the full effects of the fuel crisis has completely hit them yet. It is being passed on in small doses no doubt to prevent another revolution.

You mention the Mistinguet necklace. We have never seen them since and we pass the shop regularly. Prices for that sort of thing now have gone up to about £200 a piece as it suddenly became fashionable and also because txx of the big Paul Poiret exhibition which opened here a month or two back (and is still on). As you know he made those necklaces, and they have become museum pieces.

Do send me a copy of the Phaidon catalogue. I would like to see it when you have a moment to send one. As for the 50frs. Keep it there and we will drink it or eat it if and when I have the chance of coming over.

[handwritten in black ink]

– And that is all for this time with much love from Mô

– & me

Ronald

317 10 AUGUST 1974
Typed letter

[Printed] Ronald Searle

[Handwritten]
Dearest Jean – oops!

10th August, 1974

Casting a casual glance at the calendar it is clear that I am not 'with it' this year! In letters as bold as you like, for Friday 9th August, is inscribed in red 'JEAN'S BIRTHDAY'

I seem to have been on such a 'bat' for months, finishing off the film and moving on to a series of medals that I have to do for the French Mint by Tuesday, that days and dates are already somewhere near Christmas. Especially as I have inbetween had to deliver drawings for Christmas-cards (Gulp).

Anyway, better late than later, Mô and I send off immediately all our wishes for last Friday, and we hope that it was a

[drawings of birds]

Very Very

Happy Birthday

– with very much love

Mô & Ronald

318 SUNDAY, 22 JUNE 1975
Typed letter

4, rue Antoine-Dubois, Paris 6e
Sunday, 22nd June, 1975

Dearest Jean

You will probably drop down in a dead faint when you see this letter. Your telegram made me feel ten times more guilty than I was already feeling before it arrived, with your last note sitting there for a 'proper reply' instead of a brief word back.

This has been an awful year so far, and one packed to the hilt with problems. But I won't bore you with lots of detail.

First of all let me tell you how lovely it was to get your telegram. The first news that the OMNIBUS wasn't a disaster! I don't know anything about the programme or what is in it as I kept completely out of the way – apart from supplying what was asked of me. I haven't seen it, but I am promised that they may bring a copy here for me to see this summer.

I didn't want to make it at first. But I so liked John Pett that I thought that if it had to be made once and for all, I would prefer working with him. Then never do it again. So I gave the lot on tape (about five hours of it) and on film (for three days). What was shaped out of it and what was eventually used, was then outside my hands. But I must say I kept my fingers hopefully crossed!

As you know me, and found it 'sensitive' as well as entertaining was more than a relief. Now I don't mind seeing it when the chance comes!

The idea was to concentrate on the development of an artist. Personal life was excluded – except inso much as being born somewhere, someone had to be responsible. A mother, for example. But apart from that I refused to allow a camera even in the apartment because whether or not I have a carpet, or whether or not Mô and I take sugar in our coffee is nobody's business who doesn't know us. This seems to have upset the SUNDAY TIMES last week! They seemed to have been vitally disturbed that the film wasn't about wives and that I hadn't done a drawing worth digesting since I was a little boy prisoner (Vomit, vomit). However, the reaction I have had so far has pleased me. After your telegram one of the first enthusiastic letters I had was from Scarfe. After that Calman and Nicolas Bentley rushed in to approve. So whatever happens, the "profession" seems to approve.

So much for that.

Now back to Christmas. Because of Mô's fragile state she was told by the doctors not to be near Paris for Christmas so we went to a rented house before, down south. We had already gone to the same house at the end of August last year intending to be back at the end of September. However the journey back was changed as Mô wasn't well enough to make it, and we finally did not get back to Paris until the end of October. Nor back to Paris after Christmas until nearly the beginning of February. This was somewhat difficult from the working point of view. We then received an order expelling us from our apartment here, which we are fighting. Effie and Valerios also. All apart of the Rachmanism applied by the estate manager employed by our new young landlords. So for weeks I was compiling dossiers for our attack on them, hoping to be able to spin it all out with a decent lawyer – which we luckily have. Meanwhile the final work on the cartoon film had to be done. I more or less finished last week with the poster reshaping and merchandising checking and so on. They tell me that this hour-and-a-half of cartoon film is bringing with it stuffed toys, cheese boards, lampshades, paper napkins,

2

– prints of the designs for framing, mobiles, a repulsive book done by Cape (really horrible …) and so on and on. Apart from anything else I am keeping right out of it, and not coming over for the opening, I think in July, because Mô is too fragile to be left alone, or to come over and be involved in all that. She caught a chill and bronchitis in April and has been two months in bed with it. This dis-immunisation is a devil and Effie and Valerios are in Crete until September. So there is nobody in the house. The house is one great working site. It is being ripped apart from 7.30am each morning. They are putting in a lift and supposedly restoring it to its 17th century state (hence the lift) and hopefully expelling everybody and re-fill it with multi-millionaires who want luxury apartments. This means we may have to leave Paris. We could never afford that level. Unless we win our case. We hopefully – being totally unco-operative or sympathetic to their aims – will cling to our legal loopholes in the contract we have. But as you can see, none of this has actually aided thoughts of work, income, or peace of mind.

Things are difficult because I have lost so much time this year on having to attend to staying put and having both feet in a state of insecurity …

You will now understand why I have hardly – except occasionally to my mother and sister, written a word sitting relaxed at this typewriter. I have never had such a guilty conscience.

Maybe I am getting old but the noise is also driving me mad. For a year we have had pneumatic drills outside in the street. First to bring in new tleephone cables to the whole district. Then the gas company changed the mains. Now they have a generator in the street cleaning the façade of the medical school opposite with sand and water blasting – which also brought with it a fine carpet of sand throughout and in every book. Good thing I wear Clarks desert boots …

Going back to your Christmas letter. No, we never did get a telegram from you last year. Not that it is surprising. We have lost maybe several pounds of mail and several hundred-weights of packets through a postal upheaval and then strike which finally ended just before Christmas and took until the end of February to return to 'normal'. That is ten days for my recent letters to reach Hope and two to three days for a letter to cross Paris.

All this sounds hellish, doesn't it? But for some reason everything seems to have arrived at once on this district, on this house and on our backs, so that we feel that if we can get rid of this year, next year can't possibly be as bad.

England sounds as if it is going through a difficult time. But really it is a reflection of what is happening everywhere. Work for everybody has dropped dramatically. The franc may be stable-ish but there is an air of restlessness because it is so expensive just to exist on the basics, and the technocrat runners of the country draw us all into the computer a little more firmly every day.

Anyway. This is a year of change I feel. I don't know quite where to or for, but the upheaval is there.

We continue to live a very isolated life. With Mô's dis-immunisation (as you see, a bad cold means two months in bed) we see virtually nobody. An enjoyable conversation gives her a fever and as her temperature hasn't gone down since April, it can't afford to go up. Her morale is marvellous though despite the fact that she knows every crack in the ceiling and hasn't seen (except for visits to the X-Ray clinic) the outside world since the Spring.

All this seems a lamentable excuse for being totally out of touch. My mother is not pleased with me at all. But essentials first – and that is just coping from day to day as best as possible! End of second page, so I will stop here. But at least you will know that your telegram was a joy to receive and that it DID arrive. The phone is off completely until September, and maybe our letter-box will be forced open for the third time this week. But thoughts are unrestricted …

[handwritten]

Very much love from Mô
& from me
Ronald

319 SATURDAY 6 MARCH 1976

Typed post card

Saturday, March 6th 1976

Chez Madame S. Pouthier-Sandrini,
Rue du Chateau,
83690 – Tourtour (Var), France.

Dearest Jean –

Lovely to get word from you this morning.
The Noah's Ark card was appropriate as it is raining and snowing here today! Thanks for thinking of my birthday, Over page is me pulling my 56 years…

It is such a long time since we exchanged news that I will have to let the detail run for another time. Briefly contact was lost almost everywhere because of the monstrous year we went through in 1975. Apart from Mô having passed about 6 months in bed we received an expulsion order from the landlords from the apartment in Paris, as did Effie and Valerios – and some others in the house. All on various pretexts but xxxxxx basically to clear anyone they could out so that they could turn the joint into luxury apartments and take the ceiling off the rent. We are fighting this, with all the lawyers we can muster, jointly with E & V. but meanwhile they made life a misery with noise, workmen, water off, light off and all the tactics of slum landlords. With Mô ill in bed and pneumatic drills for months IN the house, we finally had to move her and make a move out. Secretly that is. We shifted 90% of our belongings into a furniture store in Paris on the pretext of storing archives to make more space, & left only enough to keep the place legally furnished. Then at the beginning of September when E&V returned after some two months away, we left for the South here on 'holiday' which became 'extended convalescence' under Doctor's orders. So here we have been for six months living and xx trying to work out of suitcases in this house of a friend, waiting to see what the future holds. The latest is that we are being taken to court shortly.

[handwritten]

'Officially' we are still in Paris. but with M here on convalescence. So do not talk about it. The legal situation is still too fragile. But the above address still holds for a while. That's all there is room for – for this time. Much love from Mô & me & let me have your news someday.

Ronald.

320 27 NOVEMBER 1976
Christmas card with typed post card

Christmas card

[Typed]
New address
Novella adresse
83690 – Tourtour
(Var) France

[Handwritten]

Jean & Brian
with love for a marvellous
CHRISTMAS
& everything you wish
in the NEW YEAR 1977

(Mo's writing)

Mô & Ronald
XX XX

Post card

[Handwritten]

Dearest Jean
[Typed]
27 November 1976

How are you? What are you up to?
This goes off splendidly early because we shall have gone to Germany by the time this arrives, for the opening of a Christmas show I have in Munich. As we shan't be back until just before Christmas I can't see much attention being paid to cards between unpacking and getting into the turkey. We dare not use the Paris address now. The expulsion seems definitive for us and Effie and Valerios. They are still there – but leaving for USA any moment. Our things are mostly there still but it is only a question of time before we are on the street with them. After 14 years there it's more than sad … Greedy landlords – Ugh! So future indefinite. Hope yours is nicely positive. This year of upheaval has been nerve-racking and somewhat bad for the work. I look forward very much to 1977!

Much love Ronald

[Handwritten]

& who knows I may even get to England again. It is so l-o-ng since I did …

321 7 AUGUST 1977
Typed letter with envelope

Mrs. Jean Ellsmoor,
1 Child's Walk
LONDON S.W.5,
Angleterre

[Printed]

F-83690 – Tourtour (Var),
France.

[Handwritten]

Dearest Jean ------------- 7th August 1977

Back from China?

It must have been a fascinating trip and thanks for the fascinating card. And for your Christmas letter. So much has happened since then – especially the farewell to Paris. Finally this is it and the horrible landlord got his way – and our apartment as well as that of Effie and Valerios. He said he wanted it for himself. Now we hear that it is to be rented at about £400 a month! We only paid about £60 (controlled) and that is why we were expelled. All this took took 2 years of battle and cost a legal fortune. We went up and held out until March, but that was it. After that all the business of shipping everything (out of store and out of the apartment) down here, and only now are we coming out of the confusion. At least we had bought these four walls years ago and had somewhere to go, once it was got into a livable shape. But all that swallowed time and money stopped work and correspondence and everything else.

Of course it is isolated. 2000 feet up amongst the sheep and goats. But OK for health – especially Mô's. Everything that allows for contact seems to be dominated by the figure £25. The only way of getting from Nice (the nearest airport) under two days, is a two-hour drive by taxi (£25) the nearest hotel to the village costs, naturally, about £25 a night, as it happenes to be an inefficient luxury one. A day's shopping once in six weeks down at Draguignan, the nearest town, costs £25 the afternoon. So we don't budge more than can be helped!

Until we can recover the financial equilibrium, horns are being pulled in so hard that they almost stick out of the back! E&V are in the same situation. They couldn't find anywhere else to go that had a rent within the bounds of reasonableness, that they finally had to hock their future and buy a small apartment in the 14th.

So it is farewell to the 6th, and all very sad as we loved it – despite its steady degeneration into a sort of Pigalle and den of thieves.

Fortunately the work I am doing allows me to work anywhere, so long as there is a post-office, which/there is, surprisingly enough in this 150 person village. So the pattern hasn't changed and things flow steadily to the USA, Germany, sometimes England and back to Paris. I have set up a system that allows me to go on producing my prints in Paris at least once a month and for the French Mint to issue a commemorative medal sculpted by me, once every six months. So I leap from lithograph zincs, to modelling clay, to pen and ink, to painting for some of the half-a-dozen gallery exhibitions I have a year somewhere or other in Europe. Varied, but still totally absorbing, and still as hazardous as ever!

What with this and that I never got back to England much to my mother's disappointment. But she seems OK and full of beans with my sister. She's 83 and exhausting everyone. But as it costs a small fortune to get from here to Castle Bromwich for a long weekend, I hold off until I can usefully combine a longer stay and take in London for a few days too … We shall see. The bad exchange rate has reduced the English market to something fairly unimportant compared with other countries. So projects have to be interesting if they have to compete with Germany or America for attention.

2.

Anyway, at the moment I have all I can cope with without having to budge more than necessary. If there are journeys, they are usually to Germany, which is very hot property these days.

Yes, I saw that Phaidon had pulled up its roots and gone to Oxford. And I imagined that you would be darting back and forth. Still they could have moved to a less interesting place.

Whilst we were in Paris Hope went to stay with Pat Burke and brought lots of stuff from pre-1961 from her house and from yours. I haven't had much of a chance to look at it yet, but it was bizarre to see it again. However, in about a year, given a little time and space to put it it will once more get into an ordered state. Funny to think that Hope has retired from HL&S. But she seems madly active between her burst of visiting Greece. E&V are there now and have been since May. They expect to back by the autumn and then they will start arranging their homes and lives again. What a year of confusion!

I will leave this here, otherwise it will never get to you near your birthday. I hope it will be a lovely day, with some exciting surprises. HAPPY BIRTHDAY DAY wishes from Mô and me.

— &

Love

Ronald

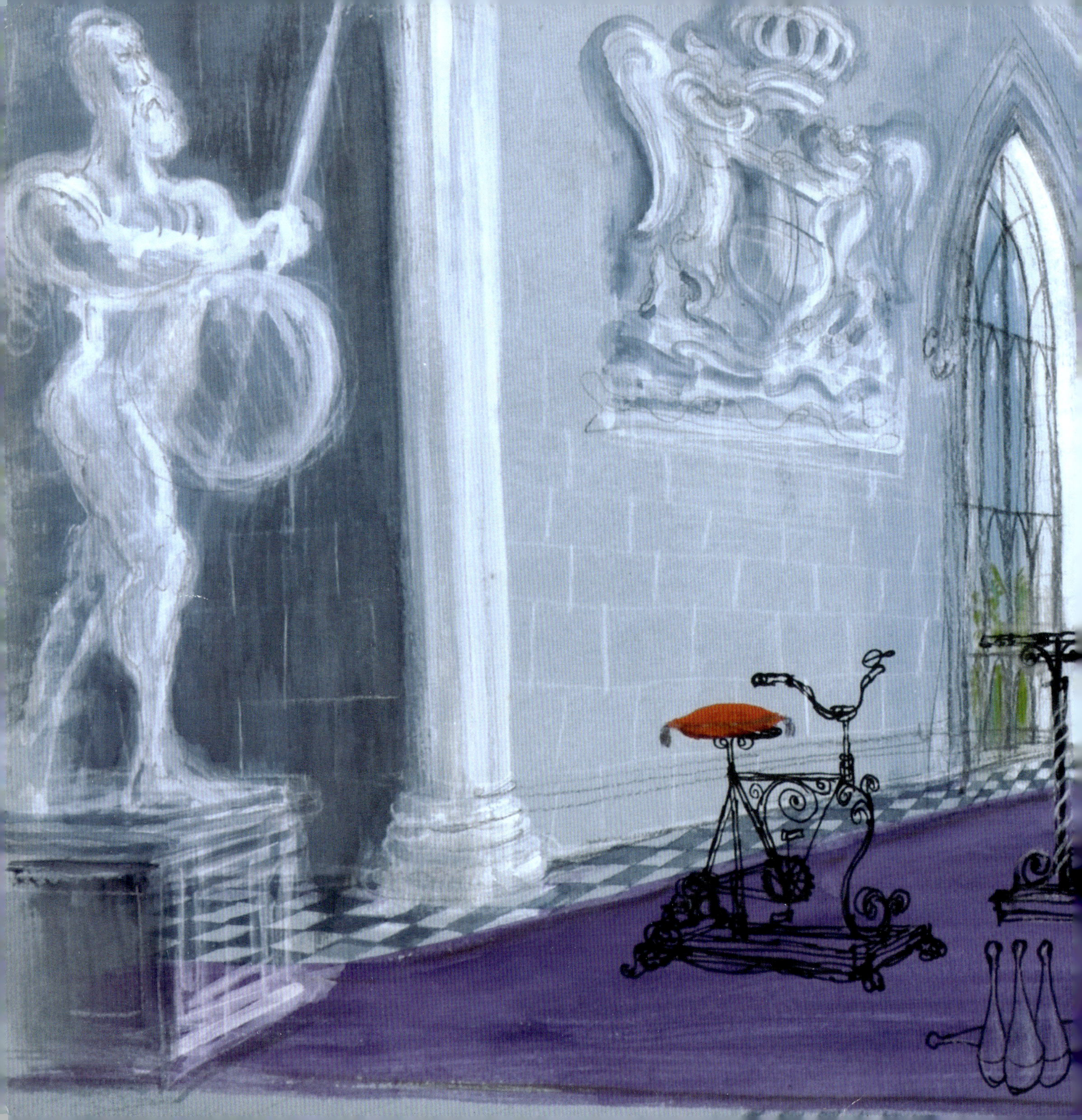